Bridging the Knowledge Divide

Educational Technology for Development

A volume in
Educational Design and Technology in the Knowledge Society
Stewart Marshall and Wanjira Kinuthia, *Series Editors*

Bridging the Knowledge Divide

Educational Technology for Development

Stewart Marshall
The University of the West Indies

Wanjira Kinuthia
Georgia State University

Wallace Taylor
The Information Society Institute (TISI)

INFORMATION AGE PUBLISHING, INC.
Charlotte, NC • www.infoagepub.com

Library of Congress Cataloging-in-Publication Data

Bridging the knowledge divide : educational technology for development /
[edited by] Stewart Marshall, Wanjira Kinuthia, Wallace Taylor.
    p. cm. – (Educational technology for development)
  Includes bibliographical references.
  ISBN 978-1-60752-109-9 (pbk.) – ISBN 978-1-60752-110-5 (hardcover)
  1. Educational technology–Economic aspects–Developing countries. 2.
Economic development–Effect of technological innovations on–Developing
countries. I. Marshall, Stewart. II. Kinuthia, Wanjira. III. Taylor,
Wallace, 1944-
  LB1028.3.B735 2009
  371.309172'4–dc22

                                                            2008054468

Printed in the United States of America

CONTENTS

SECTION 1

FLEXIBLE EDUCATION FOR EMPOWERMENT

SECTION 2

MANAGING AND COMMUNICATING KNOWLEDGE

SECTION 3

FLEXIBLE DELIVERY IN HIGHER EDUCATION

SECTION 4

PREPARING TEACHERS USING FLEXIBLE APPROACHES

FOREWORD

LEARNING FOR DEVELOPMENT

It is a pleasure to commend this book on the role of educational technology in development—not least because nearly all its chapters have been written by practitioners in developing countries who grapple every day with the challenges that they describe. Furthermore, the conceptual papers such as Neil Butcher's excellent introduction to the fashionable but difficult notion of knowledge management also come from the "south."

The themes explored in this volume resonate strongly with the work of the Commonwealth of Learning (COL), which has adopted *learning for development* as the summary of its mission. Following Amartya Sen, COL defines development as freedom. It measures the enhancement of freedom in practical terms as progress toward the goals expressed in the Millennium Declaration and the Dakar Framework for Education for All, as well as the wider adoption of the Commonwealth values of peace, equity, democracy, and good governance.

Such a stance leads COL, like the contributors to the first section of the book, to emphasize community learning as much as individual learning. Effective community learning cannot be achieved through a top-down process. It must start by empowering the community; most obviously by having its members articulate for themselves the development goals that they wish to pursue. This can be a challenging process. While it is relatively easy to facilitate the establishment of the necessary structural social capital, such as village committees, the creation of a more cohesive community through the development of social-learning capital is a longer process. However, COL's experience with its Lifelong Learning for Farmers (L3Farmers) program in India shows that the effort invested in community development does pay off in faster local economic growth. This is because many of the

Bridging the Knowledge Divide, pages ix–xi
Copyright © 2009 by Information Age Publishing
All rights of reproduction in any form reserved.

development opportunities for rural communities require collective as well as individual effort.

Contributions to the first section also highlight the role of distance learning in increasing opportunities for women. This is a vital contribution to development since women are now responsible for most of the food production in Africa and Asia. Furthermore, in COL's L3Farmers program, it is the women who have emerged as the Web programmers for the village ICT kiosks. It is particularly encouraging to see that the long tradition of women as distance learners is now resulting in women becoming managers in learning systems. For example, in the Virtual University for Small States of the Commonwealth, which is an important initiative for bridging the knowledge divide in 30 small states by networking their tertiary institutions, women constitute the majority of the specialists sent by their countries to prepare e-learning courses on development topics through online collaboration.

The second section of the book has some interesting analyses of the use of technologies. Mobile telephones are much more common in the developing world than laptop computers, so it is not surprising that Africa is the pioneer of the use of Short Messaging Service (SMS) in support of formal learning. Results are very encouraging, partly because people identify personally with their mobile phones and are pleased to use them in support of their studies.

Other contributions explore the use of open-source software and their learning equivalent, open-educational resources. Both developments have generated enormous enthusiasm, although it is too early to assess their longer-term impact on bridging the knowledge divide. When steamships appeared in the 19th century, their takeover of the passenger and cargo trade took longer than expected because of a "sailing ship" effect. Companies operating sailing ships started publishing timetables and generally becoming more efficient, thus postponing their demise. In a similar way, vendors of proprietary software are dropping their prices drastically to gain market share. Some argue that they also benefit from software piracy because it gets users accustomed to their products.

How open are open-educational resources (OERs)? Quite rightly, the book explores copyright issues, notably in Africa, where COL found some years ago that countries were spending large amounts of money needlessly on copyright clearance because they were simply unaware of the legal exemptions they had. Today there is confusion about the exact meaning of the "noncommercial" and "nonderivative" restrictions under the Creative Commons licenses that are often used for OERs. We must hope that this will be cleared up before we see "license pollution," as institutions design their own licenses in a quest for clarity.

Perhaps the greatest challenge for OERs is to create a better equilibrium between creators and users. Currently there is widespread eagerness to develop OERs, but seemingly, less enthusiasm for using the OERs produced by others. Unless this changes, we shall not see the creation of the global intellectual commons that are such an attractive ideal. Much of the answer to this riddle must lie in training people to find and adapt appropriate OERs, which is another important aim of the Virtual University for Small States of the Commonwealth.

The section on flexible delivery of higher education has a special focus on the challenges of operating dual-mode institutions. These chapters highlight situations that, in any other business than higher education, would be seem as perverse. In most dual-mode institutions, the distance-learning operation accounts for a large majority of the student body and a major share of institutional income; yet university presidents persist in regarding the campus as the core business and distance learning as the ancillary activity. But perhaps this is changing. An example is the University of London, which launched its external-studies program 150 years ago. Although that program has produced five Nobel laureates, it was gradually eclipsed by the growth of campus operations. However, with the recent spinning off of major parts of the campus as separate institutions, the external-studies program is once again becoming central to the identity of this great institution.

Finally, the section on the vital area of teacher education reminds us that there are no magic bullets for the use of educational technology for development. Creating effective e-learning requires a hard slog of curriculum design, for which traditional practitioners of distance education are well-suited. Furthermore, it is pointless simply to convert to e-learning formats and methods of conventional teacher education that are not producing teachers adapted to the classrooms of today. The expansion of teacher education using technology is a wonderful opportunity to rethink its content, as is being done brilliantly by the multination consortium TESSA (Teacher Education for Sub-Saharan Africa), which is using OERs to great effect, giving locally relevant training, carefully oriented to good classroom practice, to tens of thousands of teachers.

I congratulate the editors of this volume and their authors. They have produced a book that will help to bridge the knowledge divide, an essential task in bringing closer together the extraordinary extremes of this world in which we live.

Sir John Daniel
Commonwealth of Learning

BIOGRAPHICAL NOTES ON THE EDITORS

Stewart Marshall

Professor Stewart Marshall, PhD, is the Director of the Academic Division of the University of the West Indies Open Campus (UWIOC) and holds the UNESCO Chair in Educational Technologies. Although originally an electrical engineer with the Central Electricity Generating Board in the UK, Professor Marshall has worked in higher education since 1973. He was the foundation Professor of Communication at the Papua New Guinea University of Technology, foundation Professor of Communication Studies at Monash University in Australia, and foundation Coordinator of Academic Studies and Professor of Distance Education at the Institute of Distance Education at the University of Swaziland in southern Africa. Professor Marshall's research interests are in the role of ICT in education, especially in developing countries. He has published several books and over 90 other publications, including book chapters, as well as refereed articles and conference papers.

Wanjira Kinuthia

Dr. Wanjira Kinuthia is an assistant professor of Learning Technologies at Georgia State University. She worked as an instructional designer in higher education and business and industry for several years. She also worked in and conducted research on faculty development and e-learning. Wanjira received her PhD degree in Instructional Design and Development, a Master's degree in International Affairs, focusing on African Studies and Women's Studies, and a Master's degree in Computer Education and Technology. She has a Bachelor's degree in International Business. Before that,

Bridging the Knowledge Divide, pages xiii–xiv
Copyright © 2009 by Information Age Publishing

she attended the University of Nairobi. Dr. Kinuthia has a special interest in international and comparative education, focusing on e-learning in developing countries, and conducts research and teaching in this area.

Wal Taylor

Professor Wallace Taylor, PhD, is a founding director of The Information Society Institute (TISI), a not-for-profit academic, research, and policy development organization based in South Africa, which focuses collaborative efforts across government, business, and civil society on the social appropriation of ICT for local benefit. He was the Foundation Professor of Community Informatics and Information Society at the Cape Peninsula University of Technology, Cape Town, South Africa. He is an Honorary Professor at the University of the West Indies and a visiting Senior Research Fellow at Monash University, Australia. He is a special advisor to the Institute for the Study of Digital Inclusion, based in Florida, USA. Professor Taylor is author and co-editor of 8 books, 18 book chapters, and more than 55 papers. He sits on the executive boards of a number of international community-informatics organizations, including Community Informatics Research Network International (CIRN), which involves more than 600 researchers and practitioners from more than 60 countries. He is also an international research advisor on the Canadian Research Alliance for Community and Innovative Networks program (CRACIN). He was a keynote speaker at the Salzburg Seminar on Digital Inclusion in September 2003 and has been an invited keynote speaker and invited presenter at a number of international conferences in South Africa, Australia, France, Austria, Malaysia, Italy, Russia, the United Kingdom, the United States, and Canada. He also has more than 34 years of public-sector experience in rural and regional development.

BIOGRAPHICAL NOTES ON THE AUTHORS

Jessica Norah Aguti
Dr. Jessica Aguti was born in Teso, Uganda. She holds a BA/Concurrent Dip. Ed, Med, both at Makerere University; an MA Education and Development: Distance Education of the University of London, Institute of Education and a PhD in Curriculum, Instruction and Teaching at the University of Pretoria. She has many years experience as a teacher in schools, teachers college, and university. Since joining Makerere in 1990, she has participated in various distance education programs and forums in the country, delivered and published various papers on distance education, and carried out research on educational issues. Aguti is currently a director at the Institute of Adult and Continuing Education, Makerere University.

Wing Au
Dr. Wing Au is a Senior lecturer in Education at the University of South Australia in Adelaide. He joined the University of South Australia in 1996 after working at Massey University in New Zealand and the University of Newcastle in NSW since 1983. His main teaching interests focus on the use of information technology (IT) in education, the integration of IT in learning and teaching, and how IT can be used to enhance learning.

Cheryl Brown
Cheryl joined the Centre for Educational Technology (CET) at the University of Cape Town (UCT), South Africa in July 2003 as a researcher. Prior to that, she worked at Griffith University in Brisbane, Australia as an Educational Designer and was leader of the Multimedia Development Team with-

Bridging the Knowledge Divide, pages xv–xxiii
Copyright © 2009 by Information Age Publishing
All rights of reproduction in any form reserved.

in Flexible Learning and Access Services. She is currently working on her PhD with the Department of Information Systems at UCT and is interested in further researching issues around people's access to computers, their purpose/need for using computers, and the relationship between the two.

Neil David Loftus Butcher

Neil Butcher is based in South Africa, from where he has provided policy and technical advice and support to a range of national and international clients regarding uses of educational technology and distance education, both as a full-time employee at the South African Institute for Distance Education (SAIDE) from 1993 to 2001 and as Director of Neil Butcher & Associates. He has worked with various educational institutions, assisting with institutional transformation efforts that focus on harnessing the potential of distance education methods and educational technology as effectively as possible. He is currently working as an OER Strategist with SAIDE on its new OER Africa Initiative, which is funded by the Hewlett Foundation. He is also leading the development of South Africa's national education portal for the Department of Education—www.thutong.org.za. He has managed a range of online database and Web-development projects for various organizations, including a student portal for the Federation of Tertiary Institutions of the Northern Metropolis (FOTIM), Higher Education South Africa, International Association for Digital Publications, UNESCO, and the Southern African Regional Universities' Association.

Esampally Chandraiah

Professor Esampally Chandraiah is Associate Professor of Commerce at the Dr. B. R. Ambedkar Open University in India. He was formerly Coordinator of the Academic Studies Unit with the Institute of Distance Education, University of Swaziland. He holds a BCom and MCom (Kakatiya); MPhil and PhD (Dr. B.R. Ambedkar Open University). He has co-authored several books and has a number of research articles in commerce and in open and distance education published in refereed and nonrefereed journals. He has participated in several workshops, seminars, and conferences, and has presented academic papers in many of these meetings.

Lorenzo Cantoni

Lorenzo Cantoni is Professor in the School of Communication Sciences at the University of Lugano in Switzerland. His research interests lie in the overlap between communication, education, and new media from computer-mediated communication to usability, e-learning to e-government.

Ioana Chan Mow

Dr. Ioana Chan Mow is the Dean of the Faculty of Science at the National University of Samoa. She teaches Information systems and programming in the Computing department and also within the Master's of Samoan Studies program at the Institute of Higher Education within the National University. Her main research interests are in computer education, online learning technologies, and ICT for development.

Pier Junor Clarke

Dr. Pier A. Junor Clarke graduated from the University of Toronto, Canada (PhD), City University of New York (MA), and the University of Guyana (BSc). She has taught grades K–12, and higher education in the Caribbean, Canada, and USA for over 22 years. Her teaching experience extends to online synchronous and asynchronous environments through white-board technology, WebCT Vista, LiveText E-portfolio, and Elluminate. The multiple contexts have afforded her the richness she brings to teacher education. She has taught graduate courses and is currently the coordinator and a faculty in the teacher alternative-preparation program in secondary-mathematics education at Georgia State University.

Pamela Collins

Dr. Pamela Collins, a graduate of Aberdeen University and the University of the West Indies (UWI), is the Distance Teaching Coordinator for the online Master's in Regulations and Policy (Telecommunications) program. As a technical writer and editor, she has also assisted the University of the West Indies Distance Education Centre (UWIDEC) in the instructional design and production of blended-delivery courses in diverse disciplines. She is an e-tutor and an Associate Editor of an online journal.

Susan Crichton

Susan Crichton is an associate professor in the Faculty of Education at the University of Calgary. Her research focuses on the effective uses of ICT to inform teaching, learning, and e-training. She developed an innovative preservice course that prepares novice educators to teach in blended and online environments.

Laura Czerniewicz

Associate Professor Laura Czerniewicz is Director of the Centre for Educational Technology (CET) at the University of Cape Town, South Africa. CET builds staff capacity, develops curriculum projects, offers small grants, and develops and provides an open-source learning environment, Vula (powered by Sakai). Laura Czerniewicz has a particular interest in educational technology in developing countries, researching access to and use of

ICTs in higher education. A recent report, *The Virtual Mobius Strip*, reports on detailed findings from five higher-education institutions; another eight institutions are presently being investigated. She is also interested in the formation and nature of educational technology as a new scholarly field, in multiple contexts.

Daniel Elemchuku Egbezor

Dr. Daniel Elemchuku Egbezor is a Senior Lecturer and Head of Department in the Department of Educational Foundations at the University of Port Harcourt, Nigeria. He has written extensively in the areas of school effectiveness, teacher education, and curriculum reforms and has presented in national and international conferences. His publications have appeared in national and international journals, including chapters in books.

Francesca Fanni

Francesca Fanni got her degree in Science of the Communication and holds a Master's in Communication and Education at the University of Lugano. She is now working at the NewMinE Lab as proposals writer and as a research collaborator in the BET K–12 project (*Brazilian eLearning Teacher Training in K–12*).

Martin Franklin

Martin is a Lecturer in the Department of Economics, Faculty of Social Sciences, University of the West Indies, St. Augustine Campus. His area of specialization is mathematical economics and statistics. He has undertaken research in HIV/AIDS, Aging in Trinidad and Tobago, and issues of economic development for small island-states. He has published in several journals, including the Journal of Eastern Caribbean Studies, the Social and Economic Studies Journal, and the Journal of Global Development Studies.

Trudie Frindt

Dr. Trudie Frindt is the Director of the Centre for External Studies at the University of Namibia.

Aurelio Gomes

Aurelio Gomes, MD, is Professor of Medicine at Catholic University of Mozambique in Beira. He has worked on health and development in rural central Mozambique for many years. Current work involves the HIV/AIDS epidemic. Working with funding from the US National Institutes of Health (NIH) and a Catholic lay group based in Rome, the Community of Sant'Egidio, he has led the way to antiretrovirus medicine (ARV) treatment of 3,900 people at 13 clinics. He has a joint appointment as Research Assistant Professor at the Division of Infectious Disease at University of Pittsburgh, USA.

Roger Hosein

Dr. Roger Hosein graduated from the Cambridge University in 2000, and soon after joined the department of economics at the University of the West Indies. His research interests focus heavily on international trade with emphasis on education and economic development, especially in the Caribbean region.

Richard Kajumbula

Richard Kajumbula is in charge of the Student Support Services at the Department of Distance Education, Makerere University, Kampala, Uganda, ensuring and supervising the smooth running of regional centers and support activities to distance learners. He oversees the counseling and career guidance to all distance learners and ensures constant communication to and from students, lecturers, administrative staff, and other stakeholders using several modes, including mobile technologies. He lectures in the areas of accounting, finance, budgeting, costing and general management. He is also involved in the day-to-day running of the distance learning programs at Makerere University. His research interests are in mobile learning, distributed learning, finance, costing and management, especially of distance education.

Judith W. Kamau

Judith W. Kamau is a Senior Lecturer in the Distance Education Unit, Centre for Continuing Education, University of Botswana. Before joining the University of Botswana in 1995, where she headed the Distance Education Unit from 1995 to May 2005, Mrs. Kamau was Chair, Department of External Studies, University of Nairobi from 1991 to 1995. She has consulted widely in Africa. Judith played a pivotal role in the initiation of the Open University of Tanzania. Between 1992 and 1994, she frequently visited Kingston, Jamaica as a consultant of the Ministry of Education in the initiation of the primary teachers upgrading program. Her main areas of interest are materials development and production, management of distance education programs, and provision of learner support services.

Kim Mallalieu

Dr. Kim Mallalieu, a Fulbright Fellow and graduate of Massachusetts Institute of Technology (MIT) and University College, London (UCL), is Head of the Department of Electrical and Computer Engineering at the University of the West Indies (UWI). She is the developer and coordinator of UWI's online Master's degree in Regulation and Policy, and she has been the recipient of local, regional, and international teaching awards. Dr. Mallallieu is also a member of the Diálogo Regional sobre Sociedad de la Información (DIRSI), an academic network engaged in research on pro-poor ICT policy and regulatory intervention in Latin American and the Caribbean.

Xavier Muianga

Xavier Muianga (born March 19, 1968 in Maputo, Mozambique) is an assistant lecturer in the Faculty of Education at Eduardo Mondlane University. In 2008 he started PhD studies in the Department of Computer and System Science at University of Stockholm. He obtained his MSc in ICT in Education in 2003 and BSc in Education of Mathematics and Physics in 1994. From 1992 to 2000 he worked as teacher in several secondary schools in Maputo and as Instructor of Didactics in teacher training of teachers of primary school. He works in implementation of ICT for teaching and learning, in-service teacher training, and lecturer in statistics and research methods.

Haaveshe Nekongo-Nielsen

Dr. Haaveshe Nekongo-Nielsen is senior lecturer at the University of Namibia Centre for External Studies. Before that she was the Director of the Centre for 5 years and the University's Northern Campus for 3 years. She earned a Bachelor of Science degree from St Paul's College, Lawrenceville, Virginia, a Master's of Science degree from Long Island University, Brooklyn, New York. In 2006 she obtained a PhD in Education from the University of the Western Cape in South Africa. Dr Nekongo-Nielsen is interested in researching educational methods, approaches, and theories that facilitate learning for community economic development.

Pauline Ngimwa

Pauline Ngimwa holds a Master's of Philosophy in Information Sciences. A Kenyan born, Pauline has extensive working experience in the field of information management and African higher education. She has worked as a Senior Education Specialist and Digital Librarian at African Virtual University and as Information Manager for British Council in Kenya. She is currently a PhD student at the Open University, UK. Her research interest is in the area of electronic information resources, with specific focus on African higher education.

Nwachukwu Prince Ololube

Dr. Nwachukwu Prince Ololube is a Lecturer 1 in the Department of Business Administration at NOVENA University, Ogume, Nigeria. He has written extensively in the areas of institutional management and leadership, school effectiveness, teacher effectiveness and quality improvement, and

ICT in education. He has published in various international journals, chapters in books, and leading international conference proceedings.

Isabella Rega
Isabella Rega holds a master's in Communication Sciences and an executive master's in Intercultural Communication from the University of Lugano, Switzerland (USI). She is currently a researcher and PhD candidate with a thesis on the role of telecenters in socioeconomic development. In 2006, together with some friends, Isabella funded a nonprofit organization, seed, (www.seedlearn.org), active in the fields of ICT4D and education.

Alison Mead Richardson
Alison Mead Richardson is a freelance consultant and trainer in distance and flexible learning based in Namibia. She has worked on a number of British and European-funded distance and flexible learning programs for open schooling, teacher education, technical and vocational education, adult education, and tertiary education in Namibia, Botswana, South Africa, Zambia, and Rwanda. Alison specializes in national and institutional ODL strategy and policy, organizational management and development, and staff capacity building. Her research interests focus on the study of the processes of change in introducing new teaching and learning technologies into educational institutions in Africa.

Gail Shervey
Gail Shervey is an experienced adult educator, instructional designer, and sessional instructor in the University of Calgary's Faculty of Education. Currently, she is consulting on a variety of instructional design projects and, having completed her MA in Educational Technology in 2005, is also a PhD student in the Curriculum, Learning, and Teaching specialization area of the University of Calgary's Faculty of Education.

Correl Walter Samukelo Sukati
Dr. C. W. S. Sukati is a Senior Lecturer and Director of the Institute of Distance Education at the University of Swaziland (UNISWA). He holds a BSc, BEd (UBLS); MSc. (N. Colorado); EdM, EdD. (Harvard); and DEd (SA). He has been Acting Pro-Vice Chancellor, Registrar, Assistant Registrar, Lecturer and Head of Educational Foundations Department, UNISWA; Educational Planner and Teacher, Swaziland Ministry of Education. His research interests include educational planning and policy, comparative education, open and distance education, economics, and politics of education. He has extensive publications, including a co-published book and a number of articles in refereed and nonrefereed journals.

Jon Talbot
Dr. Jon Talbot is a Senior Lecturer in the Faculty of Lifelong Learning at the University of Chester in the UK. His principal responsibility is to deliver tailored pathways of learning to adults in the workplace using the work-based learning framework (WBIS) developed at the university. He is a professional planner by background, has taught land-use professionals for a number of years, and published widely on related matters. He has worked with Commonwealth organizations and is a passionate advocate of the potential for open and distance learning as a means of transforming access to education in all nations.

Stefano Tardini
Stefano Tardini is the executive director of the e-Learning Lab of the University of Lugano in Switzerland. His research interests include computer-mediated communication, e-learning, virtual communities, cultural semiotics, and argumentation theory.

Nokuthula Vilakati
Nokuthula Vilakati holds a BA and PGCE from the University of Swaziland; an MA in International Education and Development from the University of Sussex, UK, and a CDEP from the University of South Africa. Vilakati presently works as a Coordinator, Materials Design and Development at the Institute of Distance Education, University of Swaziland, and has contributed to part of the content developed for the Virtual University for Small States in the Commonwealth (VUSSC) Project. Previously, a publisher with Macmillan Swaziland National Publishers, and before that a high-school teacher and an examiner with the Teaching Service Commission and the National Examinations Council.

Elizabeth Walker
Elizabeth Walker, PhD, is Associate Professor in the Department of Neurobiology and Anatomy at West Virginia School of Medicine, USA. Her area of interest is medical education and health care in developing countries. She received a Fulbright Scholar Award to lecture at Black Lion Hospital, Addis Ababa University, Ethiopia in 1997 and a Rotary Fellowship to serve at the Catholic University of Mozambique Faculty of Medicine in 2001. Currently her main interest is development of online courses in human anatomy that can be available to all students.

Pauline Williams-Green
Pauline Williams-Green lectures in the Department of Community Health and Psychiatry at the University of the West Indies. She is President of the Caribbean College of Family Physicians.

Richard Wyles

Richard Wyles is the Project Leader of the New Zealand Open Source Virtual Learning Environment Project, developing open-source software and involving a consortium of 20 universities, institutes of technology, and polytechnics. Richard views the application of open-source technologies as a natural driver for innovation in our education systems and knowledge economies of the future. In early 2004 Richard led the development of Eduforge (www.eduforge.org), to support the sharing of ideas, research outcomes, open content, and open-source software for education. Eduforge now hosts in excess of 100 projects from throughout the world. His current focus is on developing a national e-learning network in New Zealand, underpinned by open source, standards, and educational resources.

Greg Yates

Dr. Greg Yates is a Senior Lecturer in Education at the University of South Australia in Adelaide. His training was in psychology, and he has contributed papers in the area of cognitive information processing and social-learning theory. He is on the editorial board of the journal Educational Psychology.

ACRONYMS

BOCODOL	Botswana College of Distance and Open Learning
CABLE	Cognitive Apprenticeship-Based Learning Environment
CCE	Centre for Continuing Education
CD	Community Development
CMC	Community Multimedia Center
COL	Commonwealth of Learning
DDE	Department of Distance Education
DE	Distance Education
EDP	External Degree Program
EFA	Education for All
EMU	Eduardo Mondlane University (Mozambique)
FOTIM	Federation of Tertiary Institutions of the Northern Metropolis
GDP	Gross Domestic Product
GPA	Grade Point Average
HEI	Higher Education Institution
IACE	Institute of Adult and Continuing Education
ICT	Information and Communication Technology
IDE	Institute of Distance Education
IT	Information Technology
LDCs	Least Developed Countries
MDGs	Millennium Development Goals
NDP	National Development Plan
NGO	Nongovernmental Organization
ODeL	Open Distance and e-learning
ODL	Open and distance learning
OECD	Organization for Economic Co-operation and Development

Bridging the Knowledge Divide, pages xxv–xxvi
Copyright © 2009 by Information Age Publishing
All rights of reproduction in any form reserved.

OER	Open Educational Resources
OSS	Open Source Software
SAIDE	South African Institute for Distance Education
SMS	Short Messaging System
UB	University of Botswana
UK	United Kingdom
UN	United Nations
UNAM	University of Namibia
UNCTAD	United Nations Conference on Trade and Development
UNDP	United Nations Development Programme
UNESCO	United Nations Educational, Scientific and Cultural Organization
UNISWA	University of Swaziland
UPE	Universal Primary Education
USE	Universal Secondary Education
USA	United States of America
UWI	The University of the West Indies
UWIDEC	The University of the West Indies Distance Education Centre
VLE	Virtual Learning Environment
WBIS	Work Based and Integrative Studies

INTRODUCTION

BRIDGING THE KNOWLEDGE DIVIDE

Educational Technology for Development

Stewart Marshall, Wanjira Kinuthia, and Wal Taylor

RATIONALE FOR THE BOOK

Regional economies and communities are facing increasing economic, social, and cultural hardship in many parts of the world as economies adjust to the demands of the new orders of the information society. A part of this is the paradox that regional economies and communities can be either enhanced or disadvantaged by information and communication technology (ICT). The potential enhancement comes from the increased social, cultural, and economic capital, which comes from harnessing ICT products and services. The disadvantage comes from the power that ICT products and services have in taking commerce, service provision, and governance away from communities that have been unable to bridge the digital divide. Education has a major role to play in resolving this paradox, but education itself is affected by the paradox. Unless ICT becomes an integral part of the development, delivery, and content of education, the disadvantage will deepen.

Bridging the Knowledge Divide, pages xxvii–xxxv
Copyright © 2009 by Information Age Publishing
All rights of reproduction in any form reserved.

This book, the first volume in the book series *Educational Design and Technology in the Knowledge Society,* discusses how educational technology can utilize ICT to transform education and assist developing communities in closing the knowledge divide. It provides comprehensive coverage of educational technology in development in different professions and parts of world. The book explores examples of best practice, case studies, and principles for educators, community leaders, researchers, and policy advisers on the use of educational technology for development. In particular, it presents examples of how education can be provided more flexibly in order to provide access to hitherto disadvantaged and underrepresented communities and individuals. It develops an integrative cross-sectoral approach in the use of ICT in education to increase social, cultural, and economic capital as a means to increased sustainability for many developing communities.

The book is divided into four sections: *Flexible Education for Empowerment; Managing and Communicating Knowledge; Flexible Delivery in Higher Education;* and *Preparing Teachers Using Flexible Approaches.*

FLEXIBLE EDUCATION FOR EMPOWERMENT

This section of the book deals with some of the key issues in flexible education as a means of bridging the knowledge divide, empowering groups, and building cohesive communities: community development, gender equality, empowering women, access to ICT, and work-based learning.

The first two chapters examine the role of flexible education in community development. As Martin Gordon Franklin and Roger Hosein say in their chapter, *Flexible Education and Community Development,* "Community development must be seen as a core element in any strategy to overcome poverty and social exclusion and to building more inclusive and cohesive communities." They explore the delivery of flexible education through community-access centers. Special attention is given to empowering women through flexible education and the integration of old and new technologies for achieving community development. The chapter ends with the identification of critical factors and constraints to the delivery of flexible education for community development.

Very often, community- and economic-development initiatives start with government or chambers of commerce setting goals for economic growth and taking steps to bring economic activities and projects to a particular community. However, the University of Namibia (UNAM) recognized that community economic development should be addressed through empowering community members who must participate in such economic activities. In his chapter, *Flexible Learning for Community Economic Development,*

Haaveshe Nekongo-Nielsen describes how through its Northern Campus, in collaboration with Regional Councillors of north-central Namibia, and two educational institutions in the USA, UNAM developed and implemented two educational programs: the New Leaders Initiative Program and the JobStart Program. The useful learning outcomes that emanated from this flexible learning opportunity were that due to a paradigm shift to more open-learning and open-knowledge systems, universities have to utilize open- and distance-learning methods in order to reach underserved communities and individuals.

In their chapter, *Contribution of the IDE in Promoting Gender Equality and in Empowering Women in Swaziland,* Walter Samukelo Sukati, Esampally Chandraiah, and Nokuthula Thembi Vilakati describe a study that aimed at analyzing the contribution of the Institute of Distance Education (IDE) at the University of Swaziland (UNISWA) in eliminating gender disparities, promoting gender equality, and empowering women. Based on an analysis of data collected from the Registrar's Office at UNISWA, the study found that the IDE has contributed significantly in increasing access to tertiary education for both men and women. It was also found that in almost all the programs offered, the number of female learners was much higher than that of males. The study further revealed that the female learners performed academically as well as, if not better than, their male counterparts. The implication of this study is that countries should promote, develop, support, and/or expand their distance education programs as these have the potential to contribute to gender equality, empowering women, and resulting in the achievement of the MDGs.

South African higher education is responding to both global imperatives as well as the need to resolve historical social tensions in an environment of resource constraints. Based on data from almost 7,000 respondents, the chapter by Laura Czerniewicz and Cheryl Brown, *A Virtual Wheel Of Fortune? Enablers and Constraints of ICTs in Higher Education in South Africa,* provides a regional perspective on how academic staff and students are enabled and constrained by access to a variety of resources and how this impacts on their use. While ICTs are generally viewed positively and considered valuable for education, there is not fair and equitable access among students. Although universities cannot resolve societal inequalities, they have a role in ensuring fair access for all.

In his chapter, Jon Talbot draws some of the lessons learned from *Delivering Distance Education for the Civil Service in the UK: The University of Chester's Foundation for Government Program.* Since 2004 the University of Chester has been running a distance-delivered work-based learning program using a dedicated Virtual Learning Environment for the British Civil Service called Foundation for Government. The program is designed to equip the broad range of Civil Servants with the essential skills for modern government.

While the program has undoubtedly been successful, it has also raised a number of issues requiring further research, such as the involvement of employers, technological versus educational imperatives, learner experience and progression, and the assumption of knowledge transfer.

MANAGING AND COMMUNICATING KNOWLEDGE

This section covers the general topic of knowledge management and then looks at some of the specific technologies that can be used in the facilitation of flexible education, including SMS communication and interactive video conferencing. It then goes on to consider issues of access to knowledge in three chapters on open-educational resources and copyright.

The first chapter in this section, *Knowledge Management Strategies For Distance Education,* by Neil Butcher, reviews the importance of effective knowledge management in education, with a specific focus on its role in supporting distance education. The chapter provides an introduction to the concept of knowledge management and then focuses attention on why it has become so important in distance learning. The chapter takes readers through a nontechnical overview of key design principles that need to govern any successful knowledge management system for distance learning.

In his chapter, *The Effectiveness of Mobile Short Messaging Service (SMS) Technologies in the Support of Selected Distance Education Students of Makerere University, Uganda,* Richard Kajumbula reports the results of an exploratory study undertaken to test the effectiveness of Short Messaging Service (SMS) communication among selected first-year Bachelor of Commerce External upcountry distance education students in Makerere University, Uganda. It is proposed that these findings will inform more effective future usage of mobile technologies in distance education in Uganda. Using a questionnaire on a cluster sample of the students and an interview guide on a deliberately selected sample of tutors and administrators, SMS communication was found to be effective in conveying information about upcoming programs and developments at the main campus. Students were enthusiastic about it.

Some would say that interactive video and audio conferencing as well as telephone tutoring and the use of the Internet have made it possible for distance education to move into the forefront of course delivery. In *The Impact of Video Conferencing on Distance Education Courses: A University of Namibia Case Study,* Trudie Frindt and Elizabeth Henning report on a case study at the University of Namibia's Centre for External Studies, which has been using interactive video conferencing and teleconferencing techniques to enhance learning among its distance education students during the past few years. They explain how 38 students who enrolled in a course on teaching methods in Economics and Business Studies received intensive interactive video conferencing to prepare them for the end-of-the-year examination due to the absence of distance education study material. Their examination results were also compared with that of the traditional full-time students, who also enrolled for the same courses. This study supports the use of interactive distance education to complement, enhance, and expand education options, as the study proved that distance education could be expected to result in achievement at least comparable to their counterpart, traditional face-to-face instruction.

Worldwide, open and distance learning (ODL) is in continual transition, and one cannot underestimate the influence of technology on the everyday life of learners and educators. There is considerable evidence amassed that documents a technology and information gap that exists between those who can afford and have access to the latest in technological tools, and those who cannot. These challenges are further complicated by the fact that higher-education institutions in developing nations generally have fewer monetary resources. In light of these trends and limitations, the purpose of the chapter, *Open Resources For Open Learning In Developing Countries: Deciphering Trends For Policies, Quality, And Standards Considerations,* by Wanjira Kinuthia, is to discuss an important emerging open-access movement, namely open educational resources (OER) and to consider recommendations for ensuring high quality.

Open source now plays a major part in mainstream information-technology economic activity and has started to dominate some market areas. Richard Wyles, in his chapter *Freedom, Innovation, and Equity with Open-Source Software,* explores the benefits, outlines the challenges ahead, and how governments and the education community can deliver on the promise of equalizing access to technology resources. He outlines five ways in which open source helps equitable access to technology. First, it can be contextualized for local conditions, thereby enhancing access. Second, it can be modified to address particular niche needs not served by commercial operations. Third, it can dramatically reduce the total cost of ownership. Open source is also driving the tenets of interoperability and thereby delivering more choice and, with that, more equitable access. There is an inherent tension for proprietary vendors to move toward open standards of their own volition. Finally, open source as a production methodology enables stakeholders to be far more involved, to collaborate, innovate, and contribute to the outputs rather than being passive end-users.

In *Copyright Issues and Their Impact on Flexible Education in Africa,* Pauline Ngimwa highlights the state of copyright in Africa and its impact on flexible education, with particular emphasis on distance education and learners with sensory disabilities. Given that education is a prime mover of socioeconomic development in any community, it is imperative that a developing continent such as Africa maximizes the educational opportunities and, in particular, takes advantage of the emerging ICT-enabled breakthroughs like the educational digital resources. Within this framework, the chapter analyzes the negative effects of the copyright laws on education in Africa in the light of the imbalance that exists as a result of copyright overprotection. The later part of the chapter is more positive and provides a discussion on some emerging solutions that are being considered to mitigate the issues raised. The chapter concludes with a prediction that if nothing is done to overcome this imbalance, not only will Africa continue to lag behind on issues of development, but the digital divide will continue to widen.

FLEXIBLE DELIVERY IN HIGHER EDUCATION

In a bid to widen access to higher education and reach constituencies that have not been provided for through the conventional mode, many universities are adopting flexible means of delivering teaching and facilitating learning. This section looks at some of the methods adopted by universities, often in very difficult circumstances.

Started in 1922, Makerere University is the oldest university in Uganda and has provided education for national and regional development ever since. However, as Jessica N. Aguti points out in her chapter, *University Education for National Development: Makerere University's Dual-Mode Experience,* that in the last few decades state funding has decreased, even though there are more people wanting places at the university. To cope with this, Makerere has adopted a number of strategies, including evening and external programs. In 1991 the External Degree Program (EDP) was launched. Since then the program has grown in both the number of courses and students. The EDP has benefited greatly because of Makerere's dual-mode status; but because the university was set up to provide internal programs, this program has continued to meet a number of challenges.

The University of Botswana, which is a dual-mode institution, promulgated the distance education mainstreaming policy in 2005 in order to tap the potential of the distance-delivery mode through the provision of life-long and continuing education. The aim of this policy is to expand participation in tertiary education by making distance education an integral part of the institutional vision, mission, values, organizational culture, and the entire decision-making process. Through this policy, academic faculties, departments, and supporting departments dealing with management and finance are expected to align their rules, regulations, and bureaucracies and budgetary requirements with the needs of distance learners. In her chapter, *Considerations for Higher Education Distance Education Policy for Development: A University of Botswana Case Study,* Judith W. Kamau discusses the challenges facing the implementation of this policy and suggests ways forward if distance education is to become part and parcel of the normal university business.

Xavier Justino Muianga's chapter, *Blended Online and Face-To-Face Learning: A Pilot Project in the Faculty of Education, Eduardo Mondlane University*, describes an intervention to explore the use of a course-management system (CMS) within a flexible, student-centerd teaching and learning strategy. The project develops new teaching and learning methods and an evaluation of the strengths and weaknesses of technologies used in education. The results include quantitative and qualitative information on the use of the CMS, such as the access conditions of students and instructors, teaching and learning methods, and the like. The conclusion identifies challenges and offers solutions to provide the human and technological needs for effective implementation of CMS.

In the chapter, *Evaluating the Impact of CABLE: A Cognitive Apprenticeship-Based Learning Environment,* Ioana Chan Mow, Wing Au, and Gregory Yates describe a study that evaluated the impact of a cognitive apprenticeship-based learning environment (CABLE) in the teaching of computer programming. The CABLE approach employs a combination of practices, such as directive support, cognitive apprenticeship, and collaborative learning. The study also evaluated the effectiveness of the online learning environment used as part of the CABLE implementation. The results of both phases indicated that students in CABLE scored more highly than those participating in the non-CABLE program. In terms of positive attitudes toward the learning environment, results of the study indicated that the participants in both CABLE and non-CABLE showed strong positive feelings toward their allocated treatment. Furthermore, the results showed positive evidence of the effectiveness of the online implementation of CABLE and pointed to the benefits of the use of technology in implementing pedagogies such as cognitive apprenticeship.

In 2003 the Catholic University of Mozambique (UCM) officially created the Centro de Ensino a Distancia (CED) long-distance learning center. The great majority of its students are teachers working in rural areas of central and northern Mozambique with no specific training in education. Currently the center has 700 students studying for a bachelor's degree in the field of education. Launching distance education in this environment has been difficult. Experience has shown that lack of interaction with faculty and the feeling of remoteness by the students hampers distance-learning success. In their chapter, *From Long Distance Learning to E-Learning in Central and Northern Mozambique,* Aurelio Gomes and Elizabeth Reed Walker outline the plan to move from long-distance education to e-education. The cornerstone of e-education will be a network of community outreach centers, based at the Catholic missions affiliated with UCM. These centers will have the technological communication capability to run long-distance courses and also serve health centers and members of the community.

This section finishes with two chapters from the Caribbean. Kim Mallalieu and Pamela Collins, in their chapter, *A Framework for the Delivery of Cross-regional Distance Education to Professionals in Developing Countries,* document the planning, development, and delivery of an online graduate program on a modest budget. It captures the scope of such an undertaking through a review of the Master's degree in Regulation and Policy (telecommunications) experience at the University of the West Indies. It may be used as a resource for the development of modest-budgeted cross-regional distance-education programs to professionals in developing countries. Although not a blueprint, its structured layout offers a framework for distance education planning and programming.

Several attempts have been made to establish postgraduate training in general medical practice/family medicine in the Caribbean. These have failed because of the archipelagic geography of the region, the disparate nature of this medical specialty, and the remote location of its practitioners. In her chapter, *Distance Learning: Challenges and Opportunities for Postgraduate Medical Education,* Pauline Mercedes Williams-Green describes the first attempt to utilize distance learning as the vehicle for this level of medical training at the University of the West Indies.

PREPARING TEACHERS USING FLEXIBLE APPROACHES

Clearly, if one is going to encourage teachers to use flexible education for students, then it is necessary to use the same flexibility for the education of the teachers. This section looks at some of the cases of the introduction of flexible teaching and learning into teacher preparation.

Susan Crichton, Gail Shervey, and Elizabeth Childs report on a four-year investigation concerning preservice teachers and online teaching and learning in their chapter, *Preservice Teacher Preparation and Effective eLearning.* They posit that simply transferring the experiences of traditional education to innovative e-learning environments will NOT encourage quality experiences, and that preservice teachers are well-positioned to become online educators. They also share thoughts arising from their recent development work in China, suggesting that international e-learning needs the same attention to teacher preparation and training if it is to provide rich learning opportunities and sustain the efforts of various development projects.

In her chapter, *Distance Teacher Training in Rwanda: Comparing the Costs,* Alison Mead Richardson describes a study to compare the costs of teacher training on two programs at Kigali Institute of Education (KIE) in Rwanda: the campus-based preservice teacher-training program and the in-service teacher-training program by distance learning. The study aimed to establish which of the two teacher-training programs produced qualified teachers at the lower cost. The chapter describes the methodology for ascertaining unit costs and identifies nine key issues in costing teacher training.

In the chapter, *Beckoning E-Learners Through Exploration of Computer Technology* by Pier A. Junor Clarke, preservice secondary-school mathematics teachers in an English-speaking Caribbean setting provide their perspectives on their experiences of transitioning from learning with computer technology to exploring in a Web-knowledge forum. The teachers' academic acquisitions in technologies is initiated by their aptitude and indicative of the collaborative approach employed during their exploration with computer-technology integration and Web-knowledge forum discussions.

Efforts to bring about rapid economic and social development are dependent, to a significant degree, on changes in the outlook and behavior of the people at all levels of an educational system. Despite extensive studies that have revealed the process of decline within Nigerian educational systems and institutions, no effective policy implementation has been put forward to remedy the situation. The chapter *Educational Technology and Flexible Education in Nigeria: Meeting the Need for Effective Teacher Education*, by Nwachukwu Prince Ololube and Daniel Elemchukwu Egbezor, has the purpose of focusing on some factors that hinder effective educational technology and flexible-education implementation and their impact on teacher education. The authors feel that the elevation of teacher education in Nigeria is dependent upon the various findings and recommendations put forward being more fully applied.

In the final chapter of this section and the book, *Fostering Digital Literacy of Primary Teachers in Community Schools: The BET K–12 Experience in Salvador de Bahia*, Lorenzo Cantoni, Francesca Fanni, Isabella Rega, and Stefano Tardini present the ongoing experience of a project (BET K–12: Brazilian e-Learning Teacher Training in K–12) that aims at introducing and assessing the use of ICTs in the training of in-service primary-school teachers who work in disadvantaged schools in the area of Salvador (state of Bahia, Brazil). The chapter shows how the introduction of ICTs in a curriculum for in-service teachers has noticeably increased their perception of self-efficacy, both in terms of being able to use ICTs and of being better teachers.

SECTION 1

FLEXIBLE EDUCATION FOR EMPOWERMENT

CHAPTER 1

FLEXIBLE EDUCATION AND COMMUNITY DEVELOPMENT

Martin Franklin and Roger Hosein

INTRODUCTION

The world population has increased continually from 3.2 billion in 1960 to 6.53 billion in 2006[1]; an increase of 116%, or an additional 3.51 billion people. This in turn has posed significant challenges to the world economy. The greatest of these challenges is the UN Millennium Development Goals (MDGs) that seek to bring the world community together in a joint effort to reduce the incidence of poverty, illiteracy, child mortality, maternal mortality, malaria, HIV-AIDS, and other communicable diseases. Virtually all countries agree on the importance of reducing poverty and its attendant problems of ill health, inequity, lack of respect for basic human rights, marginalization of masses, and the relative lack of knowledge and skills in rural communities around the world.

The World Education Report 1991 noted that

> [P]olicies aimed at alleviating poverty, reducing infant mortality and improving public health, protecting the environment, strengthening human rights, improving international understanding and enriching the national culture

Bridging the Knowledge Divide, pages 3–21
Copyright © 2009 by Information Age Publishing
All rights of reproduction in any form reserved.

are essentially incomplete if they are not specifically incorporated into an appropriate educational strategy. (UNESCO, 1991)

Data from the U.S. Census Bureau show that by 1998, 96% of the increase in the world population occurred in the developing regions of Africa, Asia, and Latin America, and this percentage was expected to increase over the period 1999–2008. According to the United Nations Conference on Trade and Development Least Developed Countries (UNCTAD LDCs) Report 2006,[2] only 6% of the population aged 20–24 in LDCs was enrolled in tertiary education in recent years, compared with 23% in other developing countries and 57% in OECD countries; technical and vocational education constituted only 2.6% of the secondary enrollment in LDCs on average in 2001, as against 10.4% in developing countries and 25% in OECD countries; and the average years of schooling of the adult population in LDCs in 2000 was 3 years less than the level in other developed countries in 1960.

One of the main objectives of developing countries, especially those in the Caribbean, that are characterized by current account deficits, fiscal account deficits, and rising debt in the presence of slow economic growth, should be the fostering of a greater degree of external competitiveness. In this regard, marked improvements in the educational system to equip people with lifelong educational skills are urgently needed. Governments in developing economies must, therefore, establish the required educational framework that will enable the public and private sectors to play a meaningful role.

Education provides utility for a variety of reasons, including the important contribution it can make to the economic growth process. Education translates into economic growth through two specific mechanisms. The first is the development of new technologies which, according to the literature, is known as Schumpeterian growth. This type of reasoning is premised on the fact that educated persons are more likely to be technicians and inventors and hence contribute to the stock of knowledge. The second mechanism relates directly to the diffusion and transmission of knowledge. Educational institutions facilitate the transmission and spread of knowledge and information, thus allowing individuals and organizations alike to build on the existing stock of knowledge.

Countries (and communities) worldwide are charged with continually adjusting their educational strategies so as to address the disparities mentioned above. Further, the evolving global-, social-, and technology- driven environment make these strategies complex.

As early as 1996–1997, Castells (1996, 1997, & 1997a) and Graham and Marvin (1996)[3] suggested that many of the problems faced by the people and communities living in the UK were linked to the technological transformation that results from the influence of the emerging "international economy" on the economic and social welfare of rural and urban communities. Communities worldwide continue to be challenged by the globalization and technological shifts that have stimulated a revolution in the information and communication industry. This revolution has meant, on the one hand, that remote communities can now have access to a vast portfolio of information to enhance their learning processes, and on the other, a transformation of the workplace and the educational environment to the extent that economic agents need to continually upgrade their educational profile to remain competitive.

The center of the technological revolution is the Internet, with its significant potential for accessing and transferring information, computer-based communication, and innovative teaching strategies, all at a global level. World Internet users per thousand have increased from 52 in 2001 (Rogers & Shukla, 2001) to 178 in 2007.[4] Notwithstanding such growth, Harris (2004) pointed to the uneven global distribution of access to the Internet, which has encouraged a digital divide that separates individuals and communities who are able to access computers and the Internet from those who have no opportunity to do so. Figure 1.1 highlights the current extent of this divide.

Some authors, such as Carnoy (1995), Shukla and Rogers (2001), Perraton (2002), CAPDD (2002), and Harris (2004) explore the digital divide and its implications for community development within small states; while others Castells (1996) and CIDA (2003) caution that the information society is potentially a new route to social exclusion of communities, with

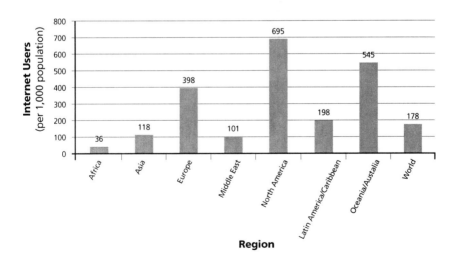

Figure 1.1 Internet users per thousand. Population by region. *Source: World Internet Usage and Population Statistics,* 2007.

the process of change creating the "information poor" or an "electronic underclass."

It is against this context of social, demographic, technological, economic, environmental, political, and other changes that communities must chart a course for their development and, in so doing, explore adopting the new information and communication technologies (ICTs).

Defining Community Development

Community Development (CD) is about building active and sustainable communities based on social justice and mutual respect, as well as changing power structures, in order to remove the barriers that prevent people from participating in the issues that affect their lives (SCCD, 2001, p. 3). CD is perceived to be multidisciplinary, in that it tends to focus on building solidarity among groups of people who share common interests and, as such, is concerned with building the capacity of people to define and address their problems and visions within the context of their own culture (IACD, 2003). It may also involve changing existing organizations so that their practices and culture embrace the empowerment of communities (SCCD, 2001, p. 8).

Frazer (2005, p. 372) points to an important role of CD in fostering a vibrant civil society and strengthening the quality of community life in disadvantaged communities. This can be done by promoting strong family, social, and community networks and a healthy infrastructure for community and voluntary organizations. In this regard, CD is also an important means of empowering individuals and groups who are at risk of exclusion and isolation. It can help these groups to overcome the fears, prejudices, and attitudes that restrict their participation and limit their self-esteem. It can also foster an environment within which these groups can act together to change their situation, collaborate with others, and overcome barriers to their active participation in society. Some of these barriers are poverty, lack of access to resources, rights, goods and services, and discrimination. CD must be seen as a core element in any strategy to overcome poverty and social exclusion and to build more inclusive and cohesive communities.

According to Schofield (2003), four interrelated concepts underpin CD:

1. A sense of community, participation, and empowerment
2. Competence, leadership, voluntarism, and creativity
3. Social capital and trust
4. Positive effect and attitude

Each of these is linked to how people and communities feel and behave as they scramble to adapt to the rapid social and economic changes at the global, national, and local levels. As a process, CD embodies a set of values and commitments as shown in Table 1.1.

The CD process has two subprocesses, namely community empowerment and enhancing the quality of life. The components of these subprocesses and the corresponding measurable outcomes are shown in Table 1.2.

TABLE 1.1 The Community Development Process

Values	Commitments
• Social Justice • Participation • Equality • Learning • Cooperation	• Challenging discrimination and oppressive practices within organizations, institutions, and communities. • Developing practice and policy that protects the environment. • Encouraging networking and connections between communities and organizations. • Ensuring access and choice for all groups and individuals within society. • Influencing policy and programs from the perspective of communities. • Prioritizing the issues of concern to people experiencing poverty and social exclusion. • Promoting social change that is long term and sustainable. • Reversing inequality and the imbalance of power relationships in society. • Supporting community-led collective action.

Source: (SCCD, 2001)

TABLE 1.2 Subprocesses and Measurable Outcomes of Community Development

Subprocess	Component	Outcome
Community empowerment	Personal empowerment	A learning community
	Positive action	A fair and just community
	Community organizing and volunteer support	An active and organized community
	Participation and involvement	An influential community
Enhancing the quality of life	Community economic development	A shared wealth
	Social and service development	A caring community
	Community environmental action	A safe and healthy community
	Community arts and cultural development	A creative community
	Governance and development	A citizens' community

Source: Adapted from (SCCD, 2001)

Informal education and mutual learning are important aspects of community development. According to the Saskatchewan Council for Community Development (SCCD, 2001, p. 8), as people get involved in community groups and activities, they acquire and discover talents, skills, knowledge, and understanding, which enable them to take on new roles and responsibilities. Such informal education and mutual learning contribute to lifelong learning, allow knowledge to be shared through critical dialogue, and can build confidence among people who have neglected or abandoned their formal education at an earlier age. The link between informal education and the development of community was also highlighted by Foster and Rosenzweig (1995), who discovered that in agricultural societies, learning by observation facilitated the transfer of educational benefits within the community.

Achieving the outcomes in Table 1.2 amid prevailing economic, political, technological, and social changes requires that communities go beyond traditional informal education and mutual learning to a new paradigm that further enhances the capacity of both formal and nonformal education to empower individual learners. Information and communication technology (ICT) will be the lever in such a paradigm, given what George and Luke (1995) call its capacity for relaxing the constraints of time, place, and pace of delivery of courses, content, learning styles, and means of entry.

Defining Flexible Education

According to Nunan (1995), some commentators argue that universities resulted from a scarcity of books and teachers and further, that producing and receiving knowledge could only be efficiently achieved by assembling students, teachers, and books in a particular location. ICTs, they contend, reverse this situation of scarcity to one of abundance, as any agency or individual has the capacity to both produce and distribute knowledge and information on a global basis through digital communication technologies. Consumers, they argue, will now drive the direction of and demand for knowledge according to their perceived needs, with the legitimization of knowledge becoming largely a factor of its demand. Existing as a provider in such an environment necessitates the structuring of information in flexible ways (courses, modules, short-term upgrading sessions, just-in-time training, or updating information, etc.) and the provision of educational services in the workplace, at home, in the community, or at an institution at times when it suits learners. Flexibility is therefore seen to be key to the survival of educational providers in meeting the needs of the new learner.

Flexible education (FE) is a learner-centered and client-focused approach that aims to foster active learning through the use of ICTs (also called educational technologies) in improving course and program design and in supporting and enhancing student learning. In its broadest sense, FE represents not only a major shift away from the traditional bipolar model of face-to-face/distance education utilized by most institutions of higher learning, but also a response by the education sector to the emerging information age, which is demanding a wider range of educational opportunities for more people.

Given that the increasing demand for tertiary education facilities has placed heightened pressure on the resources of many economies, some of which are already characterized by twin deficits in their fiscal and current accounts, FE stands out as a value-added option to help increase access of students in even remote areas to tertiary education training and nonformal education, while at the same time not placing excess pressures on the public coffers. Studying by FE gives people in communities choices in terms of how, where, when, and what to study.

FE can be seen as the high end of distance education and includes, but is not confined to, online learning or e-learning and encompasses mobile technologies and other new technological applications, such as computer-based learning, Web-based learning, virtual classrooms, and digital collaboration (George & Luke, 1995).

According to Postman (1993, p. 29),

> New technologies alter the structure of our interests: the things we think about. They alter the character of our symbols: the things we think with. And they alter the nature of community: the arena in which thoughts develop.

It is well-known that only certain things that communities "think about" become part of a taught curriculum. ICTs, however, have the potential to remove or bypass controls over what is taught, and shape the "structure of interests" by what students choose to learn. ICT has also restructured the interests of politicians and some educators to the ways in which teaching and learning can be delivered. Traditionally, the "community" in learning fits a framework called a tutorial or seminar, which is controlled by teachers through the selection of groupings, the types of interactions, and who does the interaction. However, new ICTs radically alter these structures, enabling quite different groupings, communication patterns, and power structures; thereby facilitating community development (Nunan, 1995).

FE, as a form of distance education, meets the call in the Dakar Framework of Action for Education for All (EFA) for specific provisions to reach those groups in the community that are unable to access formal education, such as out-of-school youths and adults (Intelecon Research, 1999, 2000).

Flexible education incorporates flexible delivery and flexible learning. Flexible delivery is concerned with designing learning opportunities that are economically sustainable and pedagogically defensible in the current social climate. It brings together the dimensions of student learning, forms of delivery, and content (George & Luke, 1995). Flexible learning is synonymous with open learning and is characterized by increasing access and increased control over learning. The educational value of flexible learning is based on the assertion that flexible delivery encourages approaches to learning that support deep learning. The constructivist framework for learning is therefore seen to be compatible with the processes and techniques of flexible education (Nunan, 1995).

Delivery of Flexible Education for Community Development

ICT is being harnessed across a range of educational applications to improve the efficiency, accessibility, and quality of the learning process in developing countries, with a focus on community development. Flexible education with ICTs as a lever can be used to build competence, hone leadership skills, support creativity, build social capital, foster a sense of community, and widen participation at the community level. Barrera (2001) suggests that by making suitable, well-adapted ICTs available at the community level, FE can play a role in reinforcing the efforts of these countries in providing more effective and transparent governance and enhancing democratic processes at the local level. By making this adjustments, FE facilitates some of the concepts that underpin community development and by extension, the sub-processes that comprise community development i.e., empowerment and enhancing the quality of life.

The effective delivery of flexible education to communities, however, requires an appropriate vehicle. One such vehicle is the community-access center. Community-access centers, also called telecenters (Latchem & Walker, 2001), are public places where people within a community can access computers, the Internet, and other digital technologies that enable them to gather information, create, learn, and communicate with others while they develop essential 21st-century digital skills. While each telecenter is potentially different, the common focus is on the use of ICTs to support community, economic, educational, and social development, thereby reducing isolation, bridging the digital divide, promoting health issues, and creating economic opportunities for its users. Telecenters exist in several countries, albeit by different names, such as telecottages,[5] ICT centers,[6] flex labs,[7] village knowledge centers[8] (VKCs), community learning centers (CLCs),[9] community technology centers[10] (CTCs), community multimedia centers (CMCs),[11] and citizen service centers[12] (CSCs).

The telecottage concept started in Sweden and has been well-embraced in the UK such that at last count, over 200 telecottages existed. Depending on location (rural or urban) and country (developed or developing), these vary in size, facilities, and services (ranging from basic telecommunication services such as "phone shops" to fully interactive Internet–based training). Psychologically, telecenters can work to dispel the fears and myths about technology. Examples of telecenters can be found in every continent.[13] These are discussed in the literature by researchers, such as Proenza et al. (2001), Latchem and Walker (2001), Liyanage (2001), Rogers and Shukla (2001), Mathison (2003), Slater and Tacchi (2004), Samaranayake (2004), and Franklin and Hosein (2006).

The advanced concept as developed and promoted by the International Telecommunications Union (ITU), called Multipurpose Community Tele-centers (MCTs), includes additional facilities such as a library, workshop, and teaching rooms. MCTs take advantage of the growing availability and access-speed options for Internet service, along with the variety of uses, including 2-way teleconferencing and multimedia, to offer distance education and even medical consultations, as well as to act as delivery points for government information. Potentially, MCTs have a positive impact on the socioeconomic development of the communities they serve, helping to

- develop rural and remote infrastructure,
- provide rural regions with better public services such as education, health, and administration, including the paperwork for government procedures,
- generate employment,
- integrate relatively isolated communities into the national and international information network and thus accelerate exchange of private goods and services

Accordingly, these provide a means to deliver both public and private services to rural and remote locations without incurring immediate large investments in infrastructure (Intelecon Research, 2000).

One example of telecenters is the UNESCO-funded project, APPEAL, which supports five countries (Indonesia, Lao PDR, Thailand, Sri Lanka, and Uzbekistan) in their drive to empower local communities through the provision of suitable delivery mechanisms for ICT-based activities. In Lao PDR, the project focuses on improving village incomes among rural youth; CLCs also serve as resource centers where ICT equipment is used to disseminate news and information in various areas, including life skills and income generation. In Sri Lanka, the Sarvodaya Shramadana Movement established MCTs that serve as village banks as well as six CLCs. Community databases are being developed, and information is being disseminated to villagers and entrepreneurs through Sarvodaya's Mobile Multimedia Unit. Computer training is also provided for village bank staff, village volunteers, and CLC officials. In Thailand, under the Northern Regional NFE Centre, the telecenter project is developing intervillage connectivity and shared learning, as well as empowering the members of rural communities—particularly youth—to use ICT as a tool for community development. The project shares learning experiences between villages through ICT labs. In Uzbekistan, the National Commission is helping to develop community databases and documentation for community planning and management. Other activities include establishing an ICT network among CLCs in the target areas, providing training to all personnel and community members at the project sites, and developing ICT materials for community empowerment, poverty alleviation, and improving the quality of life. In Indonesia, activities include community data collection and a program that uses the Internet to increase access to data and to improve information flow between local communities and the government (UNESCO, 2004).

Empowering Women as a Form of Community Development

Petrakis and Stamatakis (2002) found empirical evidence to support the notion that the relationship between education and growth varies with a nation's level of development. They carried out a cross-country regression comprising three groups: advanced, developed, and less-developed economies. Their findings also reveal that primary education is more dominant in less-developed countries, while higher education carries more importance in advanced economies.

Gemmell (1996) also commented on the importance of primary-, secondary-, and tertiary-level schooling for these three categories of countries. He contends that in developing economies, the effects of human capital on economic growth are most evident at the primary and secondary levels. However, the effects are greatest at the tertiary level for OECD countries.

Notably, Michaelowa (2000) observed that in African economies, the more-educated women tend to have healthier children and smaller families, since they practice better family planning. This is significant because it suggests that educated mothers can make a greater contribution to their children's academic progress, resulting in such children staying longer in the educational system as well as being more inclined to pursue lifelong learning. With regard to the generally lower literacy rates among women worldwide,[14] but more so in the LDCs, empowering women must be a key issue in the agenda for community development within developing countries.

The use of ICT is considered a critical element in the effort to empower rural women, because empowerment entails the ability and freedom to make choices in the social, political, and economic arenas. In turn, choice making is driven by both the quality and quantity of information delivered to women in rural households. The challenge facing developing countries like Ghana is that of effectively making information available to rural households to enhance choice making (Ghana, 1995, p. 6; 1996). If ICT is critical to the empowerment of women, so too is flexible education.

Nath (2001) posed the following argument as the basis of his model for the empowerment of women in Ghana through the use of ICT:

> ICT in the context of knowledge societies is understood as building the ability and skills of women to gain insight of actions and issues in the external environment which influence them and to build their capacity to get involved and voice their concerns in these external processes and make informed decisions.

Kwapong (2007) credits Nath's model with being cognizant of the various conceptualization processes that information goes through in the women's system, but goes on to suggest that it must take into consideration the various inhibiting factors and obstacles that could affect women's empowerment, for example, the sociopolitical milieu. Flexible education can provide Nath's model with the capacity to meet the challenges posed by the inhibiting factors and obstacles.

Several examples of successful FE projects for empowering women can be found in the literature. One such example is the project mounted through the Bangladesh Open University to improve the entrepreneurial and business skills of rural women. It was developed in such a way that women with little to no literacy skills were not disadvantaged. A tutor-led community-learning-group approach was adopted. Materials were developed, and female leaders were identified from communities and trained in the use of the materials. The leaders led groups of up to 20 women through the modules of the course within their communities. The tutors negotiated with the women to determine where and when the meetings would be held. To attract women to the course, it had to be delivered at a place that was not too far from their homes, and at a time that allowed them to carry out their normal activities. Most groups assembled on grass mats spread on the ground in front of the hut of one of the participants. At the conclusion of the course, all women who had participated in the full course were awarded a Certificate of Participation, which provided documentation that could be presented to the Grammeen Bank and other NGOs to access microeconomic loans to establish small enterprises (Hampton & Bartram, 2002).

Integrating New Technologies with Old Technologies for Community Development

If community development is to be effective, it must be sustainable and transcend the structure of the society from the grassroots up. According to (Barrera, 2001), integrated, sustainable grassroots community development is increasingly seen by the developing countries as the key to improving the quality of life of all citizens, particularly in disadvantaged communities in rural areas and low-income urban settlements, which are home to the vast majority of the population. Further, access to ICTs, including community radio, is seen both as a catalyst and a driving force for community development.

Accordingly, initiatives aimed at integrating new and old technologies are being pursued in some developing countries with a view to facilitating community development. One such initiative is the "Towards a Communication and Information Society for All" program for community multimedia centers. This program seeks to bring together, in a novel manner, two areas in which UNESCO and its partners have already had strong successes: community radio and multipurpose community telecenters.

Community radio is inexpensive, easy to operate, and reaches all segments of the community through local languages to offer information, education, and entertainment, as well as a platform for debate and cultural expression. As a grassroots channel of communication, it can act as a powerful agent for community and individual empowerment, as it simultaneously offers contact, content, and self-expression. MCT, on the other hand, is a sustainable, cost-effective, shared community facility offering basic telecommunication and office administration services such as telephone, fax, e-mail, Internet access, word processing, and photocopying, along with the necessary user support and training. The MCT can facilitate access to local library and information services and also offer access to national and worldwide electronic information banks in support of literacy campaigns, basic and nonformal education, government programs, and other public-service activity.

When MCTs are combined with community radio, a wealth of information can be accessed by the entire local community and not only by individuals able to use computers and related ICTs. Therefore, when community radio, access to Internet, and other ICTs are combined, new possibilities open up for the most disadvantaged communities in developing countries.

By combining community radio, access to the Internet, library services, and other ICTs, the program aims to overcome linguistic, literacy level, and other barriers that prevent the most disadvantaged communities in developing countries from engaging in and benefiting from the exchange of information and knowledge (Barrera, 2001).

Critical Factors for Flexible Education in Community Development

Given that ICT plays a significant role in the delivery of flexible education, it would be prudent to recognize from the literature critical factors for its successful implementation as an enabler of socioeconomic development. Two such works, UNDP (2001) and Heeks (1999), suggest the following factors to be critical:

1. Strong leadership
2. A shared vision and commitment by all stakeholders
3. A comprehensive and holistic approach[15]
4. Recognition of the roles played by different stakeholders
5. A "Strategic Compact" that aligns government, civil society, and business to the strategy and creates powerful linkages among organizations and communities across local, national, regional, and global levels
6. The leveraging of local, national, and global linkages
7. A functioning information chain

Given that e-learning is subsumed in flexible education, the successful implementation of flexible education depends on the competence of the practitioner to access and select quality content and then integrate it into the teaching context. This hypothesis assumes that teachers mediate ICT applications when they are successful, and that ICT's academic value relates positively to teacher competence (Kirk, 2002). This conforms to the current trend toward blended-learning approaches—those that recognize that facilitation is a key component for success.

Other writers (Coleman & Laplace, 2002) have identified a range of other success factors. These include ensuring executive and upper-management sponsorship of the FE project, visibility of the project within the community organization, the structure and accountability of the development/implementation team, and a careful deployment strategy that includes training.

Best-practice models reviewed in Eklund, Kay, and Lynch (2003) provide a set of basic preconditions for success of an e-learning venture and, by extension, flexible education.

George and Luke (1995) suggest three factors:

- Access to a comprehensive, systematic, and coordinated network of support is essential for students to learn independently.
- Training of both students and facilitators; the latter must maximize new technologies and methodologies to promote particular kinds of learning in students.
- Flexibility in assessment is central to this view of learning.

CAPDD (2002) cites further developments in the technologies, reduction in prices, a greater availability of networks, and a more user-friendly approach to the technologies as critical to flexible education.

Constraints to Using Flexible Education in Community Development

The level of Internet penetration can also be a constraint to flexible education in community development. World Internet Usage Statistics[16] show that Asia, Europe, and North America account for 37%, 27%, and 20%, respectively, of all Internet users in 2007, while Latin America, Africa, the Middle East, and Oceania/Australia account for the remaining 17%.

One of the main deterrents to distance education and, by extension, flexible education in several developing countries (Fiji, for example) is cost. Adequate financial resources form a key factor in the successful implementation and integration of flexible education. It is obvious that countries with higher financial resource bases stand a better chance than those with limited resources to reap benefits offered by ICTs. Sife, Lwoga, and Sanga (2007) recommend that higher-learning institutions adopt freeware and open-source software for teaching and learning activities; continually press for more funds from their governments; and diversify sources of funds to have a wide financial base, in addressing the problem of limited funds and sustaining donor-funded projects.

Another constraint can be the perception by some communities (or countries) as cited in (Ghana, 1995, p. 6; 1996) that the allocation of resources to ICT and FE is in conflict with the resource allocation to meet immediate needs such as food, shelter, and health as against investing these resources in computers and ICT infrastructure. Ghana (ibid) makes the point that such perception fails to recognize the symbiotic relationship between ICT and rural households' empowerment in improving their welfare.

There are as well sociocultural factors that constrain the employment of ICT in empowering rural women. For example, in Ghana, women constitute the higher percentage (42%) of the illiterate adult population.[17] Studies have shown that women experience greater poverty, have heavier time burdens, lower rates of utilization of productive resources, and lower literacy rates (GLSS 4, 2000). School participation rates for basic and second-cycle schools are 77% for men and 38% for women. Due to sociocultural factors like early marriage, teenage pregnancy, and child labor that affect women, this discrepancy widens as one ascends the educational ladder (Ghana 1995, p. 6; 1996).

Another constraint is the availability of complementary inputs such as computers, voice and video systems and, in some cases, physical access to rural locations. UNCTAD estimated the penetration of telephone mainlines and mobile phones in LDCs in 2003 to be 11% of the level for other developing countries and 3% of the level for the OECD countries.[18] In countries like Ghana, the current infrastructure for telecommunication broadcast to communities is limited to serving the major regional centers and capitals. Resources for expanding the reach of the infrastructure may be quite limited, according to the findings of a survey of budget allocations to the ICT sector (Ghana, 2003).

Finally, the Commonwealth Action Programme for the Digital Divide (2002) explores prescriptions for addressing the following issues that usually constrain the implementation of e-learning and, by extension, flexible education:

- Lack of a systemic approach to ICT implementation
- Awareness and attitude toward ICTs
- Administrative support
- Technical support
- Transforming higher education
- Staff development
- Lack of ownership

CONCLUSION

Into the 21st century, mounting debt and growing current account and fiscal imbalances typify developing economies such as the Caribbean economies. In addition, the growth performance of most Caribbean economies has also been lagging in the last 15 years. In this type of economic environment, all efforts have to be made to improve the economic growth process, and greater investments in flexible modes of education will definitely be useful.

Overall, the nature and structure of many developing countries pose significant barriers to the equitable distribution of traditional forms of educational services. As such, FE can be applied to reduce the level of inequity in the education system and hence contribute to the development of the economy, as proposed by the new endogenous growth models. Additionally, these nontraditional methods of education can also be used to reduce the level of gender inequality domestically and thus promote equitable development. Developing countries should therefore seek to adopt as far as possible the tools for the effective delivery of these alternative forms of education.

REFERENCES

Barrera, A. (2001, January). *Empowering the rural and poor suburban communities in Central America; The Infoplazas program of Panama*. Paper presented at the Seminar on Integrating New and Traditional Information and Communication Technologies for Community Development, Kothmale, Sri Lanka.

CAPDD (2002). *The Commonwealth, ICTs and development. A report to CHOGM, 2002*. Commonwealth Action Programme for the Digital Divide, Commonwealth Secretariat.

Carnoy, P. (1995). *Education and the new international division of labour*. In the *International Encyclopedia of Economics of Education*, Oxford.

Castells, M. (1996). *The information age: Economy, society and culture*. Vol.1: The rise of the network society. Cambridge, MA; Oxford, UK: Blackwell.

Castells, M. (1997). *The information age: Economy, society and culture*. Vol. 3: The end of the millennium. Cambridge, MA; Oxford, UK: Blackwell.

Castells, M. (1997a). *The information age: Economy, society and culture*. Vol. 2: The power of identity. Cambridge, MA; Oxford, UK: Blackwell.

CIDA (2003). *CIDA's strategy on knowledge for development through information and communication*, Retrieved March 2007 from http://www.acdi-cida.gc.ca/ict

Coleman, R., & Laplace, L. (2002). *E-Learning implementation*. RGS Associates Inc. Retrieved March 2007 from http://www.rgsinc.com/publications/pdf/white_papers/elearning

Dabinett, G. (2000). Regenerating communities in the UK: Getting plugged into the information society? *Community Development Journal, 35,* 157–166.

Eklund, J., Kaye, M., & Lynch, H. (2003). *E-learning: Emerging issues and key trends*. ANTA. Retrieved March 2007 from http://www.flexiblelearning.net.au/research/2003/elearning250903final.doc

Foster, A. D., & Rosenzweig, M. R., (1995). Learning by doing and learning from others: Human capital and technical change in agriculture. *Journal of Political Economy, 103*(6), 1176–1209.

Franklin, M., & Hosein, R., (2006). *Closing the digital divide in Trinidad and Tobago: The experience of community-based learning centres*. Paper presented at the Commonwealth of Learning PCF4 Conference, Jamaica. Retrieved March 2007 from http://www.openarchives.org

Frazer, H. (2005). Four different approaches to community participation. *Community Development Journal, 40*(3).

Gemmell, N. (1996). Evaluating the impacts of human capital stocks and accumulation on economic growth: Some new evidence. *Oxford Bulletin of Economics and Statistics, 58,* 9–28.

George, R., & Luke, R. (1995, November 30–December 1). *The critical place of information literacy in the trend towards flexible delivery in higher education context*. Paper presented at the Learning for Life Conference, Adelaide, Australia.

Ghana (1995). *Constitution of the Republic of Ghana*. Retrieved March 2007 from http://www.idlo.int/texts/leg5515.pdf

Ghana (1996). *Ghana Vision 2020—The first step: 1996–2000*. Retrieved March 2007 from http://www.ghana.edu.gh/prospects/vision.html

Ghana (2003). *Republic of Ghana—National ICT policy and plan development committee.* Retrieved March 2007 from http://www.ict.gov.gh/

GLSS 4 (2000). *Ghana living standards survey—Report of the fourth round.* Ghana Statistical Service, Accra.

Hampton, C., & Bartram, J., (2002). Delivering the programme. In A. K. Mishra and J. Bartram (Eds.), *Perspectives on distance education: Skills development through distance education* (chap. 7). Vancouver: The Commonwealth of Learning.

Harris, R. (2004). *Information communication technologies for poverty alleviation.* UNDP-APDIP, Malaysia.

Heeks, R. (1999). *Information and communications technologies, poverty and development.* Development Informatics Working Paper Series. No. 5. IDPM Publications: University of Manchester, UK.

Intelecon Research & Consultancy Ltd. (1999–2000). *Funds for rural telecom development: Experience in Latin America.* Rural Funds Update. Retrieved March 2007 from http://www.inteleconresearch.com/pages/forum2.html

IACD (2003). *Asset based approaches to rural community development.* International Association for Community Development. Retrieved March 2007 from http://www.iacdglobal.org/documents/resource/rsrcAssetBasedCommunityDevelopmentResourceIACDE-book.pdf

Kirk, J. (2002). *E-learning: An executive summary.* South Carolina: (ERIC Document Reproduction Service, No. ED461762)

Kwapong, O. (2007). Problems of policy formulation and implementation: The case of ICT use in rural women's empowerment in Ghana. *International Journal of Education and Development using ICT, 3*(2).

Latchem, C., & Walker, D. (2001). *Telecenters: Case studies and key issues.* Vancouver: The Commonwealth of Learning.

Liyanage, H. (2001). *Telecenters for community development—An information technology approach.* UNESCO, Paris.

Mathison, S. (2003). *Digital dividends for the poor: ICT for poverty reduction in Asia.* Kuala Lumpur, Malaysia: Global Knowledge Partnership Secretariat.

Michaelowa, K. (2000, June). *Returns to education in low income countries: Evidence for Africa.* Paper presented at the annual meeting of the Committee on Developing Countries of the German Economic Association. Hamburg Institute for International Economics.

Nath, V. (2001). *Heralding ICT enabled knowledge societies.* Retrieved March 2007 from http://members.tripod.com/knownnetwork/articles/heralding.htm

Nunan, D. (1995). Closing the gap between learning and instruction. *TESOL Quarterly, 29*(1).

Perraton, H. (2002, September). *Technologies, education, development and costs. A third look at the educational crisis.* Presented at round table University and Technology for Literacy/Basic Education Partnerships in Developing Countries, Paris.

Petrakis, P. E., & Stamatakis, D. (2002). Growth and educational levels: A comparative analysis. *Economics of Education Review, 21*(5).

Postman, N. (1993). *Technology: The surrender of culture to technology.* New York: Vintage Books.

Proenza, F. J., Bastidas-Buch, R., & Montero, G. (2001). *Telecenters for socioeconomic and rural development in Latin America and the Caribbean: Investment opportunities*

and design recommendations with special reference to Central America. FAO/ITU/
IADB. Retrieved December 3, 2008 from http://www.iadb.org/sds/itdev/
telecenters/exsum.pdf

Rogers, E., & Shukla, P. (2002). The role of telecenters in development communication and the digital divide. *Journal of Development Communication, 12*(2).

Samaranayake, V. K. (2004). *Information and communication technology for poverty reduction.* Sri Lanka Economic Association, Annual Sessions, Sri Lanka.

SCCD (2001). *Annual Report 2000–2001.* Saskatchewan Council for Community Development, Saskatchewan, Canada.

Schofield, J. (2003). *Bringing the Internet to schools effectively.* Retrieved March 2007 from http://usinfo.state.gov/journals/itgic/1103/ijge/gj09.htm

Shukla, P., & Rogers, E. (2001, November). *The Internet and the digital divide in Latin America, Africa and Asia.* Paper presented at the International Communication Association and the International Association of Mass Communication Research 2001 Symposium on the Digital Divide, Austin, TX.

Sife, A., Lwoga, E., & Sanga, C. (2007). New technologies for teaching and learning: Challenges for higher learning institutions in developing countries. *International Journal of Education and Development using ICT, 3*(2).

Slater, D., & Tacchi, J. (2004). *Research: ICT innovations for poverty reduction,* UNESCO, New Delhi. Retrieved December 3, 2008 from http://unesdoc.unesco.org/images/0013/001361/136121e.pdf

Graham, S., & Marvin, S. (1996). *Telecommunications and the city: Electronic spaces, urban places.* London and New York: Routledge.

UNDP (2001). *Human Development Report 2001.* Oxford University Press.

UNESCO (1991). *World education report (1991).* Paris: UNESCO.

UNESCO (2004). *Empowering communities through non-formal learning.* The ICT Unit, Asia and Pacific Regional Bureau for Education. Infoshare: Source and Resources Bulletin, Vol. 6, (pp. 20–25).

NOTES

1. See http://www.census.gov/ipc/www/idb/worldpopinfo.html (Retrieved December 3, 2008)
2. See http://www.uneca.org/eca_resources/news/200706unctad_launch-FACTS-aboutLDCs.htm
3. As cited in Dabinett, 2000
4. Source: World Internet Usage and Population Statistics, 2007. See http://www.internetworldstats.com
5. See http://www.the-telecottage.co.uk (Retrieved March, 2007)
6. See Slater & Tacchi, 2004
7. See http://www.telecentre.org. (Retrieved December 3, 2008)
8. See http://www.isoc.org/oti/articles/0401/balaji.html (Retrieved March, 2007)
9. See Intelecon Research, 2000
10. See http://www.ctcnet.org (Retrieved March 2007)
11. See http://portal.unesco.org/ci/en/ev.php-URL_ID=1263&URL_DO=DO_TOPIC&URL_SECTION=201.html (Retrieved December 3, 2008)

12. See http://www.edc.org/GLG/gkd/2005/May/0156.html (Retrieved March, 2007)
13. For example, Canada, UK, Hungary, Latin America, India, Trinidad and Tobago, and parts of Africa—Mozambique, South Africa, Dar es Salaam, Uganda.
14. UNESCO Institute for Statistics: Retrieved http://www.uis.unesco.org/en/stats/statistics/ed/g_%20all%20regions.jpg (Retrieved March, 2007)
15. This ensures that the strategy benefits effectively from the synergies and the optimal impact from the deployment of ICT.
16. See http://www.internetworldstats.com/stats.htm
17. Defined as people who are 15 years and above and can read and write at least a sentence (GLSS 4, 2000).
18. See http://www.uneca.org/eca_resources/news/200706unctad_launch-FACTS-aboutLDCs.htm

CHAPTER 2

FLEXIBLE LEARNING FOR COMMUNITY ECONOMIC DEVELOPMENT

Haaveshe Nekongo-Nielsen

INTRODUCTION

North-central Namibia comprises the four political regions of Ohangwena, Omusati, Oshana, and Oshikoto, collectively known as the north-central region (see Maps 2.1 and 2.2).

The Namibian economy is characterized by huge disparities, where the wealthiest 1% of the population earns 50% more than the poorest (Marope, 2005, p. 11). The north-central region faces huge economic challenges, as 70% of the poorest population lives in north-central Namibia, where subsistence agriculture and stock rearing are the dominant economic activities, which are often severely affected by the vagaries of the semiarid climate and by ongoing environmental degradation (Nekongo-Nielsen, 2005, p. 25). There are few exploitable natural resources in Namibia, but many local enterprises suffer from the competition posed by large, well-capitalized South African companies.

After independence, the Namibian government recognized that education and training, as well as knowledge and innovation, are very important

Bridging the Knowledge Divide, pages 23–38
Copyright © 2009 by Information Age Publishing
All rights of reproduction in any form reserved.

Map 2.1 The map of Namibia, with the four north-central regions highlighted (adapted from Mendelsohn, el Obeid, and Roberts, 2000, p. 2).

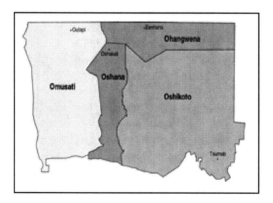

Map 2.2 The four north-central regions of Namibia.

in bringing about socioeconomic development. Furthermore, the government has supported the United Nations Declaration on meeting education for all goals which states:

> Every person—child, youth and adult—shall benefit from educational opportunities designed to meet their basic learning needs. These needs comprise both essential learning tools (such as literacy, oral expression, numeracy, and problem solving) and the basic learning content (such as knowledge,

skills, values and attitudes) required by human beings to be able to survive, to develop their full capacities, to live and work in dignity, to make informed decisions, and to continue learning. The scope of basic learning needs and how they should be met varies with individual countries and cultures, and inevitably, changes with the passage of time. (World Declaration on Meeting Education for All, 1990, Article 1, Paragraph 1)

The country has thus embarked on total educational reform. This reform has been felt equally in basic, tertiary, and nonformal education. All educational institutions were therefore tasked to ensure that the country's population is well-educated and provided with employability skills.

Accordingly, the University of Namibia (UNAM) has realized that it has a role to play in educating and preparing people to participate meaningfully in the country's development. UNAM's mission statements emphasize its commitment to national socioeconomic, cultural, political, and human resource development. Moreover, the university has realized that to provide meaningful learning for community economic development, collaboration with grassroots leadership and other educational institutions is necessary. This chapter presents the impact of two programs that have been developed in collaboration with Regional Councillors of north-central Namibia and two educational institutions in the United States. Through developing and implementing these programs, an interaction and partnership was formed to facilitate a collaborative learning process. For the purpose of this chapter, community economic development is defined as

[A]n action taken locally by a community to provide economic opportunities and improve social conditions in a sustainable way. . . . CED is a community-centered process that blends social and economic development to foster the economic, social, ecological and cultural well-being of communities. (en.wikipedia.org/wiki/Community_economic_development)

The chapter arose from the author's interest in researching the learning approaches that facilitate flexible learning for socioeconomic development and her knowledge of the UNAM Northern Campus, first as head of the Community Education and Development Unit (CEDU), under which this program resided, and as the Campus Director from 2000 to 2002. According to Nunan (2000, p. 54), the "concept of flexibility could mean whatever you want it to mean." In this chapter, therefore, flexible learning is taken, as implied by Jakupec and Garrick (2000, p. 3), as "a purposeful action undertaken by educational institutions in order to meet new, and often economic challenges." For the purpose of understanding this chapter, flexible learning is simply defined as a set of educational philosophies and systems that provides learners with increased learning opportunities, choice, and convenience of study time and place.

Through this chapter, the author shares with readers a model of flexible learning that was developed and tested at the Northern Campus of the University of Namibia. The model was developed in order to provide nonformal education that stimulates social and economic activities in rural areas and demonstrates that universities and rural communities can engage in collaborative learning for socioeconomic development. The chapter highlights the contributions these programs have made to participants' communities and the contributions that participants are making to their communities, and presents useful learning outcomes emanating from this type of collaborative learning arrangement. These learning outcomes can be replicated in other similar community economic-development activities elsewhere in the country and worldwide.

BACKGROUND TO THE NORTHERN CAMPUS

The Northern Campus was established in 1998 in Oshakati, the most densely population urban town in Namibia, to serve the north-central region, which is the most populous region in Namibia. The region is home to about half of Namibia's population, and the four north-central regions are among the most disadvantaged of Namibia's 13 political regions in terms of indices, such as per capita income, mortality rates, life expectancy, and food security. Thus, the establishment of the Northern Campus was initiated in response to the clear and significant educational needs of the community. Its continued expansion and development has resulted from constructive consultation and collaboration with all interested parties in the whole country.

The establishment of the Northern Campus in the most populous region of the country was aimed at being a community project with the objective of helping people of the region to access higher education and the general public to upgrading their skills in order to participate in the country's developmental activities. Setting up the Northern Campus as a project, which might evolve into a full-fledged university, was the University of Namibia's way of addressing three of its objectives:

- Cultivating standards of excellence in teaching research and community service
- Undertaking basic and applied research with a view to contribute to the socioeconomic development of Namibia
- Providing advisory services, consultancy, and extension services with a view to promoting education and technical know-how among rural communities of Namibia

Before, the Northern Campus of the University operated nine regional centers scattered throughout Namibia, which used to provide administrative and academic support to distance-education students. While the campus was established for the intention of extending diploma and degree programs to the most populous region of the country, due to public demand, the university also decided to "provide innovative and tailor-made programs based on the needs of the community that will be flexible and adjustable" (Harlech-Jones, 2002, p. 14).

Since its establishment, therefore, the principle of collaboration and community participation formed part of the planning process and operations of the Northern Campus. The campus vision, below, was developed in collaboration with the region's communities, and it has helped the university in developing educational programs that are relevant and address community needs.

> Our vision is of an enlightened, free, well-informed, well-educated and healthy people, living as a harmonious, integrated and caring community, guided by a democratic culture based on shared common values, open to positive interaction with other cultures, in an economy which is productive and diversified, and provides meaningful employment. (The Northern Campus Vision 2020, produced in March 1999 during the Campus' first Vision to Action Workshop)

True to its vision, and in the midst of economic challenges, the Northern Campus has developed successful combinations of outreach programs for the surrounding communities and innovative academic programs for higher-school graduates and adults who aspire to higher degrees. The strategic planning process at the Northern Campus, which includes community representation, has especially identified the expansion of the undergraduate and graduate programs as one of the critical objectives. In order to fulfill that objective, the campus has embarked on expanding its academic offerings by adding degree programs, increasing the number of courses offered via interactive video, developing programs that are offered through open and distance modes, and developing Web-based courses.

Furthermore, through various forums with the local community, it was also found that what was needed in the region was to educate the residents in realizing a sense of responsibility to their communities and for the campus to provide an educated and productive workforce. As a result, the two programs, the New Leaders Initiative Program and the JobStart Program, were developed to address issues of leadership development and the eradication of unemployment among young adults of the region. The development and implementation of the two programs were made possible by generous funding from the Ford Foundation.

PROGRAM DEVELOPMENT AT THE NORTHERN CAMPUS

As mentioned above, the development of educational programs at the Northern Campus has been guided by the principle of collaboration and community participation. Moreover, it was proposed that in developing the two programs, distance- and open-learning methods be used to widen the scope of learning and ensure that information communicated to participants located in all corners of the region would be the same in all respects. In addition, during the implementation process, local community structures and resources were used to ensure that learning was relevant to community needs and aspirations.

The two educational programs were therefore tailored, using the distance learning pedagogy and technologies, to allow access to education for rural people and meet the needs of young adults who were unemployed. The New Leaders Initiative Program was first implemented in 2000, the JobStart in 2001, and the implementation process was as described below.

The New Leaders Initiative Program

Experience has shown that every year people in rural areas of Namibia establish projects to raise awareness on issues of regional and national importance and mobilize community members to participate in those projects and take action with the purpose of improving their circumstances. However, commendable as they might be, in most cases these projects disappear from the scene without recognition and support. This results from initiators getting demoralized, stopping their activities, and some even move out of those communities to other parts of the country where their efforts are accorded the recognition they deserve. Thus, failure to recognize efforts made by up and coming leaders robs local communities, especially rural areas, of high-caliber people with workable ideas. In order to ensure that these high-caliber individuals remain to develop rural areas, the University of Namibia saw it appropriate to develop educational programs that support and celebrate local initiatives that are aimed at developing socioeconomic activities in the region.

The objective of the New Leaders Initiative Program was therefore to recognize the initiatives by these up and coming leaders that promote economic and community development and civic vitality in rural areas. It aimed at developing local leadership at the community level through appraising individuals who seek to transform the social and economic life of their communities, by recognizing their efforts, and providing them with advice and training opportunities. It was hoped that the recognition and experience gained from the training would further lead to greater involvement by these individuals and motivate them to continue engaging in community-development activities. By recognizing these leaders, the program also hoped to encourage and inspire other community members to become active and productive citizens.

In order to give impetus to genuine collaboration and partnership with the local community, selection of candidates was a joint effort by the UNAM Northern Campus and regional leaders. Each constituency in the four political regions nominated one person who qualified for the program, according to the given criteria. Eligible candidates were invited to participate in the program. The participants were selected first by finding the type of community economic-development initiatives that exist across the four north-central regions and determining the ones that qualify for the New Leaders Initiative Program. Table 2.1 highlights the type of initiatives and biographical information of individuals who tend to lead initiatives that are considered community economic-development activities. The data-gathering methods used here were guided discussions and interviews, as well as visiting and observing activities at project sites.

As seen from Table 2.1, more than half of the participants (54%) of the New Leaders Initiative Program were female. This is because females remain in the rural areas, while males "chase the bright lights of towns." Therefore, most people coming up with development initiatives are female. The initial research conducted among participants also found that females naturally tend to involve themselves in unpaid activities that are aimed at improving the well-being of a whole community, while their male counterparts seek to involve themselves in income-generation activities and those that pro-

TABLE 2.1 Type of Initiative and Individual Leading the Initiative

Type of initiative	Sex of the individual leading the initiative and number involved	Educational background of the individual leading the initiative
HIV/AIDS awareness clubs	4 male, 5 female	7 are in possession of Grade 12 and 2 Grade 10
Employment creation/ income generation	12 male, 9 female	14 are in possession of Grade 12 and 5 Grade 10 and 2 below
Civic promotion	4 male, 5 female	7 are in possession of Grade 12 and 2 Grade 10
Child welfare and development	3 female	2 are in possession of Grade 12 and 1 Grade 10
Responsible parenthood	1 female	1 is in possession of Grade 12
Senior citizens welfare	1 male, 2 female	3 are in possession of Grade 12
Total participants	21 male + 25 female (46)	34 grade 12, 10 Grade 10 and 2 below

vide opportunities to relocate to urban areas or those of a political nature. Moreover, the table shows that most candidates (45%) are concerned about the employment creation/income generation followed by HIV/AIDS and civic promotion, both with 19%. This is because these are issues that are of importance, especially for young adults in rural areas.

All 46 new leaders, 26 for the first intake and 20 for the second intake, underwent training. The training included a one-week face-to-face and a seven-month self-directed study period. All participants thus completed the Community and Leadership Development training, which covered these topics:

1. Principles of community development
2. Planning for action
3. Communication skills
4. Setting up management structures
5. Leadership and resource management

Furthermore, all 46 participants were provided with advisory services, which ranged from assisting with project-proposal formulation and writing, forming networks, and designing plans for further collaboration among themselves and the campus.

The study materials for this program were developed with the aim that most of the learning would be done through distance and only a small part was through face-to-face training. The study materials were prepared by the Northern Campus staff cooperatively with the Heartland Center for Leadership Development, an independent nonprofit organization based in Lincoln, Nebraska. The Northern Campus and the Center for External Studies' Continuing Education Department staff delivered the face-to-face training. Participants used the self-directed study materials between the one-week training and the celebration of their achievements, which took place seven months later. During that period, selected councillors and business leaders were requested to assist with participants' learning processes by acting as mentors and advisors.

The JobStart Program

Besides not recognizing individuals who initiate projects, the other concern of the region was the high level of unemployment, particularly among young people. At the time of implementing the JobStart Program in 2001, the unemployment rate in the region was 54%, which was 6.1% more than the national figures of 47.9%. Today, unemployment is still a problem at 36.7% nationally and 64% in the region (The Namibian Newspaper, 14

June 2006: pp.1–2). The problem of youth unemployment was discussed at the region's partnership workshop in June 2001, organized to develop strategies to address the problem. One of the 5-year goals identified at the workshop was that there would be a full range of vocational-skills training opportunities throughout the region, meeting the needs of unemployed young adults.

The aim of the JobStart Program was therefore to prepare participants for employment through a combination of off-the-job training and work experience. Its objective was to increase the trainees' level of self-confidence and self-esteem, and equip them with the nontechnical skills expected by employers in the work situation. The target group was school leavers who had completed grade 12 (high school).

The selection process for the JobStart Program followed an open competition. The program was advertised in the national press, at local youth organizations' offices, at all Regional Councillors' offices, and regional youth forums. The selection criteria were applied to ensure that the selected candidates had the greatest potential to benefit from the program and secure employment upon completion. Using the given criteria, 60 participants were selected for the first intake and a further 60 for the second intake of the program. In the process, 30 participants dropped out and only 90 participants successfully completed the program.

The training program consisted of five weeks off-the-job-training, mainly through face-to-face and a small part of self-directed study covering these topics:

1. Communication for Work
2. Mathematics for Work
3. Computer Literacy
4. Job Readiness
5. Career Planning

The program also consisted of 10 weeks of practical work experience. The practical work experience was implemented in collaboration with the business community and political leaders in the region. It took place between week four and week five of face-to-face training. Suitable candidates were assigned to employers, the employers were provided with a profile of the candidate, and employers in turn provided trainees with guidelines as to what was expected of them at the job.

The model of this program was adopted from Onondanga Community College of New York, which offered a similar program. The study materials and delivery of the program were the responsibility of two VSO volunteers (Volunteer Service Overseas based in Great Britain), selected community members, and the Northern Campus Community Education and Development Unit (CEDU) staff. The study materials were developed with the aim that learning would be done mainly through face-to-face mode, supplemented by self-directed study (through specially prepared worksheets). The self-directed study component was designed to offer support to participants between face-to-face sessions and during the job placement.

THE PROGRAMS' CONTRIBUTIONS TO COMMUNITY ECONOMIC DEVELOPMENT OF THE REGION

It has been said that when stakeholders share the responsibility of educating society, learning is more meaningful to individuals participating in the learning experience (Treleaven & Cecez-Kecmanovic, 2001). The two programs provided opportunities where participants, the university, and members of the community worked together to achieve shared understanding of important issues in society and co-create useful knowledge. According to Treleaven and Cecez-Kecmanovic (2001, p. 170), collaborative learning strategies require more interactions and engagements with learners to "produce deep learning of concepts, theories and the co-creation of knowledge."

Since this learning was collaboratively arranged and distance- and open-learning methods were used, it enhanced social interaction opportunities among participants, community members, and the university. It also enabled people with families and those far away from a university campus to learn in their own environment and to immediately implement what had been learned. It is further argued that through flexible learning, institutions are provided with opportunities to make the necessary arrangements of providing worthwhile educational programs to adults in the community they serve (Osorio, 2003). It was discovered later that such models provided participants with opportunities to influence each other and their communities. The methods were also found to be effective in facilitating learning that responds to the needs of society and directly contributes to participants' livelihoods as well as improving their quality of life.

Furthermore, both programs have enabled rural people to earn a living, create better living conditions, create employment, and, in the process, provide needed products and services to their communities. In other words, community economic-development activities should be able to provide people with opportunities to improve their livelihoods. The New Leaders Initiative Program was found to have made the most community impact because participants had workable ideas. Participants in the program had managed to utilize the learning experience to either create jobs or generate income, thereby sustaining project activities to date. Out of the 46 participants, 9 (20%) are continuing with their projects, with 3 doing very well. Moreover, 16 (35%) participants have found permanent employment within their local communities, while the rest (21 participants) have moved out of their communities to more developed parts of Namibia.

One participant in the New Leaders Initiative Program, Samuel Angala, is really worth mentioning. He is currently managing three projects located in the region: a student canteen at the Northern Campus, a cleaning service at a nearby agricultural college, and a bicycle courier service (Speedbike Enterprise-SBE), operating in one of the four north-central regions. Currently he employs 30 people permanently and many others as casual workers. In addition, he created an association called Namibian Youth Enterprise Fighting Unemployment (NYEFU).

He also built a shelter at one of the largest hospitals in the region, Oshakati Hospital, for patients' relatives who care for the sick. "During the official launch of the Wapandula Noyaka Shelter, Chairman of SBE, Samuel Angala, said, "the conditions under which visitors (to the hospital) previously stayed were both inhuman and degrading." The shelter will also provide health education on HIV/AIDS, TB, malaria, and nutrition" (The Namibian Newspaper, June 12, 2006, p. 5).

Samuel succeeded through collaboration with the business community and Regional Councillors, and in building the Hospital Shelter, he collaborated with the Northern Campus. Samuel Angala (July 2006) said, "it is through the New Leaders Program that I have got an opportunity to learn how to lead people, to solve conflict, and this gave me an open chance to be recognized by different institutions, including the Vocational Training Center, where I am doing my bricklaying and plastering course." At the same interview, he also said that he learned a lot from local business people, Regional Councillors, and even from people beyond Namibia's borders. "My organizations have won an International Awards from the Jet Community Award from South Africa and from the World Bank. All these are fruits of the New Leaders Program because we have learned how to win prices (prizes) and awards."

The New Leaders Initiative Program participants appreciated the opportunities to learn better ways of learning together with their communities and communicating with people in authority. According to Treleaven and Cecez-Kecmanovic (2001), through collaborative learning, participants learn new ways of communication and self-confidence. As Foibe Hailaula (July, 2006), the participant who established an HIV/AIDS Youth Club, put it, "It is good to find employment in my community. I got this job because I was able to put my ideas across to the Regional Management Committee during the interview." This young woman is now employed as an HIV/AIDS support officer with her Regional Council. This position provided her opportunities to be exposed to best practices of HIV/AIDS prevention used elsewhere in the world, enabling her to gain new perspectives on her job. As she said during the interview, "I have attended a one-week training on

Sexual and Reproductive Rights of Young People (SRHP) on a study tour to Zimbabwe in July 2002, and that helped me a great deal."

The third person worth mentioning is Julinda Nanghanda, a lady who established the stoves manufacturing project, manufacturing stoves that are appropriate for rural conditions, using corrugated iron sheets. Currently the project employs 10 people. She has also established a gardening project where young people grow vegetables and sell to local people, thereby generating income for themselves. Additionally, she has negotiated for a free venue with her Regional Councillor to enable talented young people to perform (drama and music), whereby people coming to these events pay an entrance fee, which is an income for the young artists. Not only do the artists make an income, but this has also created vibrant social evenings in her community. During the interview, Julinda Nanghanda (July, 2006) said, "The New Leaders Initiative Program helped me a lot. Through it, I had learned how to lead people with different understanding and different age groups."

When compared with the New Leaders Initiative Program, the JobStart Program had less community impact because it was designed with a very specific target audience in mind—only those who had reached grade 12. However, it has managed to equip that particular audience with the skills necessary for the workplace. The author succeeded in tracing back 42 of the 90 participants that completed the program. The data-gathering methods used here were guided discussions and interviews with participants who completed the program. The 42 participants were all employed, with 40 of them finding permanent employment, of which 5 were employed in neighboring South Africa. The other 2 participants were still working as volunteers and hoping to gain enough work experience to be able to be offered paid employment. Even though there is no visible community impact, 44% of the participants being permanently employed is significant, and it can be concluded that the program has been successful in contributing to the well-being of young people in the region. According to Prime Minister Nahas Angula (2003 Speech), at the time serving as the Namibian Minister of Higher Education, Training and Employment Creation, community economic-development activities were also found "to empower people who participate in them, thereby increasing their self-worth and decision-making powers."

In addition to enabling participants to be employed, the program has also created a new way of addressing unemployment in the region, where job creation is hard to come by. Local employers and Regional Councillors especially appreciated this approach of addressing unemployment and learning together. As one of the JobStart employers, Ms Karen Kaafuli (2001), said, "Unemployment is a national burden, and we all have a part to play in enabling young people to get the practical skills necessary to enter the workforce and for enabling the region to address developmental goals, especially that of eradicating poverty and hunger." The Honorable Nahas Angula (2003 speech) further stated that young people and community members should know that "many countries in the world are using community economic-development projects to address national problems through community participation and involvement."

USEFUL LEARNING OUTCOMES

As it was mentioned in the introduction part of this chapter, the Namibian economy is characterized by huge disparities, with the majority of the population living in extreme poverty on the one hand, and the wealthy minority controlling the economy (Marope, 2005, p. 11). The majority of poor people reside in the north-central region, with subsistence farming as the dominant economic activity (Mendelsohn et al., 2000, p. 2). In order to enable poor people to participate in the economic activities of the country, the government has encouraged educational institutions to make use of open- and distance-learning methods to educate the majority of the country's population. For the past 15 years, the University of Namibia has been utilizing open and distance methods to enable teachers and nurses to qualify for their jobs, but it has never used the methodology in developing nonformal programs. Due to a paradigm shift to more open-learning and open-knowledge systems, the university decided to engage in nonformal programs utilizing open- and distance-learning methods. It also realized that developing programs for this paradigm shift calls for collaboration with relevant stakeholders in society.

The two programs were thus developed in partnerships with the local community and other educational institutions in the United States, which provided materials and methods that have been successful in communities with similar conditions. These materials and methods were then adopted and changed to suit the Namibian conditions. The programs enabled academics to make sense of participants' messages and their aspirations in implementing community-development activities. According to Zwierzynski (2003, p. 17), community voices are powerful instruments for development. Through participation in these two programs, therefore, the university academics assisted in creating new knowledge, which is valued in local communities and could be used to enable positive progress of developmental activities in rural areas.

We have also learned that it is possible for higher education to successfully engage with local communities and provide strategies and learning approaches for addressing developmental goals. This means it is possible for higher-education institutions to collaborate with rural communities, bring about socioeconomic development, and create communities of action. As Roger Mills and Alan Tait (1996, p. 8) put it, "If faculty makes the time, place and modes of curriculum delivery more accessible, they are simultaneously opening the universities to new kinds of students." Through these programs, the Northern Campus received students who otherwise would have not come to a university campus, even though they are full of innovative ideas that have the potential to bring about development in rural areas.

Regional councillors also got an opportunity to be involved in learning activities aimed at improving the quality of life of their constituents. During the self-directed learning, participants were encouraged to approach their councillors and other local leaders if they experienced any problems. However, the researchers learned that if they are to use business and political leaders as partners in the learning process, they need to be prepared for the job and to change their mindset and attitudes toward a more participatory learning, which increases mutual understanding of issues and assists to cooperatively construct useful knowledge.

Finally, it should be mentioned that the university was criticized for engaging in nonformal education, both by academics and government. Academics felt that by engaging in such low-level education, the university was degrading its academic standards, while government felt that resources were being wasted in offering nondegree programs. However, Osorio (2003, p.94) recognized that contradictions are part of the learning process and stated, "to speak of university programs for older people may smack of utopia, if not of a contradiction in terms." Thus, contradictions are part of the adult-learning activities in a university setting. This is because university education, as we all know, has been reserved for selected groups, usually young people who meet the entry requirements for university programs. However, as the world changes, we find so many universities engaging in adult-learning activities in order to address immediate societal needs. It is also this author's conviction that universities should engage in developing and testing innovative learning approaches that facilitate community economic development; and once successfully tested, the university could transfer them on to relevant stakeholders for implementation, especially to nongovernmental organizations (NGOs) working in the adult learning sector.

CONCLUSION

Through the establishment of the Northern Campus, the university has demonstrated its commitment to providing education that is responsive to the needs of the country and is accessible to all. It has also been engaged in basic and applied research that has contributed to the social, economic, cultural, and political development of Namibia and provided good educational models to other educational institutions and organizations.

Also, the collaboration utilized in implementing the two educational programs was beneficial to all stakeholders. The university was seen as being relevant to issues affecting society; and Regional Councillors' involvement in issues affecting their constituencies was good for their political careers, because they were seen as leaders who cared and were interested in creating economic activities in their communities.

Thus, the evaluation of the two programs provided convincing data to interest other stakeholders in implementing the educational models that develop participants' knowledge, skills, and attitudes and enables them to implement worthwhile projects. With the New Leaders Initiative Program, we especially found that it developed strong community-oriented types of attitudes among all participants. As a result of participating in the training, participants were more concerned that if they do not get involved in community projects, their communities will become "ghost" communities and be forgotten by regional planners and leaders. They therefore chose to work with their leaders, both at regional and community levels, in order to "save our communities" (according to one participant). It was also concluded that in order for the participants to continue and successfully grow their businesses and projects, the involvement of local leadership and influential members of the community is of much importance.

Furthermore, and due to the unemployment situation rife in the country, it was found that some community-development and nongovernmental organizations have started to introduce similar models in their training activities. This is in line with Marcelo Zwierzynski's thinking (2003) that as people become disenchanted with current services, they tend to become increasingly interested in participating in activities that respond to their immediate needs. Therefore the high unemployment currently prevailing in the country is enough motivation for civil society and community-development organizations to search for educational models that work, and the New Leaders Initiative and JobStart programs are found to be suitable models for their training activities.

REFERENCES

Angula, N. (2003, July 19). *Creativity and entrepreneurial thinking instead of complaints to fight unemployment in Oshana region.* Speech delivered at the official launch of the Speedbike Courier Services in Oshakati, Namibia.

Bottomley, J. (2000). Reconfiguring strategies for flexible learning and delivery. In V. Jakupec and J. Garrick (Eds.), *Flexible learning, human resources and organizational development: Putting theory to work,* London: Routledge.

Harlech-Jones, B. (2002). *The northern campus: An educational seedling.* Research Project, University of Namibia.

Marope, M. T. (2005). *Namibia human capital and knowledge development for economic growth with equity.* Africa Region Human Development Working Paper Series—No. 84. The World Bank.

Mendelsohn, J., el Obeid, S., & Roberts, C. (2000). *A profile of north central region.* Windhoek, Namibia: Gamsberg Macmillan Publishers.

Mills, R., & Tait, A. (1996). *Supporting the learner in open and distance learning.* London: Pitman Publishing.

Nekongo-Nielsen, H. (2005). Developing adult education delivery methods that extend educational opportunities to rural people of north-central Namibia. In Tony Dodds (Ed.), *Open and distance learning in Southern Africa.* Pretoria: University of South Africa Press.

Nunan, T. (2000). Exploring the concept of flexibility. In V. Jakupec and J. Garrick (Eds.), *Flexible learning, human resources and organizational development: Putting theory to work.* London: Routledge.

Osorio, A. R. (2003). University and education for older adults: Development of specific programs for university education of older adults in Spain. *Convergence, 36*(1), 87–99.

Treleaven, L., & Cecez-Kecmanovic, D. (2001). Collaborative learning in Web-mediated environment: A study of communicative practices. *Studies in Continuing Education, 23*(2), 169–182.

United Nations (1990). *World declaration on meeting education for all.* Article 1, Paragraph 1.

Wikipedia. *Definition of community economic development.* Available at http://en.wikipedia.org/wiki/cCommunity_economic_development

Zwierzynski, M. (2003). On global wisdom: Some thoughts about the role of adult education in rebuilding civil society in Argentina. *Convergence, 36*(1), 5–19.

CHAPTER 3

CONTRIBUTION OF THE IDE IN PROMOTING GENDER EQUALITY AND IN EMPOWERING WOMEN IN SWAZILAND

C. W. S. Sukati, Esampally Chandraiah, and Nokuthula T. Vilakati

INTRODUCTION

The World Conference on Education for All (EFA) held in Jomtien, Thailand, in March 1990 resolved that "all people must have access to basic education, both because basic education should now be considered a right of citizens and because development, however conceived, requires an educated populace" (Samoff, 2003, p. 61). The rationale for basic education was, among others, that it is a prerequisite for creating a population that is qualified to enter higher education.

A decade later, in the year 2000, at the World Education Forum held in Dakar, Senegal, the Member States of the United Nations made a commitment in the Millennium Declaration to achieve eight goals, now called

Bridging the Knowledge Divide, pages 39–56
Copyright © 2009 by Information Age Publishing

the Millennium Development Goals (MDGs). Goal number 3, which is the focus of this chapter, is to promote gender equality and empower women (UNDP, 2005). The first deadline for this Goal Number 3 target was to eliminate gender disparity in primary and secondary education, preferably by 2005 and at all levels of education no later than 2015 (UNDP, 2005). The UNDP continues to indicate that although in the past three decades gains have been made in girls' education, which has led to and reduced gender gaps in primary-school education, it is apparent that many countries would miss the first deadline, particularly as regards higher levels of education (p. 28). Dhanarajan (2006, p. 7) declared that "the gender gap, despite our knowledge of the benefits of educating women, is still appalling." As women are about 50% of the world population, and as investing in female education is said to be the best-bet investment, Mlama (2005, p. 49) argues that it is clear, therefore, that no country can develop to its fullest without providing education to women. The relevant major questions to Swaziland on this are: Is the country on target to achieving this goal? Has gender disparity in education been eliminated?

In spite of all the evidence that points to the fact that gender disparities still persist, not many current research studies exist that inform us on gender disparities and their interrelationship with the social, economic, and cultural characteristics of the countries and communities. Similarly, few studies explore the nature of the problem caused by gender disparities, their special dimensions, the comparative situation in the various countries of Africa (Shabaya & Konadu-Agyemang, 2004; UNESCO, 1997), and thus the justification for this study.

This chapter focuses on the role of the Institute of Distance Education (IDE) at the University of Swaziland (UNISWA) in eliminating gender disparities, promoting gender equality, and empowering women. Why look at the role of the IDE? This is because distance education is a rapidly growing alternative to access to higher education and is found to be convenient because learners do not have to leave home or work in order to pursue their studies. The distance education delivery mode has become an important complement to mainstream conventional education (Srisa-An, 2006; Perraton, 2004). Indeed, in many African countries, including Swaziland, policymakers and institutional managers have come to regard distance education as a solution to widening access to university education. They regard the distance education mode as a relatively more viable option than conventional face-to-face teaching and the current residential campus model. Hence, it is taken that distance education offers the means through which the development of university education can be improved by opening up more opportunities and empowering women, despite the existing severe resource constraints faced by many African countries. The major objective of this chapter is to determine whether or not the IDE is aiding the country in achieving the goal of gender equality and empowerment of women, and as such, is sufficiently responsive to the rapidly changing needs of university education and training of marginalized women. The specific questions that guide the study are

1. How does the ratio of women in IDE compare with that in the UN-ISWA full-time face-to-face Faculties?
2. How does the ratio of women in each of the IDE programs compare with that in each one of the programs offered through conventional UNISWA Faculties?
3. How does the performance of women compare with that of men in IDE?

This study is therefore relevant in that it investigates whether the institute has opened up opportunities for women to do tertiary education or not. It determines the distribution of women across the various programs in the institute, and this helps to further throw some light on whether or not the females go for softer options in subject choices. The study progresses by probing whether or not the IDE goes beyond widening access for women by providing for gender equality through finding out the performance of the females in relation to the males and by establishing whether or not the males' performance is higher than that of the females. It is therefore an important contribution to gender equality and the empowerment of women; and other researchers and policymakers can benefit from this study.

In trying to answer the research questions, this chapter starts by looking at the existing literature on gender equality and empowering women. It then proceeds to present some pertinent and relevant information on the Swaziland educational context. This is followed by a discussion on the methodology used to collect and analyze data, and thereafter, a presentation and discussion of the results is undertaken. The final section presents the conclusions that can be drawn from the findings of the study, and whether or not the IDE is aiding the country in achieving the goal of gender equality and the empowerment of women.

REVIEW OF LITERATURE

Gender, Education, and Development

The global education agenda has raised awareness for the support of gender parity and gender equality in education. The Human Development Report for 1995 declares that if human development is not engendered, it is endangered (UNDP, 1995). The subject of gender has taken center stage in many countries, as available data shows that the persistence of widespread poverty is intrinsically related to the systematic subordination and confinement of women to positions of social, political, and economic disadvantage. The literature also reveals that countries with high levels of gender discrimination also suffer from high poverty levels (Development Studies Network, 2006, p. 23). Similarly, as Pong (1999, p. 155) has pointed out, the gender gap has been found to be negatively related to the economic growth and social well-being of a country and thus the strong justification and desire for reducing this gap. As such, developmental efforts to reduce poverty levels must be considered inseparable from initiatives to better educate and empower women who are the other half of the world's population.

Throughout the contemporary globalized world, education is held to be the key element of the emergent knowledge society. It is seen as the main instrument by which equality among diverse social groups, and especially between men and women, will be achieved (Stromquist, 2006, p.145). According to Perry et al. (2003, p. 26), the World Bank points out that "education is the most important productive asset most people will ever own." If education is thus such a powerful tool for economic and social betterment, we would expect that public policy requires that education is made accessible to all and to distribute it equitably at all levels. Mlama (2005, p. 49) adds that according to available evidence, investment in female education in low-income countries of Africa is a "best-bet" investment, which simultaneously achieves greater earning ability for families, lower fertility rates, reduced rates of infant and maternal mortality, and improvements in public health. Such benefits can be direct or indirect (Kwesiga, 2002, p. 34) and can accrue to the individual, their families, their communities, and indeed, the entire society.

There is therefore an economic rate of return and a social rate of return to girls' education. The economic rate of return of investing in girls' education is considered even higher than the rate of investing in boys' education (World Bank, 2000). When the social rates of return on girls' education, namely improved health and education levels of children, lower population growth rates, etc. are considered, the case for girls' education is even stronger. Lewin (1993, p. 17) is correct in pointing out, therefore, that it is beyond doubt "that investing in female education is a critical input for development and has a cluster of interrelating benefits."

According to Mlama (2005, p. 49), the provision and the quality of girls' education in sub-Saharan Africa have therefore attracted increasing attention over the past decade in response to the EFA and MDGs. As a result, the Forum for African Women Educationists (FAWE) was created as a response to this challenge, and this organization has been at the forefront of promoting girls' education in the African continent. While many writers argue for girls' education in terms of human capital theory and the added value of production to the economy, it is apparent that even if one's income and productivity were to remain constant, a person may still benefit from education—in being able to read, communicate, argue, choose in a more informed way, and in being taken more seriously by others (Sen, 1999, p. 293).

Issue of Equal Access

The issue of access to education became topical internationally in the 1960s through the work of UNESCO, arising from the Universal Declaration of Human Rights. The 1981 UN Convention on the elimination of all forms of discrimination against women (CEDAW) extended the debate by indicating areas in education where discrimination had to be eliminated (Kwesiga, 2002, p. 51). Kwesiga goes on to say that despite these international conventions, discrimination in education on grounds of gender is still evident, and declares, "Though progress has been made worldwide, the gender gap in education is still too wide to be ignored" (2002, p. 51). UNESCO (1997) and Mlama (2005) are also of this opinion, that despite the positive actions and the sensitization campaigns undertaken by governments, which have resulted in dramatic gains in enrollments over the past 30 years, statistics still present a grim picture of the education of African women and girls as the gender gaps persist.

Similarly, Shabaya and Konadu-Agyemang (2004, p. 396) assert that women in Africa remain the most undereducated in the world and that by virtue of their lack of education, they are still confined to the fringe of society in menial jobs, due primarily to poor access to education and training. The authors go on to present a table of the gender gap among selected African countries at the primary, secondary, and tertiary education levels and conclude that the gender gap in African education seems to be universal across the continent (Shabaya & Konadu-Agyemang, 2004, pp. 400–401). Assessing progress toward the EFA goal on gender in sub-Saharan Africa, girls' participation in primary education remains substantially lower than boys' (Lewin, 1993). At secondary and tertiary levels, the gap is more pronounced.

It appears though that much of the literature on developing countries tends to be more concerned with the issue of female students' access to education. Achieving gender equality in education implies not only access to education, but also equality of opportunities for males and females, equality in the learning process, equality of outcomes, as well as equality of external results after leaving education (UNESCO, 2005). It is therefore more of a challenge to achieve gender equality.

Issue of Subject Choices

There are many challenges pertaining to gender, education, and development, and one of these is the concentration of women in typically feminine fields, and another is the overrepresentation of men in fields perceived to be masculine, such as science, engineering, and technology (Stromquist, 1996; Smith, 1988). Francis (2000, p. 35) points out that, traditionally, the sciences, including subjects such as mathematics, science, and information technology, have been perceived as a masculine domain, while conversely, the arts, including fine art, languages, and humanities subjects such as history, have been perceived as feminine ones.

Kwesiga (2002, p. 71) presents a table showing females as a percentage of total tertiary enrollment in selected sub-Saharan African countries in the arts and in the sciences. In the arts, although the female percentage was less than 50, it was, however, much higher than that of females in the science subjects in almost all the selected countries, indicating that very few women opt for the sciences, hence, the tendency by some female students to avoid some forms of knowledge, such as science. Such subject bias in favor of the arts may just as successfully exclude females from mainstream economic, social, and political life as no education at all, and therefore, the under representation of women in highly skilled and professional employment (Fagerlind & Saha, 1992; Leach, 1988).

Comparative Academic Performance of Male and Female Students

Differentials in achievement between females and males have received increasing attention from policymakers, women feminist activists, politicians, and parents. This is the case because academic achievement is related to survival and progression in the education system. Students who do well in their studies will often proceed to the next level each year and eventually graduate from that particular program. Those who do not perform well will often be required to repeat classes, and many eventually drop out of school or tend to be expelled from school because of too many repeats. Academic performance is important, therefore, as it is related to survival in the system and to the empowerment of women. It is not just getting women in the education system, but it is also getting them to learn and graduate from their education programs so that they can enter the labor market.

To attain gender equality and empowerment, it is important to consider whether or not the females perform as well as (or better or worse than) their male counterparts. If they do not, then the question of whether the program is providing for equality and the empowerment of women is brought to bear. If women enter the program, fail and/or drop out, it is doubtful whether the program is indeed providing for gender equality and is empowering women. So, how do girls perform in relation to boys? Several studies have been conducted in this area and, in most of sub-Saharan African countries, it is found that the girls' performance is lower than that of boys, especially in mathematics, science, and technical subjects (Kwesiga, 2002, p. 49).

The Swaziland Educational Context

The kingdom of Swaziland is a small landlocked country with an area of 17,364 square kilometers and lies between the 25th and 27th parallel in southeastern Africa. It is situated between the Republic of South Africa and the Republic of Mozambique and has a population of about 965,000 people (Magagula et al., 2001). The present formal system of education in Swaziland is divided into four main subsystems. These are preprimary, primary, junior and senior secondary, and postsecondary or tertiary. The broad aim of the system is contained in the belief that "A nation's greatest assets are its human resources; Human development is therefore the great aim of education" (Swaziland Government, 1975). As a result of this, the Swaziland educational system has expanded tremendously at all levels since independence in 1968. These increases have necessitated large additions in other supporting services like teachers, schools, classrooms, and other physical facilities, equipment, etc.; and all these have entailed huge increases in the budgetary allocations to education. As available national funds are limited and are unable to meet all the needs of education, other options, which are cost-effective and can cater to a large number of students, have had to be considered; therefore, distance-education institutions have been introduced. The main ones are Emlalatini Development Center to cater to secondary education and the IDE to cater to tertiary education, with a view to providing education to individuals who for one reason or another are unable to undertake a full-time school or university education.

The challenges faced by education in Swaziland, therefore, are not very different from those faced by other developing countries, and hence, the Swaziland system has been influenced by global educational trends, one of which relates to gender parity and equality in education. At present the Ministry of Education is still developing a gender policy. Until now, however, the approach has been more or less gender neutral, that is, in terms of access (Obanya, 2004). Obanya (2004) indicates that there is an apparent gender balance at primary and secondary levels. Table 3.1 shows the situation at the secondary level.

TABLE 3.1   Secondary School Enrollments in Swaziland (1997–2000)

Year	Boys	Girls	Total	% Girls
1997	29,020	29,177	58,197	50.13
1998	30,228	30,602	60,630	50.31
1999	30,741	30,825	61,566	50.07
2000	30,003	30,252	60,253	50.20

Source: Obanya (2004, p. 30)

Looking at these figures, it is apparent that Swaziland presents a unique case in gender parity at the secondary-school level when compared with many other sub-Saharan African countries. Perhaps this is the reason why notable key gendered educational interventions in Swaziland have not been government driven. For example, science, mathematics, and technology clinics and industry attachments have been arranged for girls with the assistance of the Forum for African Women Educationists in Swaziland (FAWESWA, 2000). The main goal has been to include more girls alongside boys in science, mathematics, and technology. But does this gender parity apply across all the subjects in all the faculties at UNISWA? This study answers this question and others.

There exists some limited literature that probes the issue of gender-based differences in subject choices and in the performance of male and female students specifically in Swaziland (Kaino, 1999; Makhubu, 1999; Simelane, 1996; Nkosi, 1992; Wheldon & Smith, 1986, 1988). A study conducted by Kaino on enrollment, drop out, and performance of undergraduate students at UNISWA by gender showed that male enrollment in mathematics was much higher than that of females in all the academic years studied. Female students, it appeared, tended to concentrate in the humanities, home economics, and arts, with some in business and public administration fields, and were underrepresented in mathematics, geography, and the physical sciences (Kaino, 1999; Wheldon & Smith, 1988). This gender bias in the choice of subjects appears to be a continuation of trends observed at secondary school. At secondary-school level, Wheldon & Smith revealed:

> There are highly significant differences between the subjects selected by boys and girls. These differences are particularly marked in the technical subjects. No girls attempted Geometrical Drawing, Woodwork, Metalwork or Electricity & Electronics. Only a very small percentage of boys attempted either Food and Nutrition or Home Management. (1988, p. 17)

The literature also discusses the academic performance of male and female students. The findings on Swaziland indicate that female students performed equally with their male counterparts and sometimes even bet-ter than the male students, and thus that the overall differences in per-formance between males and females was negligible (Kaino, 1999; Nkosi, 1992; Wheldon & Smith, 1988). These results are pertinent in this study, which probes not only gender parity across programs offered at the IDE but also the academic performance of male and female students.

METHODOLOGY

The study uses secondary data collected by the researchers from UNISWA records that are kept by the Registrar's Office. Sex-disaggregated data on each of the UNISWA programs was extracted from the university enrollment books for both full-time and part-time students, for academic years 1997–98 to 2005–06. The information collected was analyzed using percentages.

The data used for the academic achievement of males and females in IDE was acquired from a study that had been undertaken to compare the academic performance of BA Humanities students in the full-time program and those in IDE (see Sukati et al., 2007). The information used in that research study had been collected from the end-of-year-results handbooks that are kept in the University Registrar's office. The data, which was stored in the computer, had been used in the Sukati et al. study (2007) to compare the academic performance of a cohort of BA Humanities students who were studying in the conventional full –time program with those who were study-ing through distance education mode. As a result, for the comparisons on performance of females and males, only information from the humanities program was available, and thus the results on performance can only apply to the BA Humanities degree and not to the other programs.

This study uses the data from the same data bank, which was analyzed us-ing the SPSS program, but this time only information on IDE was used, and the comparison on academic achievement was between males and females. The 1997–98 data compares the cohort of IDE BA Humanities students, that is, 33 males and 65 females, in their year 1 performance; the 1998–99 data compares them, then 21 males and 56 females, in their year 2 perfor-mance. The 1999–00 data compares them (17 males and 48 females) in their year 3 and the 2000–01 data compares their performance (17 males and 39 females) at year 4. The number of students decreases as you go up because some students repeat and others drop out. Hence, it is the same group of students that are being compared, from year 1 to year 4, when they complete their degree. The t-test statistic was used to compare the mean scores (which are in percentages) of the males and the females to deter-mine the probability that the difference in the means is a real difference rather than a chance difference.

RESULTS AND DISCUSSION

The results and discussion of the data falls under 3 sections, beginning with sex-disaggregated data on access to academic programs. This is followed by a section that deals with male and female students' representation in academic programs, then finally the comparative analysis of the academic performance of male and female students.

Aspect of Access

Reaching gender parity implies that the same proportion of boys and girls—relative to their respective age groups—enter the education system. It is measured by the ratio between the female and male values for any given indicator with parity equal to one (UNESCO, 2004, p. 5). Generally there is a prevalence of males in all fields of education at the tertiary level all over the world. In Swaziland, however, the trend is different, as shown in Table 3.2.

Table 3.2 reveals that the number of female students enrolled at UNISWA (without the IDE students) has been, on the average, equal to that of males at about 50%. It appears, therefore, that equal access to full-time university education between the sexes exists at UNISWA. In the IDE, as Table 3.3 shows, more females are catered to than males.

Table 3.3 shows that most students in IDE from the academic year 1999–00 to 2005–06 were females, as they were about 58% of the total student population. Further, the average over the nine-year period shows that females accounted for 55.8% of enrollments in IDE, while males accounted for only 44.2%. As these statistics show, whereas in the full-time programs the average of women over the nine years is 49.4%, in IDE it is higher at

TABLE 3.2 Student Enrollment at UNISWA from 1997–98 to 2005–06 (IDE excluded)

Year	Total Enrollment	Male (%)	Female (%)
1997–98	3,204	1,626 (51)	1,578 (49)
1999–00	3,003	1,557 (51)	1,446 (49)
2001–02	3,143	1,578 (50)	1,565 (50)
2003–04	3,518	1,738 (49)	1,780 (51)
2005–06	3,677	1,898 (52)	1,779 (48)
Average		50.6	49.4

Source: University of Swaziland Enrollment Yearbooks (percentages calculated by the authors)

TABLE 3.3   Student Enrollment at IDE from 1997–98 to 2005–06

Year	Total Enrollment	Male (%)	Female (%)
1997–98	224	115 (51)	109 (49)
1999–00	546	232 (42)	314 (58)
2001–02	1,055	438 (42)	617 (58)
2003–04	1,447	623 (43)	824 (57)
2005–06	1,943	837 (43)	1,106 (57)
Average		44.2	55.8

Source: University of Swaziland Enrollment Yearbooks (percentages calculated by the authors)

55.8%, demonstrating the fact that the institute has opened up more opportunities for women to access university education and thus promoting gender parity.

Aspect of Gender Representation Across Programs

Another issue on gender parity and equality is whether or not the female students are equally represented in all programs. Table 3.4 shows the representation of females in all the programs offered by UNISWA, including IDE, for academic years 2004–05 and 2005–06.

TABLE 3.4   Student Enrolment at UNISWA by Faculty and Gender in 2004–05 and 2005–06

Faculty	2004–05			2005–06		
	Males	Females	Total	Male	Female	Total
Agriculture	401 (57)	302 (43)	703 (100)	444 (58)	317 (42)	761 (100)
Commerce	308 (50)	306 (50)	614 (100)	312 (52)	285 (48)	662 (100)
Education	123 (38)	197 (62)	320 (100)	159 (47)	177 (53)	336 (100)
Health Sciences	99 (32)	209 (68)	308 (100)	121 (38)	196 (62)	317 (100)
Humanities	241 (42)	338 (58)	579 (100)	237 (41)	337 (59)	574 (100)
Science	241 (69)	108 (31)	349 (100)	253 (67)	337 (33)	574 (100)
Social Science	335 (52)	313 (48)	648 (100)	347 (52)	315 (48)	662 (100)
Post-Graduate Studies	23 (50)	23 (50)	46 (100)	25 (50)	25 (50)	50 (100)
I.D.E.	678 (42)	917 (58)	1,595 (100)	837 (43)	1,106 (57)	1943 (100)
Total	2,449 (47)	2,713 (53)	5,162 (100)	2,735 (49)	2,885 (51)	5,620 (100)

Note: The figures in brackets are percentages that have been calculated by the authors.
Source: University of Swaziland Enrollment Yearbooks.

From the above table, it is seen that certain programs like education, humanities, and health sciences (which includes mostly nursing) have a much higher proportion of females than males. On the other hand, programs like science and agriculture tend to have a very high proportion of males. Thus, one can conclude that despite the equal representation of males and females at UNISWA, as revealed by Table 3.2, the females tend to be underrepresented in the hard sciences and in agriculture, and overrepresented in health sciences, humanities, and education. This supports the findings of many other researchers and, in particular, what Kwesiga (2002) found in sub-Saharan Africa and what Kaino (1999) found at UNISWA with regard to female underrepresentation in fields considered to be masculine, such as science and agriculture.

Table 3.5 shows the representation of females in all the programs offered in IDE for the academic years 2004–05 and 2005–06.

The table again reveals certain programs that have a high proportion of females, like Certificate in French (languages) 75%, BA Humanities 67%, BEd 59%, BCom. 55%, and Diploma in Law 54% in the 2005–06 academic year. It is only in the Diploma in Commerce, where there are higher proportions of males than females, that it is 54% versus 46%. Again, here it is apparent that IDE female students tend to dominate in almost all the educational programs, thus making a big contribution toward gender parity and gender equality. Of concern however, is the fact that the programs offered in IDE are more on the "softer subjects," such as humanities and

TABLE 3.5 Student Enrollment in IDE by Program and Gender in 2004–05 and 2005–06

Program	2004–05			2005–06		
	Males	Females	Total	Males	Females	Total
Cert. in French	2 (33)	4 (67)	6 (100)	2 (25)	6 (75)	8 (100)
Diploma in Commerce	174 (55)	140 (45)	314 (100)	222 (54)	187 (46)	409 (100)
Diploma in Law	316 (46)	375 (54)	691 (100)	340 (46)	401 (54)	741 (100)
Bachelor of Arts (Humanities)	148 (30)	342 (70)	490 (100)	225 (33)	449 (67)	674 (100)
Bachelor of Education	26 (40)	39 (60)	65 (100)	21 (41)	30 (59)	51 (100)
Bachelor of Commerce	11 (38)	18 (62)	29 (100)	27 (45)	33 (55)	60 (100)
Total	677 (42)	918 (58)	1,595 (100)	837 (43)	1,106 (57)	1,943 (100)

Source: University of Swaziland Enrollment Yearbooks

education, which are traditionally taken by women. This then downplays the contribution that the institute is making on gender equality.

Aspect of Academic Performance and Gender

To get a good measure of gender equality, it is necessary that the academic achievement of both sexes be considered, as it is possible that one can provide the access and achieve parity in male and female representation in all the programs but have the females perform poorly and not graduate and perhaps be eventually eliminated from the programs. On this aspect, IDE data was only available for the BA Humanities program for the academic years 1997–78, 1998–89, 1999–00, and 2000–01. The results are shown in Table 3.6.

TABLE 3.6   Academic Performance in the BA Humanities Degree by Sex

Year	Subject	Mean		Probability
		Males	**Females**	
1997–98	African Languages & Literature	49.64	53.88	0.052[a]
	English Language & Literature	53.36	57.03	0.149
	History	61.19	62.38	0.693
	Theology & Religious Studies	60.45	59.63	0.720
	Overall Performance	54.18	57.15	0.062[a]
1998–99	African Languages & Literature	50.50	55.33	0.196
	English Language & Literature	61.05	60.33	0.149
	History	57.91	60.53	0.178
	Theology & Religious Studies	62.43	60.04	0.212
	Overall Performance	59.19	59.29	0.951
1999–00	African Languages & Literature	53.50	54.75	0.836
	English Language & Literature	57.11	57.50	0.918
	History	59.75	61.65	0.356
	Theology & Religious Studies	63.43	56.90	0.014[a]
	Overall Performance	59.00	56.98	0.432
2000–01	African Languages & Literature	53.50	57.93	0.470
	English Language & Literature	59.56	59.47	0.963
	History	62.00	62.44	0.821
	Theology & Religious Studies	64.50	62.35	0.394
	Overall Performance	61.00	61.54	0.681

[a] significant at the 10% level.
Source: Compiled and calculated from database created for the study by Sukati et al. (2007)

Table 3.6 shows the mean scores for both females and males for each subject in the BA Humanities degree from the academic year 1997–98 to 2000–01 in years 1 to 4. A t-test was conducted to determine if the mean scores for each subject for the two sexes were significantly different in each year. The findings are as follows:

1. In African Languages and Literature, it is seen that the average score of females is consistently higher than that of males for all the 4 years. So it appears that females perform better than males in this subject.
2. In History, again it is seen that the average score for females is consistently higher than that of males in all the 4 years. It can be concluded, therefore, that females outperform the males on this subject as well.
3. In Theology and Religious Studies, the average score for the males is consistently higher than that of females in all the 4 years. In this case, it seems that the males perform better than females on this subject.
4. Using the t-test, it is found that in 1997–98 (year 1), the mean difference between the sexes in African Languages, i.e., 49.64 vs. 53.88, is significantly different at the 10% level in African Languages, with the probability of 0.052. This means that the difference between the performance of males and females is significant, and that the females performed better than the males.
5. Using the t-test, it is found that in 1990–00 (year 3), the mean difference between the sexes in African Languages, i.e., 63.43 vs. 56.9, is significantly different at the 10% level in Theology and Religious Studies, with the probability of 0.014. This means that the difference between the performance of males and females is significant, and that the males performed better than the females on this subject.
6. The t-test again revealed that in the 1997–98 (year 1), overall performance between the sexes, i.e., 54.18 vs. 57.15, was significantly different, with the probability of 0.062. This means that the difference between the overall performance of the males and females is significant, and that the females performed better than the males overall.

CONCLUSION

On the aspect of access to university education, the above data reveals that while in IDE, about 57% of the students are female; in the conventional full-time program this percentage is about 50, showing that the IDE has provided more access to women than the conventional full-time face-to-face UNISWA programs. This finding supports the widely held view that distance education plays a crucial role in achieving gender parity and increasing the literacy rate in general and among women in particular. Thus, to increase life choices among women, distance education is a suitable alternative.

An in-depth analysis of the data further reveals that while in the conventional full-time faculties, there is a wider variety of programs; it is noted that programs offered at the IDE are limited. They are more concentrated on the "softer subjects," mainly humanities, education, and law. Data on the full-time programs, as indicated in Table 3.4, shows that there is a higher proportion of females in the courses perceived to be feminine, like education, humanities, and health sciences. There is a higher proportion of males in the subjects perceived to be masculine, like agriculture and science. However, the IDE does not offer any program in critical fields like the sciences, engineering, and agriculture. This downplays the positive strides by IDE in achieving gender equality. It seems that more of the IDE programs can perpetuate gender stereotyping in the choice of careers because areas of study are restricted at the IDE, while there is comparatively more curriculum diversity in the conventional face-to-face university. Therefore, there is a need for the IDE to introduce more market-oriented and job-oriented subjects and fields considered to be masculine, which offer sufficient means of empowerment to help both male and female students in their careers. Hence, the IDE should introduce more subjects that are traditionally taken by males, like science, agriculture, engineering, and technology, to maximize its contribution.

Coming to academic performance, our analysis has revealed that the female students who enroll in IDE perform as well as their male counterparts, if not better (as seen in academic year 1997–98). This follows our finding that in most of the subjects and academic years (with the exception of those indicated above), there was no significant difference between the performance of males and females. This means that not only does the IDE increase access to university education for females, but it also enables the females to enroll in a variety of programs, while at the same time the learning process allows females alongside males to perform as well as the males in their studies. This finding makes Swaziland different from other African countries, where it is found that female enrollments and academic-performance rates are lower than those of the males. Further research is, however, needed to determine if this is the case in all the education subsystems in Swaziland and, if so, find out what makes the country succeed in this regard when compared with the other African countries.

Based on the findings of this study, therefore, it would appear that the IDE is playing a critical role in gender parity, equality, and in empowering women. This contributes immensely to Swaziland's achievement of Goal Number 3 of the MDGs: that of promoting gender equality and women empowerment. Thus, the institute needs to be expanded to take in more students and to diversify its programs so that female students can increasingly access the traditionally male subjects. In general, therefore, this study demonstrates the power of distance education in promoting gender equality and in empowering women. It thereby supports the widely held view that developing countries like Swaziland should establish, support, and expand their distance education programs if they are to solve their myriad problems in education and if they are to achieve the MDGs. National education planners and policymakers, therefore, have to take into consideration the planning of distance education systems along with the planning of the conventional face-to-face systems, and not leave distance education on the periphery.

REFERENCES

Development Studies Network (2006). Measuring gender equality: Indicators of change. *Development Bulletin, 71.* International Women's Development Agency Inc., Canberra, Asustralia.

Dhanarajan, G, (2006). Face to face with distance education. In S. Garg, A. R. Khan, A. K. Aggarwal, U. Kanjilal, and S. Panda (Eds.), *Open and flexible learning: Issues and challenges – Prof. G. Ram Reddy Memorial Lectures.* New Delhi: Viva Books Private Limited.

Fagerlind, I., & Saha, L. (1992). *Education and national development: A comparative perspective* (2nd ed.). Oxford: Heinemann-Butterworth.

FAWESWA (2000). *Needs assessment report on teenage young mothers forum for African women educationalists – Swaziland,* FAWESWA, Manzini, Swaziland.

Francis, B. (2000) The gendered subject: Students' subject preferences and discussions of gender and subject ability. *Oxford Review of Education, 26*(1), 35–48.

Kaino, L. M. (1999) Analysis of student enrolment, dropout and performance in mathematics by gender at the University of Swaziland, *UNISWA Research Journal, 13,* 39–46.

Kwesiga, J. C. (2002). *Women's access to higher education in Africa – Uganda's experience.* Fountain Series in Gender Studies. Kampala, Uganda: Fountain Publishers.

Leach, F. (1988). Gender on the aid agenda: Men, women and educational opportunity, In P. Drake and P. Owen, (Eds.), *Gender and management issues in education: An international perspective.* Staffordshire, England: Trentham Books Limited.

Lewin, K. M. (1993). *Education and development: The issues and the evidence.* London: Department for International Development.

Magagula, C. M., Dlamini, B. M., Mkatshwa, T.D., Dlamini, N., & Shongwe, A. B. (2001). *Equity in educational resource provision in high schools of Swaziland: Implications for policy formulation.* Kwaluseni, Swaziland: Blue Moon Printing.

Makhubu, L. (1999). *Science: The gender issue in World Conference in Science.* UNESCO, Paris.

Mlama, P. (2005). Pressure from within: The forum for African women educationalists. In N. Rao and I. Smyth (Eds.), *Partnerships for girl's education.* Oxfam, Oxford.

Nkosi, T. M. (1992). Gender bias in history performance at junior certificate level. Bachelor of Education dissertation, University of Swaziland, Kwaluseni.

Obanya, P. (2004). *Promoting basic education for women and girls.* UNESCO, Paris.

Perraton, H. (2004). Aims and purpose. In H. Perraton and H. Lentell (Eds.), *Policy for open and distance learning: World review of distance education and open learning.* Vol 4. London: RoutledgeFalmer.

Perry, G., Ferreira, F., & Walton, M. (2003). *Inequality in Latin America and the Caribbean: Breaking with history?* The World Bank, Washington, DC.

Pong, S. (1999). Gender inequality in educational attainment in peninsula Malaysia. In C. Heward and S. Bunwaree (Eds.), *Gender, education and development: Beyond Access to Empowerment.* London: Zed Books Limited.

Samoff, J. (2003). Institutionalizing international influence. In R. F. Arnove and C. A. Torres (Eds.), *Comparative education: The dialectic of the global and the local.* Lanham, Maryland: Rowman & Littlefield Publishers.

Sen, A. K. (1999). *Development as freedom.* Oxford University Press.

Shabaya, J., & Konadu-Agyemang, K. (2004). Unequal access, unequal participation: Some spatial and socio-economic dimensions of the gender gap in education in Africa with special reference to Ghana, Zimbabwe and Kenya. *Compare – A Journal of Comparative Education, 34*(4), 395–424.

Simelane, Q. G. S. N. (1996). *A Comparison of female and male students' academic performance at O-level in Swaziland.* Bachelor of Education dissertation, University of Swaziland, Kwaluseni.

Smith, A. C. (1988). Females in science courses in Swaziland: Performance, progress and perceptions. *Swaziland Journal of Science and Technology, 9*(1), 65–82.

Srisa-An, W. (2006). Making distance education borderless. In S. Garg, A. R. Khan, A. K. Aggarwal, U. Kanjilal and S. Panda (Eds.), *Open and Flexible Learning – Issues and Challenges – Prof. G. Ram Reddy Memorial Lectures.* New Delhi: Viva Books Private Limited.

Stromquist, N. P. (2006). Gender, education and the possibility of transformative knowledge. *Compare – A Journal of Comparative Education, 36*(2), 145–161.

Stromquist, N. (1996). The World Bank's university education report and its implications for women. Retrieved November 22, 2004 from http://www.bc.edu/bc_org/avp/soe/cihe/newsletter/News05/textbk1.html

Sukati, C. W. S., Chandraiah, E., Simelane, H. S., Sithole, M. M., & Magagula, C. M. (2007). *Comparative analysis of the academic achievement of a cohort of BA (Hums) students studying full-time and those studying by distance learning mode.* Report for the UNISWA Research Center, Luyengo. In possession of the authors.

Swaziland Government (1975). Report of the National Education Commission 1975, Ministry of Education, Mbabane.

UNESCO (2005). *Education for all: The quality imperative.* Global Monitoring Report, UNESCO, Paris.

UNESCO (2004). *Gender and education for all: The leap to equality,* Global Monitoring Report. UNESCO, Paris.

UNESCO (1997). Common Country Assessment Report–Swaziland Government. UNESCO, Paris.

United Nations Development Program (2005). *Taking action: Achieving gender equality and empowering women—Achieving the millennium development goals.* UN Millennium Task Force on Education and Gender Equality. Earthscan, London.

United Nations Development Program (1995). *Human development report: Gender and human development.* Oxford University Press.

University of Swaziland (1997–1998 to 2005–2006). University of Swaziland Full-Time and Part-Time Student Enrollment Yearbooks, University of Swaziland, Kwaluseni.

Wheldon, A. E., & Smith, A. C. (1988). The access of girls to education, with particular reference to secondary science education in Swaziland. *BOLESWA Educational Research Journal,* (6) 14–27.

Wheldon, A. E., & Smith, A. C. (1986). Gender based differences in O-level subject choice and performance in Swaziland. *Swaziland Institute of Educational Research Bulletin,* 7.

World Bank (2000). *Engendering development through gender equality rights, resources and voice.* Oxford University Press.

CHAPTER 4

A VIRTUAL WHEEL OF FORTUNE?

Enablers and Constraints of ICTs in Higher Education in South Africa

Laura Czerniewicz and Cheryl Brown

INTRODUCTION

Globally, the increase of information and communication technologies (ICTs) in higher education is shaking up complex tertiary institutions from the inside while provoking larger questions about the overall role of higher education itself. It is evident that ICTs are being taken up in the core business within institutions while they are simultaneously integral to the various pressures that are presently being experienced by the higher education sector as a whole. South African higher-education institutions (HEIs) are being further challenged at two levels: by the pressures of global trends and by insistent local socioeconomic imperatives.

This chapter reports on the findings of a study of the five HEIs in one South African province. The study aimed to identify the enablers and constraints of ICT use in higher education, situated firmly within the wider

Bridging the Knowledge Divide, pages 57–76
Copyright © 2009 by Information Age Publishing
All rights of reproduction in any form reserved.

pressures being experienced in South African institutions; and to illuminate the ways in which broader ICT trends are expressed and refracted in the local context.

HIGHER EDUCATION PRESSURES

Since the late 1980s, the higher-education sector globally has gone through a process of reorientation and repositioning. This period of transition has seen the sector become responsible to multiple stakeholders while shifting away from dominant state authority. There has been a concomitant reduction in state funding. Higher education has been required to become responsive to many more social interests than was previously the case and to engage with the imperatives being voiced by many different groups ranging from unions and associations to industry, business, and regional authorities (Middlehurst, 2001; Maassen & Cloete, 2002). From this diversified support base, the sector is now pressured to engage with new economic forces, to resolve existing social tensions, and to transform itself in a situation of centrally imposed resource constraints.

Pressures to Respond to a New Economic Order

The rapid worldwide social and economic transformation that is captured in the notion of globalization has had an impact on HEIs, with increased pressure to produce more graduates with high-level knowledge skills (Council of Higher Education, 2001; Maassen & Cloete, 2002). The concepts of globalization and ICTs are often twinned in the discourse of the new world order known variously as "the knowledge society," "the informational economy," and "the information age." Thus, according to noted social theorist Manuel Castells, "if knowledge is the electricity of the new informational international economy, the institutions of higher education are the power sources on which a new development process must rely" (Department of Education, 2001, section 1.1, para. 6). He argues, as have so many others, that ICTs are central to this new order, indeed, "The centrality of the Internet to many areas of social, economic and political activity is tantamount to marginality for those without, or with only limited access to the Internet, as well as for those unable to use it effectively (Castells, 2001, p. 247). Others have been even more forceful, arguing that "exclusion will mean severely limiting life chances" (Burbules & Callister, 2000, p. 19). Inclusion does not simply mean access to a computer; it requires a deeper notion of access, one that incorporates the full gamut of resources that access and use require for meaningful value. It also means an informed understanding of the factors that enable and constrain ICT take-up within higher education.

Globally, ICTs are considered a basic requirement of the knowledge society for which universities now prepare their students (Castells et al., 1999; Burbules & Callister, 2000; Waema, 2002). Although South Africa does not have a specific national educational-technology policy, its commitment to this new economic order and participation in the knowledge society is evident in numerous policy documents.[1] South Africa's National Plan for Higher Education confirms that the higher-education sector has "a critical and central role to play in contributing to the development of an information society in South Africa both in terms of skills development and research" (Department of Education, 2001). While the state does not yet require tertiary institutions to provide concrete evidence of 21st-century graduate competencies, as is the case, for example, in Australia (Graduate Careers Australia, 2007), institutions are having to rethink outdated understandings of "graduateness," access, and technology use.

Pressures to Address and Resolve Social Tensions

The social demands on South African HEIs have intensified in recent years. Increased participation by a diverse range of students has resulted in massification of the sector within a context of limited or even reduced funding (Maassen & Cloete, 2002). The need to engage with the needs of a great diversity of students is particularly pressing, because the nature of the student body has changed substantially since the postapartheid government was formed in 1994. As is the case around the world,[2] there are both more and different students entering the sector. Student enrollments increased by 30%, from 569,000 in 1995 to 744,489 in 2004 (HEMIS, 2003, 2004; Council of Higher Education, 2004). South African universities have also experienced a revolution in the increase of black students in the sector[3] (Cooper & Subotzky, 2001) with African students in the majority at both universities and technikons since about the turn of the new century (Cloete, 2002).

Because apartheid institutions were racially demarcated and unequally resourced, recent years have seen the substantial restructuring of a fragmented, divided, and unequal sector, as well as the formulation and implementation of policies toward transformation (Department of Education, 2001; Gillard, 2004). These changes are currently percolating through the sector, with many institutions undergoing state-mandated, full-scale institutional mergers in 2004–2005, including one merger of two Western Cape institutions, soon after our study was concluded. These changes have in turn had an impact on the standardization, distribution, and take-up of ICTs within newly formed institutions. This adds an extra dimension to the sector's imperative to address the digital divide, resulting in what some authors have called a dilemma of justice (Broekman et al., 2002). Indeed, Broekman et al. ask whether ICTs should be introduced at all into higher-education curricula if all students cannot benefit from them. They point out the difficult choices South African universities are obliged to make when considering that providing students with the means to acquire membership in global communities may further marginalize the previously disadvantaged.

Thus, in the South African context, the take-up of ICTs should be seen as yet another thread in a complex net of transformation, especially as ICT use is so closely linked to broader socioeconomic and political trends.

Resource Constraints

The South African higher-education environment is characterized by resource constraints in terms of reduced real-state expenditure in support of the sector as a whole, a relatively poor enabling infrastructure, and the absence of an overarching educational technology framework.

There has been no effective increase in spending on higher education in South Africa in recent years. While the overall government allocation to higher education has shown a growth in "real rands" since 1995–96, the high growth of student enrollments and constancy of funding (in terms of the GDP) (Council of Higher Education, 2004) means that real funding per teaching-input unit has decreased annually (Steyn & de Villiers, 2007).

South Africa's situation echoes that of many HE sectors throughout the world; a global comparison of 18 countries indicates that higher education is relatively underfunded in terms of its proportion of the state budget, education budget, and GDP (Council of Higher Education, 2004, p. 195).

While state expenditure on computer equipment increased (in terms of percentage of the total institutional expenditure) across the sector in 2002 (1.8%), there has been a steady decline since then (1% of total expenditure in 2005). This decreased expenditure may possibly be attributed to decreasing ICT costs; but old equipment requires replacement and maintenance, and it is likely that funding is being obtained from other sources, albeit unevenly.

In addition, South African HEIs are constrained by a considerably underresourced technological environment compared with the developed world. In addition to low penetration rates—109 Internet users per 1000 people compared with 630 in the United States—the sector's bandwidth is extremely poor at 19 bits pp compared with 3,306 in the US. The costs are also high, with monthly access averaging the equivalent of $3 USD compared with $15 USD in the US (World Bank, 2005).

While the lack of an overarching educational-technology policy has not proved an obstacle to innovative practices on the ground, it can be considered a constraint if such policies actually indicate longer-term values in the intended allocation of resources. The lack of state funding is a distinct constraint in South Africa; and the absence of sectoral ICT policies may be barring South Africa from access to the kinds of support that have been shown to play an important enabling role for growth in the sector in other countries.

THE STUDY

In the light of the higher-education environment outlined above, a study was undertaken in both technikons and all three universities (a mixture of previously advantaged and disadvantaged) in the Western Cape province of South Africa. In particular, the study set out to identify the enabling and constraining factors that facilitate and deter ICT use in environments that are contending with intense pressures and competing imperatives. There is very little research of this nature undertaken to date in developing contexts and almost none in sub-Saharan Africa.

In this research, we adopted a mixed-method approach, as described by Cresswell (1994). The findings reported here are based on the data obtained from a survey of 6,577 students and 515 academic staff, as well as interviews with senior managers in the five institutions in 2004 and 2005.4 Interviews were used to provide a background context to each institution in terms of the evolution of the use of educational technology.

The sample for the survey was selected by the proportional stratified random-sampling strategy used by Sayed (1998) in a survey on information literacy in higher education conducted in the Western Cape. This approach first classifies the population into two or more strata (subpopulations) and then ensures that the ratio of the sample size to the subpopulation size is equal for all the subpopulations (Jackson, 2002).

The questionnaire comprised three parts. As we understand access to ICTs to be a complex practice, in that access and use are incessantly interrelated and that the resources to be accessed are multifaceted, Part A focused on students and staff access to four kinds of interrelated resources: technological resources (physical and practical), resources of personal agency, contextual resources, and digital content resources (Czerniewicz & Brown, 2005). Part B examined the extent and the breadth of the ICT teaching and learning resources accessible to and used by students and staff; and Part C focused on demographics in order to consider how access was differentiated for different demographic groups.

ENABLING FACTORS IN THE TAKE-UP OF ICTS

Overall, student use is enabled by access to resources of personal agency, contextual resources, and online resources, but constrained by technological resources; and staff use is enabled by technological resources, resources of personal agency, and online resources, but constrained by contextual resources.

However, these resources are fluid and are experienced differently by people in various contexts and under varying conditions. In addition, the relationship between access and use is complex.

Students Are Enabled by the Conditions Rather Than by Numbers

Comparisons of South Africa's infrastructure with developed countries are clearly not useful. Frustrations at not being able to compete in terms of provision can be addressed by not attempting to provide as many computers as elsewhere or even as many as possible. Rather, increased use can be better enabled by supportive and safe conditions, and adequate and accessible access.

In the study, the ratio of students to computers ranges with the lowest being 6:1, while the highest ratio was 12:1. This is consistent with the reported average for South African tertiary institutions of 11:1 and much better than the average for African tertiary institutions of 55:1 (Steiner et al., 2004). Internationally, this is comparable with the level of access found in secondary schools in the United Kingdom (Teachernet, 2007). However, at a university level, countries such as those in the UK and US have ceased to report on the ratio of computers to students and instead report on how many computers a student has and what the number of wireless points on campus is (Green, 2004; Mangan, 2006).

The provision of computers is generally thought to be a quick and easy (albeit not cheap) way to resolve the problems of lack of access. Given this belief, an important finding from this study is that what matters is not the numbers of computers provided, but rather the conditions of use. Of the five institutions in the study, the one with the lowest ratio of computers to students was found to have the highest student-satisfaction levels. What makes the difference is availability and ease of access, adequacy of computers and support. Related practical issues such as opening hours, booking conditions, and the conduciveness of the learning environment prove crucial.

Students Are Enabled by Equitable Access on Campus

While students across the five institutions did have different experiences of on-campus access, mainly in relation to the small number of computer facilities available centrally, the small percentage of computer facilities accessible after hours and on weekends and other restrictions on use, a significant finding of the study in all institutions was that unlike computer access off campus, on-campus access was equitably reported by most students. Socioeconomic factors such as access to electricity, hardware, software support, and even study space were constraining factors in off-campus use. With on-campus use, however, students reported equivalent and fair access to resources with only students with disabilities reporting difficulty of access. Most students (69%) across all institutions felt that Internet access and general institutional support were adequate for their learning requirements. In addition, there were no differences reported regarding ease of access across different demographic groups of students.

In an age where policymakers may be expecting students to solve access needs by acquiring personal computers, it is possible that the provision of computer laboratories, information literacy support, and an enabling technological environment may not be prioritized. However, in a developing-country context characterized by major inequalities off campus, the equity of access offered in the on-campus environment is crucial to alleviating digital divides and is likely to remain vital in the medium-term. In addition, as argued later in this chapter, the lack of specific infrastructure and support for students with disabilities is not just a constraint for these students but a missed opportunity.

Staff and Students Are Enabled by Positive Dispositions

The study found consensus about the value of computers, with both staff and student overwhelmingly positive about their benefits both generally and particularly, for teaching and learning. Indeed, 72% of students were extremely positive about the role of computers in learning and have a high opinion of their own abilities/self-efficacy. While their actual skills would need to be tested by other research methods, the findings do suggest that students' use of ICTs is enabled by their motivation and confidence. Researchers have noted the importance of the linkage between personal agency and use. Broos and Roe (2006), for example, note that psychological factors such as motivation and interest offer possible explanations for differential adoption and use of ICTs in their study of Flemish adolescents. Some researchers have specified that a lack of interest in and aptitude for using computers is a factor constraining use (Kvasny, 2002), while others have found positive student attitudes to technology an enabling factor for use (Miltiadou & Savenye, 2003).

In our study, academic staff was similarly enabled by a positive disposition (78%). More than half had availed themselves of some computer training and most (74%) expressed great confidence in their own abilities.

Students Are Enabled by Supportive Networks

Students were also enabled by supportive networks, as their family and friends placed a high value on their use of computers. Overall, students have good access to supportive contextual resources, with friends even more supportive in terms of interest (87%) and actual use (76%) than families (85% and 55% respectively). These findings on the enabling power of supportive contexts correlate with arguments that strong social networks encourage use (Kvasny, 2002). Conversely, lack of social support is observed to constrain use of technology (Warschauer, 2003a, 2003b, 2003c). The role of supportive networks has been specifically linked to settings where parents used a computer as part of their work and could provide support and guidance (Nakhaie & Pike, 1998).

ICT Use is Enabled by Existing Student ICT-Mediated Practices

Students used computers for learning even when they were not asked to do so, and they used computers informally. This was particularly evident in the case of communicative media, where 55% of staff asked students to use communicative media as part of their courses, yet 75% of students reported using communicative media regularly for their learning. As students reported using communicative media for learning more often than they were asked to do so by staff in support of particular courses, this suggests that they were more broadly engaged in ICT-mediated activities for non-classroom and informal learning purposes.

ICT Use Is Enabled by Curriculum Integration

The example above of students using a media form for learning more often than they were asked to do was echoed by other media forms and computer uses, suggesting that the amount of use did not appear to be only driven by lecturer requirements within courses. However, *variety* of use did seem to be strongly related to lecturer requirements; when different ICTs were embedded in learning activities, then students were very likely to use them. For example, when students are not required to use computers at all by staff, they exhibit more infrequent use themselves (88%) and conversely, when students are required to use a computer for all teaching and learning events, they use a computer more frequently themselves (60%). This demonstrates the importance of purpose in relation to use and echoes much of the literature, which shows that ICTs are more likely to be used and to be useful when fully integrated in the curriculum (Stensaker et al., 2007).

CONSTRAINING FACTORS IN THE TAKE-UP OF ICTS

Students Are Constrained by Lack of Home Access

This study identified that low home access is a significant constraint. Sixty percent of students who did not have use of a computer at home were low users of ICTs for learning. This finding confirms those by others, which indicates the important link between computers at home and frequency of use (Selwyn, 1998; Facer, 2002), even if on-campus/school access is adequate. A lower likelihood of owning a computer at home also translates into lower access to the Internet (Castells, 2001, p. 253).

However, Hassani (2006) also notes that while home computer access is a key factor for use, individuals who have many locations of use (e.g., home and work or home and Internet café or home and school, etc.) take greater advantage of ICTs. It is therefore heartening to note that the majority of students (78%) in this study reported some form of access to a computer off-campus. Indeed, students were creative in terms of where and how they accessed computers off-campus, with 34% employing multiple strategies and finding a computer wherever they could, including such examples as "at a friend's dad's work."

In this study, practical considerations, such as sharing of computers, affected the majority of students, with most students sharing with more than two people. Even where computers are available off-campus, they are not available when a student may need them. Additional constraining considerations relating to practical access are also reported: these being the conduciveness of the physical environment and the affordability of physical resources.5

Students Are Constrained by Inequality of Access

Given the increased diversity in the student body in the higher-education sector and the rapid adoption of ICTs within a resource-constrained environment, we were interested in how different groups of students are affected by access to ICTs and whether or not this impacts on their use.

Our findings show that access to ICTs is not equal: students from different socioeconomic groupings, languages, disability levels, and gender have different levels of access to ICTs. This is evident particularly in three areas: technological access, aptitude, and access to supportive social structures.

Inequalities of Technological Access

As explained earlier, inequalities of on-campus use were not apparent. However, off-campus, those students who had no access or only had access somewhere other than where they lived were predominantly from low socioeconomic groups (43%) as opposed to high socioeconomic groups (22%).6 Also, whereas 27% of students from high socioeconomic groups had maximum access to ICTs off- campus, this was true for only 13% of students from low socioeconomic groups.

Sixty three per cent of students from low socioeconomic backgrounds indicated that they had below-average ease and adequacy of access to computers off-campus, compared with 49% of students from high socioeconomic backgrounds. A contributing factor may be practical access, as low socioeconomic students had less autonomy in their use of computers off-campus; fewer had sole use of a computer (21% compared with 25% of students from high socioeconomic groups) and 37% shared a computer with four or more people. This finding echoes that of a World Bank study (2007) of the rise of new technologies among youth across the world, showing that globally, access is concentrated in the middle/ high socioeconomic groups.

Language differences also exist in South Africa, and we agree with researchers who assert that language is another signifier of socioeconomic class position (Wasserman, 2002). In our study, students who spoke English as a first home language had much more access to a computer off-campus than those who spoke English as a second language; 31% of English second-language speakers had no access to a computer off-campus compared with only 10% of English first-language speakers. English second-language speakers also had less autonomy of off-campus access, with 36% sharing a computer with more than four people, compared with 25% of English first-language speakers. At the same time, 64% of English second-language students also indicated that off-campus access is more difficult and less than adequate for their learning needs compared with 47% of English first-language speakers. This finding also correlates with research from South America that different ICTs are adopted differently in different language groups (Lizie et al., 2004).

While the group of students who indicated they have a disability that limited their ability to use a computer was very small (99 people: 0.01% of the entire survey), it should be noted that this group is significantly disadvantaged in terms of technological access (Brewer, 2002; Department of Communication, 2005). Nearly half (48%) of students with a disability had no access whatsoever to a computer off-campus. Among those with access, only 16% had sole access to a computer. Of those who shared access, only 10% were primary users. Understandably, 72% of students with a disability indicated below-average ease and adequacy of access off-campus compared with 56% of students without a disability. This discrepancy between students with and without a disability was also notable in terms of ease and adequacy of on-campus access, with 56% of students with a disability indicating below-average ease and adequacy of access on campus compared with 36% of students without a disability.

The lack of specific infrastructure and support for students with disabilities is not just a constraint for these students, but a missed opportunity. ICTs offer enhanced admission for, engagement with, and retention of disabled students, providing possibilities for access in ways not possible previously (Eastwood, 2005). This is manifest in organizations such as the United Kingdom's Open University, where specific strategies to ensure technological development that enhances admission and retention of disabled students (Daniels, 1996) have resulted in some 10,000 disabled students studying with the OU (R. Basi, personal communication, 2007).

In terms of gender and age, there was equal access to computers and the Internet on- and off-campus; there were, however, small differences with regard to autonomy of access. Males had more autonomy of access than females (26% of male students had sole access to a home computer compared with 18% of female students) and students older than 30 years had more autonomy of access (45% of older students had sole use of the computers off-campus compared with 18% of under-20-year-olds). However, for neither gender were there any reported differences in ease or adequacy of access.

Given that students from low socioeconomic groups, those who spoke English as a second language and those with a disability, had significantly less access in off-campus settings, the provision of ICTs on-campus is critical in order to ensure that these digital divides are minimized for these demographically marginalized groups.

Inequality of Aptitude

While students across all demographics groups (except those with disabilities) value ICTs, there were strong differences in students' reported self-efficacy across the same groupings. More students from low socioeconomic groups rated their ability to use ICTs poorly (38%) than did students from high socioeconomic groups (16%). In addition, English first-language speakers rated their ICT abilities higher; 53% in the reported high-aptitude category compared with only 33% of those who do not speak English as a home language.

Other differences included 26% of male students rating their ability as excellent compared with 15% of female students. Interestingly, 17% more males in the high-socioeconomic group rated themselves as excellent than males in the low-socioeconomic group.

Students with a disability rated their ability comparatively lower than those without a disability—few students with disabilities reported a high aptitude (14%). Indeed, most students in this group reported a low aptitude (55%); they also had a much lower attitudinal disposition toward computers than students without a disability (36% compared with 46%). Perhaps this is because despite the opportunities ICTs offer them, the difficulties and cost associated with ICTs make students wary of their use.

Inequality of Supportive Social Structures

Again, our findings showed that when it comes to value placed on ICTs, students' peers and families placed almost equal value on the use of computers for educational purposes, irrespective of social context. However, while the perceived value of ICTs is unanimous among the social networks of all socioeconomic groups, there were differences in the support students reported receiving from these social networks. This differential support is relevant, as it translates into the kind of assistance that students are likely to have access to.

Students from high-socioeconomic groups had more access to a supportive student community (52%) and family networks (37%) than did students from low-socioeconomic groups (38% and 28%, respectively). Also, 34% of students from low-socioeconomic groups reported unsupportive family networks compared with only 18% of students from high-socioeconomic groups.

Differences were also evident when language was used as a variable. Students who spoke English as a first language reported more access to a supportive student community (53%) and family networks (38%) than students who spoke English as a second language (41% and 28%, respectively). Students who spoke English as a second language also had a higher percentage of unsupportive family networks. Of English second-language speakers, 46% fall within the low part of the scale compared with 32% of English speakers. Like students from low-socioeconomic groups, English second-language students had less access to such contextual resources than English first-language students.

Students with a disability had less access to supportive student communities (45%) compared with students without a disability (32%). However, this difference was less marked for the families of students with a disability.

With regard to gender, males and females had equal access to social networks, but these were accessed slightly differently. More females (53%) solved computer-related problems by asking their families than did male students (45%), while more males (35%) than females (22%) reported that they solve problems themselves.

Staff Are Constrained by On-/Off-Campus Lack of Integration

Despite quite different institutional environments, academic staff generally had adequate access to computers on-campus. Yet academics' days are not traditionally structured; they do not work in patterns that mean they are in their offices eight hours a day, five days a week. Their commitment to being able to work off-campus was manifest in the extent to which they had invested in computers at home. This was true across the five institutions, regardless of the resource intensiveness or historical wealth of the institutions in which they work. Although we did not ask about on-/off-campus integration in the quantitative investigation, the open-ended questions revealed this to be a relevant consideration. ICT access for academics was constrained by the lack of integration between on- and off-campus systems and by the fact that, without exception, academics shouldered the cost of home access themselves.

Staff Are Constrained by Poor Access to Contextual Resources

Unlike students, academic staff was constrained by poor or ambivalent social and institutional networks, and they generally did not report access to good institutional resources. In all but one institution, staff felt that respective institutional support and vision of ICTs for teaching and learning was average or poor.

In addition, many staff didn't know whether or not their colleagues thought computers were important. When they did report knowing about their colleagues use and attitudes toward computers, they were divided about their opinions as to their colleagues' values and use, indicating limited support networks and communities of practice. The qualities and quantities of academics' use of ICTs was not being enabled or driven by formal institutional strategies or policies, except in the case of one institution where staff both knew about and felt enabled by institutional policies.

Certainly, across the five institutions, there was no common or shared language or understanding about the use of computers in higher education.

Summary of Findings: ICT Use Is Constrained by Lack of Access but not Necessarily Enabled by Access

Overall, it is easier to identify constraining factors than enabling ones, especially when considering access in relation to use. The relationship between high and low access reveals that while 73% of students with low access also made low use of ICTs for learning (indicating that lack of access was a clear constraining factor for use), the converse was not necessarily true. Only 58% of students with high access also made high use of ICTs. This indicates that high access alone is not enough to result in high use.

Our study showed that better access correlated with higher frequency of use, while those students with inadequate access to a range of resources made very infrequent use of ICTs for learning. In addition, the majority of students with high access also had a more varied use of ICTs for learning.

However, even when there was good access, a significant percentage (44%) of students did not make frequent use of ICTs for learning. In particular, students from lower-socioeconomic groups made less-frequent use of ICTs for learning, even in high-access situations. This suggests that when there is no digital divide apparent (as in the high-access group where students all had reasonable access to ICTs), there is a socially structured usage differential. Such differences have been noted in the context of developed countries (Van Dijk, 2006), but have not been previously explored in a developing-country context.

CONCLUSION

The findings of our study can be usefully viewed in light of the three major pressures outlined at the beginning of this chapter.

The first pressure being experienced by higher education is the need to participate in a new global order, specifically in the form of the information society. As a systematic clustering of meanings and beliefs, the discourse of the information society is expressed in both the policy terrain generally and the reported practices of higher education provided by our study. These findings have highlighted the extent to which ICTs are overwhelmingly considered central to a new order, and access is considered to be desirable and necessary. Our study confirmed that students value ICTs highly, as do their social networks in the form of both family and friends. Indeed, students' friends are a significant source of ICT-related problem solving. This shared confidence and membership of a supportive community is an enabling factor that is arguably crucial to the use of ICTs. Indeed, such access has ripple effects, because such social capital is not just an input into human development, but serves as a point of leverage; a "shift factor affecting other inputs since it tends to enhance the benefits of investment in human and physical capital"(Warschauer, 2003b).

Participation in an ICT-mediated social order means using ICTs widely: for formal learning, for informal learning, and for social activities (which may inform and overlap with learning). Our study found that students were keen to use ICTs as part of their learning, and many did so as part of informal social and collaborative learning activities. These kinds of activities are beneficial because of the value of peer-to-peer learning (Nicol & Boyle, 2003) and because the strengthening of social ties enables people to better learn from others (Warschauer, 2003b). In an information age where collaboration and knowledge sharing are valued (Daniels, 2006), findings of such expansive use indicate the extent to which students buy into ICT-mediated communication.

On the other hand, participation in the new global order is constrained, especially for staff. There is an expectation of flexibility of access and "anywhere anytime use." But academics expressed frustration and lament the lack of technological integration between home and work.

That staff and students wish to participate in and create an information society, and that they have access to many of the resources required are key findings of this South African study. But this desire is not experienced evenly, which echoes the second tension manifest in higher education more broadly: the pressure to resolve broader social tensions. Universities are under pressure to support bright students who have been disadvantaged by inequitable educational opportunities and systems. To date, such support is generally provided only for the development of academic literacies and numeracy skills. This study has demonstrated that students from particular groups are disadvantaged in terms of their ICT access, particularly with regard to ability and support. Institutions have a crucial role to play in assisting disadvantaged students build confidence and skills and enabling their access to communities of practice.

Access to technology for learning is therefore part of educational development, not simply an infrastructural matter. Even as an infrastructural consideration, it is evident that simply providing resources such as networked computers is not enough to enable use for successful teaching and learning. Conditions of access on-campus are more important criteria for ease and successful access than numbers of computers. In a resource-constrained environment with a diverse student body and a generally divided society, ensuring fair access on-campus is essential and is a genuine contribution to equality of access and use.

At the same time, while institutions may provide generally fair and equivalent access to all students, this does not negate the advantage of home-computer access as an enabler of use. It is not surprising that lack of home access is linked to socioeconomic group, as affordability is a key, broad social issue. While institutions cannot resolve the underlying social differences upon which differences of access are premised, they can, and do, provide thoughtful solutions to off-campus access. These may take the form of innovative laptop schemes or partnerships with Internet cafés or original uses of now-ubiquitous technologies such as cell phones, which are owned by the vast majority of South African students, even in previously disadvantaged institutions.

Universities cannot resolve all the inequalities of the broader societies in which they are located. But within their own community contexts, they can offer equal opportunities to all students with academic potential, no matter what their backgrounds, nor the specific educational disadvantages they bring into tertiary education. With regard to these disadvantages, individual institutions have a responsibility to take measures to ensure that their students can succeed. This includes ensuring that access to the resources that technological use requires are available to all. Educational-development progams need to incorporate ICT-related components. While it is encouraging that the five universities researched in this study currently provide generally fair access to all (excepting students with disabilities), there is a danger that institutions may not continue with a specific commitment to the provision of these resources given the financial pressures they are under and given the perception that ICT access in broader society is becoming pervasive. As long as South African society remains divided by class and educational opportunity, it is clear that ongoing institutional commitments to equal access to the full range of technological resources remain imperative. Otherwise, the digital divide may widen, and institutional developments may, in fact, further marginalize the already disadvantaged.

REFERENCES

Barraket, J., & Scott, G. (2001). *Virtual equality? Equity and the use of information technology in higher education.* Australian Academic and Research Libraries.

Brewer, J. (2002). *ICT and disability: World Wide Web consortium (W3C):* Web Accessibility Initiative (WAI).

Broekman, I., Enslin, P., & Pendlebury, S. (2002). Distributive justice and information communication technologies in higher education in South Africa. *South African Journal of Higher Education, 16*(1), 29–35.

Broos, A., & Roe, K. (2006). The digital divide in the Playstation generation: Self-efficacy, locus of control and ICT adoption among adolescents. *Poetics, 34,* 306–317.

Burbules, N., & Callister, T. (2000). *Watch IT: The risks and promises of information technology for education.* Boulder, CO: Westview Press.

Castells, M. (2001). *The Internet galaxy: Reflections on the Internet, business and society.* New York: Oxford University Press.

Castells, M. R., Flecha, P., Freire, H., Giroux, H. A., & Macedo, P. (1999). *Critical education in the new information age.* New York and Oxford: Bowman and Little-field Publishers.

Cloete, N. (2002). South African higher education and social transformation. *Higher Education Digest,* Autumn Issue, UK.

Cooper, D., & Subotzky, G. (2001). *The skewed revolution: Trends in South African higher education: 1988–1998.* Cape Town: University of Western Cape, Education Policy Unit.

Council of Higher Education (2001). *Developing African higher education.* South Africa.

Council of Higher Education (2004). *South African higher education in the first decade of democracy.* South Africa

Creswell, J. W. (1994). *Research design: Qualitative and quantitative approaches.* Thousand Oaks, CA: Sage Publications.

Czerniewicz, L., & Brown, C. (2005). Access to ICTs for teaching and learning – From single artefact to inter-related resources. *International Journal of Education and Development using Information and Communication Technologies, 1*(2).

Czerniewicz, L., & Brown, C. (2006). *The virtual Möbius strip.* Cape Town. Centre for Educational Technology.

Daniels, J. (1996). Implementing a technology strategy for a mega-university: The instill project. Proceedings of the 3rd International Interactive Multimedia Symposium. Perth, Australia: Promaco Conventions

Daniels, J. (2006). eLearning and free open source software: The key to global mass higher education. In *International Seminar on Distance, Collaborative and eLearning: Providing Learning Opportunities in the New Millennium via Innovative Approaches.* Universiti Teknologi Malaysia.

Department of Arts Culture Science and Technology (2002). *South Africa's national research and development (r&d) strategy.* Pretoria:Government Printers.

Department of Communication (2005). *South Africa to host SADC disability conference in preparation for world summit on information society (WSIS).* Pretoria:Government Printers.

Department of Education (2001). *The national plan on higher education.* Pretoria: Government Printers.

Department of Education (2003). *White paper on e-education: Transforming learning and teaching through ICT.* Pretoria: Government Printers.

Department of Science and Technology (2000). *National research and technology foresight ICT report.* Pretoria: Government Printers.

Eastwood, P. (2005). ICT: A major step for disabled students. In S. Fallows and R. Bhanot, (Eds.), *Quality issues in ICT-based higher education.* London: Routledge-Falmer.

Facer, K. (2002). What do we mean by the digital divide? Exploring the roles of access, relevance and resource networks. In *Digital divide: A collection of papers from the Toshiba/ BECTA digital divide seminar.* Coventry, UK: British Educational Communications and Technology Agency.

Gillard, E. (2004). *Report on the colloquium on 10 years of democracy and higher education change.* South Africa: Council of Higher Education.

Graduate Careers Australia (2007). Course experience questionnaire data. Retrieved September 11, 2007 from http://www.universitiesaustralia.edu.au/content.asp?page=/policies_programs/graduates/index.htm

Green, K. (2004). Campus computing report. Retrieved December 1, 2008 from http://www.campuscomputing.net/summaries/2004/index.html.

Hassani, S. (2006). Locating digital divides at home, work and everywhere else. *Poetics, (34)* 250–272.

HEMIS (2003). *Higher education management information system (HEMIS) for state subsidised universities and technikons 2003.* Retrieved November 30, 2007 from http://www.education.gov.za/dynamic/dynamic.aspx?pageid=326&dirid=14

HEMIS (2004). *Higher education management information system (HEMIS) for state subsidised universities and technikons 2004.* Retrieved November 30, 2007 from: http://www.education.gov.za/dynamic/dynamic.aspx?pageid=326&dirid=14

Higgs, N. (2002). Measuring socio-economic status: A discussion and comparison of methods or letting the Gini out of the bottle plus some thoughts on well-being. In SAMRA Convention 2002,. Drakensberg, South Africa.

Jackson, G. (2002). Sampling for social science research and evaluations. Retrieved June 12, 2006 from: http://www.gwu.edu/~gjackson/281_Sampling.PDF

Kvasny, L. (2002). A conceptual framework for examining digital inequality. In *Eighth Americas Conference on Information Systems,* Dallas, TX.

Lizie, A., Stewart, C., & Avila, G. (2004). *Cultural dimensions of the digital divide: Information and communications technologies (ICT) and Brockton's Cape Verdeans*: Porto Alegre, Brazil.

Maassen, P., & Cloete, N. (2002). Global reform trends in higher education. In N. Cloete, R. Fehnel, P. Maassen, T. Moja, H. Rerold, and T. Gibbon, (Eds.), *Transformation in higher education. Global pressures and local realities in South Africa* (pp.13–58) Cape Town: Juta and Company:.

Mangan, K. (2006). For many students, one computer is not enough. *Chronicle of Higher Education, 52*(26).

Middlehurst, R. (2001). University challenges: Borderless higher education, today and tomorrow. *Minerva, 39,* 3–26.

Miltiadou, M., & Savenye, W. (2003). Applying social cognitive constructs of motivation to enhance student success in online distance education. *AACE Journal (formerly Educational Technology Review), 11*(1).

Nakhaie, M. R., & Pike, R. M. (1998). Social origins, social status and home computer access and use. *Canadian Journal of Sociology, 23*(4), 427-450.

Nicol, D., & Boyle, J. (2003). Peer instruction versus class-wide discussion in large classes: A comparison of two interaction methods in the wired classroom. *Studies in Higher Education, 24*(4), 457–473.

Sayed, Y. (1998). *The segregated information highway: Information literacy in higher education.* University of Cape Town Press.

Selwyn, N. (1998). The effect of using a home computer on students' educational use of IT. *Computers and Education, 31,* 211–277.

Steiner, R., Tirivanyi, N., Jensen, M., & Gakio, K. (2004). African tertiary institutions connectivity survey. Retrieved December 1, 2008, from http://www.dgroups.org/groups/cgiar/InternetAfrica/docs/ATICS2004Report.pdf.

Stensaker, B., Maassen, P., Borgan, M., Oftebro, M., & Karseth, B. (2007) Use, updating and integration of ICT in higher education: Linking purpose, people and pedagogy. *Higher Education, 54*(3), 417–433.

Steyn, A. G. W., & de Villiers, A. P. (2007). *Public funding of higher education in South Africa by means of formulae.* South Africa: Council of Higher Education.

Teachernet (2007). *ICT key facts: Did you know...?* Retrieved September 11, 2007 from http://www.teachernet.gov.uk/wholeschool/ictis/facts/

UNESCO (2006). *Global education digest: Comparing education statistics across the world.* UNESCO Institute for Statistics, Montreal.

Van Dijk, J. (2006). Digital divide research, achievements and shortcomings. *Poetics, 34,* 221–235.

Waema, T. M. (2002). *ICT human resource development in Africa: Challenges and strategies.* Nairobi: African Technology Policy Studies Network.

Warschauer, M. (2003a). Demystifying the digital divide. *Scientific American, 289*(2), 42–47.

Warschauer, M. (2003b). *Technology and social inclusion: Rethinking the digital divide.* Cambridge, MA: The MIT Press.

Warschauer, M. (2003c). Dissecting the digital divide: A case study in Egypt. *The Information Society, 19,* 297–304.

Wasserman, H. (2002). Between the local and the global–South African languages and the Internet.. *African and Asian Studies, 1*(4), 303–321.

World Bank (2005). ICTs at a glance: Country reports. Retrieved September 11, 2007 from http://web.worldbank.org/WBSITE/EXTERNAL/DATASTATIS TICS/0,,contentMDK:20459133~menuPK:1192714~pagePK:64133150~piPK: 64133175~theSitePK:239419,00.html

World Bank (2007). World development report 2007: Development and the next generation.

NOTES

1. National Plan for Higher Education (Department of Education, 2001), the National Research and Development Strategy (Department of Arts Culture Science and Technology, 2002), the National Research and Technology Foresight ICT Report (Department of Science and Technology, 2000), and the White Paper on e-Education (Department of Education, 2003b).

2. Globally, student enrollment increased from 68 million in 1991 to 132 million in 2004 (94.1%), while in sub-Saharan Africa, student enrollment increased from 7 million to 15 million (114.3%) in the same time period (UNESCO, 2006).

3. The ratio of black students in total higher-education enrollment increased from 52% in 1993 to 74% in 2004 (CHE, 2004, HEMIS, 2003, 2004).

4. Details of the research study and methodology are available from the full project report (Czerniewicz & Brown, 2006) available at http://www.cet.uct.ac.za/virtualmobius

5. With regard to cost of access, South Africa has the highest Internet cost in Africa: four times that of the USA (World Bank, 2005).

6. We used 3 variables to determine socioeconomic group (SEG), namely occupation of primary breadwinner, education of primary breadwinner, and whether or not the student was the first person in their family to attend HE. This is in concordance with variables collected by the South African Census, such as education, occupation status, and occupation group, which determine the potential socioeconomic level of the primary breadwinner (Higgs, 2002). We also included whether or not the students were the first person in their family to attend university, as this has been determined to be a particularly effective measure of socioeconomic status (Barraket & Scott, 2001).

CHAPTER 5

DELIVERING DISTANCE EDUCATION FOR THE CIVIL SERVICE IN THE UK

The University of Chester's Foundation for Government program

Jon Talbot

INTRODUCTION

Since the 1980s in Britain, there have been ongoing attempts by governments to improve the quality of public services, including the Civil Service. In this context, the Civil Service refers to the collection of organizations that services the administrative needs and delivers services for Central Government and the devolved administrations in Scotland, Wales, and Northern Ireland. This agenda for public-service transformation has become global, often transmitted through major developmental agencies. An important aspect of reform is the education and training of civil servants to equip them with the ability to manage a more professional service, focused on efficient delivery. This chapter describes the development of a program developed

Bridging the Knowledge Divide, pages 77–96
Copyright © 2009 by Information Age Publishing
All rights of reproduction in any form reserved.

jointly between the University of Chester and the British Civil Service, which is cost-effective, flexible, and delivered largely in the workplace.

The Foundation for Government (F4Gov) program is a part-time Foundation Degree using a dedicated Virtual Learning Environment (VLE). Unlike better known programs such as Masters in Public Administration (MPAs), it is not aimed at senior personnel, but is designed for the broad mass of civil servants whose job it is to deliver services directly to the public. It aims to improve individual and hence organizational performance. F4Gov is located within Chester's prevalidated Work Based and Integrative Studies (WBIS) framework. WBIS is flexible in terms of design and delivery and enables individuals and organizations to devise learning that meets their needs. The program incorporates an emphasis upon the integration of theory with practice and facilitates reflection.

This chapter describes the rationale and development of the program and identifies key issues for future evaluation with respect to distance-delivered work-based learning programs. In particular, four key issues are addressed: employer involvement in design and delivery, the tension between technological and educational imperatives, and the impact of the program in terms of knowledge transfer and progression rates. Finally, the implications for more widespread application of the program are discussed.

MODERNIZING THE CIVIL SERVICE

In the last 10 to 20 years, there has been a global movement to modernize all public services and most notably civil services (World Bank, 2000). The impetus for reform originated with the British and New Zealand governments in the 1980s and stems from a disillusion with the performance of traditional Weberian bureaucracies. What became known as New Public Management spread to the United States in the same decade and, by the 1990s, organizations such as the World Bank, IMF, the Inter-American Development Bank, and the OECD had programs in place to encourage improved public-sector performance across the world (Karmarck, 2003).

The British Civil Service has historically enjoyed an enviable reputation for probity and neutrality, but it has been subject to the same criticisms of large government bureaucracies the world over. Traditional complaints, such as amateurishness and an aversion to innovation and efficiency, have been supplemented by a concern that public services in general are not sufficiently focused on the needs of the public they nominally serve. Critics of public services, traditionally drawn from the political right, have been joined in recent years from those on the left who see that the major global shift to customers from producers will result in the loss of all notion of public service unless there is fundamental reform (Cherny, 2001).

The immediate predecessor to the present UK Government introduced a series of reforms in the late 1980s and 1990s. These had the effect of reducing the overall number of civil servants, the creation of executive agencies whose only role was to concentrate on delivery, the introduction of performance indicators, and the contracting out of services to the private sector (Massey & Pyper, 2005).

The successor New Labour government has continued with the emphasis on performance, efficiency, and delivery and has made it a central objective of government. Each of the three heads of the Civil Service they have appointed has instituted reforms, beginning with those of Sir Richard Wilson (Wilson, 1999). His successors, Sir Andrew Turnbull and Sir Gus O'Donnell, have continued the reform process by concentrating on the development of professional staff. The Civil Service College has been recast as the National School for Government and a new training benchmark established, Professional Skills for Government (PSG), aimed at the upper echelons of the service. More recently, the drive for improved professionalism has been allied with a drive for greater efficiency (National Audit Office, 2006). At the same time, government departments have been subjected to a series of external audits designed to assess competency in key areas such as leadership, improved delivery, responding to the needs of the public, and increasing the skills of staff (Cabinet Office, 2006).

The final strand of the modernizing agenda is a commitment to the application of new technologies to the efficient working of government (HM Government, 2005). In the years since 1999 there have been numerous strands of civil-service reform. In summary these are

- Improved leadership
- Improved efficiency
- Better business planning and greater financial expertise
- Enhanced staff capacity and more professional management
- An emphasis on meeting clearly specified performance indicators
- Greater transferability of staff between the public and private sectors
- Exploitation of new technologies wherever possible

The F4Gov program is designed to help achieve these goals.

THE WBIS FRAMEWORK

In 2002, when the Cabinet Office was given responsibility to develop a Foundation Degree for the Civil Service, the University of Chester was approached to use the Work Based and Integrative Studies framework as the mechanism for its delivery. Knowledge of WBIS had been gained firsthand by members of the Cabinet Office on WBIS programs. It is a prevalidated degree framework designed to facilitate learning for people in the workplace and provide academic credit for it. WBIS has been in existence since 1998 and is informed by a distinctive educational philosophy:

- To bridge the divide between knowledge located in higher education and that in "real life," specifically the workplace, so that both are informed by one another
- Enable individuals to engage in lifelong learning by sensitizing them to their learning needs and preferred methods of learning. In short, to produce reflective practitioners
- To place the learner and their needs at the center of the learning process
- To provide low-cost flexible education that recognizes the profoundly social nature of the learning process
- To value knowledge from all sources, including that of learners, and recognize that we, as facilitators, learn from them as well as they from us

WBIS programs are tailored to the needs of either individual learners or those of an employing organization. Learners, provided they meet standard academic entry criteria, determine not only the content of their program but also the award they obtain. They can opt for Higher Education Certificate, Foundation Degree/Diploma, Degree, Postgraduate Certificate, Diploma, or Masters. The title of their program reflects their preference and the content of the program.

A fundamental aspect of the program is therefore that it is demand led. Tutors do not determine the content of the learners program: the learner does. The tutor's role is to facilitate and assist the learning process and translate it into formal academic credit-bearing qualifications.

Another distinctive feature of the WBIS approach is the intimate connection with workplace practice. In a typical WBIS module, the learner is introduced to a body of theory and wider literature and then asked to interrogate their practice. From the learners perspective, the relationship with theory becomes much more immediate than is the case in conventional programs. They select those theories/models that are relevant to their needs and use this as the basis for an internal dialogue based upon their own practice and that of colleagues. This requires a degree of sensitization to formal, reflective practice, which is usually embedded at the start of WBIS. In this way, learners are encouraged to reflect upon their current practice as a means of improving performance.

DEVELOPMENT OF THE PATHWAY

Within the UK in recent years, Foundation degrees have been developed to meet the need for an intermediate, vocational qualification. They are the equivalent of the first two years of a conventional 3-year degree program. They are intended to be more practically oriented than conventional university programs and have to combine formal academic elements with practical projects (DFES, undated). An important feature of a Foundation degree is that institutions can only develop them where they are demanded by employers. There is also a requirement for considerable employer involvement in the design of programs to ensure relevance. A Foundation degree is consistent with the Civil Service's desire for a broadly based, vocationally oriented qualification. The level, content, means, and delivery has therefore been developed jointly between the University of Chester, the National School of Government, the Cabinet Office, and the participating departments.

From an outsider's perspective, it is important to understand that the British Civil Service is not a monolithic organization. At time of writing, it is composed of 554,000 people in 26 separate bodies, which range in size from 140 (the Northern Ireland Office) to 129,110 (Department for Work and Pensions) (Office for National Statistics, 2006). Each department has its own history and culture, and in large departments like the DWP, there are considerable variations between its constituent parts (Pyper, 1999). Securing agreement among so many stakeholders has therefore presented challenges.

Following initial discussions, a research exercise was carried out among all government departments to ensure their needs were identified. The academic content of the program was then developed during 2003–04 on a working-party basis. From consultation with the employers, two requirements were paramount:

- First, the demands of the Service are such that learning has to involve minimal time away from the job. In practical terms, this has resulted in minimal face-to-face contact between tutors and learners. To compensate for this, a dedicated Virtual Learning Environment was created during 2003–04 to support distance learning.
- A second important requirement from the employer side was that the program be as relevant to practice as possible. An important issue for the employers is that individual performance and that of the Service as a whole is improved as a result of attendance on the program.

The resultant program is designed to deliver the UK Civil Service modernization agenda, as described above. It is intended to provide people with the skills necessary to run a professional, customer-focused organization. In terms of Bratton's (2001) distinction between learning for task and learning transferable skills for work, it is definitely the latter. It is the first higher-education qualification specifically for civil servants to be delivered in the UK.

Since its launch in September 2004, almost 350 students have been recruited, principally from four departments: the Department for Work and Pensions, the Home Office, the Department for Education and Skills, and the Cabinet Office. Future plans for the program include greater extension to other departments and a large increase in the number of participating departments and learners. It is envisaged that two partner universities will participate in delivery. F4Gov is therefore one of the largest Foundation degrees.

PROGRAM DESIGN AND ACADEMIC CONTENT

The traditional pattern of education in the Civil Service is for entrants to acquire a general education prior to entry and then use a combination of common sense and on-the-job training. Unlike a country such as France, it is unusual, even for senior members, to undertake an education specifically designed to facilitate management and leadership (Pollit, 1990). Even where training has existed, such as via the former Civil Service College (now the National School for Government), the emphasis has been upon policy development for high-ranking officials, not management and delivery for the broad mass of the service.

The ambitious program of reform in the Civil Service places an unparalleled strain on the ability of staff to deliver it and has necessitated a change of emphasis. F4Gov is a radical departure in a number of ways. First, it is not delivered by the National School for Government but is an accredited university program. Second, it does not rely upon the traditional (and expensive) residential approach but instead uses new technology to deliver the program to where the learner is situated. Third, as it is much cheaper to deliver, it has opened up the possibility of delivery on a mass rather than limited basis. Fourth, the content is aligned with the reform agenda outlined above and in particular on delivery rather than policy issues.

Designing the academic content of F4Gov involved a number of challenges, in addition to the usual academic issues of coherence, relevance, and progression:

- The content has to reflect what are often rapidly changing governmental priorities as well as satisfy the needs of the participating departments, each of which is autonomous.

- The program has to incorporate as much work-based learning as possible, in the sense of enabling learners to integrate practice and theory.
- There was a tension between the employers desire to prescribe which topics learners should engage within accordance with an organizationally driven learning agenda and the idea of student choice.
- Within 12 months of beginning, it became apparent that the recognized benchmark of achievement for more senior Civil Servants (Professional Skills for Government—PSG) would require the program to be aligned to ensure compatibility. What has made this especially difficult is trying to develop modules in anticipation of what PSG would finally look like.

Despite these difficulties, the program has been successfully developed and includes modules on topics included as core competences in PSG. Module titles therefore include

- Customers and Stakeholders
- Managing and Leading People
- Working with People
- Managing Resources
- Leading Organizational Change
- Project Management
- Public Finance Management

The program is prescriptive at Level 1, reflecting the employer's desire to see all those on the program demonstrate learning in what it sees as core skills. There is greater flexibility at Level 2, where learners have options and can complete negotiated project modules. In addition to the kind of generic competency modules described above, there are modules at the beginning, middle, and end of the program, which enable students to reflect on their experience and learning.

The first module learners complete is called "Introduction to Work Based Learning." Within the module, students conduct a self-assessment of past and present achievements as the basis for assessing their learning needs. From this they develop their intended learning pathway in the program. In addition to developing their Pathway Rationale, learners are also introduced to literature in respect to learning preferences and critical reflection. They learn to engage in reflective practice by applying formal theorizing to a critical workplace incident. The module is designed not only to enable learners to think about their learning needs but also to begin to adjust mentally to the process of critical workplace reflection.

At this stage, any applications of Accredited Prior Learning (APL), either Certificated or Experiential, are considered. Thereafter, learners can complete the Level 1 modules in any order, although they are encouraged to complete a module on the Civil Service itself next. This asks them to consider the rationale for a wider process of Civil Service reform, as it affects their department and themselves personally. The aim here is to enable contextualization for the whole program. After that, the program of learning varies depending upon the needs of the learner. Where learners have no strongly expressed preference, there is a recommended route.

After completing Level 1, students progressing on to Level 2 first complete a module reflecting on their cumulative learning at Level 1 and its application to practice. At the end of Level 2, there is a similar module to reflect on learning from the entire program.

At the time of writing, the first learners are completing the program and, using the WBIS framework, pathways are being developed that will enable them to complete a full undergraduate degree.

PROGRAM DELIVERY: THE VIRTUAL LEARNING ENVIRONMENT

One of the key requirements of the program, from the employers' perspective, is minimal time away from the workplace. Following an initial two-day induction, most learning in the program is facilitated via a dedicated Virtual Learning Environment. The VLE is hosted on the university's intranet system, IBIS. The VLE contains specific learning materials developed for the program as well as links to a variety of other sources. These include electronic books, parts of books scanned in, e-journals, and other relevant Web sources. For each module, learning outcomes and learning opportunities are specified. There is also a Theory Document specifically created for the module, which summarizes those theories and models appropriate to the learning outcomes. In addition, all other features, such as assignments, are on the VLE. Submission is also electronic.

The VLE attempts to meet all learner needs; and there are facilities for online discussion. In practice, these have not been well-used; and the VLE, despite recent improvements (such as the incorporation of short videos) is text-dominated and essentially unidirectional.

The requirement for minimum time away from work has greatly restricted face-to-face contact between learners and between tutors and learners. Many of the learners are from "nontraditional" backgrounds and have varying learning preferences; independent study is by no means ideal for all those on the program.

The university has attempted to overcome learner isolation. In addition to the induction process, learners are allocated a personal tutor, and there is a subject tutor for each module. Tutor support is available online or by telephone. Workplace support is provided by means of a personal mentor. Peer learning is encouraged wherever possible and if an individual employing organization requests it, the tutor team provides additional study workshops.

PROGRAM ASSESSMENT

Assessment is in the form of formal reflective reviews related to the learning outcomes for each module. In effect, learners, in consultation with the module tutor, devise their own assignment. This is formalized through a Topic Learning Plan, where the learner indicates to the tutor how the requirements of the assessment will be met. To support learning, a theory document for each module has been prepared. Learners are encouraged to read the learning outcomes and theory document and then consider ways in which they can relate materials to their own experience, which should form the basis for their assignment.

Learners are encouraged to submit drafts for formative assessment. Heavy emphasis is placed on formative assessment as a means of facilitating personal development. Most learners submit in this way before formal submission. One of the limitations of a work-based approach is that it assumes the learner is engaged in a wide variety of situations and activities upon which to reflect. In practice, many in the program perform fairly limited work roles. Assignments therefore always present learners with the option of work-based or work-related assessment. *Work-based learning* is appropriate where the learner is engaged in an activity and therefore able to reflect upon it in the light of formal theories, models, and empirical evidence, which are supplied as part of the learning resources. *Work-related learning* is suitable where the learning is contextual or where the learner is acquiring knowledge that will be applied in future.

Learners are always encouraged to engage in work-based learning as much as possible to meet the employers need for relevance. Wherever possible, learners submit artefacts or portfolios of material generated in the workplace, accompanied by a short reflective commentary. Submission is flexible, in the sense that students are free to negotiate their own pathway and deadlines.

MANAGEMENT, RECRUITMENT, AND DELIVERY

Management of F4Gov is more complex than most academic programs. In addition to the normal academic assessment and quality oversight, the program is overseen by a joint University and Civil Service Management Board, which meets approximately three times a year. This involves representatives from all stakeholders (that is, all participating departments, the National School of Government, and the Cabinet Office) in the management and development of the program. There is also a student representative. The result is that the program is not directed solely by academic considerations. Decisions also reflect employer interests.

Recruitment to the program is coordinated centrally by the National School of Government. The National School is also the key coordinator and driver of the program for the employer's side.

REFLECTIONS ON EXPERIENCE: A TUTOR'S PERSPECTIVE

In developing and delivering this program, there have been a number of challenges. It is still in its early days and there has, as yet, been no formal evaluation. There are a few observations to make about F4Gov from the perspective of a tutor (as in Schon's (1992) famous "reflection on action'") before setting out in more detail some of the issues any future evaluation is likely to focus upon.

The most important observation is that the feedback from students, government departments, and the external assessor has been uniformly excellent. Despite its highly vocational approach, there do not appear to be any major issues in relation to academic standards in F4Gov. An important element in this has been successful teamwork. Although there have been changes in personnel, the program team have worked cohesively and have striven to adopt the customer focus essential in delivering a program for an employer.

The tutor team itself has been on a steep learning curve. Coming from a conventional HE background, the tutors have discovered that writing things down is a lot more demanding than giving lectures. The formative assessment has also proved time-consuming. It is not unusual to spend two hours providing formative assessment on a draft. The tutor team have also had to learn to prepare learners for the sheer volume of learning materials available for students and the requirements for formal writing. The results have justified the hard work, and assignments are of a noticeably higher quality than would be expected from a conventional program.

Against this, there have been a number of difficulties. The Civil Service has changed dramatically in the last two years as the reform agenda has clearly swung toward a concern for greater efficiency. Very few of the initial cohorts 2 years on are still performing the same role they were when recruited. Some have had more than two job changes in that time. Changing jobs is hugely disruptive to study. Not only are there new roles to learn but there is a change in line management. Learners tend to originate from parts of the service that are supportive of learning; this is not always true of the areas they move to. It is not just that learners are performing different roles; the consequences of the Gershon (2004) report and the reduction in head count mean that most of them are also working a great deal harder, leaving less time for study.

A further consequence of rapid change is that the program itself has had to be adapted more or less continually. Each of the three heads of the Civil Service since 1999 have had different views about reform of the system. In recent years, there has also been a subtle change in emphasis reflecting the gradual transition of power within government from Tony Blair to Gordon Brown, prior to the latter becoming Prime Minister in July 2007. The point is that a government program has to be relevant, but government changes very quickly.

ISSUES FOR EVALUATION

In addition to the personal observations above, there are four major issues that require more formal research:

- The implications of employer involvement
- The conflict between technological and educational imperatives
- The nature of the learner experience and progression rates
- The assumption of knowledge transfer

Employer Involvement

Employer involvement in university programs is still a relatively new idea for many. It is an integral feature of Foundation degrees and has its advocates, not just among employers and in government (Morgan et al., 2004). While it is clear that such involvement is likely to result in programs that are more relevant to learner needs, it is not without problems.

As engagement between employers and universities has increased, so has the literature. In this context, the development of a theoretical model by Evans et al. (2006) is especially useful and resonates with our experiences. The model postulates a continuum of organizational approaches to workforce development, which are either "expansive" or "restrictive." There is not the space here to further elaborate, but for anyone familiar with organizational literature, these organizational types broadly equate to Burns and Stalker's (1961) famous continuum between "mechanistic" and "organic" companies. The British Civil Service is not monolithic and is composed of many separate organizations, but overall, the majority of learners are undoubtedly in a restrictive learning environment. The consequences of this are reflected in the observations below.

From the learners' perspective, one of the most fundamental restrictions relates to time. Understandably, employers want people at their desks; while with learners and tutors, academics want to see the creation of dedicated learning time. Work-based learning, we have discovered, is often interpreted by employers as meaning "at their desks," and a persistent difficulty for learners has been a lack of time allowed for study.

Allied to this is a further misunderstanding of the nature of work-based learning. From the perspective of the tutor team, there is an awareness from the literature, borne out by experience, that e-learning without much personal contact is likely to result in low rates of progression and completion (Garrison & Cleveland-Innes, 2003; Garrison & Kanuaka, 2004; Williams, 2002). Yet many on the employer side seem either unaware of this or are unwilling to concede it, perhaps because of pressure to "deliver."

Further difficulties have arisen with respect to employer expectations of completion of the program. A Foundation Degree is the equivalent of 2 years full-time study, yet in practice, this has been interpreted as a "2-year program." Publicity for the program is the responsibility of the employer in this instance, not the university, and there have been issues with respect to expected completion dates.

Employer control results in other difficulties. Ensuring learners are effectively represented in the management of the program is difficult on most, especially distance programs. Isolated learners may feel discouraged, thinking their problem is theirs alone. Allied to this is the difficulty of finding an effective spokesperson in a situation where people do not know one another and where the experience is highly individualized. Third is the issue of finding a platform; the student representative (if able to attend) is only one voice in a room composed of employers. Finally, in a situation where employers feel it is "their program," there may be an unwillingness to accede to the interests of learners.

Technological and Educational Imperatives

One of the most attractive features of F4Gov to employers and learners is the VLE, because it enables access to information pretty much whenever it is needed. There are also other features such as electronic submission of assignments. Attempts to facilitate communication by means of discussion boards, facilities for informal chat, personal and group blogs, and so on are also available, although usage has been low.

Most of these additions have come from learning technologists rather than being demanded by either learners or tutors, and uptake has been low.

A number of other e-learning programs attempt to encourage online dialogue by including it as part of the assessment process (Johnson & Dixon, 2006). The F4Gov tutor team have not gone down this route because of a shared view that the technology can assist in certain key educational tasks, notably providing information; but it is less well-suited to changing attitudes, inspiring interest, facilitating personal and social interest, and teaching behavioral skills—the kinds of issues Bligh (1998) so effectively demonstrated, over 30 years ago, that lectures are poor at.

The development of e-learning has been accompanied by the creation of a new group of professionals to facilitate the process—educational technologists. To date, the literature on this group is sparse and largely examines their role in terms of describing their activities (Oliver, 2002). However, the presence of a new professional group with a claim to expertise in areas beyond the competence of tutors has implications for the learning process. For example, the interlearner communication features on the VLE have not been created as a result of demand from learners or pressure from tutors but have been created by technologists. By contrast, tutors' preferences for a more multimedia, synchronous interactive approach have not been heeded. Our learning technologists seem to be a great deal more powerful than in other institutions (Vallance, 2006).

The presence of technology can have a distorting effect on effective delivery. For example, a lack of engagement is "solved" by a new blog facility; lack of progression is "solved" by automatic tracking of submissions and so on. Pressure for "technical fixes" comes from a variety of sources that may be unconsciously projecting their own preferences onto learners. Learning technologists may consider participation on an electronic discussion board a normal event; employers looking for solutions involving minimal time investment consider it a way of overcoming isolation; librarians may be keen to encourage use of e-books. The presence of technology can lead to an enthusiasm for the technological over learning imperatives, with tutor's power to assert the primacy of learning diminished.

From a tutor's perspective, increasing motivation and promoting deep learning involves more than the application of technology. For example, the most effective means of promoting thought, inspiring interest, and changing attitudes is discussion and face-to-face dialogue (Bloom, 1953). On programs where tutors have control and where there are not the same competing pressures, it is acknowledged that a "blended" approach, employing a variety of learning methods and experiences, in addition to e-learning, is likely to produce a more satisfactory learning experience, as well as improve progression (see below) (Elliot, 2002; Singh, 2003; Hughes, 2007).

Implementing optimum learning strategies for F4Gov is always likely to be challenging for a number of reasons. The innovative nature of the program and lack of fit with the culture and procedures of the rest of the university make understanding and acceptance problematic. The significant involvement of alternative centers of power (such as employers and learning technologists) in the learning process has weakened the control tutors traditionally exert over delivery. While there may be benefits in terms of ensuring relevance, there are some negative consequences on factors such as progression.

Learner Experience and Progression Rates

A casual inspection of the index of 15 standard texts on e-learning by the author revealed no references to the terms "progression," "completion," "attrition," and "drop-out rates," yet it is widely accepted that progression and completion rates on e-learning programs are low compared with more conventionally delivered programs (Greenagel, 2002). Data is available on the site. The author paraphrases Greenagel in tandem with his own observations. See url http://www.league.org/publication/whitepapers/0802.html under heading "The lack of emphasis on outcomes." The program has not been running long enough for definitive progression rates, but they are a cause for concern, and the tutor team constantly try to think of new ways to improve it.

We know from experience as well as the literature (such as Billet, 2004) that access to learning time in the workplace is an important factor in progression. A noticeable feature of those progressing most successfully is that they have been given time (say, half a day a week) to do so. But this is not typical. As previously mentioned, the employers desire for minimal time away from work often translates on the ground into learners having to find their own time for study.

A closely allied issue is that of line-manager support. In our experience, consistent support greatly facilitates progression. Again, the literature confirms this (Allen & Lewis, 2006). We have also observed, and this is again validated by research, that progression is a function of individual motivation, mediated by the degree to which the work environment is supportive of learning and is unaffected by social characteristics such as gender (Fuller & Unwin, 2004). Surprisingly, and we cannot compare with our experience, but the evidence suggests progression is unaffected by learning preferences (Walsh et al., 2003). More recently Bryson et al. (2006) have demonstrated that access to learning time is mediated by status in the organization. Since learners in F4Gov are by definition mostly in relatively low-status positions, progression is adversely affected.

While the research is useful in highlighting particular factors that affect progression, there are gaps. Many of our slow-performing learners have experienced disruption in their working and personal lives. As we have already noted, the Civil Service went through an intense period of organizational change and only a minority of those on the program remained in the same job for more than 2 years. During that time, some had four different posts. Each time they started a new job, they were absorbed in learning a new role, and progress in F4Gov suffers.

Perhaps an even greater gap in the literature, and closely allied to the notion of learner motivation, is the degree of learner *compulsion*. Although we have noted that individual learners have very different personal experiences, there are some common factors. F4Gov is employer-funded, but in practical terms, payment is on a modules-completed basis. In bald terms, there is no financial penalty to the employer if learners do not progress; as a result there is a corresponding lack of pressure on learners. On other WBIS pathways where there is a far greater deal of compulsion (on one, failure to complete results in learners losing their job!), progression and completion are not an issue. On a more positive note, in circumstances where learners are allocated time by a line manager, motivation may be increased by the need to demonstrate progress.

Knowledge Transfer

The final issue requiring more thorough investigation is the assumption that completion of the program leads to enhanced individual and hence organizational capacity—knowledge transfer. Advocates of work-based learning routinely assume that such capacity enhancement occurs, but there is very little direct empirical evidence to support this contention (Nixon et al., 2006).

The belief in the efficacy of educations as a means of transforming human capital goes back to the early 1960s and, in particular, the work of Schultz (1963) and Becker (1964). Schultz, an agricultural economist, was interested in raising agricultural output. The solution to improved yields was not so much greater investment in fertilizers and farm machinery, but in educating farmers to better exploit technical progress. Schultz then extended his approach to demonstrate that the yield on investment in people across all sectors was greater than the returns from investment in physical capital such as manufacturing plants and machinery.

Becker extended Schultz's analysis to demonstrate that public investment in education and even health care could be regarded as investments in human capital. Lucas (1988) has demonstrated how the accumulation of human capital is facilitated by both formal education and learning by doing. Barro and Sala-i-Martin (2004) have produced strong empirical evidence on the positive effect government spending on education has on a national economy.

While human-growth theory appears to offer insights into how technological development allied to education can enhance economic growth, the theory is an extremely broad brush. There is little reason to believe that all education for all individuals benefits all organizations they work for in all circumstances. To begin with, not all individuals learn equally well. Nelson and Phelps (1966) drew attention to the limitations of peoples' ability to learn; that is, the stock of human capital is not equally distributed.

The pervasive belief in the effectiveness of educational programs has resulted, until recently, in few attempts to even identify it, an omission regularly identified by writers on the subject (Bassi et al., 1996; Philips, 1997; Woodall, 2000). There are many practical and conceptual difficulties in identifying effects, such as clarity about the notion of learning itself, separating out informal from formal learning, and even, in many cases, identifying what is meant by "performance," but none of these in themselves appears to explain why there are so few studies. There are some exceptions to this: Clarke (2004), for example, found that the impact of training is more effective in organizations that monitor and evaluate outcomes. More recently, a number of other studies have reinforced the impression that knowledge transfer is more effective in supportive learning environments (Beattie, 2006; Brown et al., 2006; Kirwin & Birchall, 2006; Al-Emadi & Marquardt, 2007). None of these studies refer to the expansive-restrictive continuum of Evans et al. (2006), but it would appear where knowledge transfer occurs, it is likely to do so in a "learning organization."

As previously stated, the British Civil Service is composed of a number of organizations, at least some of which fall into the restrictive camp. If this is so, and there is a link with the degree to which learning is applied, this would accord with the experience of our learners, some of whom feel frustrated with the lack of recognition they receive in the workplace. One of the ironies of our experience is that to date, for the most part, employing departments often show little interest in the enhanced capacity of their staff. They are interested in progression in the sense of learners completing the program, but remain largely uncurious about their changed capabilities. Whether this will change over a period of time remains to be seen.

FINAL COMMENTS

The Foundation for Government program has enjoyed many remarkable successes in its short lifetime. It has developed a syllabus closely aligned with the needs of modern government, it is flexible and low cost, it has embraced new technology to deliver wherever learners are located, and it has reached a broad swath of practitioners for whom access to such a program was simply impossible until recently. It is the first accredited program of its kind for the British Civil Service, and we suspect the first of its kind anywhere. Its future development seems assured. But like anything truly innovative, it requires careful, long-term evaluation. That evaluation will contribute to knowledge in a number of fields, where at present, it is compartmentalized. For example, there is a body of literature on work-based learning and another on e-learning, yet rarely are the two united, despite this being common practice (Bates, 2005).

There are many benefits from developing a program in close collaboration with an employer, but there are also constraints. The technology is a vital asset in developing a distance program, but there are dangers in seeing technology as the solution to all problems. There are concerns about the student experience and progression, and the employers themselves need greater awareness of not only their learners' needs but also their enhanced capacity. The role of tutors is very different from that in a traditional program, and it is our perception that our ability to ensure optimum learning is far more constrained. As the program matures and evaluation is put in place, the tutor team, the employers, and the learners will continue to progress with these and other issues.

As such, like all programs, it is a work in progress, as it is continually refined to better serve the needs of its stakeholders. As other Civil Services around the globe engage in modernization, there will be lessons to be learned from it.

REFERENCES

Al-Emadi, M., & Marquardt, M. (2007). Relationship between employees' beliefs regarding training benefits and employees' organizational commitment in a petroleum company in the state of Qatar. *International Journal of Training and Development, 11*(1), 49–70.

Allen, B., & Lewis, D. (2006). Virtual learning communities as a vehicle for workplace development: A case study. *Journal of Workplace Learning, 18*(6), 367–383.

Barro, R., & Sala-i-Martin, X. (2004). *Economic growth* (2nd ed.). Boston: MIT Press.

Bassi, L., Benson, G., & Cheney, S. (1996). The top ten trends. *Training and Development Journal, 50*(1), 28–42.

Bates, T. (2005). *Technology, e-learning and distance education.* London: Routledge.

Beattie, R. (2006). Line managers and workplace learning: Learning from the voluntary sector. *Human Resource Development International, 9*(1), 99–119.

Becker, G. (1964). *Human capital.* New York: Columbia University Press.

Billett, S. (2004). Learning through work: Workplace participatory practices. In H. Rainbird, A. Fuller, and A. Munro (Eds.), *Workplace Learning in Context.* London: Routledge.

Bligh, D. (1998). *What's the use of lectures?* (5th ed.). Exeter, UK: Intellect:

Bloom, B. (1953). Thought processes in lectures and discussions. *Journal of General Education, 7,* 160–169.

Bratton, J. (2001). Why workers are reluctant learners: The case of the Canadian pulp and paper industry. *Journal of Workplace Learning, 13*(7/8), 333–343.

Brown, L., Murphy, E., & Wade, V. (2006). Corporate e-learning: Human resource development implications for large and small organizations. *Human Resource Development International, 9*(3) 415–427.

Bryson, J., Ward, R., & Mallon, M. (2006). Learning at work: Organizational affordances and individual engagement *Journal of Workplace Learning, 18*(5), 279–297.

Burns, T., & Stalker, G. (1961). *The management of innovation.* London: Tavistock.

Cabinet Office (2006). *Capability reviews: The findings of the first four reviews.* Prime Minister's Delivery Unit: London. Retrieved December 1, 2008, from http://www.civilservice.gov.uk/reform/capability_reviews/publications/pdf/summary.pdf

Cherny, A. (2001). *The next deal: The future of public life in the information age.* New York: Basic Books.

Clarke, N. (2004). HRD and the challenges of assessing learning in the workplace. *International Journal of Training and Development, 8*(2), 140–145.

Department for Education and Skills (DFES) (n.d.). Retrieved December 1, 2008, from http://www.foundationdegree.org.uk

Elliot, M. (2002). Blended learning:The magic is in the mix. In A. Rossett, (Ed.), *The AJTD e-learning handbook.* New York: McGraw Hill.

Evans, K., Hodkinson, P., Rainbird, H., & Unwin, L. (2006). *Improving workplace learning.* London: Routledge.

Fuller, A., & Unwin, L. (2004). Expansive learning environments: Integrating organizational and personal development. In H. Rainbird, A. Fuller, and A. Munro (Eds.), *Workplace learning in context,* London: Routledge.

Garrison, D., & Cleveland-Innes, M. (2003). *E-learning in the twenty-first century.* London: Routledge.

Garrison, D., & Kanuaka, H. (2004). Blended learning: Uncovering its transformative potential in higher education. *The Internet and Higher Education, 7*(2) 95–105.

Greenagel, F. (2002). *The illusion of e-learning: Why we are missing out on the promise of technology.* League for Innovation in the Community College White Papers: Phoenix. Retrieved December 1, 2008, from http://www.league.org/publication/whitepapers/ 0802.html

Gershon, P. (2004). *Releasing resources to the front line: Independent review of a public sector.* London: HMSO.

HM Government (2005). *Transformational government: Enabled by technology.* Cabinet Office: London Cm 6683. Retrieved December 1, 2008, from http://www.cio.gov.uk/documents/pdf/transgov/transgov-strategy.pdf

Hughes, G. (2007). Using blended learning to increase learner support and improve retention. *Teaching in Higher Education, 12*(3), 349–163.

Johnson, H., & Dixon, R. (2006, October 30–November 3). *Using blended teaching approaches to upgrade qualifications: The experience of in-service industrial technology/ TVET teachers in Jamaica.* Paper presented to the Fourth Pan Commonwealth Forum on Open Learning, Ocho Rios, Jamaica.

Karmarck, E. (2003). *Government innovation around the world.* Cambridge, MA: John F. Kennedy School for government. Retrieved December 1, 2008, from http://unpan1.un.org/intradoc/groups/public/documents/APCITY/UN-PAN015626.pdf

Kirwan, C., & Birchall, D. (2006) Transfer of learning from management development programmes: Testing the Holton model. *International Journal of Training and Development, 10*(4), 252–268.

Lucas, R. (1988). On the mechanics of economic development. *Journal of Monetary Economics, 2*(1), 3–42.

Massey, A. and Pyper, R. (2005). *Public management and modernization in Britain.* Palgrave, Basingstoke.

Morgan, A., Jones, M., & Fitzgibbon, K. (2004). Critical reflection on the development of a Foundation Degree. *Research in Post Compulsory Education, 9*(3), 353–370.

National Audit Office (2006). *Progress in improving government efficiency.* London: The Stationary Office. Retrieved December 1, 2008, from http://www.nao.org.uk/publications/nao.reports/05-06/0506802i.pdf

Nelson, R., & Phelps, E. (1966). Investment in humans: Diffusion in economic growth. *American Economic Review, 61,* 69–75.

Nixon, I., Smith, K., Stafford, R., & Camm, S. (2006). *Work-based learning: Illuminating the higher education landscape.* Higher Education Academy: York, UK. Retrieved from http://www.heacademy.ac.uk/research/wbl.pdf

Office for National Statistics (2006). *Public Sector Employment Quarter 3.* ONS: London. Retrieved December 1, 2008, from http://www.statistics.gov.uk/pdfdir/pse1206.pdf

Oliver, M. (2002). What do Learning Technologist do? *Innovations in Education and Teaching International, 39*(4), 245–252

Phillips, J. (1997). *Return on investment in training and performance improvement programs: A step by step manual for calculating the financial return on investment.* Woburn, MA: Butterworth Heinemann.

Pollit, C. (1990). *Managerialism, the public services: The Anglo American experience.* Oxford: Blackwell.

Pyper, J. (1999). *The British Civil Service.* Basingstoke, UK: Palgrave Macmillan.

Schon, D. (1992). *The reflective practitioner: How professionals think in action.* (2nd ed.). San Francisco: Jossey Bass.

Schultz, T. (1963). *The economic value of education.* New York: Columbia University Press.

Singh, H. (2003). Building effective blended learning programs *Educational Technology, 43*(6), 51–54.

Vallance, M. (2006). Responsibility without power: Reflections of an IT coordinator in education. *Perspectives, 10*(4), 109–114.

Walsh, E., Wanberg, C., Brown, K., & Simmering, M. (2003). E-learning: Emerging uses, empirical results and future directions. *International Journal of Training and Development, 7*(4), 245–258.

Williams, C. (2002). Learning on-line: A review of recent literature in a rapidly expanding field. *Journal of Further and Higher Education, 26*(3), 263–272.

Wilson, R. (1999). *Civil service reform: Report to the prime minister.* London: Cabinet Office.

Woodall, J. (2000). Corporate support for work-based management development. *Human Resource Management Journal, 10*(1),18–32.

World Bank (2000). *Reforming public institutions and strengthening governance.* World Bank: Washington, DC. Retrieved December 1, 2008, from http://www1.worldbank.org/publicsector/Reforming.pdf.

SECTION 2
MANAGING AND COMMUNICATING KNOWLEDGE

CHAPTER 6

KNOWLEDGE MANAGEMENT STRATEGIES FOR DISTANCE EDUCATION

Neil Butcher

INTRODUCTION

A dominant feature of global society in recent decades has been the rapid development of the information society. Wikipedia defines the information society as "a society in which the creation, distribution, diffusion, use, integration and manipulation of information is a significant economic, political, and cultural activity. The knowledge economy is its economic counterpart whereby wealth is created through the economic exploitation of understanding" (Wikipedia, 2007).

One of the manifestations of the information society has been massive growth in the quantity of information that is accessible to individuals and organizations. Some commentators point out that this information explosion can be traced as far back as the 15th century, when Gutenberg produced the first modern books printed using movable type on paper. However, during the 20th century, this process was given new momentum with the development of information and communication technologies (ICT). In

Bridging the Knowledge Divide, pages 99–121
Copyright © 2009 by Information Age Publishing
All rights of reproduction in any form reserved.

particular, three trends have led to an exponential growth of information in recent decades, which looks set to continue for the foreseeable future:

1. The invention of the single-chip microprocessor in 1970, which laid the platform for growing numbers of individuals to gain access to the tools needed to produce new information of different kinds and, increasingly, using different media. This trend has gathered momentum as the cost of the hardware and applications needed for content authoring have declined rapidly in price.
2. New storage technologies have made it easier to collect and store all types of data. Data can be managed and stored in structured relational databases; in semistructured file systems (such as e-mail); and as unstructured, fixed content (like documents and graphics files). As hardware storage costs decline, the amount of data that is stored electronically expands exponentially.
3. The growth of computer networking, which allows people to interact with each other and share digital information relatively easily, the most obvious example of which is the Internet.

As R. S. Wurman has pointed out, "a weekday edition of The New York Times contains more information than the average person was likely to come across in a lifetime in 17th Century England" (Softpanorama, 2007). For many people, the information explosion has led to an overwhelming feeling of information overload, a feeling created when people have access to more information than they can readily assimilate. This problem is exacerbated as the proportion of useful information found to all information found declines. Growth of information has meant that people's searches for relevant information to solve their problems yields a growing number of results that are unrelated or only tangentially useful to their needs, while growing amounts of information are also of poor quality.

The above trends have created a growing demand to manage information and knowledge effectively if it is to be of practical value. As information proliferates, it becomes increasingly important to develop strategies to be able to store, search, sort, and analyze it effectively. If this is not done, this information will either quickly overwhelm us or become useless to us. This is of particular importance in the field of education (and even more so in distance education), where information plays such an important role in processes of teaching and learning. In response to these challenges, there has been a significant growth in the field of "knowledge management," mostly in the business world, but also, to a lesser extent, in education itself. As Lisa Patrides and Thad Nodine note,

In light of the external and internal demands for accountability and improvement in education, combined with the many demands on the time of teachers, faculty, and staff, educational institutions and systems at all levels are seeking to understand how they can more effectively collect, disseminate, and share information. As organizations dedicated to education, moreover, they understand only too well that knowledge is their key asset—and many educational institutions are seeking better ways to transform that knowledge into effective decision-making and action. (Petrides & Nodine, 2003)

Before exploring why this knowledge management has become so important in education and steps that can be taken to manage knowledge more effectively in distance education, however, it is important to begin by defining a few terms more clearly. In particular, it is worth exploring the difference between information and knowledge.

WHAT IS KNOWLEDGE?

Many people tend to use terms such as "information" and "knowledge" interchangeably. However, in the field of knowledge management, these terms are quite distinct and provide critical insight into some of the key challenges in managing knowledge. In fact, most experts add a further term to the mix, differentiating between data and information. Thus, the three terms can be defined as follows:[1]

- Data is a collection of facts and quantitative measures, from which conclusions can be drawn. The most important issue here is that "data" is typically regarded as facts that exist outside of any context. Thus, by themselves, data have very little value to us.
- Information is regarded as data placed in a meaningful context through interpretation that seeks to highlight, for example, patterns, causes, or relationships in data. Information is thus data endowed with relevance and purpose. So, reports or strategic-planning documents might place data in context and thus constitute information. From the perspective of this chapter, the most important issue here is that data is only converted into information when *people* place them in context.
- Knowledge is the understanding that develops as people react to and use the information that is available to them: an activity that can either be individual or organizational. Thus, it is the aggregation of information and human expertise that produces knowledge.

Some people also distinguish between explicit knowledge and tacit knowledge:

- Tacit knowledge is subconsciously understood and applied, difficult to articulate, developed from direct experience and action, and usually shared through highly interactive conversation, storytelling, and shared experience.
- Explicit knowledge is more precisely and formally articulated, although removed from the original context of creation or use.

At an organizational level then, a key challenge is to find ways to recognize and share tacit knowledge so that it becomes more explicit.

Thus, as we migrate from data to knowledge, complexity increases, but so does the usefulness of what is produced and shared. These concepts can be represented diagrammatically as shown in Figure 6.1.

Although it is about schools, not distance education, the following case study of the different terms illustrates the difference between them:

There is a clear progression along the path in which value is added to data, as context is combined with it to create information. A further transformation occurs when human experience is added to information to make value judgments about, and comparisons of, different information. The progression from data to knowledge can be seen both as a temporal process in which data, imported into a system's architecture, aggregates individual facts into summaries and averages that are then presented in an appropriate context. In an educational setting, this might be a report of student test performance by grade, ethnicity, race, and gender. The addition of deeper contextual information about local school leadership, particular organizational character-

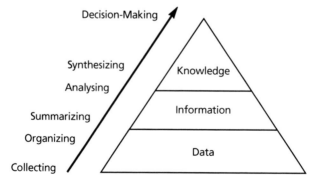

Figure 6.1   From data to knowledge. *Source:* Landcare Research, 2007.

istics, or other less quantifiable factors can be combined with mechanistically generated test-score results to describe variance in outcomes that could not be extracted from the more traditional reports. It is this application of personal knowledge and of well-designed models that differentiates information systems from knowledge systems. (Thorn, 2001)

These concepts may seem somewhat abstract, but they contain important insights into the challenge of managing knowledge effectively. From the above descriptions, two important points emerge. First, people are at the center of processes of converting data into information, as well as those of using information to create and share knowledge. Thus, people, not systems, manage knowledge. Second, the concept of tacit knowledge demonstrates that, contrary to much of the rhetoric, knowledge cannot always be easily captured, managed, and shared. Indeed, the knowledge that is often most useful organizationally is that which is hardest to make explicit. A key challenge of knowledge management is to find ways to structure the sharing of knowledge so that tacit knowledge can be made more explicit more efficiently. If this is not done, significant value is quickly lost when people move on from an organization, taking tacit knowledge with them. In educational settings, an obvious example of this occurs in many traditional universities, when academics leave a position, taking with them all of the tacit knowledge associated with running a particular course before it can be passed on to their successor.

Knowledge management, then, is the attempt to improve or maximize use of knowledge that exists in an organization or system. It aims to stimulate its creation and encourage its capture, sorting, sifting, access, linking, storage, and distribution. The levels of leveraging knowledge can be summarized as follows:

- Knowledge held by a particular person allows that person to be more effective.
- If people interact to share their knowledge, everyone involved increases their knowledge and becomes more effective.
- If knowledge is codified in a material way (i.e., written down or otherwise captured), then it can be shared much more widely both in terms of audience and time duration.
- If knowledge is encapsulated or automated, it is leveraged still further because it creates tools that factor out the need to apply individual knowledge to a task or range of tasks (HCI, 2001b).

Learning Organizations, Knowledge Workers, and Education

A learning organization can be defined as

An organization that is able to transform itself by acquiring new knowledge, skills, or behaviours. In successful learning organizations, individual learning is continuous, knowledge is shared, and the culture supports learning. Employees are encouraged to think critically and take risks with new ideas. All employees' contributions are valued. (ASTD, 2007)

It is thus clear that effective knowledge management strategies sit at the heart of learning organizations. In a business context, these ideas are typically associated with competition for customers. Organizations that "learn" more effectively should theoretically be best positioned to meet the needs of customers, although they do not necessarily see the customer as part of the learning organization. This approach also changes the role of employees. As lower-level and repetitive tasks become increasingly automated, the need grows for knowledge workers, who have to apply greater knowledge and adapt quickly through learning.

These concepts should resonate in an educational context, as educational institutions should logically function as "learning organizations" and educators as the ultimate "knowledge workers." Any institution operating in the field of education should pride itself on creating structures that enable the organization itself to learn, as this can play a major role in fostering learning environments that stimulate the achievement of educational objectives. Sadly, though, it seems that many institutions offering education to learners do not reflect in their form the core function that they have been established to perform.

Educators are prime examples of knowledge workers because they typically have considerable personal discretion and responsibility in analyzing, developing, and implementing their curricular goals. The most exciting part about applying these ideas in an educational context is that the primary "customers"—the learners—can also become an integral part of the learning organization, as they can play a critical role in helping to create and share knowledge throughout the system. Thus, in an educational context, learners need not simply be perceived as passive customers, but can rather become knowledge workers themselves, playing a unique role in producing and managing knowledge within the learning organization. One of the key challenges posed by the advent of the knowledge economy is to develop the role of educators and learners as knowledge workers within broader, integrated education systems.

Creating learning organizations and harnessing educators and other employees effectively as knowledge workers demands effective strategies for managing knowledge. Unfortunately, however, many prevailing working practices militate against such strategies. Below is a list of problems that organizations often experience in this regard:

- Techniques used rely on close contact between individuals, so the benefits of the knowledge generated have tended to be local rather than necessarily organizationwide.
- Relatively little emphasis has been placed on documenting processes for audiences wider than immediate team members, thus limiting the ability to leverage the new knowledge generated.
- Beyond the "workplace team" level, management and communication structures generally do not exist to support process improvement on divisionwide and companywide levels.
- Initiatives that share process-oriented approaches are often kept separate with their own implementation teams. For example "Quality Assurance" is seen as different from "Continuous Improvement," and in turn, "Best Practice" is often made distinct from "Business Process Reengineering (HCI, 2001a).

With some interpretation, it is easy to see how these problems map directly onto many educational institutions and systems. And the problem is not simply one of bad management. As Caroll et al. have noted,

> The greatest obstacle to effectively managing teacher professional knowledge is the attitude—even among teachers—that teaching is basically common sense . . . the generally dismissive view of teaching knowledge, the highly personal nature of individual teachers' concepts and techniques, and the lack of shared vocabulary and representations militate against the articulation and accumulation of professional knowledge by teachers. (2004)

The ability to harness information effectively is a crucial differentiator in the performance of organizations. Educational institutions have played a crucial role in using information of different kinds to generate knowledge, as any reader of academic texts will know. Likewise, the process of education is, in many ways, the construction of a set of services around information, which focuses on helping learners to convert that information into meaningful knowledge that they can act upon to improve the quality of their lives, whether it be intellectually, financially, socially, or personally. In principle, then, universities should be well-placed to compete for resources.

Regretfully, however, many educational institutions have actually paid remarkably little attention to consolidating the information resources that they have created since their inception. Significant time and energy have been expended on the above-mentioned activities; yet institutionally there is very little to show for it. Information within educational systems often resides largely with individuals, with the result that easy, well-ordered access to it often becomes impossible when academics leave for whatever reason. Institutional strategies for harnessing these extensive information resources—so that they can either reduce the investment necessary in future educational and knowledge production activities or increase their relative value—are completely inadequate. This means that investments made in generating information are largely dissipated when individuals resign or retire.

Likewise, there are very few clear strategies for turning management information into an organizational asset. For example, information about potential, current, and future students—a highly valuable potential marketing asset—is not stored in formats that facilitate easy access or analysis, particularly across years. Similarly, accurate and relevant financial information is notoriously difficult to extract from financial systems (except in very specific, rigid formats), even for people at higher levels within the institution. Consequently, its potential for supporting decisions taken by people managing educational programs or research projects is negligible, which severely hampers attempts to introduce cost-effectiveness into operations. Clearly, then, the challenges of effective knowledge management in education are significant.

Knowledge Management and Distance Education

Distance education can be defined as a set of teaching and learning strategies (or educational methods) that can be used to overcome spatial and temporal separation between educators and learners. These strategies or methods can be integrated into any educational program and potentially used in any combination with any other teaching and learning strategies in the provision of education (including those strategies which demand that learners and educators be together at the same time and/or place). One of the key attributes of distance education programs is their requirement to approach educational planning and implementation more systematically than their face-to-face counterparts. To compensate for separation in time and space between educators and learners, well-functioning distance education institutions make significant up-front investments in development of structured curricula and materials, creation of flexible learner-support systems, and maintenance of carefully designed administrative systems to support learners studying at a distance.

Based on the introductory overview provided for what knowledge management is, it is relatively simple to identify various ways in which well-designed and effectively functioning distance education systems already engage in practices of managing knowledge.

1. Typically, well-functioning distance education systems demand extensive investment of time and resources in rigorous processes of program and course design and development. These investments usually involve diverse groups of experts, collaborating to produce programs, courses, modules, and learning materials that enable independent study by learners. They can all justifiably be considered as investments in managing knowledge effectively. Importantly, they represent a process of taking knowledge that once was tacit (curriculum design, learning outcomes, teaching and learning strategies, and subject matter) and making it explicit by documenting it thoroughly. It is possible to leverage even more institutional value from these investments if the resulting materials are stored in a centrally accessible repository. In many cases, this value is not created because the resulting knowledge "products" are not shared or made accessible beyond an individual department or faculty.

2. Cost-effective distance education systems require enrollments of large numbers of students in individual programs in order to achieve the economies of scale needed to reduce the cost of learning per student. In order to be able to assure quality of delivery in such circumstances, well-functioning distance education programs create standardized approaches to the way in which learners are supported (within learning materials, through student counselling and administrative systems, during tutorial support, and via feedback on assessment tasks). Again, providing this support typically requires processes of making tacit knowledge explicit, so that it can be documented and shared with often large, decentralized networks of tutors and facilitators, who constitute the primary point of reference between the student and the institution. Such systems are often very sophisticated in the way in which they structure and manage communication across the institution.

3. Provision of distance education and management of communication with large, dispersed groups of students across wide geographical areas also usually requires investments in very efficient administrative systems, which gather and store large volumes of data about learners and learning. In best-case scenarios, such systems will now harness the power of computers and databases to support student administration. Although these systems are not, in and of themselves, knowledge management systems, they are critical sources of data and information about what is happening within the distance education institution. Such systems are potentially enormously valuable build-

ing blocks within an overall knowledge management strategy, as they can feed reliable information reports on many critical aspects of the educational process into the institution, thus supporting the creation of learning organizations that are able to adjust how they operate based on knowledge of what is and is not working successfully. As a Commonwealth of Learning (COL) Knowledge Guide on *Managing Student Records in Distance Education* notes, "educators often underplay the value of keeping student records, yet accurate records, interpreted as meaningful information, can significantly and positively impact the quality of the learning and teaching environment" (Randell, 2005).

4. Extensive literature has been produced about quality assurance in distance education, and robust, vibrant quality-assurance systems are typically a feature of well-functioning distance education systems. Although quality-assurance systems are by no means unique to distance education, the requirement to provide high-quality learning experiences to large numbers of learners and the involvement of many employees in delivering such experiences has created a strong imperative for their development in such environments. The process of designing a quality-assurance strategy is an important precursor to its successful implementation and should involve a wide range of staff members at various phases. Below are some principles in the design and implementation of such a strategy. The principles are based on national quality standards developed for distance education in South Africa. They are as follows:

   a. Management ensures that, in its day-to-day work, program activities meet quality standards set nationally, as well as institutional and program policy for different elements of specific programs.
   b. There is an organizational culture that encourages efforts to improve the quality of education.
   c. There is a clear cycle of planning, development, documentation, reporting, action, and review of policy and procedures for specific programs.
   d. Staff development is seen as fundamental to quality service provision. There are clear routines and systems for quality assurance, and staff are familiar with those that relate to their work.
   e. Staff, learners, and other clients are involved in quality review.
   f. Internal quality assurance processes are articulated with external processes.

It is hopefully clear by now that developing quality-assurance systems that operate according to the above principles demands effective knowledge management across the organization.

As these illustrative examples show, distance education systems work hand-in-hand with knowledge management strategies. It is important to understand that many of the features of well-functioning distance education already constitute effective strategies of managing knowledge. Thus, knowledge management is not a new, "high technology" concept that is beyond the reach of the average distance education institution. Nor is it a concept that should induce fear in distance educators, many of whom have for some time grasped its key principles intuitively in the way in which they have set up and manage distance education systems and programs. However, many distance education institutions could benefit from approaching knowledge management more explicitly and working systematically to improve how knowledge is managed across the enterprise. The next section in this chapter, thus, provides an introductory overview of how to tackle this task effectively. First, however, it is worth brief summarizing key issues emerging from the above discussion.

Summary of Key Issues

From an educational perspective, the following key issues emerge:

1. Data, information, and knowledge are separate but linked concepts. Knowledge can only be produced through the aggregation of information and human expertise.
2. People are at the center of processes of converting data into information, as well as those of using information to create and share knowledge. Thus, people, not systems, manage knowledge.
3. Tacit knowledge—that uncodified knowledge that is based on personal experience, absorption of organizational norms, and other factors—is a vital component of knowledge in any system. A key challenge in knowledge management is to find ways to structure and record tacit knowledge so that it becomes explicit.
4. At an institutional level, knowledge management is an essential part of creating learning organizations. This should be a fundamental objective of any educational institution, as learning is its core function, and this should be reflected in the way in which the organization itself operates.
5. Several of the practices of well-functioning distance education systems already reflect attempts to manage knowledge. Thus, the key challenge in distance education institutions is to create and build on these good practices, in an effort to integrate knowledge management more systematically into all aspects of the institution's operations.

IMPLEMENTING A KNOWLEDGE MANAGEMENT STRATEGY

Assuming then that one sees value in managing knowledge more effectively, what are the points of departure? The first point to note is that knowledge management is not a one-size-fits-all strategy. What works well in one institutional context may well fail in another. The design of knowledge management strategies, systems, and tools depends on—and needs to consider—the people involved, the organization's context of operations and its history, and the goals that have been defined for the knowledge management strategy. Thus, knowledge management brings together three core organizational resources—people, processes, and technologies—to enable an organization to use and share information more effectively. This can be represented diagrammatically as shown in Figure 6.2.

Each needs to be considered in turn when preparing a knowledge management strategy. In the discussion below, the focus is on organizations; but it is important to note that all of these principles could equally be applied at a systemic level, for example, to a country's schooling or higher-education system.

People as the Starting Point

Although the challenge can be tackled on many levels, it is possibly best to start by understanding, considering the most complex part of a knowledge management system, the people who inhabit it. It is worth noting that,

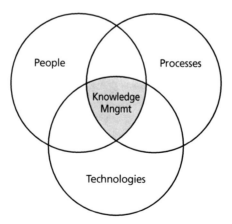

Figure 6.2 Knowledge management in the organization. *Source:* Petrides & Nodine, 2003.

in certain key respects, a system is nothing more than a set or rules and procedures by which groups of people agree to cooperate. Sometimes people fall into the trap of confusing systems with technologies, but technologies that underpin systems are typically just ways of structuring these rules and procedures so that they are easier to follow.

The success of any system thus depends on ensuring buy-in and support from those people who are going to drive and use it. As levels of engagement increase, so does the success of the system. In exactly this way, knowledge management depends on engaged, proactive participants if it is to succeed. The simplest way to achieve this is to connect the design of knowledge management strategies and systems to the needs of their users. The more people see the benefit of managing knowledge effectively and the easier it makes their jobs, the more successful knowledge management strategies will become.

Adison Na Uborn and Chris Kimble (2002) have identified some key elements that illustrate some of the human aspects that need to be considered in designing effective knowledge management systems:

- Community: Community is a group of people bound together by certain mutual concerns, interests, activities, and institutions. This is essential in knowledge management because knowledge in an organization is often built up and generated by small, informal, self-organizing networks of practitioners. Thus, the concept of community provides an excellent point of departure for dynamic, productive knowledge creation and sharing in education.
- Collaboration: Most organizations realize that they will improve performance if their staffs work together. However, building collaboration is not an easy task. Techniques such as meetings, forums, and discussions are used extensively to create knowledge through the processes of social interaction and collaboration. Tools such as e-mail and intranets are also used to encourage active collaboration among people in organizations.
- Trust and Knowledge-sharing: Trust is an essential condition for people to share knowledge and expertise. People are often reluctant to share their knowledge because of the risk of loss of control and influence. Overcoming this reluctance is key to successful implementation of knowledge management strategies.
- Shared Understanding: For effective knowledge-sharing, individuals need to have the same meaning in their communication processes and need to converge it to shared understanding. Shared understanding and a common ground among people in a community are essential for collaboration and productive knowledge transfer. Without it, individuals will neither understand nor trust one another.

To be effective, knowledge management strategies must maintain a strong focus on people (educators, administrators and managers, and learners) and ensure that these strategies will meet their needs. Policies and practices are necessary that will foster the elements outlined above. It is also likely that all existing policies and practices within an institution will need to be reviewed in order to assess the extent to which they support or inhibit attainment of these elements. The most well-designed knowledge management strategies will fail if they are not implemented within a broader environment that facilitates collaboration, builds trust and shared understanding, and encourages creation of communities of practice.

For example, it will be necessary to review human-resource policies to assess the extent to which they reward information sharing or encourage territorialism and competition between employees. So, if compensation and reward systems are based only on what people know, then there will be few incentives to share information. However, if they are based on what people teach others in the organization, then the prospect of information sharing flourishing is likely to increase dramatically. Likewise, organizational structures will need to be analyzed to establish whether they encourage the creation of organizationwide communities of practice or promote the maintenance of departmental silos.

Finally, information systems will need to be opened in order to promote wider access by all people to the information they need to produce and use knowledge effectively. It is worth noting here that information has historically been regarded as a source of power within many educational institutions, with the result that people responsible for managing information have often tended to build "empires" around this information, hoarding and only selectively sharing it. These practices need to be systematically dismantled in order to promote effective knowledge sharing. As Patrides and Nodine note,

> When the owners of information start to get nervous and anxious, that is an early sign that the practices of knowledge management are having some effect. On the flip side, organizations benefit enormously when people who have been formerly excluded from the feedback loop now begin to gain access to information and join with others to actually change the system. (Petrides & Nodine, 2003)

Organizational Processes

All organizations are characterized by various processes of many different kinds. Some are formal, some informal. In a distance education setting, procedures govern all aspects of operations, including administration, course design and development, provision of learner support, student assessment, and quality assurance. These processes exist "whether or not the people within an institution choose to participate in or pay attention to them" (Petrides & Nodine, 2003). All institutional processes can be made more robust through effective knowledge management, while also providing a vehicle through which the value of knowledge can be structurally integrated into the operations of an institution. Knowledge management entails all processes associated with the identification, sharing, and creation of knowledge. Kidwell et al. have provided an excellent series of grids, outlining applications and benefits of knowledge management for different institutional processes. Although these grids are not designed specifically for distance education institutions, they are very helpful, because they illustrate well the relationship between institutional processes and knowledge management strategies. They can be found at http://net.educause.edu/ir/library/pdf/EQM0044.pdf.

The Role of Technologies

As was noted in the introduction, the explosive growth of information and communication technologies has been a key driver behind the growing need for effective knowledge management. Fortunately, these technologies also have a key role to play as an enabler of effective knowledge management. Thus, modern knowledge management strategies will typically always incorporate these technologies as one of the key pillars required to manage knowledge effectively.

The rapid growth in functionality of ICT opens possibilities for building and exploiting information and converting it into knowledge in ways that were simply not possible even a few years ago. In particular, the following developments are worth noting:

- Developments in the digitization of information of all kinds, whether it be text, graphic, audio, or video.
- Growing functionality of electronic databases, particularly allowing people to
  - Store any kind of information in digital format, with corresponding capacity to run increasingly sophisticated data queries on information once it is organized into a well-designed management information system; and
  - Run data queries—and receive the results of these queries—using HTML-based browsers, whether across the Internet or secure intranets.

- Exponential growth in the speed of central processing units and storage capacity of computer hard drives, matched with corresponding reductions in the relative prices of this hardware. These developments contribute significantly to functionality of databases, both in terms of quantity of data storage and speed of manipulation of this data.
- Rapid developments in cheap electronic communication, more and more aspects of which can increasingly be automated. This is further facilitated by convergence in information and communications technologies, which allows communication such as e-mail or fax to work automatically in tandem with information databases if well designed.

Of course, the above sounds, in many ways, like the marketing jargon of information technology suppliers, elements of which have almost been repeated to the point of cliché. Indeed, such is the speed of communication and effectiveness of information-technology marketing that, taken on their own, none of the above points necessarily even sounds particularly innovative, notwithstanding their relative novelty as developments. Nevertheless, many distance education organizations have not yet devised systematic strategies for harnessing these trends effectively, indicating clearly that their real potential is not yet well understood.

These technological developments make it essential to find ways to use information quickly in as many different ways as possible before it loses its value. These need to focus on reusing information in different ways without generating significant additional cost. In order to achieve this, it is necessary to establish effective information systems, which can allow for quick and easy sharing and manipulation of information once it has been developed or gathered. It is also advisable from this perspective to invest slightly more money in gathering and compiling information (which would focus on making it as generically applicable as possible), with a view to increasing its versatility and the strategies that can be used to disseminate it. Although this creates some additional costs initially, these can easily be amortized across the range of options that then become possible for communicating this information or using it to support a diverse range of educational opportunities. In this way, the resources used to generate information can be used much more effectively.

Possibly most importantly, it becomes essential to develop effective strategies for storing information in ways that allow it to be very easily manipulated for future purposes. If information about educational resources, courses, and programs is stored effectively, it then becomes easily available for future applications. In this way, research can build on growing knowledge bases, rather than repeating basic work already conducted. This can maximize the value of money spent on course design and development or educational research. It can then also—where appropriate—be easily made available via the World Wide Web for access by other distance educators around the world, thus contributing usefully to developing an effective distance education resource and research base globally. However, in instances where security of information is important, it is easily possible to restrict access to it by adding a range of security strategies.

Another point emerging from the above discussions is that, increasingly, value lies not in possessing information, but rather in developing the skills and capacity to manipulate it effectively for new applications. This becomes particularly important for distance education institutions, as it is becoming clear that educational providers will be able to generate significant income streams not from the information itself (which can usually be found from several sources), but rather from the services they provide around this information: interaction with educators, measured assessment and accreditation, pacing of work, and tailoring information to local needs and requirements. Thus, the future of educational institutions will depend not on the information they have—as it has tended to historically—but rather on the services that they are able to provide around that information.

Management Information Systems

As has been noted above, distance-education institutions should, as a crucial component of building their knowledge management strategies and systems, focus on developing management information systems that allow for cheap, easy, and logical storage and retrieval of information. These demands arise from dual pressures created on administrative systems of larger numbers of students—whose details will need to be kept in an accessible format—and the need to monitor more administrative processes for these students.

It is essential to ensure that such systems are capable of providing the types of management information that a distance education institution actually needs, at all levels and without adding either unnecessary bureaucracy or administrative labor (particularly as so much reporting can be automated in well-designed database environments). One of the major considerations in designing such systems is to understand the questions that will be asked of data, in order to ensure that the data being gathered by a management information system is capable of answering these questions. The grids produced by Kidwell (http://www.educause.edu/ir/library/pdf/EQM0044.pdf) provide an overview of the kinds of information that such a system should seek to contain in a distance education setting.

There is added benefit to creating interfaces to information that enable users to engage with certain types of information themselves with little or no intervention by other people. If a simple Web interface were added to such data-warehousing systems, it would be possible for educators and learners to select their own search criteria and extract relevant resources very quickly and at no additional cost. This simple search level adds tremendous strength to the resource and is very cost-effective, because changes made to the database are reflected automatically via a Web interface. Possibly most importantly, the integration of levels of security into the database infrastructure will allow for decentralized entry of data by the people responsible for that data (for example, academics taking responsibility for entering student marks). A Web interface simplifies hardware and software requirements for almost all users and can be used to create user-friendly computer interfaces.

The successful design of management information systems is strongly founded on a clear understanding of the type of information one might wish to extract from databases developed. This extends beyond the brief of this chapter, but two useful resources that the reader might wish to consult if interested are

- The COL Knowledge Guide on *Managing Student Records* – available at http://www.col.org/colweb/webdav/site/myjahiasite/shared/docs/KS2005_records.pdf
- An article by the author of this chapter on *Student Management Information Systems for Distance Education Institutions*, available at http http://www.africaodl.org/resources/0000001539/0000000763/0000001039/Student%20Management%20Information%20Systems%20for%20Distance%20Education%20Institutions.pdf

ICT Knowledge Management Investments

In summary then, ICT can be harnessed to support many key processes within knowledge management:

- Capturing knowledge;
- Designing, storing, categorizing, indexing, and linking digital objects that correspond to knowledge units;
- Searching for (pulling) and subscribing to (pushing) relevant content stored digitally;
- Presenting information and content with sufficient flexibility to render it meaningful and applicable across multiple contexts of use (Barnes, 2001).

For all the above to be harnessed effectively within a broader knowledge management strategy, distance-education institutions will have to invest financial and human resources in

- Establishing the types and combinations of information needed to support teaching and learning environments, target learners, and strategies for making this information accessible to all participants in the educational process.
- Developing an appropriate conceptual framework for computer-based management information systems. Many investments in ICT systems lead to disappointment and serious waste of resources. More often than not, this can be traced back to incomplete definition of the business requirements of ICT systems, insufficiently detailed technical specifications, and lack of user input during design and development. A key objective in designing effective ICT systems to support knowledge management should be to leverage existing processes by computerizing and automating them.
- Designing an electronic database architecture that can be used to organize, store, and allow for multiple uses of information. This may include some combination of
  - Databases, data-warehousing systems, and content repositories.
  - Computer networks that allow users to connect via distributed computer networks. Increasingly, as the amount of information available in knowledge management systems expands, it is becoming essential that these are broadband networks, capable of supporting the movement of large quantities of data. This takes on particular relevance in developing country contexts, where communication between the various centers of a distance education institution is hampered by poor quality and expensive telecommunications. For distance education institutions to be able to harness the power of technology in supporting effective knowledge management, it is becoming increasingly important to ensure that affordable broadband connectivity is established to allow all elements of the distance education system to stay in ongoing contact with one another and to be able to share information seamlessly and effectively. This is a significant challenge in overcoming the growing digital divide that exists between developed and developing countries.
  - Communication systems that facilitate interaction and collaboration between members of the institution. These would include e-mail systems, discussion lists, and collaborative tools designed to support knowledge sharing (for example, online project-management systems and collaborative authoring tools). There

has been rapid development recently of rich, interactive tools for collaborative authoring of content that can support effective institutional knowledge management.

Key Design Principles for a Knowledge Management Strategy

Based on the above discussions, it is possible to extract a set of principles that should inform the design and implementation of a knowledge management strategy. These can be summarized as follows:

1. *Start with Strategy*

   Be clear what the objectives of a knowledge management strategy are in order to ensure that knowledge management does not come to be seen as an end in itself. Document these carefully so that they can be used to assess every aspect of the design of evolving systems and tools. In an educational context, it seems reasonable to expect that these objectives must, in broad terms, be to advance and improve student learning. If knowledge management investments cannot be linked to this overall objective, it would seem to be difficult to justify them in an educational organization.

2. *Involve users in the design of the knowledge management strategy and systems*

   This chapter has stressed throughout the centrality of people to knowledge management. The most successful strategies and systems will harness the people who are expected to drive the system from the outset, building from an existing organizational context and from an understanding of patterns of use of information already present within an institution.

3. *Clearly distinguish knowledge management strategies from technology implementation and information systems management*

   Although the previous section has outlined many ways in which technologies can be harnessed to support knowledge management, it is critical to keep remembering that technology is not the driver of knowledge management. Technology should be an enabler, facilitating the establishment of solutions to real problems. Once technology becomes a problem that needs its own solutions, it stops being useful to its users.

4. *Ensure that the broader organizational environment supports and rewards creation and sharing of knowledge*

   There is little point in attempting to layer a knowledge management strategy on top of an organization that is structurally unsupportive of knowledge creation and sharing. Thus, establishing an effective knowledge management strategy will require thorough review of all organizational polices and practices in an effort to ensure that people are encouraged to become true knowledge workers. These policies and practices should encourage a spirit of enquiry and curiosity while rewarding information sharing and collaboration. They should also work actively to break down internal boundaries within an organization in order to make it easier for people to work in teams, so that they are able to develop their own knowledge further through innovation and interaction with others. This process of organizational change will require strong institutional leadership if it is to work successfully.

5. *Approach knowledge management as an iterative process*

Knowledge management is not a one-off investment in which a system is created and then left to run by itself. It will thus be critical to ensure that support for knowledge management strategies is long term and that it assumes an ongoing need for iterative improvements. Again, this will require strong institutional leadership if the strategies and systems of knowledge management are to become truly embedded into the operations of the organization.

6. *Measure the impact of knowledge management*

As noted in point one above, managing knowledge is not an end in itself, but rather should be informed by clear objectives. To close the loop, it is critical to integrate into knowledge management strategies and systems some processes of measuring the impact of these investments. This may be difficult to do, as it may be difficult to quantify the benefits that knowledge management brings, but reflective review of the effect that knowledge management is having remains an important element of ensuring that its evolving design and implementation has the greatest impact possible.

CONCLUSION

Hopefully, this chapter has provided an overview of the concept of knowledge management, explained its importance, and provided an overview of how it can be harnessed to support distance education. The final word goes to Patrides and Nodine (2003):

> The power of knowledge management, particularly when compared to other change efforts, is that it maintains focus on people—on faculty, staff, and students—and their needs. There is no quick fix for managing knowledge in an organization. And there is no single system, no matter how complex and

integrated, that can manage knowledge. In the final analysis, it is people who manage knowledge, and it is the role of organizations to promote policies and practices that help people want to share and manage knowledge effectively.

REFERENCES

ASTD, (2007). *Learning Organization.* Retrieved from http://store.astd.org/Default. aspx?tabid=143&action=ECDProductDetails&args=17094

Barnes, P. (2001). *A Primer on knowledge management.* Retrieved December 2, 2008, from http://www.accaglobal.com/students/publications/student_accountant/archive/2001/18/57627

Carroll, J., Choo, C., Dunlpa, D., Isenhour, P., Kerr, S., Maclean, A., & Rosson, M. (2004). *Knowledge management support for teachers.* Retrieved December 2, 2008, from http://choo.fis.utoronto.ca/FIS/ResPub/ETRD/KM4T.pdf

HCI (2001a). *Knowledge management primer: Part 1 – Why?* Retrieved December 2, 2008, from http://www.hci.com.au/hcisite3/journal/Knowledge%20Management%20primer%20part%201.htm

HCI (2001b). *Knowledge management primer: Part 2 – How?* Retrieved December 2, 2008, from http://www.hci.com.au/hcisite3/journal/Knowledge%20Management%20primer%20part%202.htm

Landcare Research (2007). *Communicating science–Reflecting on practice.* Retrieved December 2, 2008, from http://www.landcareresearch.co.nz/research/social/communicationinfo.asp

Na Ubon, A., & Kimble, C. (2002). *Knowledge management in online distance education.* 3rd International Conference on Networked Learning. Sheffield, UK. Retrieved December 2, 2008, from http://www.cherrycorner.com/download/Knowledge%20Management%20in%20Online%20Distance%20Education.pdf

Petrides, L., & Nodine, T. (2003). *Knowledge management in education: Defining the landscape.* California Institute for the Study of Knowledge Management in Education. Retrieved December 2, 2008, from http://www.iskme.org/what-we-do/publications/km_education.pdf

Randell, C. (2005). *Managing student records in distance education.* Vancouver: Commonwealth of Learning. Retrieved December 2, 2008, from www.col.org/colweb/webdav/site/myjahiasite/shared/docs/KS2005_records.pdf

Softpanorama (2007). *Workaholism, anxiety and obsession with computers and Internet.* Retrieved December 2, 2008, from http://www.softpanorama.org/Social/Overload/anxiety_and_obsession_with_computers.shtml

Thorn, C. (2001). Knowledge management for educational information systems: What is the state of the field? *Education Policy Analysis Archives, 9.* Retrieved December 2, 2008, from http://epaa.asu.edu/epaa/v9n47/

Wikipedia, 2007 Information Society. Retrieved December 2, 2008, from http://en.wikipedia.org/wiki/Information_society

NOTES

The definitions presented in this section have been amalgamated from:

Petrides, L. & Nodine, T. (2003). *Knowledge management in education: Defining the landscape.* California Institute for the Study of Knowledge Management in Education.
Barnes, P. C. (2001). *A primer on knowledge management.*

CHAPTER 7

THE EFFECTIVENESS OF MOBILE SHORT MESSAGING SERVICE (SMS) TECHNOLOGIES IN THE SUPPORT OF SELECTED DISTANCE EDUCATION STUDENTS OF MAKERERE UNIVERSITY, UGANDA

Richard Kajumbula

INTRODUCTION

Distance education (DE) providers face the challenge of improving student-support services so as to enhance the performance of students who are in most cases dispersed. Learner support is a system designed to assist the learner in using the study materials offered to him or her to study effective-

Bridging the Knowledge Divide, pages 123–147
Copyright © 2009 by Information Age Publishing
All rights of reproduction in any form reserved.

ly and efficiently and be in a position to adjust his or her lifestyle and study steadily so that he or she can complete the course embarked on. It aims at reducing the isolation of a distance learner, increasing peer and instructor interaction, inculcating self-discipline among the students and avoiding loss of interest. Support includes, among others, peer-support sessions (study groups), tutorials, teaching in assignments, and Internet communication including Short Messaging System Service (SMS), all attempting to close the gap between the learner and the tutor, who are separated in space and time for more than the usual time (Bbuye, 2005). Usun (2004) says that effective learner-support systems contribute to the success and motivation of students, hence leading to improved quality of distance programs, while ineffective support systems lead to their failure. Keegan (2004) points out that the new missions and challenges facing open universities today, as in the past, are linked to development in technology.

As Manjulika and Reddy (2000, p. 1) noted, institutions involved in distance and open education have been at the forefront of adopting new technologies. This can increase access to education and training opportunities. Distance education has evolved through generations: correspondence mode based on print technology was the first, followed by multimedia mode based on print, audio, and video technologies. The third was the tele-learning mode, based on applications of telecommunications technologies to provide opportunities for synchronous communication; and fourth, the flexible learning based on online delivery via the Internet. A fifth generation that is already emerging is one that utilizes the Internet and the World Wide Web. In all these, learner support is crucial. As Makerere University (MAK) begins to embark on the third generation, SMS communication will be essential.

Nix, Russel, and Keegan (2006) define SMS as a mobile-phone technology that allows short text messages to be sent and received on a mobile phone. Typical messages are 160 characters in length.

History and Management of DE at Makerere University

Makerere University, a dual-mode institution, has been running DE degree programs since 1991 (Aguti, 2000, p.256). The programs are managed by the Department of Distance Education (DDE) in the Institute of Adult and continuing Education (IACE) in collaboration with academic faculties. DDE carries out student-support activities for students scattered in many parts of Uganda, who utilize the various regional centers as shown on the map in Appendix I. The most common medium of communication to students is radio. However, this medium has no room for the recipient to store the message for future reference, and there is uncertainty as to whether, at the time the announcement passes, the target audience is listening in.

Development of Distance Education at Makerere University

DE is not a recent mode of study in Uganda. Aguti (2000, p.256), while describing the development of DE in Makerere University, points out that the first DE programs in Uganda as a country were held in the 1960s, when a number of individuals registered for correspondence courses run for England. In 1965 Makerere College began to run its own correspondence courses. However, by 1987 the number of correspondence students in the Makerere programs had dwindled to only eight.

Makerere University, which was established in 1922 as a technical school and later achieved university status in 1970, has been running DE programs since 1991. To run the External Degree Program (EDP), there is an Advisory Committee. This committee has members including

- Director of the Institute of Adult and Continuing Education
- The Academic Registrar
- Deans of Collaborating faculties/schools/institutes
- A representative from the Ministry of Education
- The Head of Department, Distance Education, who is also the secretary of this committee

According to "The Proposal for Starting the External Degree Program (EDP)," the Advisory Committee shall consider and offer guidance on all matters concerning academic standards, curriculum development, evaluation, support services, and resource mobilization.

The Department of Distance Education has a university mandate to offer DE courses. In 1990 the EDP was launched with two programs: Bachelor of Commerce (BCom) and Bachelor of Education (BEd). Currently, the programs have expanded to include the Bachelor of Science (BSc) and the Commonwealth Youth Program (CYP) diploma in Youth in Development Work.

Over the years, the number of students in the programs has been fluctuating as shown in Table 7.1.

As shown in Table 7.1, the number of students has been fluctuating over the years. From academic year 2002–03, the university started reducing the number of admitted students so as to ensure that the few available resources were well-utilized among manageable numbers of students. This is why there is a reduction in the registered students. Apart from the above

TABLE 7.1 Registered Students

| Year | Number of Registered Students | | | |
	BEd	BCom	BSc	CYP Dip.
1991–92	148	98		
1992–93	0	135		
1993–94	132	207		
1994–95	89	160		
1995–96	132	620		
1996–97	450	650		
1997–98	300	480		
1998–99	693	850		
1999–00	1,640	1,149		
2000–01	1,046	1,300		
2001–02	328	1,016		32
2002–03	388	619	66	0
2003–04	387	861	28	32
2004–05	707	794	94	33
2005–06	514	795	90	0
2006–07	381	556	88	0

Source: DE Registration records.

credit programs, the department also runs several short training programs in computer packages and management of income-generating projects.

Administration of the DE Programs at Makerere University

The DE programs have been running together with the already existing internal programs, both day and evening. Makerere University is therefore a dual-mode institution (Siminyu, 2003). The curricula of the degree programs are similar to those of the respective internal programs, and the examinations are the same, where timing allows. DE programs are managed by the Department of Distance Education (DDE) in the Institute of Adult and Continuing Education (IACE) in collaboration with the various academic units of the university, depending on the program. In the collaboration arrangement, the specific roles of the DDE, the administrative unit, are

1. Orientation of students and staff to the DE mode of study
2. The development of study materials
3. Procurement of study materials from external sources

4. Distribution of study materials
5. Guidance and counselling of students
6. Planning and management of face-to-face sessions
7. The collection of assignments and return of assignments to the students
8. Provision of support services to each student throughout the duration of his or her course
9. Planning and managing up-country tutorial programs
10. Planning and administering examinations
11. Preparing payments for all services rendered to the program
12. Collaborating with other distance education institutions for the refinement of the programs

The Specific roles of the collaborating academic units are

1. The development and implementation of the curriculum
2. Identifying academic staff to teach on the various courses
3. Identifying and seconding writers and reviewers of the study materials
4. Vetting study materials and recommending for purchase
5. Carrying out progressive assessment of students
6. Setting and marking examinations
7. Presenting results to the University Senate
8. Development and refinement of the program
9. Any other academic duties required of the academic unit

As already pointed out, management of DE programs is the mandate of the DDE, headed by a Head of Department. The package that DE students enjoy includes

- Face-to-face sessions
- Written study materials
- Student study groups
- Audio cassettes
- Other student-support services, including counseling, library services, and constant communication

The State of Student Support

The underlying assumption of DE is the separation of a tutor from the student for more than the usual time or for all the time (Keegan, 1986). Since the students are separated in space and time, they need to have at least an artificial communication medium that will deliver information and also provide a channel of interaction between them (Moore, 2000; Tait, 2003).

Bbuye (2006) says that learner support is a system designed to assist the learner in using effectively and efficiently the study materials offered to him or her for study. This is usually done by providing on-campus tutorials, lectures, laboratory-work, counselling sessions, and other face-to-face interaction with tutors and fellow students, as well as Internet use through e-mail, online discussions, downloading of study materials, and computer teleconferencing.

Bbuye (2006) further points out that student support in Makerere University is not yet well-developed with many services centralized. Counseling and library services are largely available centrally. Through the Department and Academic Registrar, both prospective and registered students receive information and counseling about courses and study requirements. The department does not have a full-time counselor, but academic and administrative staff members give students advice and counseling on many issues, ranging from coping with difficult employers to dealing with fee problems. In addition, the department offers information through circulars, mails, e-mails, telephone calls, and notice boards.

The learner-support system was not inbuilt within the DE systems. This inadequacy of policy and regulations adversely affected the provision of learner support for the distance education students. Strengths of the learner-support systems were as shown below:

1. Counseling services to the students, up-country tutorials, provided information booklets, the book bank for reference materials were key strengths of the support system.
2. Giving information to students was one of the routine works of administrators.
3. Study groups, though self-initiated by students, but occasionally tutors participated.
4. Study centers gave opportunity to students in various regions to use as a stopgap, which prevented them from frequenting the headquarters if they had minor administrative queries and to congregate as a group outside face-to-face to discuss issues.
5. In some of the Makerere University centers, there were competent staff at degree level to run study centers and ICT courses.

Weaknesses of Support Systems

The socioeconomic conditions of Uganda affect the development of learner support in universities. Uganda is not fully electrified, the telephone lines that are landlines and could be cheaper are not well-distributed in the rural areas; the post office is also unreliable. The telecom industry in Uganda is still in its infancy and expensive for the ordinary Ugandan. What has spread so rapidly are mobile phones that cover over 7 million people in over 365 towns, but have not yet been tapped by distance providers for use in the support systems of students.

Learner-support systems are still developing, lack a two-way communication system, and hardly use ICTs. Though there seems to be a concrete system of temporary staff running regional centers, these are not well-grounded in the practice of DE and often refer to the headquarters for queries that sometimes could be settled easily. Most support services are centralized, and this creates a tendency of program administrators managing and serving mostly students in urban areas. The lack of information flow has also led to students missing out on vital information and at times having to travel physically to the main campus to access information that would appear seemingly accessible.

Despite the existence of study centers up-country, the percentage of enrolled students using them are too low. One percent of the students of Makerere University based in Fortportal used the center, and only 20% of the students based in Mbale, with 200 students enrolled in the course in the region, used the center. Ninety-eight percent of the students enrolled used the Kampala center located at the main campus. There was evident underutilization of the up-country centers and over utilization of the Kampala center, overburdening and straining the services provided, especially the computer services. The underutilization of support was due to

- Inaccessibility of centers due to poor roads
- Lack of timely information
- Lack of key facilities like accommodation, photocopying, library, and Internet
- Lack of competent human resources at centers with skills of handling a distance learner.
- Books placed at the centers being very few

Distance learning support programs at the centers were wanting because

- Most study centers were supervised by absentee resident tutors and mostly managed by personnel organizers and clerks who lack capacity and are not competent in computer use or grounded in distance education theory to assist students, indicating a poor management system of existing learner systems.
- Unfavorable opening and closing hours of offices. A distance learner who works full time finds the offices of the center locked by

5 pm. During the day, also the center coordinator may not be available, and the center is run by a typist or clerk who could not fully attend to students' problems.

Students seemed not so eager to use facilities at centers because of their study habits, as indicated below.

- Students had other commitments or responsibilities at place of work or home, with inflexible work timetables and no time to visit centers.
- Poor communications, since the majority of students were located in remote areas and took much more time to reach centers.
- The spouses were not always supportive; it was difficult for a married woman to stay in the center for a large part of her evening or for the weekend without the spouse raising a finger.

The support needs of the learners were

- Communication about coursework, current books available in the book bank and other libraries, an integrated booklet or study guide, and study skills for each particular course that were not yet in place
- Key information, such as information on activities due, fellow students' contacts, ICT usage, and assignment deadlines, especially in Makerere University, where flow of information was a bit sluggish
- Overhauling of the materials distribution process, since in most cases, students received course materials and manuals late and could not collect enough information for the course assignments because of lack of extra study materials from the Internet or from the libraries;
- Sessions on study skills, flexible handing in assignments dates, tutoring outside face-to-face sessions, and an improved communication systems

DESCRIPTION OF THE PURPOSE OF THE STUDY

To enhance communication between students and staff and ensure that students do not miss out on important activities or even feel isolated, which may cause them to drop out, DDE acquired a software program known as DDE Broadcast System from SOCNET Solutions Limited, a software development company in Uganda. This program has the capacity to send instant messages to the mobile phone of a student and to the e-mail address provided by the student. The tool communicates to two out of the three mobile service providers in the country. It can be compared with the

Chikka Network in the Philippines (Mariano & De La Rosa, 2004). The most efficient PC-to-mobile service available for free on the Net in the Philippines is Chikka (Mariano & De La Rosa, 2004). This Chikka system is truly Philippine-made, as it was developed and is being run by Filipinos. This tool can communicate to all mobile service providers in the country, as well to students who are traveling abroad and are using roaming facilities. It is interesting to note that Filipino students, especially in modes of education like open learning and distance education systems that have less face-to-face and classroom interaction, often use SMS and e-mail messaging systems to foster interaction and learning.

The role of SMS communication in universities is not new in the developing world. In the Philippines, which is known as the "texting capital of the world," and Mongolia, SMS is one of the students' favorite means of communication with faculty and other students (Pabico, 2003; Mariano & De La Rosa, 2004). This was the same finding by Nonyongo, Mabusela, and Monene (2005) about University of South Africa (UNISA) students. Since on average, mobile phones have a capacity of 160 letters per message, abbreviated spelling has evolved to extend messages and, at the same time, get the messages clearly to the other person. This has made communication to students easier (Mariano & De La Rosa, 2004). Ramos (2006) further notes that although telephony is already available in many areas of the Philippines and Mongolia at almost every level of society, it is important for educators to tap this vital access model.

SMS has been used in student administrative support in the University of Ulster in Northern Ireland. Nix, Russel, and Keegan (2006) report that the University of Ulster has had great success in the use of SMS for keeping students in the programs. Sending SMS to students who have been identified as being at risk has been a very successful approach for keeping students in the system. They further add that a frequent cause of drop-out is that "nobody cares."

However, there is always a fear in introducing new technology. Even if it has worked elsewhere, to Makerere University it is like "leaping into the dark." Steven Gilbert, President of the Teaching, Learning, and Technology (TLT) wrote an article called "Why Bother." He asked,

> Why bother making great investments of money, time, and effort to increase educational uses of information technology in colleges and universities? Why should an academic leader risk making a technology investment decision that may make him/her look wasteful or foolish in 12 to 24 months? Or sooner!

His short answer was "Because more people will be able to learn and teach better."

Given that question, the introduction of technology has benefits, if applied properly. A huge sum of money has been invested in purchasing the software, and if not applied well, this money may end up among the department's sunk costs. The use of the cellular phone as well as the popularity of SMS is increasing in Uganda and in other countries, and Makerere University has to find the most appropriate way of applying the technology. This being the first time such an application of technology is happening in Makerere University, many skeptics still question whether this will be successful in enhancing management of the distance education program, especially the student-support component. It is noteworthy that there is very limited use of multimedia in supporting distance learners in Uganda (Bbuye, 2006). This study, therefore, sought to establish the effectiveness of SMS communication among selected DE students and to recommend a method of applying this technology at the maximum benefit to the student and minimum cost to DDE. Effectiveness of SMS communication in this study will be measured by measuring the percentage of students who received the messages, how students felt after receiving the messages, and whether the medium should be used.

Since this pilot study aimed at administrative support like at the University of Pretoria (Keegan, 2004), communicating programs to students so as to enable them to manage their studies is a key indicator of effectiveness of the system. An effective communication system in student administrative support should be one that can reduce isolation, increase participation of students, instill self-discipline among students, avoid loss of interest, and motivate students, all aimed at enabling them to continue in the program.

METHODOLOGY

The research design was exploratory, since effectiveness of a new technology was being tested. The survey population included distance education students. Using cluster sampling, 58 out of 78 (74.4%) up-country students were selected. The cluster involved first-year Bachelor of Commerce External up-country distance education students of Makerere University, Uganda, since the technology had been introduced with their entry. The students were invited during a face-to-face session and interviewed. Up-country centers include Jinja, Mbale, Lira, Arua, Fort Portal, Hoima, and Mbarara. The source of data was primary. Interviews were also carried out with tutors and administrators using an interview guide, and students were surveyed using the questionnaire method. This study borrows some methods as applied by Nonyongo, Mabusela, and Monene (2005), which carried out a study on student SMS usage at the University of South Africa (UNISA).

This was a pilot study and therefore focused on administrative support, as was the case in the University of Pretoria (Keegan, 2004). The primary focus was on a communication approach for administration and learning support rather than a content approach as such, because of the comprehensive paper-based study materials the students are provided with.

FINDINGS

Characteristics of Respondents

The students selected were of varying age and gender, as shown in Table 7.2.

Most of the respondents fell in the age range of 20–29 years, followed by 30–39 years, implying that students were of varying age. Most of these students were male. There was, however, a deliberate effort to increase the university entry of women with the coming up of the affirmative action scheme in Uganda. Under this scheme, female students are awarded 1.5 points during the admission process. This enables the number of those admitted to increase beyond that, which would otherwise have been admitted.

Students' Nearest Makerere University Regional Center

Students enrolled in the Makerere University External Degree program are scattered across the countryside, as shown in the map in Appendix I, and the results of this study reflected this. They were from seven up-country centers, as shown in Table 7.3. Because of this, reaching them physically was difficult, hence the need for a good communication system to help them

TABLE 7.2   Age and Gender of Respondents

	Gender			
	Male		Female	
Age Bracket	Frequency	Percentage	Frequency	Percentage
20–29	17	41.5	12	70.6
30–39	23	56.1	4	23.5
40–49	1	2.4	1	5.9
50 and above	0	0.0	0	0.0
Total	41	100.0	17	100.0

Source: Primary data.

TABLE 7.3 Students' Makerere University Regional Center

Center	Frequency	Percent
Kampala	6	10.3
Mbale	19	32.8
Lira	5	8.6
Arua	3	5.2
Fortportal	4	6.9
Jinja	12	20.7
Mbarara	9	15.5
Total	58	100.0

Source: Primary data.

save costs of travel to the main campus for information. See also the map in the Appendix, which gives the location of these centers in the country.

From Table 7.3, it can be seen that students interviewed were from several regional centers. The number of students at regional centers was still low compared with those in the central region who were nearest to the main university campus. Of the cohort from which the up-country students were selected, 752 were from the Kampala region. The students from the Kampala region could access the main campus at any time as compared with their counterparts outside Kampala. The study focused on up-country students, since they were far from the main campus. The distance from various regional centers to Kampala can be established from the map in Appendix I using the scale.

The few students up-country was mainly due to the low level of publicity, since the university policy does not provide for advertising programs. Another reason is the centralized nature of administering the program. All administrative activities including, but not limited to, admission processing, registration, and communication take place at the main university campus. The only academic activities that take place at the centers are the tutorials that occur once a semester. The center coordinators also provide information to the students.

However, the university is now in the process of developing a policy for distance education, which has been lacking. The university has also indicated that distance education is one of the priority areas in the next strategic planning period. This will open up avenues for decentralizing services and decongesting the center. Decentralization is advantageous in that it adds on the critical components of staff personal responsibility and ownership. If the services are nearer to the students, quicker response to local demands of the students and a stronger loyalty to the organization at the support centers is possible. With more decentralization, the SMS program will become even more useful, since most of the students will be in the countryside.

Students' Access to Mobile Phones

Access to mobile phones among the students is increasing. Out of the 58 students reached, 56 (96.6%) have mobile phones, with only 2 (3.4%) without mobile phones. One of the students without a mobile phone said that he could not afford it because he was not working and was using his uncle's phone. The other said that at his home there is no network. He would therefore find it difficult to use the mobile phone. However, the level of access is high generally. This level of access to mobile phones compares quite well with Mbarika and Mbarika's (2006) findings that in Uganda, more than 50% of the population have mobile cellular coverage. This level of access implies the mobile phone has huge potential to improve communication between Makerere University and its students and, therefore, the need for the DDE to deliberately seek to exploit the availability of this technology in its support services. Keegan (2004) notes that because of lack of infrastructure of ICT in rural areas in Africa, the growth of wireless infrastructure is enormous.

Nix, Russel, and Keegan (2006) note that never in the history of the use of technology in education has there been a technology so widely available to citizens as mobile technology. It is forecast that ownership of mobile phones will reach 3 billion as early as 2010. This is for a world population of just over 6.5 billion. To further the debate of whether SMS can be used in education due to its accessibility, the British Broadcasting Corporation in 2004 stated that respondents in the 16–24 age group ranked ownership of a mobile phone as a necessity, and this is the age bracket of students at universities.

Keegan (2006) noted that one of the characteristics of mobile learning (m-learning) is that it uses devices that citizens are used to carrying everywhere with them, which they regard as friendly, devices which are cheap and easy to use, constantly in all walks of life and in a variety of different settings. He defines mobile learning as the provision of education and training on mobile devises like Personal Digital Assistants (PDAs), smart phones, and mobile phones. He emphasizes that the justification of mobile learning comes from the "law" of DE research, which states "it is not technologies with inherent pedagogical qualities that are successful in DE, but technologies that are generally available to citizens." This view aligns well with the fact that a mobile phone is available to students and can also be used in administrative support as this paper suggests.

The use of SMS communication in education and student support is common in developing countries like the Philippines and Mongolia. The Philippines has been named the world's texting/SMS capital, with more than 2 million SMS sent each day from over 13 million cellular phone subscribers (Pabico, 2003). Cellular phones and SMS have become an important aspect of Filipino life, and usage of this communication system is wide, ranging from the more personal use to business and education (Coronel-Ferrer, 2002). Mongolia and the Philippines are some of the countries where technology has been noted to have the most promise in terms of using texting as a possible tool in providing education (Ramos, 2006).

Findings on SMS Communication

SMS communication is applicable where students' mobile telephone numbers are available. In Makerere University, the students are asked to submit their numbers so that communication to them is possible and, as already said, 96.6% of those interviewed have mobile-phone numbers and submitted these numbers to the department. Having phone numbers of the students is vital, because the department can communicate to them and provide feedback on whatever they need to know. Students are also reminded to come to the department and submit any changes in their mobile-phone numbers. Those who have no telephones at the beginning of the program are advised to submit the telephone numbers of their next of kin.

Students' Receipt of SMS from the Department Before Installing the Program

At the beginning of the semester, before the software was installed, students were asked whether they had ever received any SMS communication from the DDE. Only 10 (17.2%) had ever received an SMS, while the majority, 47 (81%), had never received any. One student did not respond to this question. The few that had received it had only gotten messages from individual program coordinators. Prior to installation of the program, whenever there was an activity like briefing, face-to-face, tutorial session, examinations and test coming up, individual program and year coordinators would send text messages to the few students whose numbers they had. They would also send messages to a few students in the event that their results were missing and their numbers were available.

When students were asked whether they wished to receive SMS messages from the Department of Distance Education, 57 (98.3%) wished to receive such communication, except one who said that he uses his uncle's mobile phone to communicate, and worse still, in their region, network is on and off. This implies that if the department is to fully employ SMS for student support, it should remember that not all students will have access to the mobile-phone network. Such students would need to be traced and given alternative support. They need to be written to. Further, programmed contact sessions by administrative staff at various centers can enable the university to reach out to these students to avoid the loneliness and possible loss of interest in their studies.

To those who wished to receive the messages, these findings emphasized that SMS is one of the students' favorite means of communication with DDE and other students. Moreover, PC-to-mobile-phone-messaging-system costs the user nothing when connected to the Internet (Mariano & De La Rosa, 2004). The student, however, will incur a cost when accessing the department through sending SMS or when they are sending the messages to other members of staff. Mariano and De La Rosa (2004) further noted, that the Chikka network in the Philippines had one limitation in that there is no provision for mathematical symbols, so in using it, there is a need to put every mathematical symbol into words. This emphasizes that there are limitations with using SMS that should be taken care of, and the system needs to be studied thoroughly before full implementation.

Students' Receipt of SMS from the Department After Installing the Program

Two months after installation of the SMS software, students were sent messages. On the follow-up study, they were asked whether they had received the messages, and Figure 7.1 shows that 68.6% of the students received the communication, while 31.4% did not.

On further inquiry from the systems administrator as to why some students did not receive, it was established that the program takes time to deliver the messages and, at times, if the person is in a place with poor network, the message may not be delivered at all. Ninety percent of those who did not receive the messages said that at the time the messages were sent, they were in places without network. However, the delay in delivering

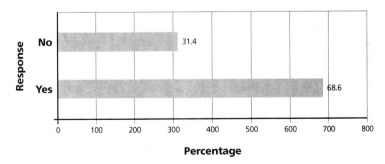

Figure 7.1 Whether students had received SMS messages from the department.

of some messages by the program was to be rectified, since the program was still in the piloting and testing phase.

The above findings also inform the administration of the department that SMS cannot be the only reliable mode of communication. Other means should be used. Some students said that they received the messages after the activity that they were announcing had passed or when it was too late for them to respond in time. Therefore, upgrading the program as well as proper planning and scheduling of activities and events is necessary so that students estimate the time when certain events will occur and also expect communication. However, students said that SMS messages played a crucial role of reminding them and informing them of new and upcoming programs that they could have otherwise missed.

The Type of Information Students Wished to Receive through SMS

SMS being a medium of communicating information to students, students were asked the type of information they wished to be communicated. The results are presented Figure 7.2.

Students wanted to know when results were out. This is because as soon as students finish exams, they return to their areas of residence. Since some of them stay far from the main university campus, it is difficult for them to frequently check physically at the main university campus to know when results are out. SMS can therefore be used to inform them that the results are displayed. Unfortunately, the details or scores of each student by course or subject cannot be communicated to them using SMS because of the need for confidentiality. However, the Academic Registrar's office is testing a program that will make it possible for each student to access their result on a database online, using a password that will be provided to them.

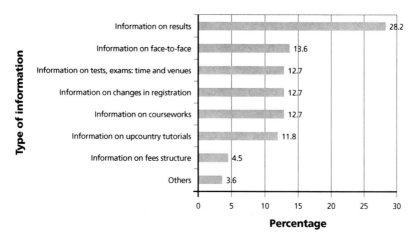

Figure 7.2   The information that students wished to receive through SMS.

It was found that 13.6% of the students also wanted information on face-to-face to be sent to them using SMS. Face-to-face information involves the dates, the place, room(s), timetable, and tutors. If students do not receive the above information, they are likely to miss the sessions or report late. To supplement SMS communication, the Department of Distance Education passes radio announcements prior to the face-to-face session, inviting students for the face-to-face sessions and what is expected of them. The department also provides a year planner at the beginning of the semester to enable students to schedule their activities. However, reminders are still needed.

Students also wanted information on changes in registration (12.7%). Sometimes a program is provided and dates indicated when registration will take place. However, there are cases when the dates and/or requirements are changed. In such cases, to avoid students traveling and not registering, SMS messages can be sent out to them informing them of the changes. Information on tests and exams was also one of the items students needed to be communicated to them using SMS. The particular information that the students mentioned was the time and venue of exams.

Students also wanted information on coursework to be communicated to them using SMS. The particular information they needed in this regard included the assignment questions, due dates, the tutors, grading, and the results from such assignments. This will enable them to plan for the examinations. In distance education, assignments are used as a tool for teaching and learning. It is important that the students get comments about the questions asked. There is therefore a plan to use SMS to send students' comments about the assignments. This information should include the approach to the question and the areas where students tended to go off track. If this is sent to each student about each of the courses that they offer, they will be motivated to read more in a focused manner and hence perform well.

The department also carries out tutorial sessions at various regional centers. These take place between face-to-face sessions. The students therefore indicated that they needed information about up-country tutorials, especially to do with the time, place, and timetable. Currently, the students are given a schedule of these tutorials after a face-to-face session as they return to their various centers. However, for those who may have missed getting the schedule, SMS reminders can play an important role in encouraging all students to attend.

The fee structure of the department for its four programs, that is, Bachelor of Commerce, Bachelor of Education, Bachelor of Science, and the Commonwealth Diploma in Youth in Development work, has been constant for some time. However, the tuition for Bachelor of Education was increased. This means that fee structure can change. Students therefore said that they would like information to that effect communicated to them using SMS. These are private programs where all the students pay tuition for themselves. This means that they have to be informed in time of any changes so that they can plan their finances or even enable their sponsors to plan.

The reasons classified under "Others" included course units to be covered, timetables, fee updates, and new stock of textbooks. From these responses, the kind of information students wanted to be given using SMS covers critical areas in the life of a distance education student. This implies that SMS communication is necessary and should be well-integrated in the department's communication strategy. This is in line with the findings in the Philippines. It is interesting to note that Filipino students, especially in modes of education like open learning and distance education systems, which have less face-to-face and classroom interaction, often use SMS and e-mail messaging systems to foster interaction and learning. The use of these messaging systems in education has become an indispensable communication system and an important aspect of teaching and learning (Pabico, 2003). Its implications for distance education policymaking, administration, curriculum development, and instruction are, therefore, worth examining.

Nix et al. (2006) also noted that students enrolled in all higher- and further-education institutions today have a frequent need for information from their institutions about timetable changes, assessment deadlines, feedback from tutors, and other urgent administrative details like cancellation of a lecture on short notice. The post and e-mail are not always effective means of communicating urgent information to students.

Effectiveness of SMS Communication

Effectiveness of SMS communication in this study measured the percentage of students who received the messages, how students felt after receiving the messages, and whether the medium should be used. Since this pilot study aimed at administrative support, communicating programs to students so as to enable them to manage their studies and reduce isolation is a key indicator of the effectiveness of the system.

Whether Students Received the Messages
Before the program was installed, students were asked whether communication between them and the department was effective, that is, if they received information on upcoming events in time, got feedback on queries, and other relevant communication from the university. Twenty-six (44.8%) said communication was effective, while 27 (46.6%) said it was not yet effective. The introduction of the software was to enhance such.

After installing the program, SMS messages were sent during the semester. Students were again invited after two months to comment on whether communication between them and the department had improved. From this follow-up survey, in which 52 students participated, 42 (80.7%) agreed that they had received relevant and timely information from the department about important events at the main campus and at centers, while 10 (19.3%) said that more should be done to reach them, because information reached late to some and others did not receive any messages. They suggested that radio communication and actual telephone calls should continue to supplement the SMS communication.

How Students Felt When They Received SMS from the Department

This question was necessary because, since most of the distance learners were isolated for most of the time, frustration is a common problem. Establishing the feelings SMS elicits from students would be an indicator of how SMS deals with frustrations associated with isolation. The responses received showed that students have positive feelings when they receive the messages from the department. Their feelings have been categorized and Figure 7.3 shows the findings.

The majority of them (26.9%) felt connected to the university. This satisfies one of the objectives of student support, which is to reduce the isolation the students felt and to reduce the distance they felt as a result of being far from the main campus. Being connected to the university also implies having a sense of belonging, which is vital for the students' morale and esteem.

Comments by Tutors and Administrators about SMS Communication with Students

Tutors and administrators commented that SMS communication can enhance both academic and administrative support to students. Students can know whether their marks are missing, dates for tutorials, face-to-face sessions and examinations, venues, and meeting times with research supervi-

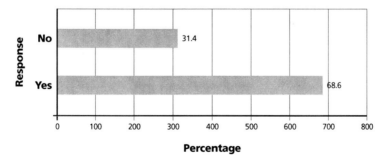

Figure 7.3 How students felt when they received the SMS from the department.

sors. This enhances effectiveness of communication between students and staff as Stone, Briggs, and Smith (2002) also emphasized. SMS communication creates a one-to-one teaching/learning interaction, as students can study the learning material for many hours and then pick a phone and send a text message to the tutor. The tutor can then respond to the various queries raised by a student. One tutor commented that

> SMS can be used to give students reminders about assignment questions and deadlines. I can also provide answers to questions, especially short answers and answers to multiple-choice questions.

SMS therefore facilitates tutor-to-tutor interaction and vice versa, tutor-to-administrator interaction and vice versa, and administration-to-student and vice versa. It also facilitates student-to-student and administrator-to-administrator interaction.

Information Flows that SMS can Facilitate

The discussion with tutors and administrators enabled identification of several information flows that SMS can facilitate, as can be seen in Figure 7.4.

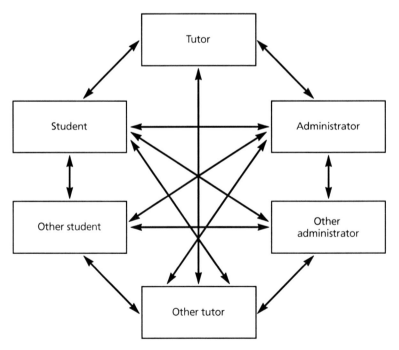

Figure 7.4 Information flows that SMS can facilitate when supporting distance learners.

However, some tutors were reluctant to open up to students. The reason they gave was that students, at times, call late in the night. This tends to irritate them. If this is the case, then students may not be able to get responses to their queries in time. Different students have different learning and studying habits. A student may decide to study late in the night and, at a certain point, may require clarity from the tutor. There is, therefore, need to brief the tutors on the uniqueness of the students and also encourage the tutors to provide the time when students can call them and/or send them text messages.

It was further noted that the SMS program would also enable interaction among tutors and between tutors and administrators. This interaction will create systematic provision of services to the students. Tutors can use it to share information on available reading lists and new knowledge, which they can then use to improve the material and methodology that they use when lecturing. Administrators can also use the same medium to communicate to tutors by giving them information on upcoming face-to-face sessions, tutorials, meetings, new books in the library and book bank, and online sources of materials.

SUMMARY AND CONCLUSIONS

This study has revealed that students' access to mobile-phone technology is very high and, therefore, the mobile phone presents a very attractive option to easing communication between the students and the department. The majority of the students wished to receive SMS, and they considered it favorable. However, other methods of communicating to students, like radio announcements and actual calling, should be maintained. The study also shows that there are a number of advantages that accrue from the use of SMS for communication. Students prefer SMS because it keeps them informed of what is happening at the university. Students wished to receive information about results, face-to-face sessions, course works, exam times and venues, registration and fee structures. When SMS messages were sent, most students connected to the university, felt special, glad, impressed, happy, and important. This satisfies one of the objectives of student support; reducing the isolation that students feel and reducing the distance they feel as a result of being far from the main campus.

Tutors and administrators, on the other hand, felt that use of SMS can enhance academic and administrative support. They said that students needed guidance on assignments, areas of the syllabi, and counseling. SMS also facilitates tutor-to-tutor interaction and administrator-to-tutor interaction and vice versa. This means that SMS is an effective medium to use in communication among students, tutors, and administrators and encourages distance education students to receive proper support, both administrative and academic, from the university.

Use of SMS can also save the department a lot of money spent on announcements over radios and newspapers. Tutors and staff too can provide both academic and administrative counseling to students and give feedback to students' queries at no cost. This shows that SMS communication is an effective way of supporting distance education learners.

RECOMMENDATIONS

To move this initial study forward, it is recommended that

- A policy involving proper authorization and approval of whatever information is going out needs to be designed. An officer in the department should be entrusted with the responsibility of checking and passing whatever information is going out. This will help to ensure that the messages are complete, clear, and relevant. This officer will also ensure that only authorized messages go out. The systems administrator will be entrusted with the responsibility of uploading the messages. An authorization form will be developed on which the systems administrator will rely before uploading a message.
- The department engages in negotiations with mobile-phone companies so that students can respond to the messages immediately using their mobile phones to a dedicated line, which will transmit to them the e-mail address of the department from where they can be forwarded to the concerned member(s) of staff. This would probably help reduce the costs to students of responding to SMS messages— something that sometimes hinders the use of the mobile phone.
- Negotiations with phone companies should also include provision of a toll-free line in remote centers so that a tutor can be called. The tutor would then analyze, correct, and gear the study of the individual student to the requirements of the certification and examination process.
- Encourage staff to acquire smart phones that can accommodate a lot of data and encourage transmission of lectures.
- To encourage the programmers to make it possible for the students to be able to get auto replies when they make inquiries by SMS to the department.
- This study should be extended to all distance education students of Makerere University gradually.
- The program should be tested for academic support as well where quizzes and revision questions are given to students and answers later on. SMS tutoring should also be tested.

REFERENCES

Aguti, J. N. (2000). Makerere University (Dual Mode University) Uganda. In V. V. Reddy and S. Manjulika, (Eds.), *The world of open and distance learning*. New Delhi: Viva Books Private Limited.

Bbuye, J. (2005, September 9 –28). *Distance education in Uganda*. Paper presented at the Seminar on Modern Distance Education. Jilin University, Peoples Republic of China.

Bbuye, J. (2006). *Towards developing a framework for support services for universities in Uganda*. Paper presented at the Fourth Pan-Commonwealth Forum On Open Learning. Retrieved from http://pcf4.dec.uwi.edu/viewabstract.php?id=52

Coronel-Ferrer, M. (2002). Politics of mobile phones. *A Philippine Journal of Third World Studies, 17*(2), 3–6.

Keegan, D. (2004, November 28–30). *Mobile learning–The next generation of learning*. Paper presented at the 18th Asian Association of Open University Annual Conference. Shangai, China. Retrieved from http://learning.ericsson.net/mlearning2/files/Des_paper_AAOU.pdf

Keegan, D. (1986). *The foundations of distance education*. London: Croom Helm.

Keegan, D. (Ed.). (2006). *Mobile learning: A practical guide*, p.150. Dun Laoghaire, Ireland: Ericsson,

Manjulika, S., & Reddy, V. V. (2000). Open and distance learning in transition. In V. V. Reddy and S. Manjulika (Eds.), *The world of open and distance learning*. New Delhi: Viva Books Private Limited.

Mariano, M. L. D., & De La Rosa, N. P. C. (2004). Beyond an institutionalized learning environment: Fostering interactions and learning using synchronous and asynchronous messaging systems. *Turkish Online Journal of Distance Education, 5*(3). Retrieved December 2, 2008, from http://tojde.anadolu.edu.tr/tojde15/pdf/mariano.pdf.

Mbarika, V., & Mbarika, I. (2006). *Burgeoning wireless networks connect Africans to the world and each other*. A publication in *Spectrum Online (IEEE), Africa Calling*. Retrieved December 2, 2008, from http://www.spectrum.ieee.org/may06/3426.

Moore, M. (2000). Is distance teaching more work or less? *The American Journal of Distance Education, 14*(3).

Nix, J., Russel, J., & Keegan, D. (2006). *Mobile learning/SMS (Short Messaging System), Academic administrtion kit*. Retrieved December 2, 2008, from http://www.eden-online.org/contents/publications/SMS/Ericsson.Mobile.A5.pdf.

Nonyongo, E., Mabusela, K., & Monene, V. (2005). *Effectiveness of SMS communication between university and students*. Institute for Continuing Education, UNISA Publication. Retrieved December 2, 2008, from www.mlearn.org.za/CD/papers/Nonyongo&%20Mabusela.pdf

Pabico, A. (2003). *Teaching through mobile technology debuts in schools*. Retrieved December 2, 2008, from http://ipsnews.net/interna.asp?idnews=18701

Ramos, A. J. O. (2006). *The viability of mobile SMS technology for non-formal distance learning in Asia: Promoting education for all*. A publication for Molave Development Foundation, Inc. Retrieved December 2, 2008, from www.pandora-asia.org/downloads/05-AAOU_Ramos.pdf

Siminyu, N. S. (2003). Distance education in universities in Uganda: An inventory. Paper presented at All Africa University Day Conference, Makerere University. (Unpublished).

Stone, A., Briggs, J., & Smith, C. (2002). SMS and interactivity—Some results from the field, and its implications on effective uses of mobile technologies in education. In *IEEE international workshop on wireless and mobile technologies in education* (WMTE02) (pp. 104–108).

Tait, A. (2003). Reflections on student support in open and distance learning. Retrieved December 2, 2008, from http://www.irrodl.org/index.php/irrodl/article/view/134/604.

Usun, S. (2004). Learner support services in distance education system (A case study of Turkey). *Turkish Online Journal of Distance Education, 5*(4). Retrieved December 2, 2008, from http://tojde.anadolu.edu.tr/tojde16/articles/s_usun.htm

APPENDIX
MAP OF UGANDA SHOWING MAKERERE UNIVERSITY CENTERS

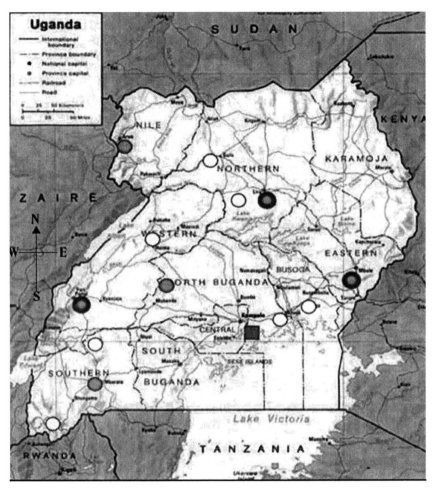

Key: ○ Regional Centres (with teaching); ◉ and with ICT Facilities
○ Resource Centres (for materials)
Available at http://distance.mak.ac.ug/de/centers_more.php

CHAPTER 8

THE IMPACT OF VIDEO CONFERENCING ON DISTANCE EDUCATION COURSES

A University of Namibia Case Study

Trudie Frindt

INTRODUCTION

It will be true to say that the demand for distance education in Namibia has been amply demonstrated over the years. Throughout the years, many Namibian citizens have enrolled at the University of South Africa (UNISA), while various vocational and school-certificates courses were offered by commercial South African correspondence colleges.

When the academy was established in 1980, it was realized that the demand for education in Namibia was increasing, and educationalists called for renewed commitment to expand educational efforts in Namibia. In 1984 the Distance Teaching section was established. It started with the Education Certificate Primary (51 students). In 1986 the Higher Primary

Bridging the Knowledge Divide, pages 149–161
Copyright © 2009 by Information Age Publishing
All rights of reproduction in any form reserved.

Education certificate was introduced (191 students). In 1989 the Distance Teaching section was extended, and new courses were introduced. With the establishment of the University of Namibia (1993), the academy as an institution ceased to operate. After the University of Namibia came into operation, distance education was reformed and restructured to offer education at the tertiary level. In the restructuring process, the Department of Distance Education, together with the newly established Department of Continuing Education, became the Center for External Studies (Beukes, 1998, p. 93).

Student support at the Center for External Studies (CES) is provided through nine regional centers that handle registration and fees, academic counseling, face-to-face tutorials, library resources, examinations, and local advertising. The northern campus, which is the largest regional center, is located at Oshakati and predominantly serves the four northern regions: Omusati, Ohangwena, Oshana, and Oshikoto. According to the official statistics of 2001, the total population of Namibia in 2001 was 1,830,330, of which 780,149 lived in the four northern regions. This equals 42.6% of the total population. Nearly half of the Namibian population is thus potentially served by the northern campus, which was established in 1998. At this point, it expanded UNAM's programs offered in the north beyond those offered by CES by open and distance learning and the full-time training program for nurses offered by UNAM's Faculty of Medical and Health Services. One of the main reasons for the establishment of the campus was to support UNAM distance education students who resided in the four northern regions. Apart from providing a registration point and place for students to write examinations, nearly half of the population lives 700 km or more from the capital city of Windhoek. Furthermore, apart from the main campus, the northern campus is also the only regional campus in Namibia that employs a video conferencing facility. The Ford Foundation sponsored this facility (see the distribution of UNAM centers in Appendix A).

In the mission of the University of Namibia, it is stated that learning throughout Namibia should be encouraged and promoted. In the light of this, the CES caters to the needs of persons who for a variety of reasons cannot attend residential classes at UNAM. CES therefore helps UNAM to fulfill its larger mission in terms of providing accessible and quality higher education through flexible and mixed-mode approaches to the people, wherever they may be located. In providing an enabling environment and leadership through innovative teaching methods, CES has enabled the university to increase its numbers of distance education students to 45% of the total number of UNAM students, making UNAM a dual-mode institution (CES Policy Document, 2005).

The focus of this case study was to see whether the introduction of video conferencing as a delivery mode could provide sufficient learning experiences and interactivity to enable distance education students to study successfully, while allowing for different learning styles. Thirty-eight distance education students at the Oshakati northern campus had to rely on interactive video conferencing to prepare them for their end-of-the-year examination. These students enrolled for their final year course in one of the two teaching-methods subjects, namely, Teaching Methods of Business Studies and Teaching Methods of Economics.

This research had its origin in 2005 when the above-mentioned students were informed that there was no study material available for the two subjects they had enrolled in. This information had the implication that the students would not be able to sit for their final exam in November 2005. Knowing what effect that could have on student performances, CES sought help from the full-time lecturer on the main campus, but soon discovered that the full-time students only made use of handouts and class notes, which obviously was not suited for distance education learning. The CES student-support staff then decided to find out where students were located. As it was clear that the majority of the students resided in the northern region of the country, CES was then confronted with three options. The first option, to ask students to attend full-time classes at the main campus, was rejected almost right away, as staff realized that it was unrealistic to expect distance education students to travel every week to the main campus. The second option of sending a lecturer to the Northern campus on specified dates also became a problem, as it was costly to travel to Oshakati, not to mention the financial implications of traveling allowances and accommodation. The next best thing was to concentrate on video conferencing. As the majority of students lived close enough to the Northern campus, it was possible to negotiate with the students to attend a three-hour video conference twice a week, stretched over a period of one month.

The choice to make use of video conferencing was therefore in line with what Cavanaugh (2001, p. 75) and others said with regard to distance education delivery methods. They claim that distance acquisition of knowledge is often an expensive and time-consuming process to institute and maintain, and that it is important to know whether distance education actually improves student performance and which distance education delivery methods and techniques are more effective, "so students get maximum benefit from society's investment in distance learning technology." This study will therefore discuss the effectiveness and interactivity of video conferencing on a group of distance education students at the Oshakati Northern campus, who had to rely on interactive video conferencing to prepare them for their end-of-the-year examination.

CONCEPTUAL FRAMEWORK

While research on technology-enhanced learning dates back to the beginning of the last century (De Vaney & Butler, 1996), research on video conferencing in Namibia is still in its infancy, as very little has been reported on the effectiveness of video conferencing in Namibia. In addition to the work done by Sherry (1996) and Alhalabi, Anadaptuam, and Hamza (1998), Heath and Holznagel (2002) and Amirian (2002) are all in agreement that video conferencing has a unique ability to promote interaction in the classroom. If the course encourages interactions, active learning models that follow the social constructivist model of Vygotsky (1978) predict that successful learning is likely to result. These learning models require students to construct their own knowledge in a self-directing manner and to take on more responsibility for their own learning.

In the well-known theory of distance teaching, conceptualized by Holmberg (1995), the notion that distance teaching will support student motivation and promote learning pleasure and effectiveness if learners are engaged in discussions and decisions is stressed and that the program should provide for real and simulated communication to and from the students. This means that distance education is believed to work well and produce results as effective as traditional classroom instruction (Kearsley, 1996, pp. 55–58). However, the distance education currently in practice has the potential to provide more effective learning with updated pedagogy, more experience, and greater understanding and knowledge of methods. Wagner (1998, p. 417) reported that distance learning practitioners tend to view interaction as the "single most significant attribute that defines a contemporary distance learning experience." Moore and Thompson (1990) suggested that improved distance education practices have the potential to enhance educational outcomes, especially when the amount and kind of learner interaction is increased and there is student-to-student interaction and teacher-to-student feedback.

The above findings resonate with that of Sherry (1996), who claims that interactivity represents the connectivity the students feel with the distance education lecturer, the facilitators, and their peers. Sherry (1996) states that without connectivity, distance learning degenerates into the old correspondence-course model of independent study. The student becomes autonomous and might experience feelings of increased isolation. In the worst situation, such students might drop out.

In a well-researched literature review on video conferencing, Amirian (2002) found that interaction is critical to any video conferencing-based learning situation. She argues that video conferencing should be used in ways that make full use of its unique qualities. Specifically, she says, "interaction is the key component of this use of the technology to support a more social learning, negotiating meaning through interaction." From research conducted by Irele (1999) on how video conferencing enables remote learners to be part of a social and socializing environment, it is evident that there is a greater awareness that in a video conferencing-based learning situation, a combination of media increases the chances of positive learning outcomes by increasing the range of learning styles that can be accommodated. Additional findings from Irele suggest that using several technologies to meet different instructional needs and learning styles will result in a richer, more effective instructional experience, not only for the lecturer but also for the student.

PURPOSE OF THE STUDY

The purpose of the study was to see whether the introduction of video conferencing as a delivery mode could provide sufficient learning experiences and interactivity to enable distance education students to study successfully while allowing for different learning styles. As mentioned earlier, this case study focused on 38 students who enrolled for a course in teaching methods of Economics and Business Studies; but due to the absence of distance education study material, they received intensive interactive video conferencing in preparing them for the end-of-the-year examination.

Although it was not the purpose of the research to compare the examination results of the two distance education groups with that of the full-time students on campus, the researcher saw it as a further opportunity to prove what impact video conferencing had on the performance of distance students when comparing them with their full-time counterparts, since both groups had different lecturers but sat for the same examination paper, which was compiled by the full-time lecturer at the main campus.

DESIGN AND METHOD

For the purpose of this case study, a qualitative method was employed. Results of the design are outlined as indicated below:

A literature review with particular reference to the interactivity of video conferencing was made.

Data Collection:
- Personal interviews were conducted with the student-support staff at CES, while several interviews were conducted over the phone with the tutor who was responsible for the video conferencing.

   – End-of-the-year examination results of distance education, as well
   as full-time student s' results were obtained and compared to support the study.

Data Processing:

   The research design followed a qualitative approach where descrip-
   tive statistics were applied.

Sampling:

   The sample considered in this study consisted of 38 distance education students, of whom 16 were enrolled for the course in Teaching
   Methods of Economic and 22 for the Teaching Methods of Business
   Studies. The language of instruction was English, and for all students, this was their second language.

The instrument:

   The study was done by means of personal interviews with the student-support staff at CES, while several interviews were conducted
   over the phone with the tutor who was responsible for the video
   conferencing.

PROCEDURE

As mentioned earlier, it was decided to use interactive video conferencing
on a group of 38 undergraduate distance education students who enrolled
for the course in Teaching Methods of Economic and Teaching Methods
of Business Studies, when CES student-support staff realized that these students were not going to have their study material in time to prepare them
for the end-of-the-year examination. Student-support staff at the main campus traced the students and informed them about the video conferencing
classes that were going to be held over a period of one month in order to
assist them with their studies and thus eliminate the problem of the non-
delivery of their learning materials. Since 32 of the students resided in the
northern regions, it was possible to organize video conferencing classes,
because it was much closer for the students to go to the Northern campus
than to travel to Windhoek. The remaining 6 students were living close to
the main campus and were able to travel to Windhoek every Tuesday and
Thursday. A survey was therefore conducted to determine how many students had access to e-mail, facsimile, and cell phone or telephone facilities.
As the majority of the students were teachers, it was possible to e-mail or fax
class notes to those schools that were equipped with fax or e-mail facilites.
Those students who had no access to fax or e-mail could collect copies from
the northern campus when they came for their classes.

   The CES student-support staff was also faced with the further problem of
finding a suitable tutor for the video conferencing teaching, since this sub-

ject was not offered before at distance education. After long discussions and many hours of interviewing various teachers and lecturers, it was decided to appoint a very dynamic teacher from one of the local senior secondary schools, who was teaching these two subjects at her school.

When interviewing the teacher who was responsible for the tutoring, she mentioned that she felt somewhat overwhelmed at first but felt that she could cope because of the simplicity of using the video conferencing system. She devoted much more time in preparing for the video conferencing classes then for her normal teaching at school. Rather than being a mere substitute for face-to-face interaction, she stated that a readjustment of teaching style and methodology was necessary. According to her, the greatest challenge of video conferencing was to make sure that the students received their handouts well in advance and remained involved in the course. She would e-mail handouts to those students who had access to the Internet and, at the same time, e-mail notes to the student-support staff at CES to be distributed to those who had access to fax facilities. Staff would also phone students, reminding them about classes and informing them where to pick up their class notes to prepare them for their next video conference class. During this one-month period, students wrote class tests, which were invigilated by staff from the northern campus and were collected and posted the following morning to the main campus. Assignments were faxed, e-mailed, or brought to the northern campus to be posted to CES.

The following quotation provides something of the flavor of the personal involvement that the tutor had with the students:

> I spent a lot of time on the telephone with the students. I told them to phone me if they had a problem. If they were not sure about their assignments, I told them to send me what they've got, and I would tell them if they're on the right track. Some of my students traveled more than 50 km to come to class; so, it was very important to make them feel part of a group and wanted. (Interview with lecturer, July, 2006)

When asked how she ensured interaction between her and the students and among the students themselves, she said that she encouraged them to work in groups and then also to have students report back in groups. She also mentioned that it was difficult to "read" the students, because the picture was not always clear, so she had to make sure that the presentation was lively to ensure that students did not loose interest.

> The greatest challenge was to get the handouts to the students before each session so that students could prepare well in advance, so that we did not waste any time on lecturing, but rather to concentrate on what they did not understand from the notes.

Although the tutor mentioned that it demanded lots of planning and hard work from her side, she was convinced that the high achievement rate scored by the distance education students came as a result of their determination and self-motivation to complete the course. She said that the students took responsibility for their own learning. They knew what they wanted, and nothing could stop them from achieving their goal.

The end-of-the-year results of this one-month interactive video conferencing and other technology-based support for the two distance education groups were satisfactory, to say the least. When the researcher discovered that the distance education students and the full-time students wrote the same examination paper at the end of the year, she saw it as a further opportunity to prove what impact video conferencing had on the performance of distance students when comparing their examination results with their full-time counterparts.

RESULTS

Teaching Methods of Economics

When comparing the examination results of the distance education students with those of the full-time students, it was surprising to find that the distance education students scored much higher in the examination than their full-time counterparts. Their highest score was 83%, with an average of 72%, while the highest score of full-time students was 71%, with an average of 65.2% (see Figure 8.1).

It is also worth mentioning that all 16 distance education students passed, while 5 obtained distinctions, whereas 3 of the full-time students failed.

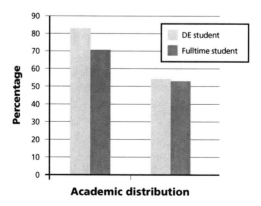

Figure 8.1 Distribution of academic performances of distance and full-time students.

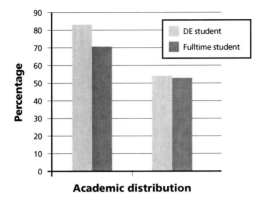

Figure 8.2   Distribution of academic performances of distance and full-time students.

Teaching Methods of Business Studies

When looking at the course in Teaching Methods of Business Studies, we found that of the 22 distance education students who enrolled for the course, only 2 were male, while the remaining 20 students were female. Their ages ranged from 32 to 58, with the average age being 42 years. Strangely enough, the same number of full-time students enrolled for the course. Their ages ranged from 22 to 30, with the average age being 26. Five of the 22 students were male, while 17 were female. Figure 8.2 illustrates the academic performances of the two groups of students.

As with the previous subject, all distance education students passed, while 7 students obtained 80% and higher. Although there were two full-time students who obtained 80% and higher, 4 of the 22 students failed the course.

DISCUSSION

A major conclusion from this case study is that video conferencing requires a different teaching methodology from any that the tutors in this case study have used before. The technology itself necessitates different ways of interacting, different ways of presenting information, and different ways of judging the meaning of the messages going in both directions.

At first impression, video conferencing appears to be a substitute for the usual classroom interaction and is, therefore, appealing as a teaching medium as it promises face-to-face experiences for teaching at a distance. The aim is for the technology to be clear so that interaction takes place as it would if the individuals were in the same room. When video conferencing is used effectively, a high level of interaction will occur between people who may be separated by many kilometers. Considerable preparation time is required for a video conferencing session. An interview with the tutor responsible for the video conferencing revealed that preparation for video conferencing sessions required additional effort for her to acquire and develop skills in the preparation of the teaching materials. Many of these skills relate to the preparation of distance education material such as print and nonprint resources to support a video conferencing session.

Video conferencing is not merely another version of face-to-face teaching; major modification of teaching strategies is essential so that focus is on interaction. First, video conferencing involves simultaneous teaching of two or more classes at different sites through the use of technology. Considerable effort is required to maximize interaction between the sites.

Second, just as with all types of teaching, there is need for variety of presentation techniques within video conferencing sessions. If a lecture strategy is necessary, the "talking" component of the lecture should be kept short, it should be supplemented by graphics or other visual material to emphasize and illustrate, and questions should be asked frequently to challenge the students and to check whether they are still on the same level of understanding.

Third, the capability of transmitting close-up images of small, two- and three-dimensional objects via the graphics camera at each site enables video conferencing to contribute a unique element to teaching and learning. For example, disclosure of the points being made during a lecture adds variety to a presentation as well as giving a conceptual overview.

Finally, while teaching in a face-to-face mode requires particular teaching competencies and presentation skills, teaching in a distance education mode requires equally demanding but different skills in which interaction is via printed material that has to be prepared a long time in advance of the student working on it. In video conferencing, both modes of interaction are used. As well as being an effective presenter, a video conferencing lecturer has to be highly organized ahead of time as he or she can't send teaching materials to the other members of the class at other sites during the session itself. Prior planning is essential so that materials are prepared and distributed well in advance of the session (Mitchell, 1993).

CONCLUSION AND IMPLICATIONS OF THIS STUDY

The traditional distance education student within the Namibian context has been that of a remote student, an independent learner, with a stand-alone package of study materials. The findings of this case study concurs with the general body of knowledge that distance education can be as effective as traditional face-to-face instruction since the methods and technologies used were appropriate to the instructional tasks. There have been numerous occasions of interaction between student and lecturer as well as between the students themselves, however there were significant differences between the two groups with regard to age and the final exam scores. Distance education students scored higher in both subjects. Yet, this is not sufficient evidence to conclude that distance education is superior to traditional education. Other factors may have contributed to these results. For example, the fact that the age of the distance education students may make up for motivation, determination, and life experience. This study also proved that instruction can be successful if lecturers identify themselves with the needs of the students and when they have empathy with their students.

A major implication from this study is that the use of video conferencing needs to be carefully planned and the rationale for its use clearly identified. It is not merely an electronic means of transmitting lectures to another site. When used as one of a range of "mixed mode" strategies and techniques, including use of intensive face-to-face workshops, distance education print packages, e-mail, telephone tutoring, and other means of teaching and learning at a distance, video conferencing becomes a powerful medium for interacting at a distance.

Through new technologies, video conferencing enables use of familiar face-to-face teaching/learning strategies with students at other locations. However, it also necessitates variations in teaching style and methodology to accommodate the characteristics of the technology. Therefore, initial use needs careful planning and considerable support. Because of the need to restructure existing material, to learn new techniques, and to change one's approach to teaching when using video conferencing, an emphasis on staff development is critical. Video conferencing confronts staff and challenges teaching methodologies. It demands a reassessment of the way in which a lecturer interacts with students and poses different limitations on students interacting with students at the other end. Techniques such as the use of a graphics camera to show summaries of notes, close-ups of pictures, diagrams, etc., and the need to vary the length and pace of a video conferencing session can all be essentials in an induction workshop, as lecturers will have initial anxieties about its use. These workshops should focus on the actual operation of the video conferencing system with an emphasis on "hands on" operation and should highlight the major, essential teaching strategies for effective initial use. According to Mitchell (1993, p. 55), "information overload" at this initial stage sometimes occurs when experienced users of video conferencing try to alert the new user of all the variations and even the pitfalls of video conferencing they have experienced, sometimes forgetting that the beginner user's needs are quite basic as they focus on "survival" strategies in initial use.

Finally, development of any new subject in which video conferencing should be a component should be developed as a mixed-mode subject, in that a variety of distance education techniques should be planned and implemented. Video conferencing should be used in those elements of the subject in which interaction is important. Different distance education strategies should be used for other components of a subject.

REFERENCES

Alhalabi, B., Anadaptuam, S., & Hamza, M. (1998). Real laboratories: An innovative rejoinder to the complexities of distance learning. *Journal of Open Praxis,* 24–30.

Amirian, S. (2002). Pedagogy and video conferencing: A review of recent literature. In A. Greenberg, *Navigating the sea of research on video conferencing-based distance education.* Wainhouse Research, Polycom, Inc., February 2004.

Beukes, H. (1998). The Center for External Studies (CES) at the University of Namibia. In *Learner support services: Case studies of DEASA member institutions.* Pretoria, South Africa: UNISA Press.

Cavanaugh, C.S, (2001). The effectiveness of interactive distance education technologies in K-12 learning. *International Journal of Educational Telecommunications, 7*(1), 73–88.

De Vaney, A., & Butler, R.O. (1996). Voices of the founders: Early discourse in technology. In D. H. Jonassen (Ed.), *Handbook of research for educational communications and technology.* New York: Simon and Schuster Macmillan.

Heath, M. J., & Holznagel, D. (2002). Interactive video conferencing: A literature review. *NECC,* June 2002.

Holmberg, B. (1995). *Theory and practice of distance education.* London: Routledge.

Irele, M. (1999). Relative effectiveness of distance learning systems. In *Lucent Technologies and the World Campus,* Pennsylvania State University Press.

Kearsley, G. (1996). Education as usual: Comments on Chris Dede's article. *The American Journal of Distance Education, 10*(2), 55–58.

Mitchell, J. (1993). Interacting at a distance: Staff and student perceptions of teaching and learning via video conferencing. *Australian Journal of Educational Technology. 9*(1), 41–58.

Moore, M. G., & Thompson, M. M. (1990). *The effects of distance learning: A summary of literature.* Research Monograph No. 2. University Park, PA: American Center for the Study of Distance Education.

Sherry, L. (1996). Issues in distance learning. *International Journal of Educational Telecommunications, 1*(4), 337–365.

Vygotsky, L.S. (1978). *Mind in society.* Cambridge, MA: Harvard University Press.

Wagner, E. (1998). Interaction strategies for online training designs. Paper presented at the 14th Annual Conference on Distance Teaching & Learning, Madison, WI.

APPENDIX:
DISTRIBUTION OF UNIVERSITY CENTERS IN NAMIBIA

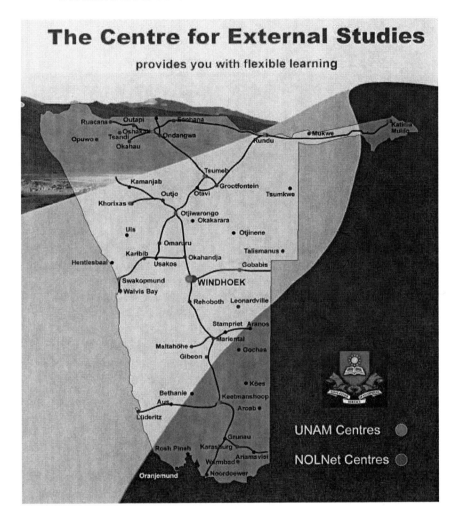

CHAPTER 9

OPEN RESOURCES FOR OPEN LEARNING IN DEVELOPING COUNTRIES

Deciphering Trends for Policies, Quality, and Standards Considerations

Wanjira Kinuthia

INTRODUCTION

Globally, higher education throughout is in continual transition, and one cannot underestimate the influence of technology on the everyday life of learners and educators. There is considerable evidence of a technology and information gap that exists among those who have access to information and communication technology (ICT) (Hess & Leal, 2001). Access to ICT in developing nations has lagged, keeping poor, rural, and minority populations from participating and benefiting from the ICT revolution. This trend is inevitably carried into the higher-education environment (Hamilton, 2001). Educational institutions encounter challenges pertaining to ICT infrastructure, training, and content development. Open and distance

Bridging the Knowledge Divide, pages 163–181
Copyright © 2009 by Information Age Publishing
All rights of reproduction in any form reserved.

education (ODL) and similarly, e-learning, are among the forces influencing higher education. A major role of higher education is to ensure learners are suited to, and competent for, their social and occupational roles (Herman, 1995). These attributes include the commitment to providing the less advantaged with an opportunity for education with an emphasis on learning and scholarship. In light of these trends and limitations, the purpose of this chapter is to discuss emerging ICT trends in the development and use of open educational resources (OER) and to review recommendations for ensuring high quality and sustainability.

OPEN AND DISTANCE EDUCATION

For the purposes of this discussion, it is necessary to clarify the terms, especially when making a case for the use of OER. Distance education encompasses print-based and electronic learning resources used to connect learners, resources, and instructors, where the learning group is separated by time and/or geographical distance. Distance learning, on the other hand, is the system and a process that connects learners with distributed learning resources that include electronic resources. The mode can be synchronous or asynchronous and is generally characterized by separation of place and time in a learning community (Hill, 1997; Willis & Dickinson, 1997).

Open learning is an approach that allows learners flexibility and choice over what, when, at what pace, where, and how they learn, and is commonly delivered via distance education. The complexity of open-learning terminology is in it's close association with ICT development (Davis, 1996). Thus, open and distance learning (ODL) commonly utilizes ICTs to provide or enhance learning. It focuses on expanding access to learning and is characterized by its philosophy of removing barriers and increasing access and choice by utilizing ICT (Perraton, 2000). In many developing nations, ODL is not necessarily used as a cost-saving approach, but rather to promote wider objectives that aim to reach learners in remote areas.

E-learning is the delivery of instructional content via electronic means, including the Internet, intranets, satellite broadcasts, audio tapes, video tapes and conferencing, virtual classrooms, digital collaboration, and CD-ROM (Gabriel, 2000, Klein & Ware, 2003). Simply put, e-learning is merely another mode of technology-aided teaching and learning. It is viewed as a blanket term for its predecessors: computer-based learning, Web-based learning, online learning, and other buzz terms of the 1980s and 1990s. In its present form, many learners engaged in e-learning may not be geographically distanced from the institution. In fact, some observers see distance learning as not being synonymous with e-learning.

E-learning has moved toward automation of administrating teaching and learning via software known as Learning Management Systems (LMS). LMS are not pedagogically neutral technologies, but through their design, they can influence and guide teaching. A growing trend is the "hybrid" or "blended" or "multimodal" instructional approaches that replace or supplement partial face-to-face instruction with online instruction that takes advantage of LMS. To facilitate e-learning, institutions have embraced proprietary LMS tools such as WebCT and Blackboard (Bennett & Bennett, 2003). The adoption of LMS worldwide has been fueled by several issues: 1) Possible means of increasing the efficiency of teaching; 2) Possibility of enhancing the learning process; 3) New student expectations that are fueled by advancing technologies; 4) Competitive pressure between institutions; 5) Proposed means of responding to increasing demands for access to higher education; and 6) A culture shift occurring in higher education (Coats et al., 2005).

OPEN EDUCATIONAL RESOURCES

The term Open Educational Resources (OER) came out of the United Nations Educational, Scientific, and Cultural Organization (UNESCO) Forum on the *Impact of Open Courseware for Higher Education in Developing Countries* (2002) and the *Second Global Forum on International Quality Assurance, Accreditation, and the Recognition of Qualifications in Higher Education* (2004), based on sharing of knowledge and information, the goal of which was to "increase human intellectual capacity" (Johnstone, 2005). A common definition of OER is "digitized materials that are offered freely and openly for educators, students and self-learners to use and re-use for teaching, learning, and research."

Cedergren (2003) uses the term "open content," where he views "content" as being produced collectively for nonprofit purposes. Further, he states "content is just about anything that is not executable and can be anything digital (not software) that can be distributed or accessed electronically, including images, audio files, movies and text." Examples include open-library resources, open-access journals, and e-books, which challenges traditional modes of scholarly research, publication, and research dissemination. This is creating new forms of information distribution and supply in the publishing industry, prompting a reevaluation of how research is accessed and distributed (May, 2005; Schopfel, 2005; Snowhill, 2001).

The term has grown to include: 1) Learning resources that encompass courseware, content modules, learning objects, learner-support and assessment tools, online learning communities; 2) Resources to support educators including tools, support materials, and training; and 3) Resources to assure the quality of education and educational practices. OER have common defining features (Hylén, 2006): 1) Open courseware and content; 2) Open software tools such as LMS; 3) Open material for e-learning capacity building of faculty staff; 4) Learning objects repositories; and 5) Free educational courses. For instance, there are over 150 universities in China participating in the China Open Resources for Education initiative, with over 450 courses online. Likewise, there are over 2000 courses offered through OER projects in Australia, Brazil, Canada, Hungary, India, Iran, Ireland, the Netherlands, Portugal, Russia, South Africa, Spain, Thailand, the United Kingdom, the United States, and Vietnam (Hylén, 2006).

Alongside the growth of OER has been the continual development of open-source software (OSS), which refers to software programs that are distributed with the source code. OSS licenses allow users the flexibility to run programs for their purpose, to study and modify them, and to freely redistribute copies of the original or modified program (Coppola & Neelley, 2004). Although OSS development has been around for over two decades, it has developed mainly in infrastructure domains such as network, server, and browsers. Contrary to popular belief, many OER projects have not arisen spontaneously from the goodwill of freelance software developers and educators, but rather are the result of government or foundation funding where developers, whether contractors, university employees or contractors, are paid to work on projects (Dalziel, 2003). Table 9.1 presents examples of currently available OSS.

There are many options for OER currently available, and the list continues to grow. Many of these are university or foundation initiatives, for example the Andrew Mellon Foundation. Table 9.1 provides a noncomprehensive list of resources that purposefully take into account global users. Many OER and OSS overlap in their features, output, and goals. Therefore, Table 9.2 presents a list of currently available OER listed in alphabetical order.

TABLE 9.1   Examples of Open-Source Software (OSS)

Function	Resource	URL
Web browser	Mozilla	http://www.mozilla.org
Web filtering	Dansquardian	http://dansguardian.org
E-mail filtering	Spam Assassin	http://spamassassin.apache.org
Office Suite	OpenOffice	http://www.openoffice.org
Image editor	The GIMP	http://www.gimp.org
Course Management	Moodle	http://moodle.org
Web Server	Apache	http://www.apache.org
Database	MySQL	http://www.mysql.com
Operating System	Linux	http://www.linux.org
Content Management/Web Application	Joomla!	http://www.joomla.org

TABLE 9.2   Examples of Open Educational Resources (OER)

Open Educational Resource	Resource Description and Features
Connexions http://cnx.org/	• Collaborative environment for developing, sharing, and publishing scholarly content on the Web. • Content is organized into modules that are connectable to larger collections or courses. Free to use under Creative Commons "attribution" license.
Commonwealth of Learning (COL) WikiEducator http://www.wikieducator.org	• Portal for development of free educational content. • Uses similar software to Wikipedia for courses. • Creates online communities for example Virtual University for Small States of the Commonwealth.
Dspace http://www.dspace.org/	• Digital library system to capture, store, index, preserve, and redistribute output of university's research faculty in digital formats. • Developed jointly by MIT Libraries and Hewlett-Packard (HP). • Freely available to research institutions worldwide.
Fedora http://www.fedora.info/	• Jointly developed by University of Virginia and Cornell University. • Scalable general-purpose digital-object repository system that supports repositories, digital libraries, content management, digital asset management, scholarly publishing, and digital preservation.
Harvard Open Collections Program (OCP) http://ocp.hul.harvard.edu	• Provides online access to Harvard's libraries, archives, and museums. • The goal is to offer a new model for digital collections for users around the world.
The Open University "LearningSpace" http://openlearn.open.ac.uk/	• Provides free access to Open University course materials. • The LearningSpace is open to learners anywhere in the world.
Learning Activity Management System (LAMS) http://www.lamsinternational.com	• Tool for designing, managing, and delivering online collaborative learning activities. • Provides educators with visual authoring environment for creating sequences of learning activities. • Managed by Macquarie University, Australia.
Massachusetts Institute of Technology's (MIT) OpenCourseWare (OCW) http://ocw.mit.edu/OcwWeb/index.htm	• Large-scale electronic publishing initiative funded jointly by William and Flora Hewlett Foundation, Andrew W. Mellon Foundation, MIT, and Ab Initio software company. • Provides free, searchable access to MIT's course materials for educators, students, and self-learners globally. • Aims to extend the reach and impact OER concept.

(continued)

TABLE 9.2 Examples of Open Educational Resources (OER) (continued)

Open Educational Resource	Resource Description and Features
Moodle http://www.moodle.org	• LMS designed to help educators create online courses. • Has strong grounding in social constructionist pedagogy. • Downloadable, modifiable, and distributable under terms of the GNU General Public License. • Runs without modification on most servers in a single database. • Available in 40 languages.
Multimedia Educational Resource for Learning and Online Teaching (MERLOT) http://taste.merlot.org/	• Searchable collection of peer-reviewed learning materials created by registered members, and a set of faculty development support services. • Goal is to improve the effectiveness of teaching and learning by increasing the quantity and quality of peer reviewed OER that are easily incorporated into instructor designed courses.
National Science Digital Library (NSDL) http://nsdl.org/	• Created by the US National Science Foundation (NSF) to provide organized access to high-quality resources and tools that support innovations in teaching and learning at all levels of science, technology, engineering, and mathematics education.
Open Archives Initiative (OAI) http://www.openarchives.org/	• Develops and promotes interoperability standards that aim to facilitate the efficient dissemination of content. • Has roots in efforts to enhance access to e-print archives as a means of increasing the availability of scholarly communication.
Open Directory Project (ODP) http://www.dmoz.org	• Large project with over 3 million hierarchically organized links that are edited by over 50,000 volunteer editors. • Operated by Netscape/America Online. • Google and other search engines access data from ODP. • Requires that in return for the use of its content a small banner, recruiting new editors.

Open Knowledge Initiative (OKI) http://www.okiproject.org/	• Collaborative project started at Massachusetts Institute of Technology (MIT) in 2001 with funding from Andrew W. Mellon Foundation with collaboration among leading universities. • Provides a modular development platform for building both traditional and innovative applications. • Designed for broad adoption in the higher-education domain and is scalable and adaptable.
Open Learning Support (OLS) http://mit.ols.usu.edu/index_html	• Utah State University's (USU) self-managed OER for educators and learners worldwide. • Supports USU's mission by engaging the public, cultivating diversity of thought and culture, and supporting learning. • Linked to 2,200 modules in Connexions collection and provides discussion services for MITs OCW initiative.
Open Source Portfolio Initiative (OSPI) http://www.osportfolio.org/	• Collaborative, open-source, software development project based on the University of Minnesota's (U of NM) Enterprise System's electronic portfolio software in collaboration with University of Delaware. • Collaboration to develop nonproprietary, open-source electronic portfolio software.
Sakai http://www.sakaiproject.org	• Free and open-source product that is built and maintained by the Sakai community. • Development model is called "Community Source" because many of the developers creating Sakai are drawn from the "community" of organizations.
Uportal http://www.uportal.org/	• Free, sharable portal under development by institutions of higher education. • Provides community tools, such as chat, forums, survey to build relationships among campus constituencies.
Wikipedia http://www.wikipedia.org	• Global contribution to a Wiki-based collaborative project. • Goal is to build a collectively created online encyclopedia. • Available in multiple languages.
Wikimedia Commons http://commons.wikimedia.org/	• Media repository created and maintained not by paid-for by volunteers. • Part of the Wikimedia umbrella. • Provides a central repository for freely licensed photographs, diagrams, animations, music, spoken text, video clips.

As an example, the MIT OCW site is increasingly global, although there is a predominance of North American visitors. On average, 36% of the visitors came from North America; 16% each from East Asia and Western Europe; 11% each from Latin America and Eastern Europe; and 9% from the Middle East, Africa, the Pacific, Central Asia, and the Caribbean combined. Typically, self-learners make up 48% of users: 31% are students, while only 15% are educators (Hylén, 2006). These statistics can be interpreted to imply that either potential users from developing countries are unaware of the options available or that they lack the infrastructure to access them. An examination of benefits and challenges would therefore help potential users tap into the available resources.

BENEFITS AND CHALLENGES
OF OPEN EDUCATIONAL RESOURCES

The open-source development model in higher education has the advantage of having educators involved in the development software (Coppola & Neelley, 2004); and in the last decade, higher education has begun to develop OER such as LMS, content-management systems (CMS), and electronic portfolios, influencing the move away from proprietary software. The growth of OER has also been driven by dissuading factors that include limited budgets and growing resentment of vendor power. The collaborative nature of OER across boundaries and cultural appeal in higher education has also influenced its growth. Advocates regard OER as an agile, practice-led initiative that addresses the issue of cost, as most products are usually freely available for public download (Fitzgerald, 2004). Benefits of OER include 1) Low or no cost to users, as products are generally free to access and download; 2) Shorter developmental cycle than proprietary software due to the collaborative, parallel efforts of developers; and 3) High-quality products, for example Apache Web server, Linux operating system, and Mozilla Firefox browser.

By the same token, OER faces challenges that include targeting and maintaining development talent, maintaining code quality, project initiation, code modularity, stability, and standardization. There is skepticism over the motivation behind open resources, where critics equate open source to open standards (Coppola & Neelley, 2004). Concerns have also been raised about the "sudden availability" of educational resources. This is countered by residents and advocates (Fitzgerald, 2004) of developing countries, who cite imperialistic views of the critics, noting that when resources are shared, it means that knowledge is shared, and "knowledge is power." Altruistic motivation to bridge the knowledge and technology divide is seen to be a leading reason behind OER (Johnstone, 2005). Further, Cedergren (2003) presents other reasons behind developing open resources:

1. Collaborative environment;
2. Learning new information and skills;
3. Benefit for end users;
4. Receiving feedback;
5. Intrinsic motivation;
6. Altruism, even when content is used commercially;
7. Open content as a new business opportunity;
8. Possibility of publicity; and
9. Indirect revenue.

Witten et al. (2002) state, for example, that digital libraries are a key technology for developing countries. Many countries have to grapple with human-development issues, and digital resources can provide a noncommercial mechanism for distributing humanitarian information on topics such as health, agriculture, nutrition, hygiene, sanitation, and water supply. In particular, various areas can benefit from open content:

1. Dissemination of humanitarian information, particularly where traditional publishing and distribution mechanisms have failed;
2. Preservation and propagation of indigenous cultures by opening the possibilities of flexible and coherent multimedia collections that are searchable and browsable in multiple dimensions and allow active participation by local and indigenous people in preserving and disseminating their own culture;
3. Locally produced collections of information, for example, teaching materials. Such collections have the advantage of providing relevant information that is readily available locally, yet is easily adaptable to other contexts; and
4. New opportunities to enter the global marketplace by saving costs associated with a fair competitive edge.

The growth of OER is occurring quite rapidly, leaving several issues to be examined. First, the debate as to what "open" really means remains unresolved. Some dichotomize open as commercial versus noncommercial, while others classify open according to the four freedoms: copy, modify, redistribute, or redistribute modified versions. Still others would argue that with freedom comes responsibility to contribute back to society (Downes, 2007). In response, content developers can determine the extent to which resources can be open. Second, in developing nations, limited access to high-speed Internet connection has meant that users may not be able to maximize on the extent of available resources. Third, differing curricula often require the instructor to modify the structure of OER to make it contextually relevant. Hence, much of the content is often used to supplement other instructional materials and learning tools. Fourth, the presumed lack of support (especially technical) that comes with proprietary software when OER does not perfectly meet the end-user's needs is challenging (Dalziel, 2003). In response, many contributors and users take advantage of social learning networks such as blogs and discussion forums to share experiences and recommendations.

SUSTAINING OPEN EDUCATIONAL RESOURCES

"Sustainable does not equate to cost free" and the production of open resources can result in a large-scale investment. As an example, the Open University of the United Kingdom spends about $3 million USD per course on content development. It has over 200 undergraduate courses in the inventory, representing a total investment of $600 million USD (40% of the budget). Sustainable does, therefore, not imply "cost free" (Downes, 2007). Sustainability should go beyond the cost of the resource itself to include additional costs such as training, making certain infrastructural considerations:

1. Technology that includes hardware, software, connectivity, and standards;
2. Organizational structure that accounts for technical competencies and training; and
3. Policies that address openness and the business model.

The difficulty in sustaining external funding-dependant projects is that they are susceptible to collapse when project funding ends. This is a problem that may not be well-understood by governments or foundations (Dalziel, 2003). However, this does not mean that there are no useful outcomes from such funded projects, because even when the project ends and the community of developers disbands, the source code is still useful to others or other projects, particularly if it is widely available and well-documented. Downes (2007) discusses four considerations to ensure OER is sustainable: Funding, technical, content, and staffing (organizational). Various models of funding are currently in place in several projects and organizations:

1. Endowment Model: The project obtains base funds that are sustained from interest earned, for example, the Stanford Encyclopedia of Philosophy.

2. Membership Model: A coalition of organizations contributes funds as seed money, annual contributions, or subscription. The funds generate operating revenues, for example Sakai.
3. Donations Model: The project receives donations from the community. Funds are managed by a nonprofit foundation, for example, Wikipedia, Apache, and Mozilla Firefox.
4. Conversion Model: First the consumer gets something for free and is later converted into a paying customer, for example, Learning Activity Management System (LAMS).
5. Contributor-Pay Mode: Contributors pay for the cost of maintaining the project, and thereafter the provider makes the contribution available for free. Wellcome Trust and Public Library of Science (PLoS) have adopted this model.
6. Sponsorship Model: The model ranges from commercial messages to sponsorship messages, for example, the China Open Resources for Education (CORE).
7. Institutional Model: Funding is part of a university's regular program and is justified in its organizational mission, for example, MIT's OCW projects.
8. Governmental Mode: Similar to the institutional model, the model represents direct funding for projects by agencies, for example, Canada's SchoolNet project. The United Nations is also involved in similar funding models.
9. Partnerships and Exchanges: Partnerships depend less on funds and more on exchange of resources. For example, a UNESCO conference for an Open Source Congress was proposed to be a voluntary, collaborative effort where universities would use their technical and functional expertise to work on the high-level design and planning for the next generation open source, administrative systems.

Technical considerations must also be taken into account (Downes, 2007). There are two models that are commonly used: 1) Resources are downloaded and used by putting together a collection of resources; and 2) Resources are downloaded, adapted, and sent back to the system repository for potential use by others. There needs to be an organizational structure that promotes continuity of a project. Two models that are generally used are 1) the community model, where the reputation of the project is a natural outgrowth of interactions, and mutual use and respect is developed; and 2) the emergent model where reputation is an outgrowth other larger organizations but users have less of a contributing authority, except in the aggregate.

Content should be developed in a manner that ensures a long lifespan, to determine that it will be used (and reused) in the most efficient manner.

This call for flexibility and sustainability of OER calls for the development of reusable learning objects and should be developed in a manner that is applicable on a local context level (Wiley, 2000). It is important for the following content considerations to be in place: 1) resources stored in distributed databases; 2) resources are downloadable for adaptation and use; 3) a centrally maintained index of resource; 4) resources are dynamic and regularly updated; and 5) the index includes a full history of the version cycles and users feedback (UNESCO, 2002a).

Access and usability issues should be addressed to ensure browsing, searching, and data-mining tools are available to users. Mechanisms to assist dissemination, adaptation, evaluation, and use of resources must also be in the organizational plan. UNESCO has taken initiatives toward this goal by establishing a Global Index System, which helps potential users to easily locate existing resources. UNESCO/IIEP hosts a Wiki with OER resources, and lists several other portals, gateways, and repositories (UNESCO, 2002a, 2005).

QUALITY ASSURANCE: IMPLEMENTING STANDARDS AND POLICIES

Dalziel (2003) brings up the debate between open standards and open source, noting that the answer is obviously not so simple. He states that "open standards are transparent descriptions of data and behavior that form the basis of interoperability" (p. 5). ODL is often criticized, because governing policies are often not coordinated with provision of resources, development of supporting infrastructures, and training of users of distance education. Further, ODL tends to be introduced without adequate understanding of the organizational culture and context, and the political, physical, economic, social, and technological environment (Kinyanjui, 1998). In addition, ODL is sometimes introduced hastily or arbitrarily in a top-down manner, when instead, decisions should be made as to whether a top-down or a bottom-up approach should be used to integrate ICT. The top-down approach assumes that formulating goals, organizational structures, management approaches, and implementing technological advancements should bring about change. On the other hand, the bottom-up approach is one that should facilitate change from the point of view of middle-level administrators, educators, and learners, who work directly with the technology (Surry & Farquhar, 1997).

Lack of clarification of policies to guide the use of OER is a barrier to participation for potential educators. These polices can be categorized into several areas: 1) Academic policies refer to quality, accreditation, grading, program evaluation, admissions, credentialing, mission compliance, and curriculum review; 2) Fiscal, geographical, and governance policies cover fees, interstate or intercountry relationships, consortia agreements, and contracts with collaborating agreements; 3) Educator-related e-learning policies that address compensation, workload, design and development, incentives, staff development, support, evaluation, and intellectual freedom issues; 4) Legal policies refer to intellectual property agreements, copyright, and educator/learner/institutional liability; 5) Learner-related policies address support, access, advising, training, financial aid, assessment, access to resources, equipment requirements, and privacy; 6) Technical polices define reliability, connectivity, technical support, hardware/software access; 7) Philosophical policies are developed to define a clear understanding of approach, faculty autonomy, organizational values and missions, enhanced public access, organization, governance, partnerships, and financial support; 8) Instructional design and course-development policies that address learning goals and content presentation, interactions, assessment, instructional media and tools, and learner support; and 9) Program evaluation, a meta-activity that incorporates all the aspects of the e-learning experience (Frydenberg, 2002; Gellman-Danley, 1997; Simonson, 2002).

There are other barriers to implementing quality-assurance (QA) systems due to incompatibility and acceptance of systems between institutions and countries. However, the use of OER calls for well-defined frameworks and methods that are ratified by high standards, because without well-elaborated quality management, it is difficult to attain high user satisfaction (Kefalas et al., 2003). Information on the quality of the courses and programs needs to be clear to the educational sector, learners, employees, and decision- and policymakers. The QA should consist of the policies, actions, and procedures necessary to ensure high standards are maintained and enhanced.

The QA system should address coursework, educators concerns, technology, instructional methods, services provided, and organizational and managerial structure. To do so, it should specify certain attributes: 1) Availability and reliability of the platform and staff; 2) Usability that is effective and efficient; 3) Learning effectiveness; 4) Performance within given constraints such as time and resources; 5) Security and action plan in response to online threats such as hacking, protection of intellectual property (where applicable), and safekeeping of personal information.

In recent years, several universities, as discussed above, have chosen to release their LMS under open-source licenses, for example the Sakai Project and MIT's Stellar. These have grown in collaboration with a standards-development program, the Open Knowledge Initiative (OKI), drawing interest in its potential to forge industrywide standards (Coats et al., 2005). There are over 30 nations currently supporting open universities and conventional universities establishing open-learning programs that take advantage of OER (UNESCO, 2002). In addition, there has been a larger scope of adoption of standards by e-learning vendors, particularly through the adoption of the Shareable Content Object Reference Model (SCORM) from Advanced Distributed Learning (ADL) (Dalziel, 2003). SCORM is a standard for Web-based e-learning that defines how individual instruction elements are combined on a technical level and sets conditions for software needed for using the content.

For governments and foundations to intervene in addressing the challenges tied to standards, there should be channels that assist in the development and implementation of standards, which utilize OER, and pilot the practicalities of implementing standards. The formation of standards testing/certification organization that are monitored by government bodies, for instance the UNESCO, can potentially encourage wider adoption of standards through assurance of standards conformance. As noted earlier, the approach adopted by MERLOT is to invite volunteer contributions and then subject the material to professional review by peer committees. Although this slows down the process of making the resources available, it ensures that content meets established standards.

While many universities have committees tasked with putting policies in place, many do not explicitly address the overall technological strategic plan toward OER and in many cases, educators are not involved in the actual development of institutional policies. Additionally, many educators are unfamiliar with existing policies, although some would be interested in being more active in the policy-development process but lack the time to do so. Educators are, however, bound by policies, which in most cases require that the institution holds all the rights to any content developed on behalf of the institution. In addition, many educators are unclear about intellectual-property-rights policies, and the information is not always clearly communicated. In the end, potential participants are apprehensive about developing coursework for the Web environment until they have clear knowledge of who owns the material, as it is often unclear as to who owns the rights to the instructional material (Kinuthia, 2003). OER policy should cover a wide range of areas (Rahtz, 2006). These include

1. Resource acquisition that considers open resources alongside proprietary solutions in procurements;
2. Institutional, national, or international standards for data storage;
3. Research contracts and exploitation of inventions;
4. Work contracts; and
5. Training plans.

Based on individual institutional missions, it is important to form program-evaluation advisory committees with representation from administration, educators, and learners, with representation from academic affairs, information technology services, library services, and partnerships and liaisons that work with the programs (Lape & Hart, 1997). Thus, before institutional policies can be changed, each individual institution should determine what the administration knows about OER and the importance that is placed on the policies. To address policies for successful OER integration, several approaches are recommended. First, policies should be integrated gradually and seamlessly to incorporate the concept of distant delivery of instruction. Second, learners should be defined by their enrollment in a course, not by whether they are distant or on campus. Third, initially, policies should be separate from existing policies. Ultimately, policies can be integrated to indicate that OER are regular components of instructional delivery, as learners and educators become more proficient with the ICT.

When making recommendations for policies, several questions should be considered before settling on developing and using OER. Each organization should respond to existing or potential concerns: 1) Do educators have portability rights to take the material with them when they leave? 2) In the event that another educator teaches the course, does the developer receive compensation? and 3) Should copyright be in the name of the developer or the school? If these questions cannot be clearly answered, it is unlikely that educators will be willing to participate. Based on these questions, the following is recommended:

1. Copyright ownership policies written to allow educators to have reasonable latitude with their own work;
2. The extent to which institutions have the authority to determine, suggest, or decide use of OER should be clearly addressed;
3. It is to the advantage of the institutions and the educators to define each participating member's ownership rights, and all parties should know who owns the final product; and
4. Compensation and workload, design and development incentives, support, and promotion and tenure should also be taken into account.

When faculty have leverage with their work and they are part of the decision-making process, they will be more likely to take initiative and ownership of the OER development process and the end product (Gellman-Danley, 1997).

Creative Commons (2006), a nonprofit organization, was founded on the notion that some authors may not want to exercise all of the intellectual-property rights the law affords them. Creative Commons works to define an alternative to copyrights by filling in the gap between full copyright, where use of resources is not allowed without explicit permission, and public domain, where permission is not required at all. Creative Commons Licenses allow users to copy and distribute their work under specific conditions, general descriptions, and legal clauses. To this end, Creative Commons has developed a set of free public licenses to enable authors to share their work with others. Authors have the flexibility to specify that the use of their resources would require attribution, that it be noncommercial, or that the product be shared under the same license. Thus, while "open" on the one hand can mean "without cost," it does not necessarily translate to "without conditions" (Downes, 2007).

The key to collaborative decision making when incorporating technology into education is for both bottom-up and top-down administration to ask the following questions when reviewing guidelines: Are there mission-critical problems that are unresolved under the current practices? Do the problems affect a majority of the educators and learners? Does ICT provide any real value educationally, and is OER a solution for these problems? If the answer is no, then perhaps the institution may not be ready to move in the OER direction.

CONCLUSION

The area of integration of technology in education is a continuous effort that revolves around looking for factors and practices that can be applied to encourage faculty to integrate technology in their areas of teaching. With the exponential growth of Internet resources, the challenge that remains is to keep the practices and guidelines current and accurate. While each institution has its own administrative approach, it is important for administrators and educators to communicate with each other and to work together in policy development. The question of suitability of OER for both institutions and learners is an area of concern for many. Is quality assurance an initiative of administrations or voluntary action on the part of the faculty? If it is voluntary, how much input from educators is taken into account? Is policy formation a top-down or bottom-up approach? When planning, implementing, and maintaining OEI, governing policies must be carefully developed, guided by needs analysis, examination of barriers, and a participatory evaluation process.

Education had often been cited as a major instrument of economic and social change. Moreover, this is emphasized more in developing nations and addressed in the millennium development goals (MDGs). Further, developing countries lack the requisite hardware and dependable bandwidth, especially in rural settings. Thus, OER implementation requires a different approach in developing countries. This requires engaging governments, institutions, and communities on a sustained basis. In addition, the percentage of bandwidth users seems dismal in most of these countries, but the absolute number of potential users of educational material are actually greater than many developed countries, due to a large population base. As opposed to simply implementing uniform OER structure, the availability of good educational material tailored to the requirement of a local population, for example, would have a ready market in many settings in developing nations. Because technology is constantly changing, the policies also require regular revision and updating. It is not suggested that OER should completely replace institutionally supported ODL. Rather, it should be viewed as a source for sharing resources, especially for those who would have limited access. As technology continues to evolve, the policies governing instructional ICT will become more complex and accumulative, requiring continuous review to remain current and valid.

REFERENCES

Bennett , J., & Bennett, L. (2003). A review of factors that influence the diffusion of innovation when structuring a faculty training program. *Internet and Higher Education, 6,* 53–63.

Cedergren, M. (2003). Open content and value creation. *First Monday, 8*(8).

Coats, H., James, R., & Baldwin, G. (2005). A critical examination of the effects of learning management systems on university teaching and learning. *Tertiary Education and Management, 11,* 19–36.

Creative Commons (2006). Choosing a license. Creative Commons.

Coppola, C., & Neelley, E. (2004). *Open source–opens learning: Why open source makes sense for education.* Retrieved from http://dlist.sir.arizona.edu/453/01/Open-SourceOpensLearningJuly2004.pdf

Dalziel, J. (2003). Open standards versus open source in e-learning. *Educase Quarterly, 4,* 4–7.

Davis, H. J. (1996). A review of open and distance learning within management development. *Journal of Management Development, 15*(4), 20–34.

Downes, S. (2007). Models for sustainable open educational resources. *Interdisciplinary Journal of Knowledge and Learning Objects, 3,* 29–44.

Fitzgerald, B. (2004). A critical look at open source. *Computer, 37*(7), 92–94.

Frydenberg, J. (2002). Quality standards in e-learning: A matrix of analysis. *International Review of Research in Open and Distance Learning, 2*(3), 1–15.

Gabriel, A. (2000). E-learning can be worlds apart from plain distance learning. *Business Journal, 20*(30), 28–29.

Gellman-Danley, B. (1997). Who sets the standards? Accreditation and distance learning. *New Directions for Community Colleges, 99,* 73–82.

Hamilton, K.H. (2001). Historically black colleges strive to bring campus communities up to technological speed. *Black Issues in Higher Education, 18*(2), 30–33.

Herman, H. (1995). School-leaving examinations, selection and equity in higher education in South Africa. *Comparative Education, 31*(2), 261–274.

Hess, F. M., & Leal, D. L. (2001). A shrinking "digital divide"? The provision of classroom computers across urban school systems. *Social Science, 82*(4), 765–788.

Hill, J. (1997). Distance learning environments via the World Wide Web. In B. H. Khan (Ed.) *Web-Based Instruction.* Englewood Cliffs, NJ: Educational Technology Publications, Inc.

Hylén, J. (2006). Open Educational resources: Opportunities and challenges. Paris: OECD-CERI.

Johnstone, S. M. (2005). Open educational resources serve the world. *Educause Quarterly, 28*(3), 15–18.

Kefalas, P., Retalis, S., Stamatis, D., & Theodoros, K. (2003, May). Quality assurance procedures and e-DOL. *International Conference on Network Universities and e-Learning.* Valencia, Spain.

Kinuthia, W. (2003). *An exploratory study of faculty participation in Web-based instruction at historically black colleges and universities.* Unpublished dissertation, University of South Alabama, Mobile, Behavioral Studies and Educational Technology Department.

Kinyanjui, P. (1998). Distance education and open learning in Africa: What works or does not work. *.EDI/World Bank Workshop on Teacher Education through Distance Learning.* Addis Ababa, Ethiopia.

Klein, D., & Ware, M. (2003). E-learning: New opportunities in continuing professional development. *Learned Publishing, 16*(1), 34–46.

Lape, D. H., & Hart, P. K. (1997). Changing the way we teach by changing the college: Leading the way together. *New Directions for Community Colleges, 99,* 15–22.

May, C. (2005). The end of scholarly publishing as we know it? Open source journals and other forms of open distribution of information. Annual meeting of the International Studies Association, Honolulu.

Perraton, H. (2000). *Open and distance learning in the developing world.* London: Routledge.

Rahtz, S. (2006). *Developing an open source policy.* Retrieved from http://www.mc.manchester.ac.uk/eunis2005/medialibrary/papers/paper_134.pdf

Schopfel, J. (2005). Between open access and copyright: Document supply in France. *Interlending & Document Supply, 33*(3), 158–161.

Simonson, M. (2002). Policy and distance education. *The Quarterly Review of Distance Education,* 3(2), v–vii.

Snowhill, L. (2001, July/August). E-books and their future in academic libraries. *D-Lib Magazine,* 7(7/8).

Surry, D. W., & Farquhar, J. D. (1997). Diffusion theory and instructional technology. *Journal of Instructional Science and Technology, 2*(1). Retrieved from http://www.usq.edu.au/electpub/e-jist/vol2no1/vol2no1cont.htm

UNESCO (2002). *Free access to 2,000 MIT courses online: A huge opportunity for universities in poor countries.* Paris. Retrieved from http://portal.unesco.org/en/ev.php-URL_ID=4316&URL_DO=DO_PRINTPAGE&URL_SECTION=201.html

UNESCO. (2002). *Forum on the impact of open courseware for higher education in developing countries.* Retrieved December 2, 2008, from http://portal.unesco.org/ci/

en/files/2492/10330567404OCW_forum_report_final_draft.doc/OCW_fo-rum_report_final_draft.doc

UNESCO. (2004). *Second Global Forum (2004): Widening access to quality higher educa-tion.* Retrieved December 2, 2008, from http://portal.unesco.org/education/en/ev.php-URL_ID=41187&URL_DO=DO_TOPIC&URL_SECTION=201.html

Wiley, D. (2000). Connecting learning objects to instructional design theory: A defi-nition, a metaphor, and a taxonomy. In D. Wiley (Ed.), *The instructional use of learning objects.* Retrieved from *http://reusability.org/read/chapters/wiley.doc*

Willis, B., & Dickinson, J. (1997). Distance education and the World Wide Web. In B.H. Khan (Ed.), *Web-based Instruction.* Englewood Cliffs, NJ: Educational Technology Publications, Inc.

Witten, I. H., Loots, M., Trujillo, M. F., & Bainbridge, D. (2002). The promise of digital libraries in developing countries. *The Electronic Library, 20*(1), 7–13.

CHAPTER 10

FREEDOM, INNOVATION, AND EQUITY WITH OPEN SOURCE SOFTWARE

Richard Wyles

THE PREMISE OF OPEN SOURCE SOFTWARE

The increasing uptake of open source software, spearheaded by increasing adoption of the Linux operating system, represents a paradigm shift in the emergent information society.

Open source now plays a major part in mainstream information-technology economic activity and has started to dominate some market areas. Over 50% of all Internet activity uses open source software and anyone who surfs the Web will visit sites using open source software since the Apache Web server dominates the server market. Open source is used from supercomputers to mobile phones, plus underpins mission critical functions in banking, defense, education, government, and telecommunications. Google, Amazon, and Ebay use open source technologies, and global technology corporations such as IBM, Sun Microsystems, and Novell are building successful commercial models around the open source paradigm.

Much of the success is also obscured by the reality that it is small reusable scripts, compilers, debugging tools, and building blocks that are reused

Bridging the Knowledge Divide, pages 183–198
Copyright © 2009 by Information Age Publishing
All rights of reproduction in any form reserved.

for bespoke or in-house solutions. In this sense, open source underpins an enormous amount of technology-based economic activity.

FREEDOM

Software applications are built from source code, in essence the software's blueprint, made up of computer-readable instructions. The key difference that open source delivers is that this blueprint or *source code* is open for anyone to evaluate and alter. In general, this freedom does not come with proprietary software.

Richard Stallman started the Free Software Foundation (FSF) in the mid-1980s with the GNU project to create an operating system. Although the most widely used license in open source software projects is the GNU General Public License, there are some important nuances between Richard Stallman's original conception of "free software" and the common notions of what open source stands for.

It is reasonable to sum up the split by describing Richard Stallman's position as holding a strong moralistic and political stance relating to the freedom to use, modify, and redistribute software code.

The term "open source" began in the late 1990s and was viewed as a more corporate-friendly term to describe a software-development methodology. Part of the rationale for new terminology is the understandable confusion over the word "free."

> "Free software" is a matter of liberty, not price. To understand the concept, you should think of "free" as in "free speech," not as in "free beer."[1]

The freedom that Stallman extols is consistent with the liberty to teach, pursue, and share knowledge common in academia.

> The advances in all of the arts and sciences, indeed the sum total of human knowledge, is the result of the open sharing of ideas, theories, studies and research. Yet throughout many school systems, the software in use on computers is closed and locked, making educators partners in the censorship of the foundational information of this new age.[2]

As with many freedoms, governance is prescribed by various laws and protocols. The Free Software Definition and the Open Source Definition are both underpinned by the stated freedoms to copy, make derivative works, and redistribute the software. The legal framework that supports these fundamental freedoms are defined by different licensing structures, with a a spectrum of constraints over the core freedoms.

The GNU General Public License (GPL) is the most popular open source license. A key tenet is that it requires derivative works to be distributed under the same conditions. Sometimes described as the viral clause, the GPL allows commercial distributions, but it prevents proprietary vendors from incorporating open source code into their closed source products for redistribution. Proponents argue that the GPL protects open source freedoms by making it more difficult for corporations to exploit the work of others. At the more permissive end of the spectrum, BSD licenses do allow open source code to be incorporated into proprietary commercial products.

In addition to the legal framework of licensing, open source developments frequently adhere to the guiding principles of open standards. A open standard is an agreed-upon set of guidelines for interoperability. In terms of standards the word "open" refers to being free and publically available without any proprietary contractual constraints.

Many proprietary-software vendors attempt to "lock-in" their customers to using their products by ensuring they are not compatible (interoperable) with their competitors, either in terms of formats used or so-called standards applied. As Grace Hopper, the software pioneer, once said, "The wonderful thing about standards is that there are so many of them to choose from."[3] Proprietary software vendors can use the myriad standards to their advantage by picking and choosing which to apply.

Once locked in, proprietary vendors have an advantage over their customers, as the costs of switching becomes higher. Subsequent common behaviors include regularly increasing support costs, forcing expensive upgrades by not supporting older versions, and selling extensions at a premium.

In contrast, open standards are characterized by collaborative and consensus-driven processes. Similarly to successful open source developments, a meritocracy emerges. In the wider software ecosystem, the trend to open source is playing a vital role as a major driver toward the adoption of open standards by commercial firms. With open source solutions, there is no reason to adopt nonstandard formats, while there are many reasons to maintain open standards to make the code more useful and more widely adopted.

The emergeance of open source and open standards is certainly intertwined with higher education, and it is the tenets of academic freedom that often support the application of, and experimentation with, open source technologies within educational institutions.

Total Cost of Ownership

Total cost of ownership comparisons between proprietary and open source products is a hotly debated topic, with no definitive answer to cover all circumstances. The argument for open source is strong, but it does depend on the maturity of the software and the support options.

The most obvious advantage for open source is the cost of licensing, which is often free. Sale price is only part of the equation, however. Support costs over the software life cycle is a major component, and this is where open source has a distinct advantage if support services are available internally or broadly in the marketplace. Most proprietary vendors have their customers locked into support contracts, as it is only the vendors who may access the source code. With open source, contestability for support is advanced, as any ICT service provider may access the codebase. Costs become more transparent and directly related to the services received and can be brought in-house.

In addition, because most mature open source applications often comply with open standards, the switching costs are significantly reduced.

Quality

How can it be that open source is more robust and secure than proprietary software? While it's easier to detect security flaws, the majority of programmers reviewing code are there to fix bugs and security flaws, not to exploit them. In the same way that Wikipedia is an increasingly high-quality online encyclopedia, open source software from vibrant communities can often advance more rapidly than closed, commercial software.

For example, the Washington Post compared 2005 patch times between Mozilla's Firefox Web browser, which is open source, and Microsoft Internet Explorer. Mozilla averaged approximately 21 days compared with 135 days for Microsoft to address software vulnerabilities.[4] Because inherently more programmers have access to open source, security flaws are often fixed more rapidly and robustly. "Many eyes makes all bugs shallow" is known as Linus's Law.

In contrast, in a commercial setting, the development team can only apply so much time to undertake testing prior to release. When it is released, the premise by the commercial vendor is that the software is of high quality. It is typical for open source code to be released much earlier, when bugs abound and functionality is far from complete. Given that the software meets a need, relatively larger numbers of users will access and review the code, fix bugs and security flaws, and advance the functionality.

However, the notion of open source being of higher quality in a general sense is too idealistic. Open source is a generic term and does not automatically equate to good software no matter the philosophical persuasions of proponents. If the objective is to deploy mission-critical application software, then there are a number of considerations before embarking on the open source direction.

> People think just because it is open-source, the result is going to be automatically better. Not true. You have to lead it in the right directions to succeed. Open source is not the answer to world hunger (Torvalds, 1999).

The success of the Linux operating system is well-documented, but for application software, the success of open source still appears confined to relatively few projects. There may be over 130,000 open source projects registered on SourceForge, but very few of them are active or will flourish into successful projects.[5] In this harsh Darwinian context where only a few survive, what characterizes the successful open source projects?

This is a difficult question, as a successful open source community is as complex as all the human interactions and community dynamics that they contain. It is easy to postulate that no two open source projects are the same.

In general, as the research from Stürmer (2005) describes, positive preconditions include great initial source code, meeting an identified need, level of innovation or novelty factor, the programming language used, visibility, and presence on a collaboration platform such as EduForge or SourceForge.

The human element cannot be underestimated. Leadership skills and behaviors are paramount. The leader needs to not only be a highly skilled developer with a clear vision to attract other skilled contributors, but also exhibit the personality traits necessary for leading or being the figurehead for an essentially voluntary community. It is small wonder that many open source initiatives fail to reach a critical mass of participation.

Different Models—Myths and Realities

The suggestion that the open source movement is analogous to a utopian society is as erroneous as the rose-tinted notion that most open source software is the output of a group of altruistic hobbyist-programmers undertaking some niche activity.

The motivations of individuals and the structures within open source communities tend to reflect the same complexities of any small society or grouping. While the underlying ethos advanced is one of collaboration, the reality in many successful open source projects can be described as a meritocracy, centred by a strong-minded but charismatic leader.

> Open source may sound democratic, but it isn't. At the LinuxWorld Expo on Wednesday, leaders of some of the best-known open source development efforts said *they function as dictators.* (Torvalds, 1999)

The presumably benevolent dictatorship that Linus Torvalds expresses is tempered by the underlying freedom for anyone involved in an open source project to fork the code and start a new community. A project fork occurs when the community splits and one group takes a copy of the code and develops it in a new direction. Therefore, successful open source projects are often characterized by a type of servant-leadership. While assertive, leaders of open source projects necessarily have a high profile within the community and rely on persuasion and their own coding prowess to convince others to follow a particular development roadmap.

The community consists of a meritocracy, which is fluid in its make-up, as interested parties come and go from the project. However, at the heart of seemingly open communities is a small close-knit group of core developers who are trusted with access to the version control system of the codebase. Weber (2004) likens open source developers to artisans, in contrast to the Fordist development methodology typical in commercial software projects.

Beyond this core, there is a wider community of users that may discover bugs, contribute ideas, swap experiences, ask for help, and, of course, download software and its updates. A vibrant community of users does not require funding nor be encouraged in their use and support of a project. It is self-interest that drives participation in open source communities.

Moodle has a large and diverse user community with over 100,000 registered users on Moodle.org, although it is fair to point out that many would have low levels of participation. In larger projects such as Moodle, it is atypical for much of the code to be developed by volunteers rather than employees of companies or educational institutions that see benefits accruing from the project.[6]

INNOVATION

The saying goes that necessity is the mother of invention. Innovation is somewhat different; it can be incremental improvements, a new way of using something, or the thinking that underpins radical invention. When it comes to innovation, there are two quite distinct drivers. One is the norm in the proprietary software world, that is, supplier-side innovation. To differentiate a product, suppliers will invest in research and development and commercialize and often protect their innovations with patent law. While this model is reasonably efficient in open competitive markets, a significant problem remains in that it largely ignores end-user or demand-side innovation. Not totally, because any successful proprietary-software vendor will, of course, take demand signals such as customer feedback into account when designing new releases. The problems are that there are time lags, inefficiencies in communication flow, and inherent prioritization of resources that ignore both niche and emergent need. Patents are also designed to limit the diffusion of innovation and thereby protect the competitive advantage that the innovation provides.

Not surprisingly, the open source production methodology has distinct advantages in terms of both the quantity and quality of ideas, as it embraces everyone as a potential innovator, not just the Research and Development team within a company. For a start, a problem shared is a problem solved. Notwithstanding the benevolent dictatorships that characterize many open source communities, end-users can also be producers, and therefore, broad-based, networked innovation is made possible. Innovations become cumulative, which is why modular architectures are common. A meritocracy emerges where the best ideas combined with quality code become part of the core code, while an outer tier of localized innovations are often shared as unofficial modules or plugins.

Innovations may be very localized, for example, a new language pack. With access to the source code, the software interface can be altered to reflect regional community cultures. Large proprietary-software vendors will tend to focus their efforts only on large and profitable markets and ignore less-widely spoken languages. For local users, this incremental innovation of having software that reflects their cultural mores is a vital component of harnessing the benefits of information and communication technologies.

The sheer scale and speed of innovations can outstrip even the most well-resourced proprietary products. This mass-networked innovation is made possible via the Internet, but is only apparent when a software product reaches critical mass in its growth curve. The point where this community-based synergistic effect is reached is usually identifiable by the growth curve in software adoption and community engagement.

Moodle provides a cogent example. Growth in the community started to accelerate during the middle of 2004. Approximately one year later, Moodle 1.5 was released, incorporating many of the innovations and enhancements of the growing community. The release of Moodle 1.5 was a catalyst for a sharp increase in adoption rates. Looking for the inflection point in the growth of open source community software is a good indicator of the sustainable success of that product. It is an indicator of the synergistic effects of networked innovation.

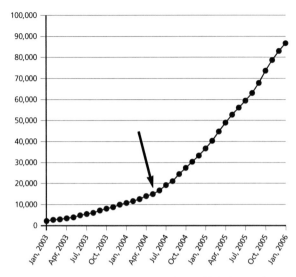

Figure 10.1   Growth of Moodle community 2003–2005. *Source:* Statistics from www.moodle.org.

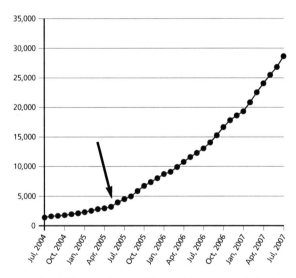

Figure 10.2   Growth of Moodle sites 2003–2007. *Source:* Statistics from www. moodle.org.

EQUITY

Why is the consideration of open source in the context of social justice and equity so important? Software is ubiquitous and permeates all aspects of life in 21st-century developed societies. Equitable access to technology is a key question, and open source is part of the answer.

There are further challenges than simple access, however. "Digital divide" is a term that describes the chasm between the "haves" and "have nots" in information and communication technologies, both in terms of information literacy and available infrastructure.

At worst, open source remains as a significant and cost-effective technology transfer from those who have it to those who need it. The choice is often not between proprietary and open source, it is between open source or nothing at all. Robust, established open source software enables an escape route from technological dependence for international corporations. However, even this seemingly self-evident proposition can be challenged. Based on the assumption that the open source development methodology is more efficient in many instances, it thereby becomes a catalyst for progress in an information society. So, while the "have nots" can readily gain access to the code, the "haves" are accelerating ahead and increasing the digital chasm.

Rather than simple adoption, it is embedded participation through the development of local expertise and support that holds the key to technological self-determination and equity in the information age. "Freedom in general may be defined as the absence of obstacles to the realization of desires."[7] While one obstacle is removed on the road to freedom, many others remain. If you're able to progam in the software language of the open source application in question, you have the freedom to change it. With skill and effort, you may edit and extend the software to do as much or as little as you require. But if you lack the technical skills and the resources to make any changes, then the fundamental freedoms provided with open source are rather moot. It may be easy to post a feature request on an open source software project's home page, but that is not the same as having the wherewithal to make the customizations within your own team or at least commissioning the work from a pool of talent on a contestable basis.

The digital divide, in terms of end-user adoption, is reduced, but the freedom and social justice that emerges from self-reliance is harder to attain. Software development at a higher level, whether open or closed, requires expertise, and this is often paid for. How do regional economies and communities develop the requisite local expertise in open source to start to bridge the digital divide? Market demand to provide livelihoods and education are the realms where leadership is required.

MEETING THE CHALLENGES

With the prospective benefits of freedom, innovation, and equity being advanced through adoption of open source solutions, how do we address the significant challenges that remain for tangible participation beyond ad hoc end-user adoption? Open source is changing the information society in fundamental ways, and developing economies can't afford to be left behind.

Instead, there is the potential for developing economies to be the harbingers of a paradigm shift toward this mode of production and distribution. The growth of the open source movement presents developing countries with an opportunity to escape from technological dependence while also providing a catalyst for innovation and self-determination in the emergent information society.

When exploring the political economy of open source, it is worth outlining the subthemes and how each may become a building block to achieving national development goals.

Policy Framework

As many governments are doing, a key first stage is to create the policy environment whereby open source solutions can at least be evaluated without prejudice, through procurement and development policies.

In 2003 Taiwan launched the "National Open Source Plan," with the goal of establishing a free software industry on the island nation. The Taiwan government has been investing heavily in the areas of skills development, open standards, and removing legal impediments. The Open Source Software Application Consulting Center, an initiative by Taiwan's Ministry of Education, trains and supports school teachers in an effort to diversify the ICT curriculum.[8]

The United Kingdom's government policy on open source, in place since 2002, states that the government will consider open source software solutions alongside proprietary solutions. Solutions must adhere to open standards, and the government will seek to avoid lock-in and "explore further the possibilities of using open source software as the default exploitation route for government-funded R&D software."[9] Throughout Europe, there are similar policy initiatives at central and local government levels.

Peru was one of the first countries in the world to introduce legislation explicitly mandating open source. However, after a visit from the US Ambassador and a donation personally delivered by Bill Gates himself, the legislation was softened. In 2005 further legislation was introduced, which ensured that open source was considered on the same basis with price and capability being the appropriate metrics for evaluation.[10]

Venezuela, China, Japan, and Norway are planning at least partial migration to open source.[11] China is becoming a major stronghold for open source, as it has a policy of not being reliant on foreign software.

However, government commitment doesn't mean that success automatically follows. After first announcing the decision in 2003, the Munich City Council in Germany has moderated its goals and now intends to migrate 80% of its workers to open source desktops by 2009. The initiative has been plagued with patent wrangles, delays, and rising costs.[12]

Brazil is often referred to as having a strong policy supportive of open source and local software industry. However, there are also reports of routine violations of the GNU General Public License, inefficiencies, hype, and situations where poor-quality code has been deployed in mission-critical situations.[13]

Notwithstanding, the undoubted problems with some large-scale policy initiatives to implement open source as the trend are unmistakeable. There is an increasing amount of legislation globally that is weighted toward or even mandating open source in government.

The benefits of governments moving in this direction are clear. Governments are very large spenders in information and communication technologies. Adopting open source can reduce budgets, plus substitute software imports, thereby alleviating balance-of-payments deficits. Accessibility can be improved as the impediments of commercial licensing are removed. Most importantly, government procurement and adoption of open source legitimizes the trend with significant flow-on benefits for other sectors in the economy.

Human Capacity

Even with the optimal policy framework in place, the shortage of the requisite human capacity can mean that developing nations remain as consumers of software, albeit open source, rather than active participants in a globalizing information society.

Education and training takes time. To avoid the initial capacity, deficit skills may need to be centralized or brought in from international suppliers. Firstly, lack of know-how or organizational cultural barriers remain a barrier to adoption for many organizations. Cost remains a significant factor, despite the cost benefits of royalty-free open source licensing. Secondly, objections to open source in general often focus on a perceived lack of credibility in comparison with that normally associated with the backing of a large proprietary-software vendor.

However, unless there are capacity-building activities in parallel to the initial procurement of support, technological self-reliance and prosperity will be constrained.

The education sector needs to spearhead the capacity building by adopting open source and fostering its support through educational progams of study and research.

Were the majority of universities, schools, and colleges to eliminate the costs of commercial software licensing fees, they would soon become enablers, both through development and capacity building. A key benefit of accessible software is that those interested in learning software development can hone their skills. Surely, a great way to learn how to write good computer progams is to study what has been written by others and then perhaps even tinker with improvements, even if that means learning through mistakes.

To deliver skilled software developers as graduates, open source is ideal for learning, as it reveals the workings of actual software progams and allows for change and imrovements. Deliberate bugs can be introduced by the tutor for the students to resolve. There can be no better a practical environment in which to test a learner's skills. Experienced progammers are more easily able to mentor learners. Open source is having an effect on business worldwide, so it is paramount for developing economies to have graduates with these skills to achieve technological self-determination.

The author's own experience with addressing these challenges is primarily within the context of New Zealand, a geographically remote country, although relatively developed and prosperous. The population, at approximately four million, is relatively small and spread across a geographical area comparable to Britain, meaning there is internal geographical remoteness as well as external remoteness. The challenges for spreading an inherently limited budget for the uptake of information and communication technologies have some commonality with other regional economies. There is uneven access and know-how both geographically and across ethnic groupings. Cost is a significant barrier to entry for small organizations, thereby contributing to a digital divide within the educational system. Across the economy, there is significant duplication of investment and activity. In the education sector, those able to invest in platforms such as BlackBoard and WebCT, while e-learning enabled, have commented on the lack of flexibility, lack of cultural identity, and rigid constructs in pedagogy, partly due to their inability to innovate with the code base.

In 2003 the New Zealand government designated funding, to be administered by the Tertiary Education Commission, for e-learning capability-development initiatives throughout New Zealand, spanning a time period of 2004 to 2007. The e-Learning Collaborative Development Fund (eCDF), a contestable funding model available to New Zealand tertiary educational organizations, was designed to improve the tertiary educational system's capability to deliver e-learning that improves education access and/or quality for learners.

The New Zealand Open Source Virtual Learning Environment (NZOSV-LE) project was a consortium-based project, involving 20 further- and higher-education institutions, focused on developing open source application software for education. The NZOSVLE Project was designed to strengthen system capability and quality, while simultaneously reducing the total cost of ownership for New Zealand e-learning across tertiary and secondary education, industry, and enterprise growth sectors. Many tertiary organizations in New Zealand have fewer than 2000 students. To date, these organizations have not been able to afford licensing and support of an e-learning environment. A key goal, that has been widely met, has been to lower the barriers to entry in using e-learning technologies.

Another key motivation for considering open source solutions was the need to accommodate alternative pedagogical approaches and different contextual interfaces with an emphasis on Te Reo Maori and Pacific Island cultural requirements. One group of tertiary organizations has focused on contextual interface development of the virtual-learning environment, including cultural look and feel themes, creating technical help, pedagogical support files, and tutorial packages, in appropriate languages, to assist learners and instructors in becoming familiar with the e-learning environment created.

Once Moodle was selected, the development team started in earnest and has been working on Moodle full time since June 2004. The project has had an enormous impact across New Zealand's educational system, with Moodle now the most widely deployed LMS in New Zealand's further-education sector. Moodle was selected for its following strengths: 1) open and active developer community; 2) good system help files and end-user documentation; 3) quality of the code and modular system architecture; 4) ability to interface with other systems; 5) course-centric rather than tool-centric; and 6) flexibility, including the ability for instructors to adjust courses on the fly.

The NZOSVLE project also facilitated the establishment of a shared hosting facility, which delivers economies of scale on hardware, hosting, disaster-recovery systems, availability of appropriate expertise, bandwidth, and 2nd/3rd-level support services. By collaborating on shared infrastructure, commercial service levels are available for mission-critical systems at a significantly lower cost than if individual institutions were to set up these systems and services individually.

The promise for an economically sustainable ICT investment pathway for NZ education using open source technologies is evident throughout the sector, with cogent evidence available by exploring individual cases. In 2003 the Nelson Marlborough Institute of Technology established a project to select and implement a commercial LMS.

However, up-front costs of hardware, licence and local technical support proved too great a barrier in difficult financial times and we lacked experience or confidence in utilising Open Source systems. The advent of the NZO-SVLE project has changed all this. Moodle is a highly functional, stable and relatively intuitive LMS compared to many of the commercial products. An external service provider now hosts our installation of Moodle and the quality of the support available via the NZOSVLE project and the wider Moodle user community has been outstanding. Rather than pay for expensive hardware and license fees, a greater percentage of available funds have been able to be used to establish an internal support team.[14]

Early in the NZOSVLE project, it was recognized there was a need for an online environment for project collaboration. Instead of being focused on a specific project, Eduforge (www.eduforge.org) was established as an open-access environment designed for the sharing of ideas, research outcomes, open content, and open source software for education. The goal with Eduforge is to try to bring software developers and educators into the same space and provide a focal point for development, distribution, and maintenance of open source software for education.

The commitment to open standards, modular, flexible, and extensible architecture underpins the systems framework of the NZOSVLE and interrelated open source projects in New Zealand. A key strength of these projects lies in the philosophy of building upon established, well-regarded open source communities. The intent is to contribute to and harness the synergy from a collaborative, international community of expertise. The result is a virtual learning environment raised to a new level of competitiveness, with proprietary alternatives and a catalyst for further innovation across the sector.

The interwoven open source projects have set the foundations for continuing innovations in education delivery and have enabled the potential for deeper levels of collaboration across consortia and networks between industry and education. To date, the combined open source initiatives are having far-reaching implications for New Zealand's e-learning environment and knowledge economy.

The growth of the open source movement in education presents economies with an opportunity to escape from technological dependence through a sustainable technology-investment strategy, providing a catalyst for innovation, and delivering a means of helping achieve social justice. This is the premise of the One Laptop Per Child project, the goal of which is to provide a very low cost, powerful, and robust laptop to the world. The laptops are Linux based and have wireless broadband, which enables them to operate as a peer-to-peer mesh network. They are also designed to operate with a range of power inputs including wind-up! The concept is to distribute them in very large numbers directly to governments.

CONCLUSION

Open source communities do not equate to ideal societies. Human foibles are as much on show in open source communities as anywhere else. As such, open source projects do not necessarily mean quality outcomes. Often quality correlates with the vision, leadership, and competencies of the project's figurehead, such as Martin Dougiamas [Moodle] or Linus Torvalds [Linux].

However, while due care is important, and selection of open source solutions encompasses risk, it is a risk worth embracing. Risks and benefits go hand in hand, particularly with software. The benefits of getting open source right are enormous, especially for learners of the future, as ICT becomes part of both the delivery and content of education.

The adoption of open-source software by governments, while accompanied with a number of challenges, is vital to help remedy inequities in access to information technology. Government adoption helps normalize its use. In parallel, educational institutions must become more proactive in the teaching of open source and growing the number of open source software programmers, to increase society's capacity to harness the power of ICTs with the ultimate goal of achieving improved social equity.

Open source helps equitable access to technology. First, it can be contextualized for local conditions, thereby enhancing access. Second, it can be modified to address particular niche needs unserved by commercial operations. Third, it can dramatically reduce the total cost of ownership. Open source is also driving the tenets of interoperability and thereby delivering more choice, and with that, more equitable access. There is an inherent tension for proprietary vendors to move toward open standards of their own volition. Finally, open source as a production methodology, enables stakeholders to be far more involved, to collaborate, innovate, and contribute to the outputs rather than being passive end-users.

REFERENCES

Stürmer, M. (2005). *Open source community building.* Master's thesis submitted to Prof. Dr. Thomas Myrach, pp. 103–105. University of Bern.

Torvalds, L. (1999, December). In N. Bezroukov, A second look at the cathedral and bazaar. *First Monday, 4*(12). Retrieved from http://firstmonday.org/issues/issue4_12/bezroukov/index.html

Weber, S. (2004). *The success of open source.* Cambridge, MA: Harvard University Press

NOTES

1. Free Software Foundation. Retrieved December 2, 2008, from http://www.fsf. org/licensing/essays/free-sw.html
2. Vessels,T. (2001). *Why should open source software be used in schools?* Retrieved December 2, 2008, from http://edge-op.org/grouch/schools.html
3. Wikequotes. Retrieved December 2, 2008, from http://en.wikiquote.org/ wiki/Grace_Hopper
4. Brian Krebs. Retrieved December 2, 2008, from http://blog.washingtonpost. com/securityfix/2006/02/2005_patch_times_for_firefox_a.html
5. Open, but not as usual. *The Economist,* March 16, 2006. Retrieved December 2, 2008, from http://www.economist.com/business/displaystory.cfm?story_ id=5624944
6. Open, but not as usual. *The Economist,* March 16, 2006. Retrieved December 2, 2008, from http://www.economist.com/business/displaystory.cfm?story_ id=5624944
7. Bertrand Russell, Welsh Philosopher: 1872–1970.
8. Retrieved December 2, 2008, from http://www.p2pfoundation.net/FOSS_ in_Taiwan
9. Open Source Software – Guidance on implementing UK Government Policy. Retrieved December 2, 2008, from http://www.ogc.gov.uk/documents/ Open_Source_Software.pdf
10. Peru lawmakers vote to give open source software equal footing with Microsoft. Retrieved December 2, 2008, from http://www.itbusinessedge.com/ item/?ci=7370
11. Cuba to migrate to open source software. Retrieved December 2, 2008, from http://news.com.com/Cuba+to+migrate+to+open-source+software/2100-7344_3-6160496.html?tag=st.ref.goo
12. Munich fires up Linux at last. Retrieved December 2, 2008, from http://news. com.com/Munich+fires+up+Linux+at+last/2100-7344_3-6119153.html
13. Retrieved December 2, 2008, from http://www.linux.com/article.pl?sid= 07/01/17/2018227
14. David Sturrock, Flexible Learning Team Leader, Nelson Marlborough Institute of Technology. Retrieved December 2, 2008, from http://moodlemoot. org.nz/moodle/mod/resource/view.php?id=7

CHAPTER 11

COPYRIGHT ISSUES AND THEIR IMPACT ON FLEXIBLE EDUCATION IN AFRICA

Pauline Ngimwa

INTRODUCTION

Educational institutions are both creators and users of copyrightable content. Copyright protection is intended to promote creativity within these institutions of learning. It allows the creators of original work to be rewarded with financial and other incentives in order to continue to generate intellectual capital without fear that their work will be stolen or misused. In this scenario, institutions of learning recognize the value of copyright in education. However, in order for these institutions to progress their core mission of scholarship, teaching and research, they require access to the world's scholarly and research works. Unfortunately, the reality is an imbalance in the way copyright is applied, particularly in a continent such as Africa, which is struggling with economic-development challenges. Overprotection of copyright and the restrictive intellectual property (IP) systems hamper the wide diffusion of educational content. Worse still, the emergence of the digital era has introduced technological measures that tend to restrict the access and usage of educational content instead of promoting their spread.

Bridging the Knowledge Divide, pages 199–211
Copyright © 2009 by Information Age Publishing
All rights of reproduction in any form reserved.

This makes it difficult to access quality education in developing countries, which are the poorest regions of the world, with a large proportion of the population still living on less than $1 USD per day, and the most heavily indebted countries. UNESCO (2004) estimates that there are about 46 million out-of-school children in sub-Saharan Africa.

Besides education being a basic right, it is the backbone of national economies worldwide. Even in the African context, where literacy levels are still low, as demonstrated by the above statistics, there is evidence that literacy levels do indeed contribute toward economic development and, indeed, uplift standards of living. According to UNESCO (2004), an adult with a primary education earns twice as much as an adult without any schooling; in Niger, the incidence of poverty is 70% in households headed by adults with no education, compared with $56 for households headed by adults who have been to primary school. In Uganda, four years of primary education raise a farmer's output by 7%.

However, a literate society alone is not enough to contribute toward improving a nation's economy. Education needs to be pitched a little higher to tertiary level. This is the level that contributes significantly to research, science, and technology, which are the main drivers of technological and telecommunication innovations leading to modern global-knowledge economies. Bloom, Canning, and Chan (2006) present some analysis of two distinct channels to demonstrate that increased higher education can enhance economic growth in Africa. Their study shows that if Africa would increase the tertiary education of its population by one additional year and hence contribute to the production frontier, the GDP per capita growth rate in Africa would raise by 0.24 percentage points in the first year. Their second channel is based on the potential the tertiary-education graduates have on the economic growth if they were to apply technological advancement, and they argue that this would increase the GDP per capita growth rate by 0.39 percentage points in the first year. This indicates a need for widening access to tertiary education. Unfortunately, universities do not have capacities to provide quality education to all qualified students. UNESCO (2004) puts gross enrollment rates for tertiary education for about half of the African countries at 2.5%. This is why flexible education in Africa is so relevant. Flexible education not only gives more eligible population access to university education, it also means that qualified students with disabilities, particularly those of a sensory nature, have a better opportunity. In this context, open and free access to knowledge is fundamental in promoting flexible education. This explains why when access to educational content and the free flow of information are undermined or interfered with, the quality of learning is lowered, and this in turn affects the overall contribution toward economic development.

The following discussion highlights the negative effects of the overprotection of the copyright laws on flexible education in Africa from a practitioner's point of view. As a way of mitigation, the chapter has also highlighted some of the positive initiatives that are emerging to create a desirable balance and open up the access to the educational content.

ISSUES

Excessively Expensive Books and Journals and Their Copyright-Related Fees (Collection Societies, Copyright Clearance Fees, etc.)

The quality and success of education, and in particular distance education, is highly dependant on access to a wide range of information resources including journals and books, both in print and digital formats. More specifically, the presence of digital resources advances opportunities for better and quality e-learning. But access to these resources is not determined by their availability alone. There is the issue of affordability as well. The cost of these resources is often prohibitive, particularly to scholars in developing countries. Such high costs are mainly as a result of the copyright protection imposed on these resources. Usually, the producers of the resources sustain profits from assigning and licensing copyright to the materials they produce. They are the ones who determine the prices, which in most cases are beyond the reach of the developing world. Consumers International (CI) conducted a comparative survey on book prices in 11 countries in Asia and observed that developing countries end up paying more for copyrighted educational materials, and this imposes a barrier to access to education. For example, a book at $27 USD in Indonesia is equivalent to $1,048 USD in the US. The study concluded that

> Although retail prices of books in developing countries are generally lower in absolute terms, when the prices are considered in the context of a country's GDP per capita, it becomes clear that consumers in developing countries are in fact paying more than consumers in developed countries for the same books. (Consumer International, 2006, p. 3)

This is confirmed by another study conducted in the Ivory Coast, which showed that books and educational materials used in schools, especially for scientific subjects, were usually bought at a high cost from Europe (Loupis, 2000).

The high cost of copyrightable resources is not the only cost that African scholars have to endure. Other related costs include the price of Internet access and ICT infrastructure such as computers. The ultimate result is that scholars are denied access to quality resources that they would otherwise enjoy if there were appropriately balanced copyright. More often than not, such scholars end up defying the copyright law by illegally photocopying the available printed resources, which in effect undermines the quality of education.

Another complication is in the clearance of third-party materials. Instructors and course designers often use third party copyright materials in developing their courses. This applies both to distance and residential education programs. For instance, an online learning program can be created using many different third-party sources involving many different "owners." Examples are software programs used in teaching and learning; content prepared by a team of writers and instructional designers that draw on additional nonoriginal sources, including graphics and artwork, photographs, musical extracts, and video clips, most of which would require copyright permission to be obtained before they are used. In this case, clearance of the third-party materials becomes very important, but in most cases, this is a very tedious, costly, and frustrating process. As illustrated above, there are so many rights from owners whose permission must be sought before the program can be completed. Sometimes it takes so long to obtain the permissions, and this may delay the development of the program. If clearance is not done beforehand, and just one rights-owner challenges the inclusion of his materials without his clearance, it can lead to a whole program being canceled and even a possible third-party lawsuit.

For delivery purposes, most of these materials are copied and distributed to students. Use of these copyrighted materials without permission or following laid-down instructions for use is illegal in most worldwide jurisdictions. This is particularly so with digital resources, as the limitations and exceptions provided internationally for educational purposes are often overlooked. Unfortunately, while developed countries have taken advantage of the legal flexibilities in international intellectual-property agreements for distance education, African countries have rarely done so. This only makes access to education for the distance learner more costly.

In addition, there are very few reprographic-rights organizations to facilitate clearance of photocopying permissions, and where they exist, only a few are fully functional. There are only about eight African countries where such organizations exist, and these include South Africa, Kenya, Togo, Zimbabwe, Uganda, Nigeria, Malawi, and Zambia. Even in these countries, educational institutions and libraries often find themselves battling with the reprographic-rights organizations, particularly those that are not streamlined and which lack transparency in their operations.

Technological Restrictions

Technological Prevention Measures (TPMs) imposed on digital content have, to a great extent, impacted negatively on the flow of information. TPMs give rights-owners control over access and use of digital content by using software or hardware or a combination of both. They enable rights-owners to lock up content, including the local lawful exceptions and limitations. Because they are either embedded in the hardware, software (or both), they often assume a readily available technical infrastructure, which in developing countries is not always present. Unfortunately, TPMs are legally protected under the WIPO Copyright treaty, making it illegal to circumvent them.

So, how does this affect education in developing countries? The presence of TPMs in digital content means that distance education cannot enjoy cheap electronic instructional content, because TPMs increase the cost by placing barriers to storing, transmitting, and using this content. Take an example of a distant learner based in a remote area in Africa who receives an instructional-content CD with a TPM embedded in it. He loads it into a borrowed PC because he cannot afford to own one, but the next time he wants to use the CD in a different PC, he discovers that he cannot access the content because the TPM in the CD cannot allow a reload. The CD would perhaps have cost the learner some money, but he cannot freely use the content as he wishes because it has been locked up!

Further, TPMs deny sensory-disabled people (people who are partially or fully blind or deaf) the opportunity to fully take advantage of the technological advancements that would otherwise widen access opportunities. For instance, technology provides for audio editions of e-books, which would benefit a visually impaired reader. Unfortunately, a rights-holder can switch off this capability with a TPM. To illustrate just how disadvantageous this is to this category of people, Nicholson uses the following scenario of how TPMs have negative effects on flexible education in Africa:

> Copyright law prohibits a blind student from converting his textbook, or even a portion of it, into a more accessible format, e.g. Braille. He tries to access an electronic book but copyright technological protection measures block the 'text-to-speech' software. He tries to download an electronic article from an electronic database to email, but the license prevents this, so he is unable to access the information via a voice-synthesizer. He cannot browse in the library, since there are no facilities or legal provisions for him to convert even a small portion to Braille. Copyright protection measures prevent him from exercising his fair use rights. (2006, p. 312)

While most copyright laws recognize the exceptions and limitations for sensory-disabled people, TPMs come to undermine these rights and create inflexibility in the access to information and educational opportunities for this group of people, who are already very disadvantaged by their disability.

In the context of the libraries, TPMs contribute to less sharing and more costs involved in trying to obtain permissions from rights-owners to circumvent and allow exceptions and limitations in order. Anticircumvention laws prevent the libraries from enjoying copyright exceptions already provided for in the international laws, thereby making it difficult to provide effective information services such as sharing of materials and providing current awareness services. Libraries are forced to spend a lot of money to negotiate for permission to circumvent or obtain TPMs free content. Libraries in Africa cannot afford to pay for these privileges.

TPM-protected materials can remain permanently locked up, even after their protection term has expired. When this happens, content that would have otherwise been in the public domain becomes difficult to access, as it is still locked up. This is a great disadvantage for libraries, learners, and educationists in developing countries. It is important that all stakeholders in the categories mentioned above push for circumvention of these TPMs in order to benefit education and development in Africa.

Bilateral and Multinational Agreements

Intellectual property is governed by a complex collection of international treaties and agreements. North-south investment agreements are being used by developed economies to enhance or provide alternative routes for further IP protection, a move that is creating certain pressure on countries, mainly in the developing world, to sign up for stricter copyright laws. This undermines the flexibilities already available under the World Trade Organization (WTO) Agreement on the Trade-Related Aspects of Intellectual Property Rights (TRIPS) and other international IP agreements. Instead of taking advantage of the flexibilities and limitations present in these international agreements to protect and enhance access to education, some developing countries are succumbing to the pressures by developed countries to adopt such agreements and ending up with copyright regimes that are stricter and with extended copyright terms. Implications are serious, as they ultimately affect access to information and cross-border exchange of knowledge, and in turn, this affects education, libraries, and general development.

Cumbersome and Unaffordable Licensing Schemes for Digital Content

Libraries are the pillars of research and critical to tertiary education, particularly in open, distance, and e-learning. Digital technologies have brought about an evolution in the ways libraries provide access to information resources. Libraries are now taking the advantage of the proliferation of electronic resources to support scholarship and research. These resources come in dozens of major databases in all areas and disciplines, and these are now benefiting students, academics, and researchers, even in developing countries. This is a positive development, especially because of its contribution toward uplifting standards of education in the developing world. It has, for instance, created equal opportunities where scholars in these economies are able to access the same high level of resources that are being accessed by their counterparts in the developed world. Unfortunately, this is not always straightforward, as most of these resources are acquired through a negotiated license that states clearly what the user can and cannot do with the material. A license is a contract between the user and the rights-owner. On one hand is the user, whose main focus is to use the resource as conveniently as possible to him. On the other hand is the rights-owner, whose interest is to maximize his profits by holding on to as much of his rights as possible. This is problematic for the user, who must negotiate as much of these rights as possible for reasonable prices. This is a typical challenge created by what is perceived as a copyright imbalance. Copyright is not just about protecting the rights-owner.

Besides these license contracts being expensive, they tend to override the statutory exceptions and limitations mentioned above, and in the process, the libraries are forced to enter into complex negotiations with the rights-owners. These negotiations are often time-consuming and unfriendly in the African context. For example, inclusion of clauses that prevent photocopying in Africa, where Internet connectivity is not always guaranteed, undermines proper and adequate usage of these resources.

Worse still, most of these licenses do not provide for perpetual access to the materials that have been paid for, as they only cover a specified period of time, beyond which the user can no longer access the materials. Whereas libraries can choose to either keep back issues of journals in print format and bind them for later use or discard them after use, the electronic licenses do not provide access to these back. Libraries have to pay exorbitantly to obtain resources for only a period of time, and if they want to have access to these resources in the future, they have to pay extra for archival access.

Such unbalanced copyright laws are real challenges for libraries, and they are a hindrance to equal access to information, as they impose unrealistic costs on already disadvantaged societies. Besides, there is not always a guarantee that even after paying all the costs, the materials will be utilized to the optimum, given that the Internet access is not always adequate to allow smooth access to digital content in Africa.

In attempts to overcome this, initiatives such a elFL.net and INASP have come up with support systems for libraries, particularly in developing countries, where they offer their expertise in license negotiations as well as formation of consortia among various libraries aimed at increasing the bargaining power at the time of subscription, hence bring down the subscription costs.

Erosion of the Public Domain Work

Public domain work is creative work that is not protected by copyright and is thus free to be used by anyone. Creative work can become public domain work when its protection term expires or when the creator does not want it protected or renounces copyright. Making their proposals to the 3rd Session of WIPO Development Agenda (IFLA, 2007), the International Federation of Library Associations, Library Copyright Alliance and Electronic Information for Libraries argued that public domain works may be used without expending resources in tracing rights-holders to obtain permission or buy licenses. It is easier and cheaper to create distance-education content from this collection, as one does not have to seek for third-party clearance from multiple rights-holders. Similarly, a publisher can publish low-cost educational textbooks for developing countries from public domain materials, hence making it easier and cheaper to access textbooks that would otherwise be unaffordable, as discussed above. Distance education in developing countries in particular therefore stands to gain from this collection, because in a real sense, this is mainly open- and free-access information.

Unfortunately, some countries are choosing to extend the protection period and, in so doing, increase private rights on content, while material in the public domain gets decreased. While the minimum copyright term in the Berne Convention and TRIPS Agreement is 50 years after the author's death, some developing countries are choosing to add 20 or more years. This is most unfortunate for such countries where access to information is critical to their economic development. It simply means that information that would otherwise be accessible to everyone is removed from this collective ownership, and this in turn affects education, innovation, and ultimately their levels of development. Besides, this extension only benefits rights-owners and their estates, who in most cases are in the developed world, at the expense of the already disadvantaged information-users in the developing countries. Instead of such countries developing their own educational content from the materials in the public domain, they continue to be importers of information from the developed countries at a high cost.

Education initiatives in developing countries that are attempting to digitize content in the public domain stand to be affected adversely because they resort to older, out-of-copyright, and more out-of-date materials, which impedes academics and research.

In the era of digital advancement, there is even a greater threat to the public domain works, introduced by the TPMs discussed above. TPMs do not expire when the copyright protection expires. Due to the volatile nature of technology, it means that if there are no new TPMs compatible with the technology of the day, the digital resources in the public domain that have been protected by TPMs will remain locked up in perpetuity and implying that digital content in the public domain becomes inaccessible to future generations.

One area that has great promise for the improvement of the distance education is the creation and widespread use of the Open Educational Resources (OERs). African institutions of higher learning have a lot to gain by embracing this technological advancement, as it creates educational content and allows for reuse of the same to create new knowledge. Unfortunately, locking up digital content limits this possibility.

This shrinking of public domain content should be discouraged, as it robs users and, in particular, learners of vast amounts of relevant content that would otherwise be freely available. Preservation and protection of public domain content should be a priority, particularly in Africa, where students and scholars are rarely able to afford the high cost of learning materials.

SUGGESTIONS ON WAYS TO MITIGATE THE ISSUES RAISED ABOVE

Open Content/Access

With the emergence of the knowledge economy, debates on the future of the IPR have dominated the last few years, with world and regional players developing varying movements and initiatives. While some rights-owners continue to erect barriers that threaten sharing of knowledge and are aggressively pursuing protection of IPR, there are those who promote the free sharing of knowledge, which has been facilitated by advancements in ICTs.

These supporters of Open Access, Open Content, or Open Educational Resources are challenging the "ownership" barriers that limit access to knowledge. They seek to debunk the current limitations to accessing digital content imposed by intractable copyright laws that fail to realize that the nature of knowledge creation and dissemination has moved on. As described above, in many cases, TPMs and expensive database license fees have now become a hindrance to the flow of knowledge and innovation at global, regional, and national levels.

The "Open Access" concept involves access to scholarly works via digital files accessible through the Internet and electronic networks. Researchers are afforded the opportunity to publish their research in academic journals (without payment) for the sake of knowledge and inquiry, thus enabling other researchers, scholars, lecturers, and students to access peer-reviewed journals freely at no cost. This accelerates research and enriches education, in that knowledge sharing becomes far more egalitarian.

The Open Access concept creates an environment where the user is granted a wide range of specific rights to use and adapt online works. This also encourages online collaboration among many people in the development of content. One good example is the Creative Commons, which has developed a set of licenses that enable producers and consumers of works to exchange and share these among themselves in accordance with a set of predefined criteria to which they each agree. These alternative licensing systems encourage a wide diffusion of knowledge. The idea is to create "common spaces" where knowledge is shared and, where appropriate, controlled by those within that space.

Developing countries should embrace these initiatives by contributing toward developing their own open content as well as making use of what is already available. Further, they must ensure that public-funded research and such works are made open to the public.

Create Reforms on the African Copyright

This will entail review of existing domestic copyright laws, particularly where they have ignored or left out limitations and exceptions provided in the international agreements. This is especially relevant to countries with outdated laws from the colonial era that are too restrictive. In countries that are going through amendments to their copyright laws, educationists, librarians, legal experts, and legislators must actively get involved and ensure that the greater flexibilities provided by the international agreements are indeed considered in line with the countries development goals, such as literacy and education.

Further, such reforms and reviews should consider recommendations provided by education experts and advocates of access to knowledge, such as the International Federation of Library Associations, the Library Copyright Alliance, and Electronic Information for Libraries. The Commonwealth of Learning has documented recommendations on the international exceptions and limitations to copyright that are necessary for a fair education policy.

Become Activists for Access to Knowledge

African educationists, librarians, and education policymakers must speak out and protect the interests of the education content users, i.e., the students. This entails active participation in copyright-law reforms and amendments to ensure that international provisions and exceptions are included in these amendments. They must advise the lawmakers against incorporating the international investment agreements into domestic agreements, as these undermine the international exceptions and limitations. Further, they must encourage their governments to support international debates and advocacy initiatives instead of giving in to the pressures from developed economies on the international IP agreements such as the TRIPS Plus. They should support WIPO activities such as the Development Agenda and the call for a Treaty on Access to Knowledge (A2K), which seeks to redress the balance between the rights-holders and the users.

African countries must work together to challenge the introduction of laws that undermine their development goals and find appropriate solutions for copyright laws that suit their circumstances. They must also work together to review their outdated laws and liberalize and harmonize them to ensure that they support their development agenda.

Formation of Communities That Act as Watchdogs Against Practices That Perpetuate Imbalanced Copyright Laws

In cognizance of the imbalance of copyright laws on the continent and of the developmental gap created by this imbalance, the African Copyright and Access to Information Alliance (ACAIA) was established in November 2005 during a conference held in Uganda and attended by educationists, librarians, copyright experts, and activists, as well as copyright owners. The alliance strives for equitable and practical copyright laws, including harmonization that reflects the socioeconomic, cultural, and political realities of individual countries and societies in Africa. Similar associations or chapters should be formed and education stakeholders encouraged to participate in order to ensure that their interests are covered in their respective domestic copyright laws.

Formation of Consumers/Rights-Owners Partnerships

There is a need to enter into mutual agreements with the rights-owners, particularly those who understand that there is the need for balanced copyright. The Springer Open Choice initiative creates certain flexibilities by allowing the authors of journal articles the choice to have their articles made available with open access free to anyone, any time, and anywhere in the world, in exchange for payment of basic fees. If authors choose open access in the Springer Open Choice program, they are not required to transfer their copyright to Springer either. This is a perfect example of a rights-owner ready to make exceptions and thereby open up access to knowledge.

CONCLUSION

In conclusion, copyright issues have never been so important in Africa as now, when access to knowledge resources impacts so heavily on socioeconomic development. Africa must strike a balance between encouraging knowledge creation (by rewarding those responsible for its creation) and the control mechanisms in place for the use and access to this knowledge. This is very important because, as a result of the exorbitant cost of information resources, the continent has for a long time been deprived of the opportunity to benefit from the world's knowledge as well as to share its own knowledge. Unbalanced and disproportionate copyright laws undermine the free flow of knowledge and have negative effects on flexible education, which in turn affects the level of socioeconomic development of a country. Such an imbalance creates a double tragedy in a developing continent: on one hand, the continent is struggling to improve its level of economic development by encouraging the governments to widen education opportunities, but on the other hand, it has to deal with the restrictions of access to knowledge created by this imbalance.

Besides, if nothing is done to reduce this imbalance, the continent will never be able to reap the benefits of this electronic era. Instead, the digital divide will continue to widen and, as Walker (2005, p.1) stresses, "...without the global knowledge to meet their needs, many African countries are in danger of becoming failed states."

REFERENCES

Bloom, E., Canning, D., & Chan, K. (2006). Higher education and poverty in Sub-Saharan Africa international. *Higher Education, 45,* 6–7.

Committee on Copyright and other Legal Matters (CLM), (2007). IFLA, Netherlands. Retrieved August 11, 2007 from http://www.ifla.org/III/clm/p1/ CLM-pr08032007.htm

Consumers International (2006). *Copyright and access to knowledge: Policy recommendations on Flexibilities in copyright law.* Consumers International Asia Pacific Office, Kuala Lumpur, Retrieved August 5, 2007 from http://www.idrc.ca/ uploads/user-S/11417705291COPYRIGHT_Final_16.02.06.pdf

Loupis, Leila (2000). *Increased participation with local expertise and materials.* UNESCO, Paris. Retrieved August 10, 2007 from http://www.unesco.org/education/ wef/en-leadup/rmeet_afric_ivorycoast1.shtm

Nicholson, Denise R. (2006). Intellectual property: Benefit or burden for Africa? *IFLA Journal 32*(4), 310–324. Retrieved August 8, 2007 from http://www.ifla. org/V/iflaj/IFLA-Journal-4-2006.pdf

UNESCO (2004). *Why is education important?* UNESCO, Paris. Retrieved August 14, 2007 from http://portal.UNESCO.org/education/en/ev.php-URL_ ID=28703&URL_DO=DO_TOPIC&URL_SECTION=201.html

Walker, K. (2005). Bandwidth and copyright: Barriers to knowledge in Africa? *Carnegie Reporter*, Spring 13–18.

SECTION 3

FLEXIBLE DELIVERY IN HIGHER EDUCATION

CHAPTER 12

UNIVERSITY EDUCATION FOR NATIONAL DEVELOPMENT

Makerere University's Dual Mode Experience

Jessica N. Aguti

INTRODUCTION

Makerere University was established in 1922 as a technical school and in 1949 became a University College linked to University of London; then in 1963 became a constituent college of the University of East Africa. Makerere finally achieved its full university status in 1970. Prior to 1971, when Idi Amin came to power, Makerere University was held as the "Harvard of Africa." It was then famous for its programs and quality of its graduates. The Amin era did wreak havoc on the university because, like many other social institutions, the university suffered gross neglect, and many academics left the country out of fear for their lives and out of the desire to find better working conditions. The post-Amin era was a time for rehabilitation, and gradually both the infrastructure and staffing situation improved greatly. Makerere has since grown and transformed itself into a major player in

Bridging the Knowledge Divide, pages 215–229
Copyright © 2009 by Information Age Publishing
All rights of reproduction in any form reserved.

the provision of university education in the region with day, evening, and external programs being offered at its 22 schools, faculties, and institutes. By introducing external programs, Makerere University is now a dual-mode university. The student population as of this writing is about 30,000 undergraduate and 3,000 postgraduate students.

When it was started, Makerere offered only a few courses, which were meant to help train blacks to support the colonial government and eventually take over from the colonialists. Over the years, however, the number of courses being offered has grown in variety, and so have the student numbers. For example, by 2005, the University had 77 bachelor's programs; 14 undergraduate certificate programs; 10 postgraduate diploma programs; 60 master's programs; and 12 PhD programs; up from 22 bachelor's programs; 2 certificate programs; 8 postgraduate diploma programs; 9 master's programs and 4 doctoral programs in 1993 (Wabwire, 2007, p. 19).

The graduate output in the same academic year, 2005–06, was 9,667 in the various undergraduate and postgraduate programs, with 44% of these female. The growth of the courses and student numbers has been in response to the growing demand for higher education and the university's desire to train the required human resources vital for national development. In its effort to meet this growing demand both in-country and regionally, Makerere has recently become an example of a public university that has transformed itself from an institution relying entirely on government subsidies to a university with diverse programs, some that generate income. For example, the 2005–06 financial year generated 53 billion shillings (approximately $9.6 million USD) from internally generated income, representing nearly 50% of the total university budget (Wabwire, 2007).

All these efforts are a direct response to the increased demand for higher education in the face of dwindling government subvention and as a response to new market demands for graduates with new skills, knowledge, and attitudes.

MASSIFICATION AND DEMOCRATIZATION
OF EDUCATION IN UGANDA

The government White Paper on Education acknowledges the role of education in fulfilling the national goals of development, and so the national objectives of education are stated in conformity to these goals. Uganda also perceives education as "...a basic human right for all Ugandan citizens regardless of their social status, physical form, mental ability, sex, birth or place of ethnic origin..." (The Republic of Uganda, 1992, p. 162). In conformity with these, the Ministry of Education and Sports has as its mission, "to provide for, support, guide, coordinate, regulate and promote quality education and sports to all persons in Uganda for national integration, individual and national development" (Ministry of Education and Sports, 2006). Therefore, to ensure that these goals and objectives are achieved, a number of national policies were put in place, including the introduction of Universal Primary Education (UPE) Universal Secondary Education (USE), and liberalization of the education system. However, in spite of all these efforts at massifying education, the system in the country has still not provided adequate facilities and opportunities for all the citizens to access education. The demand for both school and higher education, therefore, still far outstrips the existing facilities and resources.

There has been tremendous growth in the number of tertiary institutions. For example, in 1962, when Uganda became independent, Uganda had one university, one technical college, and one National Teachers College (for the training of diploma teachers); by 1999 the numbers had grown to 10,500 primary schools, 625 secondary schools and 2 universities; by 2002 the number of secondary schools had risen to 2,198, while the universities had grown to 14. The greatest change has perhaps been since 2003, for by 2006 the universities rose to 27, with six of these as public universities (Ministry of Education and Sports, 1999: p. 5; Wabwire, 2007, p. 12).

The implementation of UPE has boosted school enrollment figures in the primary-school system, and this is creating a UPE bulge that will demand specific strategies to ensure that the huge number enrolling in primary school will continue to secondary education and later to tertiary/university education. In 2004 a total of 433,010 students sat the primary leaving examinations; if by 2010, when this cohort is expected to sit for Advanced (A) Level examinations, 30% will have dropped out, and 303,107 will sit the examinations; if only 50% of these complete and pass the examinations, then in 2011 nearly 150,000 students will be eligible for university education. In 2005 the total admissions to all the universities and tertiary institutions was 124,314 (Ministry of Education and Sports, 2006). If, therefore, these institutions maintain the same capacity, more than 25,000 students will not gain admission into any institution of higher education. To do so would require alternative means of providing higher education. Figure 12.1 represents this scenario.

In an effort, therefore, to democratize education, government recommended provision of continuous and life-long education. The White Paper recommends that "tertiary institutions, especially the universities should expand the activities of their Centres for Continuing Education and Extension work" (The Republic of Uganda, 1992, p. 183). Dual-mode universities like Makerere University were therefore expected to diversify their programs so as to ensure provision of continuing and extension education. However, although, as said earlier, the number of universities has grown tremendously, admission figures from the other universities remain low while Makerere

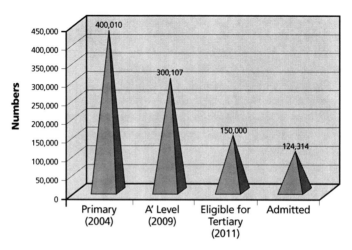

Figure 12.1 Projected Student Numbers Joining Tertiary Education in 2011. *Source:* Admissions office, Makerere University.

continues to have the highest enrollment. For example, in the academic year 2005–06, Makerere had a total enrollment of 33,108 (60.8%) out of the aggregate enrollment of 71,279 in all the public universities (Wabwire 2007, p. 12).

In 2005, 59,329 students presented themselves for the advanced-level examinations; out of these, 35,172 passed with a minimum of two principal passes, which is the required minimum pass for entry into undergraduate programs in the public universities (Ahimbisibwe & Mugisa, 2006). However, Makerere University, with the highest intake, admitted only 2,493 on government scholarship, another 13,116 as private fee-paying students, and 1,309 (7.7% of total admission) as external students. In spite of the enormous increase in enrollment at Makerere, many young people are still left without hope of accessing higher education. This is compounded by the fact that a number of students admitted as fee-paying students do not always pay the required fees and ultimately drop out of the university.

Uganda is certainly interested in massifying and democratizing education, and the efforts in place have increased the number of students enrolling in the school and higher-education system. In the latter case, Makerere continues to be a major player.

Makerere and Massification of Education

Makerere's response to this increasing demand for higher education has been through the diversification of its programs to include evening and

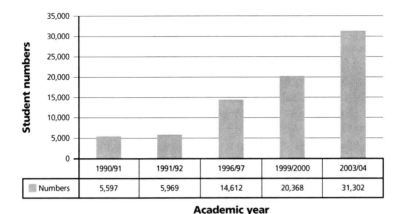

Figure 12.2 Undergraduate Student Numbers in Makerere University 1990–2004.
Source: Makerere University Annual Report 2004.

external programs. The introduction of evening programs was to open up access to the working class wishing to study and to increase the number of school leavers admitted; while the introduction of external degrees was to provide access to a cross-section of clients, including adults working and living in the countryside. The impact of all this has been an enormous increase in the students enrolling in programs in Makerere. Figure 12.2 gives the growth of student numbers in Makerere since 1991, when the External Degree Program was introduced. By 1991 Makerere had a total enrollment of 5,597 undergraduate students; by 1999 this number had grown to 16, 042, and to 31,302 by 2005, reflecting a 459% increase. In the academic year 2006–07 Makerere admitted a total of 17,019 undergraduate students.

This is a clear illustration of Makerere's attempt at fulfilling the government vision of massifying higher education, but a lot more is still expected of the university. Makerere recognizes this and has in the Strategic framework: 2007–08/2017–18 identified the use of open, distance, and e-learning (ODeL) as one of the key strategies for the next 10-year plan. One of the goals in this new plan is therefore "to increase the supply capacity of the University to provide increased access opportunities to meet increasing demand for higher education at national level"; and one of the measures of success for this plan shall be "increased number of Programs offered using ODeL approaches" (Makerere University, 2007). As the new plan is rolled out, the hope is that the External Degree Program will expand much more than it has done in the last 16 years of its existence.

The next section will focus on exploring the specific role that Makerere's External Degree Program has so far played in massification and democratization of education in the country.

EXTERNAL DEGREE PROGRAM

Objectives

The External Degree Program (EDP) was launched in 1991 at the then Centre for Continuing Education (CCE), now the Institute of Adult and Continuing Education (IACE) with the following aims in mind:

> To introduce degree courses by distance education and so increase university intake in some fields of higher education that meet urgent national needs;

> Produce good quality course materials, which would also be used by the internal students and other people in the near future;

> Strengthen the university's distance-education organization on the basis of enrollment and practice

> Develop Makerere University's capability to offer a good distance-education service, which will meet national, community, and individual needs at undergraduate and postgraduate levels (CCE, 1990, p. 19).

Management

Under the EDP scheme, the Department of Distance Education can, in collaboration with any other department, run any program as a distance-education program. The department therefore collaborates with the Faculty of Economics and Management in running the Bachelor of Commerce (External), the School of Education for the Bachelor of Education (External), and the Faculty of Science for the Bachelor of Science (External). Under this arrangement, the department is responsible for the management and administration of the program, while the collaborating faculties are responsible for the teaching functions. However, although this arrangement seems quite plain and clear, it has created some problems. These are discussed later as part of the challenges distance education faces in a dual-mode institution.

Programs

The External Degree Program was launched with only two courses: Bachelor of Education (BEd) for the upgrading of both primary- and secondary-school teachers from the diploma level to the degree level, and Bachelor of Commerce (BCom) for both A level leavers and those with diplomas in business subjects. Since then the department has introduced two other programs: Bachelor of Science (BSc) and Commonwealth Youth Program (CYP) Diploma in Youth Work and Development. The department's strategic plan envisages that by the year 2017–18, when this new plan comes to a close, there will be a total of nine external programs.

Study Package

The study package for the EDP consists of written study materials, student study groups, face-to-face sessions, assignments, and audiocassettes. The study package is therefore a blended package, although because of inadequate study materials, the program is skewed toward heavy reliance on face-to-face sessions, and there has been no integration of modern technologies. There have already been efforts at integrating e-mail and mobile-phone technologies in the provision of student support. Although this has been a pilot study, the results indicate huge promise that the department ought to pursue further.

Quality Assurance

The learning materials given to the external students are developed using clear and strict guidelines to ensure that these materials are appropriate for distance learners. Some of the key steps in the process include the training of writers, peer review, editing, and adherence to a specific house style. Also, all programs offered under the EDP are subject to the university general quality-assurance guidelines and mechanisms and the recently approved Quality Assurance Policy. Curriculum design for the external programs is therefore subject to the approved university processes; the same external examiners are involved in assessing both the internal and external students; and all programs employ the same general university examination regulations. Also, as far as is practically possible, students sit the same examinations with the internal students, as in the case of Bachelor of Commerce. In February 2007, as one of the strategies of working toward developing a culture of quality assurance at all levels in the university, a Quality Assurance Unit was established, with the responsibility for the quality-assurance function. The activities of this unit are meant to benefit all university programs including the external programs. These are the different ways in which Makerere is attempting to achieve parity of esteem for all the programs.

These quality-assurance strategies have helped promote acceptance of the external students in both the university and in the job market. Although again no empirical research has been carried out to establish acceptability of the graduates, anecdotal evidence is available to show that all graduates are employed without discrimination.

ACHIEVEMENTS

Enrollment

The Department of Distance Education has helped boost the university intake numbers through its EDP. Since its launch in 1991, the EDP enrollment has grown from 245 registered students in 1991 to an enrollment of approximately 6,500 in 2007. This enrollment is almost 20% of the total university enrollment.

Prior to the launching of the BEd (External), Makerere University did not have any students for this degree, except for students who were studying at the then Institute of Teacher Education Kyambogo (ITEK), now Kyambogo University—and registered for this Makerere degree. Even then, only about 300 students were admitted each year. While with the BCom, each year the university admitted about 60 students, today more than 500 students are admitted each academic year. Also, with the introduction of the EDP, more and more adults are retuning to school, as opposed to only 10% who were admitted each year prior to the introduction of both the external and private students' scheme. The introduction of the EDP therefore gave Makerere University the opportunity to expand its intake, diversify its clientele, fulfill the nation's objective of massifying education, and provide the much-needed human resource for national development.

Also, the programs currently being run are programs that are expected to have a direct impact on national development; for example, BEd is meant to upgrade teachers from diploma level to graduate level with the hope that this would make them better teachers. The BCom (External), on the other hand, was started with hope of increasing the much needed human resource, with knowledge and skills on business subjects a particularly urgent need as Uganda seeks to expand its hitherto largely agro-based economy. However, there have been no tracer studies carried out to establish the impact of the EDP graduates on the economy. This is an area that requires urgent attention.

Overall, the Makerere student population has expanded greatly (by 459% between 1999 and 2005), raising fears that perhaps the expansion is at the expense of quality. In response to this, the University Council resolved to decongest the university by annually reducing the intake figures by 10%. This seems like a contradiction, considering that the nation as a whole expects increased admissions, so it is now felt that one way of decongesting the university main campus, increasing overall enrollment while at the same time maintaining quality, is through expanding and strengthening the External Degree Program.

Increased Income for the University

The EDP was the first fee-paying degree program at Makerere University and can therefore be said to have paved the way for the introduction of fee-paying programs in Makerere. This innovation was in the midst of a lot of doubt and skepticism about the feasibility of any university program levying fees. Until this time, all university programs received full funding from government. However, due to pressures of reconstruction and rebuilding the nation, and the donor conditionalities, government subsidies were shrinking, and Makerere was under pressure to find alternative sources of funding. Introduction of fee-paying programs was therefore one way of diversifying funding while at the same time increasing access to the much demanded university education.

In the financial year 2006–07, the budget of the Department of Distance Education was 2.5 billion Uganda shillings (approximately $1.5 million USD). Out of this, the department contributed a total of nearly 320 million Uganda shillings to the central administration, while the rest of this income was used for running the department and its programs. In addition to the contribution made from tuition fees, the university also receives additional income from the functional fees that the students pay. As mentioned earlier, internally generated income has greatly enhanced the university's ability to meet its financial obligations, and there have been some initiatives that have been implemented through these internally generated funds, and these include

- A staff-development fund, which has enabled the university to train both academic and nonacademic staff by funding, especially graduate studies and research. Over the period between 2000 and 2007, a total of 51 staff were funded for PhD studies.
- A number of new buildings have been put up. This is significant, considering the increasing student population and therefore the growing need for office and classroom space.
- Salary enhancement. The government no longer funds the entire salary bill, and the university is now contributing toward enhancing all the salaries. Although there are debates about the sustainability of this strategy, considering that it is dependant on the university's ability to continue generating income, for now, this strategy has helped assuage the staff.
- Research funds that can be accessed for either graduate research, any other appropriate research, and for publications.

All in all, the Department of Distance Education has also contributed to all these initiatives through the income it generates from tuition fees and functional fees.

Developing High Quality Materials

As pointed out earlier, the EDP uses a study package that includes written materials, student study-group meetings; face-to-face sessions, audiocassettes, and radio. Both the external and internal students of the university are using the study materials that have been developed. In so doing, the program has helped address the problem of lack of reading material in the university.

Another related development has been that the department trains all its writers in the development of high quality and relevant learning materials that take into account the unique nature of distance learners. This training has contributed to enhancing the writing skills of lecturers, and some of them have gone further and written and produced other books. This is a huge contribution toward building up the capacity of the university staff to write learning materials.

Strengthened University's Capacity to Run Distance Education Programs

After the correspondence courses of the 1960s collapsed, the university lost its capacity to run distance education programs. However, since the launching of the EDP, the university capacity has grown stronger as evidenced by

- Establishment of the Department of Distance Education in 1992;
- Increase in the number of staff in the Department of Distance Education, with some of them undertaking various studies in the field of Distance Education;
- As part of the university's growing confidence in its ability to run distance education programs, a Bachelor of Science (External) was launched in 2002. It is often feared that distance education cannot be used to offer courses with practical components, but the university is now convinced that this can be done as long as there is adequate preparation for the practical component.
- The university is also looking to expanding the External Degree Program. This is evidenced in the inclusion of distance education as one of the strategic directions in the Strategic framework for the development of the Strategic Plan for 2007–08/2017–18.

Influencing National Policy on Distance and Open Learning

Makerere University is a key stakeholder in the development and provision of higher education in the country and has therefore been involved in a number of national efforts. For example, with regard to the development and growth of distance education in the country, the university is involved in lobbying for the development of a national policy on distance and open learning and the development of minimum standards for institutions seeking to offer distance education. This is important for the overall growth and development of distance and open learning in the country. The launching of the EDP has certainly helped rejuvenate distance education activities at both Makerere University and the country at large.

CHALLENGES DISTANCE EDUCATION FACES IN A DUAL-MODE INSTITUTION

Management

All the programs currently offered are on a collaborative basis, involving the teaching faculties and the Department of Distance Education. As earlier mentioned, the responsibilities are shared, but the demarcation into administrative and academic function is not that obvious. The case of the BCom (External) best illustrates this. At the launch of the program, BCom (External) was run in collaboration with the Faculty of Commerce, however when this faculty became Makerere University Business School (MUBS), there was no clear agreement between the Department of Distance Education and the Business School over what constitutes administrative and what constitutes academic functions, and disagreements erupted.

Also, distance education requires specialized skills and management, which is not often found in universities running internal programs. Introducing distance education therefore brings in new demands, creating tensions and pressures that Makerere does not seem to have given adequate thought to. The uniqueness of the department, its staff, and student population does not seem to have been taken into account. As a result, the department establishment is as for any other academic department, with the resultant effect that the department is understaffed, and there are key positions that are not catered to. Such inadequacies are likely to compromise the quality of the service delivered to students and the quality of the programs as a whole. To address this issue, the university is developing a comprehensive policy that will guide all the operations of the distance education unit and its programs.

Funding

As a fee-paying program, the EDP has long been classified as an evening program and has for many years been contributing 41% of its income to the Central Administration of the university. No special arrangement was made for the EDP taking into account its uniqueness. As a result, the department has been dissatisfied with the way this is being handled, while the Central Administration seemed baffled by the department's position. Clearly this was lack of clear understanding and appreciation of the uniqueness of DE programs. This has been addressed with the university recognizing the department's unique demands; therefore the department only contributes 20%. However, this decision was taken only as a temporary measure. Reverting to the old strategy will certainly not help strengthen the program as envisaged.

This is compounded by the fact that all running costs of the program, with the exception of salaries for some staff, is meant to come from fees collected, and yet the students pay very low fees. At the time of launching the program, fees were deliberately kept low so as to open up access to the underprivileged. However, the current fees have been overtaken by inflation and should change. The department also needs to diversify sources of income.

The Department's Mandate

Although the proposal to establish the EDP gave the department the mandate to develop any other programs in collaboration with other faculties, this mandate seems to be either not well-understood or not well-appreciated by other departments, which now want to independently run distance education programs and have little or no association with the department. The major reason for this is that in all the current programs, the department has control of the finances generated, which has become a bone of contention.

This raises the question of what the department's mandate ought to be and what model of management of programs Makerere should adopt. The hope is that the draft Policy on Distance Education being debated will put to rest some of these dilemmas.

Low Enrollment

The enrollment figures for the external programs in Makerere are still low. Although the current figures appear massive considering the total university population (6,500—nearly 20% of total enrollment), the full potential of distance education to reach many more students has not been fully exploited. The major handicap is inadequate development of critical systems necessary for the expansion of programs. For example, the student-support system is very weak, thus there are no effective learning centers in all the major towns in the country. A highly centralized student-support system does not reach out to the very persons for which the program was designed.

Inadequate Study Materials Development

Written materials were supposed to be the core medium of instruction in this program. However, the rate of development of the study materials has been extremely slow. A lot of study units have been written, but only a few have been published. This seems to be a major handicap of this program, for as it is pointed out

> Unfortunately, the EDP still relies heavily on face-to-face sessions as the major form of support. This is partly because of lack of sufficient study materials which should really be the core of the study package. (Department of Distance Education, 2001, p. 1)

The department still faces the same problem. Study materials coverage is still low. Bachelor of Science (External) is the only program with nearly 70% of all the required modules already developed, but this was only because this program benefited from donor funding for the materials development.

Any distance education program that has inadequate learning materials is running the risk of compromising the standard of its programs. Makerere University is therefore running this risk and should make every effort to address the need for more study materials and for the integration of other technologies in its programs. Some work is being done in exploring the integration of mobile technologies in student support, and initial research indicates huge promise. Some work has also been done in trying the integration of e-learning, but this has been done with internal students, although there is pressure now to integrate it in the current distance education programs. A major challenge still is access to technology and the poor infrastructure at the regional centers.

If Makerere University is to remain relevant in both the type of programs run and the study package being used, modern technologies must be exploited in the provision of high quality and relevant learning materials.

LESSONS LEARNED

The Makerere University dual-mode experience in contributing toward the development of the country provides a number of key lessons that can be learned:

- Introduction of distance education programs in a traditional university requires careful planning to avoid disenfranchising the students. New systems and structures that cater for the needs of distance learners will need to be put in place.
- Universities intending to become dual mode must also invest in the development of distance education learning materials, structures, and systems. It is a fallacy to believe that because a university already has structures and systems these will be sufficient for distance education as well.
- Quality-assurance mechanisms employed should help achieve parity of esteem for both the internal and external students.
- The opportunity to offer distance education programs provides opportunity to traditional universities to open up access to university education.
- Dual-mode universities can maximize the utilization of resources since the physical facilities and the academic and nonacademic staff can be involved in reaching more students than is permitted in a traditional university.
- Distance education offers universities opportunities to reach more people and exploit the changing work and study demands in changing economies.
- To fully exploit the benefits of distance education and for dual-mode institutions to thrive, there must be a conducive national environment, including the existence of clear national policies, rules, and regulations on distance and open learning.

CONCLUSION

Makerere University has attempted to address the national demand for higher education and the need for human resource through the diversification of its programs by offering day, evening, and external programs. The External Degree Program, in particular, has opened up access to hitherto neglected clients and has gone a long way in facilitating the acceptability of distance education in the country and in the job market.

With the increasing demand for higher education in many countries in sub-Saharan Africa, distance and open learning are strategies that could be utilized to increase access and promote development. Since, however, most governments do not have adequate funds to build more new universities, traditional universities can adopt distance education to diversify strategies, but for this to work effectively, the right systems and structures for distance education should be put in place.

REFERENCES

Ahimbisibwe, F., & Mugisa, A. (2006). S6 results released. *The New Vision*, Wednesday, February 23, 2006. Retrieved July 31, 2006 from http://newvision.co.ug/D/8/12/419660/uneb%20results%20statistics

Centre for Continuing Education (1990). A proposal to start the external degree program. Centre for Continuing Education, Kampala, Uganda.

Department of Distance Education (2001). Tutoring section report. Department of Distance Education, Kampala, Uganda.

Makerere University (2004). *Makerere University annual report 2004*, Makerere University, Kampala, Uganda.

Makerere University (2007, April). Repositioning Makerere to meet emerging development challenges: strategic framework: 2007/08-2017/18. Makerere University, Kampala, Uganda.

Ministry of Education and Sports (1999). *The Ugandan experience of Universal primary education (UPE)*. Kampala, Uganda.

Ministry of Education and Sports (2006). *Education sector annual performance report 1st July 2005–30th June 2006*. Kampala, Uganda. Retrieved August 17, 2007 from http://www.education.go.ug/Final%20ESAPR%202006.htm#_Toc149034303

Republic of Uganda (1992). *The education policy review commission report on education for national integration and development*. Government white paper (pp. 6–8,162–185). Republic of Uganda, Kampala.

Wabwire, J. K. W. (2007, February). Makerere University towards 2017 strategic choices. (pp. 11–24. Makerere University, Kampala, Uganda.

CHAPTER 13

CONSIDERATIONS FOR HIGHER EDUCATION DISTANCE EDUCATION POLICY FOR DEVELOPMENT

A University of Botswana Case Study

Judith W. Kamau

DISTANCE EDUCATION POLICY AS A NATIONAL AGENDA

The earliest government initiative in Botswana to apply distance education in solving socioeconomic problems dates back to 1962, when untrained primary-school teachers were enrolled on an Elementary Teachers Certificate to upgrade their academic and professional qualifications using correspondence materials obtained from a correspondence college in Salisbury, present day Harare (Mphinyane,1993). Learners were also supported with face-to-face tutorials and radio broadcasts aired over weekends. By the time this program came to an end in 1965, it had demonstrated that the distance delivery mode was a viable alternative for teacher upgrading. Following independence in 1966, there was need to expand education

Bridging the Knowledge Divide, pages 231–244
Copyright © 2009 by Information Age Publishing
All rights of reproduction in any form reserved.

at all levels to promote socioeconomic development. This demand led to unprecedented enrollments at the primary-school level with no trained teachers to teach or even replace expatriate teachers who were leaving the country (Mphinyane, 1993). In 1986 the government responded to this challenge by initiating the Francistown College Teacher Training project by distance mode. By the time this project came to an end in 1973, over 700 teachers had been trained through a combination of correspondence materials supported by radio broadcasts and face-to-face sessions (Nhundu, Kamau, & Thutoetsile, 2002).

The success of the two ad hoc initiatives discussed above prompted the government to formalize the provision of distance education programs. In 1973 the Botswana Extension College was started to run secondary-level correspondence courses. In 1977 the management of these courses was transferred to the newly created Department of None-Formal Education in the Ministry of Education, (Nhundu, Kamau, & Thutoetsile, 2002). With no proper structures to run a distance education program, the department experienced various problems, such as limited resources in the form of personnel, space, and budget, including lack of understanding and lack of institutional and professional status, which made it difficult for the department to respond promptly to learners needs (Report of the National Commission on Education, 1993). To minimize these constraints and strengthen the status and legitimacy of the distance education, the National Commission on Education of 1993 recommended the creation of a Botswana Distance Education college and the strengthening of the Centre for Continuing Education at the University of Botswana to enhance the expansion, diversification, and development of the distance-delivery mode (Report of the National Commission on Education, 1993, p. 303).

The Revised National Policy on Education (RNPE) (1994) and Vision 2016: Towards Prosperity for All (1996) also recognized the potential of distance education as part and parcel of the entire educational system and, in particular, as a tool for redressing regional and gender imbalances and preparing citizens for life and the world of work, through continuing and lifelong learning. To make distance education part of the decision-making process at the national level, the government of Botswana established the Botswana College of Distance and Open Learning (BOCODOL) by an Act of Parliament in 1998. The role of BOCODOL is to expand education and training opportunities to out-of-school youth and adults through the use of distance education methodology. Through BOCODOL, the government is extending formal education and entrepreneurial skills to out-of-school youth and other adults as a strategy for socioeconomic development and to prepare them for participation in higher education in the future (Tau and Thutoestile, 2006).

DEVELOPMENT OF DISTANCE EDUCATION AT THE UNIVERITY OF BOTSWANA

The earliest distance education program at the UB was the Certificate in Adult Education (CAE), launched in 1982 by the then Institute of Adult Studies (IAS), to prepare literacy teachers for the eradication of illiteracy. Through this certificate course, the government has been able to train literacy teachers for combating ignorance, disease, and poverty, which were perceived as the main enemies of socioeconomic development in many developing nations, including Botswana, between the 1960s and1980s. Since that time, the university has diversified its programs to diploma and degree courses and is venturing into postgraduate courses.

In 1991 the Centre for Continuing Education (CCE) was created from the (IAS) and mandated to expand participation in tertiary education through the distance-delivery mode. Since that time, the CCE has been the administrative and professional unit through which the university extends some of its diploma and degree courses to the public. The CCE is responsible for course development and delivery, which entails instructional design, writing, editing, production, and distribution of study materials and management of student-support services, while academic faculties are responsible for curriculum decisions, including content and structure of courses, quality assurance, and assessment. To maintain parity of standards between the conventional and the distance-taught programs, academic faculties are expected to provide lecturers for materials development and tutors for course delivery.

The University of Botswana recognizes the potential of the distance education delivery mode in various planning documents. For example, in the 2004–2009 Development Plan "Shaping Our Future," the university undertakes to expand access to tertiary education through

> Self-development, franchising, partnership arrangements with other universities, academic and professional institutions, and interactive video-conferencing...*including*...access to ICT driven information resources through partnerships, cooperative ventures and contractual agreements. The Centre for Continuing Education (CCE) will be re-conceptualized as a technology driven open and distance tertiary learning centre for the nation. (Shaping Our Future 2004–2009, p. 3)

DISTANCE EDUCATION BEFORE THE
MAINSTREAMING POLICY

Before 2005 distance education programs were implemented using the traditional face-to-face regulatory structures, which are not compatible with the special nature and requirements of distance learners. Within this context, distance education had evolved as an add-on to the extramural and on-campus extension activities that made the existing rules and regulations irrelevant to the requirements of distance education. Adapting these rules and regulations to the operations of distance education did not solve the problems either, because distance education still remained on the periphery. As a result, the CCE encountered various problems, ranging from lack of materials developers and tutors to grade students' work and providing feedback, including unavailability of physical facilities for tutorials and practical work. Where an external stakeholder approached the CCE to provide a course that was not offered by any academic faculty, the CCE had to look for an appropriate academic home from various faculties to register, assess, and accredit distance learners, because as a service department, the CCE has no mandate to register and accredit any academic program. These constraints negated the expansion of academic programs via the distance mode and hence the need for the DE mainstreaming policy.

The peripheral position of distance education within the current dual-management structures has resulted in significant challenges in the development and delivery of distance education programs. At the operational level, it has been difficult for the CCE to introduce distance education programs in the current organizational structures due to institutional cultures and attitudinal barriers that make mainstream academicians cast doubt on the credibility of distance education as a viable delivery mode, in comparison with traditional teaching methods. These barriers may be a result of misplaced fears and psychological dissociation with distance education programs by the mainstream faculties, thinking that the quality of conventional academic programs would be compromised and that the time-tested traditional teaching methods are superior to distance teaching and learning (Hope, 2006).

The DE mainstreaming policy was therefore meant to address these barriers and bring distance education from the periphery by infusing it with the decision-making organs and core business of the university. To achieve this goal, the policy has identified a number of operational activities and responsibilities where the CCE and collaborating departments need to converge:

- **Program initiation:** participation in joint program initiation, materials development, and review including syllabus approval by collaborating academic departments;

- **Materials development:** maintaining quality assurance through content review for quality assurance by staff members from academic departments;
- **Materials adaptation:** subject experts from academic departments carry out materials inspection for adaptation of study materials to determine their appropriateness, gaps, and contextualizing them to local academic enrollment;
- **Recruitment of writers/content reviewers, tutors and markers:** in consultation with academic departments, the CCE to determine criteria for selection and appointment of part-time staff;
- **Delivery of instruction and assessment:** subject experts from academic departments to conduct face-to-face tutorials, set assessment items, moderate examination questions, and mark students scripts;
- **Record Keeping:** both the CCE and academic departments to maintain up-to-date student and tutor records;
- **Program review:** both the CCE and academic departments to carry out joint and continuous monitoring and major program reviews. (Distance Education Mainstreaming policy, pp. 13–14).

It is hoped that this collaboration will bring about quality assurance and parity of standards between the conventional and distance-taught programs. The policy articulates areas of responsibility at the institutional, faculty, departmental, and individual level. At the institutional level, the university undertakes to monitor faculty, departmental, and individual accountability in the development and delivery of distance education programs, including ensuring that distance learners get the same quality administrative, advisement, and instructional support as their on-campus counterparts. The university will also provide incentives and rewards such as attractive part-time payments for services rendered on distance education programs so as to encourage full-time staff to invest more time and effort in the development and delivery of distance education programs across the university. Faculties and departments are expected to infuse distance education into their missions and strategic plans to enable them to initiate new courses or convert existing ones into the distance-delivery mode. At the individual level, academic departments are expected to provide part-time staff to develop learning materials, conduct tutorials, and provide learners with academic advisement and prompt feedback (Distance Education Mainstreaming Policy, 2005, pp. 12–13).

COLLABORATIVE PROGRAM DEVELOPMENT
AND DELIVERY

Program initiation, planning, and development, including course design, development, and production is a labor-intensive activity that requires a systematic team-approach strategy (MacDonald-Ross, 1995). At the program initiation and development stages, the mainstreaming policy requires the CCE to form a Program Planning and Development Committee (PPDC), comprising representatives from CCE, collaborating academic departments, and Library and Information Technology (IT) representatives to plan the nature, structure, and volume of learning materials and establish whether the regulations are flexible and responsive to the needs of distance learners. Thereafter, the Course Development Team (CDT) takes over to design interactive and user-friendly, self-instructional materials within the agreed-upon deadlines. The role of the library is to ensure that the necessary reading materials are available and accessible to distance learners while the IT department ensures the availability and functionality of media, such as the video-conferencing suites and computers for the e-learning.

For parity of standards, the majority of course writers, content reviewers, tutors, and markers are recruited from collaborating departments through internal advertising circulated via the UB intranet and the local media to attract additional part-timers. After training part-time staff in course development and tutorial skills, CCE program coordinators work with the collaborating departments to ensure that learning materials adhere to the distance-teaching instructional design pedagogy. In addition, the CCE has developed clearly documented procedures and processes in the form of style guides that spell out instructional design components and how the subject matter is to be structured, and contractual agreements that spell out roles and responsibilities of part-time university staff. These measures have been put in place to ensure that distance education programs are consistent with their on-campus equivalents in terms of curriculum, outcomes, resource availability, and staff qualifications, and that distance learners are not disadvantaged by the assessment and program-evaluation procedures, which are the same as those applied to on-campus students.

In addition, the distance education mainstreaming policy recognizes the need for the systematic provision of appropriate learner-support services in the form of regular interaction between distance learners and their teachers, accessibility to tutors by individuals and groups of learners, and provision of feedback on assessment within a reasonable turnaround time so as to judge their progress and access to physical facilities, such as libraries, quiet space for studies, laboratory, and equipment for practical work. Within the distance education mainstreaming policy framework, information on distance education programs is provided through students' information booklets, such as the students' assignment handbook. The students' handbook contains information about program/course overview and structure, admission requirements, learning outcomes, total costs, assessment requirements and processes, rules and regulations, and appeals procedures. It also specifies to the students the rules of the distance education administrative unit and the collaborating academic faculties and departments. The students also receive the university calendar to familiarize themselves with the university general regulations governing the structure, assessment procedures, and processes and awards of the programs and courses they are studying.

INTEGRATION FOR DISTANCE EDUCATION
IN ACADEMIC FACULTIES

It is one thing to make policy pronouncements and quite another to make them operational. A distance education system is not a series of separate entities, such as course content and course design and development, but a system of interrelated components that function together under the auspices of organizational and administrative arrangements (Kamau, 2004). This systems-based relationship should bring together different aspects of distance education and align them with corresponding components of the traditional delivery mode in a dual-mode institution such as the UB. The DE mainstreaming policy was not accompanied by implementation strategies, and three years later, certain questions related to its implementation still beg answers. For example, what changes in current policy structures and procedures were needed to promote better quality distance education provision in this dual-mode institution? Was the DE mainstreaming policy going to be embraced without introducing changes in the existing organizational structures? What monitoring mechanism would enable the university to assess the acceptance or otherwise of the DE mainstreaming policy and as a result, make distance learning an integral part of the more established traditional higher-education system within the university? These questions still need answers.

However, in order to widen access, UB has commissioned a national needs-assessment survey to determine the demand and priorities of the country in higher education that can be met via the distance education programs. The results of the survey will enable the university to develop and provide more demand-driven academic programs and create a comprehensive, more decentralized learner-support system that is responsive to learners' needs nationwide. It will also enable the university to develop information and communications strategies that will enhance access to Information and Communications Technologies (ICT) resources and promote the delivery of educational services to distance learners across distributed study centers. The spread and accessibility of ICT to potential distance learners will enable the university to determine whether it can establish learner-friendly registration systems that allow learners to initiate and complete registration formalities from their nearest centers without coming to the main campus. Finally, the survey will also inform the university about availability of subject expertise outside the university walls that can be tapped for program development and delivery through collaborative or other franchising partnerships.

Currently, the UB does not have its own learner-support physical infrastructures. However, it is committed to the provision of learner-support services through collaboration with other tertiary institutions in the country. Already, distance learners receive face-to-face tutorials at designated study centers based in other tertiary institutions. The university is also collaborating with other institutions in the region such as the University of South Africa (UNISA), from where it obtained start-up learning materials in 2003, to fast-track the launching of four business degree programs in accounting, finance, marketing and management. Plans are underway to automate registration processes so that students can register at specified centers in the country and not have to travel to the main campus to register for their courses.

Access to ICT facilities for distance learners at the regional level has been enhanced by the government ICT Policy, which undertakes to make ICT accessible to its citizens in every village (Botswana National ICT Policy Initiatives, 2005). The government ICT strategy focuses on community access and development, learning, health, government, economic development, the ICT sector, and provision of technical infrastructure. This policy supports the university's media-diversification technology initiatives in the development and delivery of distance education programs, because potential distance learners have access to technology close to their homes. In addition, this policy will reduce the current disparities between rural and urban access to information and services, which for a long time has limited provision of distance education to the print media only.

Implementation of the DE Policy

Attempts to integrate the distance education mainstreaming policy have revealed other difficulties that hinder implementation of changes in traditional institutions, whereas Hope (2006) observes, the weight of entrenched vested interests promotes inertia, and processes of institutional governance grind exceedingly slowly. A distance education system requires tighter control, which is difficult to exercise in a dual-mode university environment such as the University of Botswana. Managers of distance education programs require authority to enforce policy in the form of rules and regulations, otherwise the operational aspects of distance education become difficult to manage, compromising successful achievement of goals. Currently, many academic faculties and departments consider distance education as a foreign newcomer within their systems. It has been difficult to advance distance education management issues in this context due to lack of framework to facilitate implementation of the policy between the CCE and collaborating academic departments.

An open and distance education mainstreaming plan must contain the implementation strategies and time frames within which certain activities should be achieved, and a monitoring mechanism to identify and address shortcomings (Siaciwena, 2006). This will ensure that parity of standards is not unidirectional, where students studying at a distance are forced to conform to regulations governing the conventional programs that are not relevant to the circumstances of distance learners. Furthermore, the influence of the existing institutional culture impedes program development and delivery because the appointment of writers and tutors from outside academic faculties, for example, must be vetted by Academic Boards of collaborating faculties and departments as a quality-assurance measure. This is despite the fact that oftentimes, full-time academic staff has no time to write course materials or conduct face-to-face tutorials on distance education programs, citing their "normal" workload as a major constraint. Needless to say, workload constraints have been observed in other dual-mode institutions as impeding factors toward the development of a fully integrated dual-mode system of delivery, particularly because the design and development of distance-teaching materials and tutoring distance learners carries little weight in terms of career-path aspirations for academic members of staff (Hope, 2006).

Rewarding Academic Staff for Participating in Distance Education Programs

Another constraint has been in the area of rewarding mainstream academicians who participate in the distance education program. Establishing an equitable reward or remuneration system for writers and tutors has been one of the most difficult management tasks facing administrators of distance education programs in dual-mode institutions. Recognition of learning modules as publications in the same category as journal articles, books, and chapter in books, for example, but not just as teaching materials for purposes of promotion and tenure requires addressing. Course writers as well as copy and content editors argue (and rightly so) that the rigor and amount of time they invest in researching and writing a module of 12–15 units (chapters)—in compliance with UB requirements—and editing distance learning materials is the same, if not more than, the time they put to writing or editing a journal article, a book chapter, or even a book. Secondly, long payment procedures due to bureaucratic requirements have discouraged many faculty members from participating in distance education programs. The Taxation Act requires all the money earned by an individual, whether from full-time employment or part-time fees, to be combined for taxation purposes. As a result, lecturers' fees from part-time work on distance education programs are combined with their monthly earnings and taxed. This taxation procedure has demotivated many faculty members from participating in distance education programs because to them, participation is a waste of their time since it has no added monetary value. As a result, many academicians opt to go out to carry out research and write for publications that carry more weight during their promotion and tenure processes. These disparities in the reward system stress the need for processes that enhance meshing distance and traditional education in the same institution.

CHALLENGES

The extent to which collaborating faculties and departments have accepted and are comfortable with distance education can only be assessed in terms of the congruence between the intent of the policy as stated and its implementation. One problem of policy implementation seems to center on the understanding and acceptance of the policy by the faculty members who are the implementers of distance education policy in their departments. This is borne out by the delays experienced in service delivery in the areas of materials writing, content review and copy editing, reluctance to conduct tutorials, invigilate scheduled tests and examinations, and mark students' assessment work on time as contracted academicians cite heavy workloads in their departments and unattractive part-time payment packages, which make them unable to deliver on time (Kamau, 2004). The CCE does not have mechanisms for disciplining part-time staff who do not perform their duties well, apart from refusing to renew their contracts next time round. Secondly, the distance education mainstreaming policy seems to imply that academic departments will participate in distance education programs without question, in addition to their teaching loads. Even though many faculty members are initially excited about participating in distance education activities, they find distance education unappealing or threatening if they are forced to meet agreed deadlines. Although the mainstreaming policy has a provision for the recruitment of a teaching assistant to replace lecturers who are engaged in program development for distance education, this has not been implemented due to logistical constraints. As such, and given the expanding enrollment on the conventional programs, it has been difficult for lecturers to be released from conventional classes to write materials for distance education since they cannot be replaced. Materials developers, for example, can only write during their spare time, which makes it difficult for them to meet the agreed-upon deadlines. It should be noted that nonparticipation of mainstream academicians may erode the credibility of distance education programs, since the policy states that quality assurance of all distance education programs will be carried out by academic departments.

This scenario is in contrast with Australia, where dual-mode institutions have operated very successfully, and the quality and reputation of distance education programs is assured by the development of an integrated structure in which the courses are planned, developed, and taught by the same academic staff to both full-time and part-time students (Jevons, 1987). In this Australian dual-mode model, distance learners get systematic support from lecturers, and both distance and on-campus students can move between the study modes at their convenience, since on- or off-campus terms describe a mode of study but not learners (Jevons, 1987). At the University of Botswana, moving from the distance to the conventional mode is discouraged in some academic programs, as many distance students could opt for the conventional classes where they are taught on a full-time basis.

DISTANCE LEARNERS AND THE DEMAINSTREAMING POLICY

Systemic components of distance education include students and curricula. However, the distance education mainstreaming policy does not suggest any curriculum change in terms of pedagogy so as to accommodate the needs of distance learners. Admission requirements that do remain unchanged, but that do not address logistical difficulties faced by distance learning students. While having a mainstreaming policy may be considered a strategy for widening access, the reality is that nondifferentiated admission policies that do not take into consideration the known profiles and problems faced by potential and enrolled distance learners, could militate against this strategy. For example, the proposed development of foundations courses to enable those currently barred by the prevailing admission requirements to get access to university education is still to be realized. Secondly, distance learners studying various courses have to conform to the same rules that regulate semesters for conventional students. These learners are expected to demonstrate their ability to meet the expected progression and completion criteria, without being given more time to overcome logistical difficulties such as traveling to the campus for tutorials and examinations, and simultaneously attend to their jobs and other commitments. The result is that there are many requests for retakes from students who could not write scheduled examinations for one reason or other.

In addition, distance education students pay the same tuition fees per credit hour per course as conventional students, although the costs of producing a module and conducting tutorials per distance education student have not been aligned to costs of conducting a one-hour lecture within the credit-hour cost-analysis system. No cost equivalencies have been worked out so far. These fees may have impeded expansion of enrollment, since they are unaffordable to the majority of distance learners, many of whom are self-sponsored. Unlike conventional students who are younger and just out of the formal schooling, distance learners are mature, with the majority of them being working adults. Although they are earning salaries, many distance learners have expressed their inability to meet their schools fees because they are paying fees for their children or younger siblings. Secondly, costs in distance education are driven by, among other things, course populations; the number of courses offered; the lengths of course lifetimes; the media and technologies chosen; teaching and assessing students; administration of learner support and providing infrastructure; planning and managing the distance education programs; and the extent to which cost-inducing actions, for example, the use of copyrighted materials, are avoided (Rumble, 2001, p.76). These variables have not been critically analyzed and cost equivalencies between distance and on-campus students established. If carried out, this analysis would enable UB to decouple the fees charged to distance learners from full-time rates since the drivers of costs between the two deliveries modes are not necessarily the same.

CONCLUSION

In this chapter, I have argued that the distance education mainstreaming policy was meant to integrate the provision of distance education programs within the university core business, and as a result, enable the university to widen access to higher education by expanding enrollment in line with the socioeconomic needs of the nation. While the distance education mainstreaming policy seeks to uphold parity of standards between the conventional and traditional programs, it is not understood, and as such, academic faculties have not as yet incorporated it in their teaching, research, and service activities. To achieve this wider goal, there is need for academic departments to address existing regulations, procedures, and processes that were initially created for the provision of conventional face-to-face programs because these regulatory measures are not compatible with the development and delivery of distance education programs. I have also argued that institutional policies related to promotion and professional development of academic staff need to be revisited so that work done by academicians in distance education programs is recognized and rewarded accordingly. For the policy to be embraced widely, there is need for a universitywide consultation so that academic departments and other support departments can appreciate their roles, responsibilities, and accountability in the implementation of the distance education mainstreaming policy, and in turn, widen access to higher education, which is an intrinsic objective of the mainstreaming policy.

REFERENCES

Hope, A. (2006). *Factors for success in dual mode Institutions.* Vancouver: Commonwealth of Learning. Retrieved December 2, 2008, from http:www.col.org/colweb/site/pid/3975

Jevons, F. (1987). Distance education and campus-based education: Parity of esteem. In P. Smith and M. Kelly (Eds.), *Distance education and the mainstream* (pp. 12–23). London: Croom Helm.

International Labor Organization (1994). The Revised National Policy on Education, March 1994—Botswana. Retrieved December 2, 2008, from http://www.ilo.org/public/english/employment/skills/hrdr/init/bot_6.htm

Kamau, J. W. (2004). Management of learner support services. Unpublished workshop paper in possession of the author. University of Botswana, Gaborone.

Macdonald-Ross, M. (1995). The development of printed materials: A view of print production for distance learning in the light of recent developments. In F. Lockwood (Ed.), *Open and distance learning today.* London: Routledge.

Mphinyane, O.P. (1993, September). Distance education in Botswana: Its present and potential role in human development. A dissertation submitted in partial fulfillment of the Master of Arts in Education and Development (Distance Education), University of London and Institute of Education.

Nhundu, T. J., Kamau, J. W., & Thuthoeitsile, T. (2002). From correspondence to distance education: The Botswana experience. A paper presented at the Second Pan Commonwealth Forum on Open and Distance Learning, Durban, South Africa, July 29–August 2, 2002. CDROM prepared by Commonwealth of Learning.

Republic of Botswana (2005). Botswana national policy initiatives. Ministry of Communications, Science and Technology. Gaborone, Botswana; Government Printer

Republic of Botswana (1996). Vision 2016. Gaborone, Botswana: Government Printer

Republic of Botswana (1994). Revised National Policy on Education 1994. Gaborone, Botswana: Government Printer.

Republic of Botswana (1993). Report of the National Commission on Education, 1993. Gaborone, Botswana: Government Printer.

Rumble, G. (2001, September). The costs and costing of networked learning. *Journal of Asynchronous Learning Networks, 5*(2).

Siaciwena, R. (1999). *Dual–mode distance education at the University of Namibia: A case study.* A study commissioned by the World Bank, Washington, DC.

Siaciwena, R. (2006). *Challenges of a dual mode institution: The case of the University of Zambia (UNZA).* Retrieved December 2, 2008, from http://pcf4.dec.uwi.edu/viewabstract.php?id=426

Tau, D.R., & Thutoetsile, T. (2006). Quality assurance in distance education: Towards a culture of quality in Botswana College of Distance and Open Learning (BO-CODOL). In B.N. Koul and A. Kanwar (Eds.), *Perspectives on distance education: Towards a Culture of Quality.* Vancouver: Commonwealth of Learning.

University of Botswana. (2004). *Shaping our future: UB's strategic priorities & actions to 2009 and beyond.* Gaborone.

University of Botswana. (2005). *Shaping our future: Strategic plan.* Retrieved May 22, 2006, from http://www.ub.bw/about/documents/shaping our future.pdf

University of Botswana. (2005). *Distance education mainstreaming policy.* Retrieved December 2, 2008, from http://www.ub.bw/documents/Distance_Education_Mainstreaming_Policy.pdf

University of Botswana. (2006). Distance education mainstreaming policy. University of Botswana, Gaborone.

University of Botswana. (2008). *Planning UB for the National Development Plan 10 (NDP10) Period, 2009–2015.* University of Botswana, Gaborone.

CHAPTER 14

BLENDED ONLINE AND FACE-TO-FACE LEARNING

A Pilot Project in the Faculty of Education, Eduardo Mondlane University

Xavier Justino Muianga

INTRODUCTION

Mozambique's National Information and Communication Technology (ICT) Policy (2002) provides principles and objectives that will allow ICT to be a driving force for national development and for better governance. Other goals are to increase the participation of the country in the global economy, to widen the access to the information society, and to convert the country from a mere consumer to a producer of ICT. In this way, ICT contributes to the poverty eradication and to the improvement of living conditions of Mozambicans.

Mozambique's national university, Eduardo Mondlane University (EMU), has a Strategic Plan (EMU, 1998) that supports the application of ICT in order to support education research and to improve teaching and learning processes. The plan specifies that

Bridging the Knowledge Divide, pages 245–265
Copyright © 2009 by Information Age Publishing
245

- The use of ICT can offer access to a wider student body across the country through the provision of distance education programs;
- The use of ICT can offer opportunities to extend the teaching and learning methods;
- ICT can provide the basis for developing focused, profitable lifelong learning programs;
- ICT can support the promotion of postgraduate programs.

CONTEXT

Increases in the numbers of students, diversity, and rapid changes in technology and work practices have changed the relationship between universities and the wider community. The EMU, like many other educational institutions worldwide, has responded by identifying specific required graduate competencies. As part of this response, the Faculty of Education (FacEd) has adopted curriculum-based competencies that integrate ICT into teaching and learning processes.

Despite the changes in the curriculum, many faculties continue to use a traditional teaching and learning pedagogy that is characterized by an emphasis on face-to-face lectures. For self-study, the students use libraries. The instructors lecture through the use of the chalkboard and textbooks, while the learners listen; sometimes the instructors use handouts or overhead projectors.

Most faculties are only in the very early phase of using computers to promote student learning. In some faculties, both students and instructors have access to computers, but these are often used for administration tasks, e-mail, and to consult Web sites that not always have a clear relationship with teaching and learning processes. Most instructors at EMU do not have experience in the use of computers for teaching and learning processes. They are also lacking in teaching skills in a student-centered way and have little experience using methods/strategies that incorporate the use of ICT. Furthermore, the instructors have limited access to examples that illustrate the use of ICT in teaching their subjects. Students are in a similar position: when the computer competencies of students, in the beginning of academic year, were evaluated through a questionnaire, more than 80% of the students answered that they had poor basic computer skills (like the use of Windows and Office). These results demonstrate the need to integrate a basic computer-skills module into the FacEd curriculum.

RESEARCH QUESTIONS

This chapter sets out to demonstrate that the new teaching and learning strategies through ICT in the Faculty of Education at EMU can contribute to improve the quality of education programs offered at EMU. Also, there is a pilot project that can be used to provide recommendations for processes to roll out the use of ICTs in teaching on a larger scale across the university.

The central research questions for the study are

- Can the introduction of a course-management system improve flexibility and reduce face-to-face teaching time at the Faculty of Education of EMU?
- How does the adoption of a course-management system affect courses in the Faculty of Education?
- What kind of pedagogical model is best suited to the context of teaching and learning in the Faculty of Education?
- Which framework is applicable to describe the costs and benefits of adopting a course-management system in the Faculty of Education?
- How can EMU prepare an effective roll-out of a course-management system across the institution?

The effective use of ICTs in teaching and learning processes is simplified by the use of an Internet or intranet-based course-management system. "A WWW-based course-management system is an environment created on the World Wide Web in which students and educators can perform learning-related tasks" (Jones & McCormack, 1997, p. 1). It is not simply a mechanism of distributing information to students; it also supports tasks related to communication, student assessment, and course management. "A WWW-based course-management system is a comprehensive software package that supports some or all aspects of course preparation, delivery and interaction and allows these aspects to be accessible via a network" (Collis & Moonen, 2001, p. 78).

According to de Boer (2004), the overall aim of the intervention was to increase flexibility of course delivery and reduce the amount of face-to-face teaching by using the course-management system to facilitate blended learning. "Blended learning is a way to design courses that blends different kinds of delivery and learning methods that can be enabled and/or supported by technology with traditional teaching methods (de Boer, 2004, p. 17). The intervention itself had two elements: the implementation of a WWW-based course-management system as a pilot project and the redesigning of two master's-level courses with the application of acquisition and contribution pedagogy (Collis & Moonen, 2001).

SELECTION OF A COURSE-MANAGEMENT SYSTEM

The WWW-based course-management system used in the Faculty of Education in EMU is TeleTOP, which was developed by the Faculty of Behavioral Sciences at University of Twente in 1997. TeleTOP is a useable system that requires limited training of students and instructors. It includes multiple functions in an integrated system, including News, Course Information, the Roster, Discussion, Questions & Answers, and Assignment Submissions. The University of Twente made TeleTOP available for the pilot project at EMU.

LITERATURE REVIEW

The combination of innovative, increasingly learner-centered pedagogy and new learning technologies inevitably has implications in the teaching and learning methods used at universities. According to Collis and Moonen (2001, p. 9), flexible learning is related to a variety of forms of study used in higher education. They say that

> Students in higher education have for a long time chosen from a variety of courses, studying their textbooks in a variety of locations and times, and selected from a variety of resources in the library. Learning also takes place outside of explicit course settings, as students interact with others or take part in events such as guest instructors or debates and use built-in tutorials to help them to use a software package.

Flexible learning has a variety of characteristics that collectively differentiate it from other models of education. It can be mapped according to several dimensions, such as time, content, entry requirements, instructional approach and resources, delivery, and logistics, as described in Table 14.1.

EDUCATIONAL MODELS

Collis and Moonen (2001) differentiate between the acquisition model and the participation model of learning. The acquisition model is focused on learning activities that are predetermined and are based on the acquisition of prespecified knowledge by individuals; whereas the participation or contribution model is focused on the learning activities where the student interacts and communicates with other participants in a learning community. Because participation alone is not enough, contribution-oriented activities also play an important role in the learning process in such environments. Collis and Moonen (2001) suggest that both models should be reflected in pedagogy with more emphasis on contribution-oriented activities.

Collis and Moonen (2001) show the relationship between flexibility and pedagogy by using the flexibility-activity framework that is similar to the ideas argued by Rich, Gosper, Love, and Wivell (1999). By combining an

TABLE 14.1   Dimensions of Learning Flexibility: Options Available to Learner

Flexibility related to time:

Fixed time <==> Flexible
Times (for starting and finishing a course);
   Times (for submitting assignments and interacting within the course);
   Tempo/pace of studying;
   Moments of assessment.

Flexibility related to content:

Fixed content <===> Flexible
Topics of the course;
   Sequence of different parts of a course;
   Orientation of the course (theoretical, practical);
   Key learning materials of the course;
   Assessment standards and completion requirements.

Flexibility related to entry requirements

Fixed requirements <==> Flexible
Topics of the course.

Flexibility related to instructional approach and resources

Fixed pedagogy and resources <=====================================> Flexible
Social organization of learning (face-to-face; group, individual);
   Language to be used during the course;
   Learning resources: modality, origin, (instructor, learner, library, WWW);
   Instructional organization of learning (assessments, monitoring).

Flexibility related to delivery and logistics

Fixed place and procedures <=======================================> Flexible
Time and place where contact with instructor and other students occur;
   Methods, technology for obtaining support and making contact;
   Types of help, communication, available technology required;
   Location, technology for participating in various aspects of a course;
   Delivery channels for course information, content, communication.

Source: Collis & Moonen, 2001, p. 10

educational-model dimension with activity goals focused on acquisition or contribution with a flexibility dimension with categories relating to less and more flexibility, we can define a flexibility-activity framework (Collis & Moonen, 2001), as shown in Figure 14.1. Rich et al. (1999, p.12) assert that

> The student-centred approach underpinning flexible learning requires a different relationship between instructors and students than other models of education. There is less reliance on face-to-face teaching, often reserving such an approach for those circumstances where it is particularly valuable. There is more emphasis on guided independent learning; instructors become facilitators of the learning process guiding students to appropriate resources, tasks and learning outcomes.

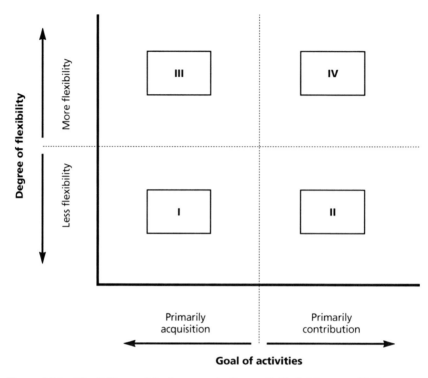

Figure 14.1 Flexibility–activity framework. *Source:* Collis & Moonen, 2001.

This framework is used to describe the changes associated with the intervention in the Faculty of Education at EMU.

The student-centred approach underpinning flexible learning requires different teaching methodologies and also a different relationship between teachers and students. In comparison to traditional educational models, flexible learning is broadly characterized by:

- Greater reliance on high quality learning resources using a range of technologies (e.g., print, CD-ROM, video, audio, Internet, and WWW-based course management system, etc.)
- Greater opportunities to communicate outside traditional teaching times.
- An increasing use of information technology (IT), but IT is often central to much of the implementation of IT flexible learning, for example in delivering use of Flexible learning is not synonymous with the learning resources, providing a communications facility, administering units and student assessment, and hosting student support systems.

- The employment of multi-skilled teams rather than the academics responsible for undertaking all stages of unit planning, development, delivery, assessment and maintenance, other professionals are often required to provide specific skills, for example in instructional design, desktop publishing, web development, administration and maintenance of progam.
- Less reliance on face-to-face teaching and more emphasis on guided independent learning; teachers become facilitators of the learning process directing students to appropriate resources, tasks and learning outcomes" (Rich, Gosper, Love, & Wivell, 1999, p. 14).

METHODOLOGY

Reeves (2000) argues that research concerning the use of information technology in education is characterized by researchers with action goals that are focused on a particular progam, product, or method, usually in an applied setting, for the purpose of describing and improving it or stimulating its effectiveness and worth. The analysis of this case study draws on an adaptation of Reeves' development-research model, as shown in Figure 14.2.

In the adapted model, the feedback and redesigning of the courses are not included since the study allowed only two months for the design of courses, implementation in TeleTOP, and data gathering. Both qualitative and quantitative data were collected in this case study. Different methods of data collection were used. The research instruments used to obtain the relevant information for the study were questionnaires (two questionnaires, one at the beginning of the modules and other at the end) for instructors and students; observations; discussions with instructors; analysis of TeleTOP sites; and some interviews.

From the first questionnaires, a total of 22 were returned from instructors and 52 were returned from students. The interviews were conducted only for some students and all instructors who were using TeleTOP in their courses. Notes from most of the interviews were written in an exercise book.

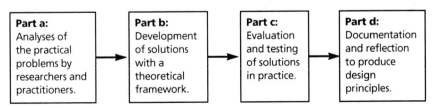

| Part a:
Analyses of the practical problems by researchers and practitioners. | Part b:
Development of solutions with a theoretical framework. | Part c:
Evaluation and testing of solutions in practice. | Part d:
Documentation and reflection to produce design principles. |

Figure 14.2 Adapted development research approach. *Source:* Reeves, 2000, p. 9.

From the second questionnaires, in the final evaluation and distributed only for postgraduate students, in total of 14, all were returned.

DESIGNS AND PLAN

The preliminary selection of the courses was planned for the new academic year, with new students in the first two courses, namely Science Technology and Society (Ciência Tecnologia e Sociedade) and Educational Program Evaluation (Avaliação de Programas Educacionais), in the master's program. Many instructors were contacted and asked if it was possible to use TeleTOP in their courses; most of them were not interested because they did not know how TeleTOP works and how to use it.

Two of the instructors accepted the challenge. The courses were designed in consideration of the pedagogy model that fitted with TeleTOP and was planned to decrease the number of lectures and give chances to the students to work independently or in groups; also the activities planned were combined with TeleTOP use. Students could contribute to the course learning materials through what they submitted in TeleTOP. A clear conception of what is to be learned in a course was, perhaps, the major target of course design. It was planned to use most of TeleTOP functions like News, Course Information, the Roster, Discussion, and Questions & Answers. Functions like Discussion, Questions & Answers, and News were planned to be used during the courses, and other functions were to be used from the beginning of the courses until the end. In the Roster, the three learning cycles were taken into account (before, during, and after activities), also other functions inside of the Roster, like Submission of the assignments, and others (see Figure 14.3).

Training for Instructors and Students

The instructors as well as the students had a training of two hours in TeleTOP use. The training for students was organized in three groups: master's students constituted the first group (only 15 students); graduate students constituted the second one and the third one. It was necessary to split the group because of the large number of students (57 students), and the computer room has only 30 computers.

In this training, after all students were registered in TeleTOP and also in the course environment via TeleTOP, the task was to show how to enter the different parts of the site, how to submit assignments, how to participate in Discussions, how to upload attachments, and how to add URL links.

Figure 14.3 TeleTOP roster options. *Note:* The English language interface of
TeleTOP is not a problem for Mozambican higher-education students who study
English in secondary and higher education.

For the instructors, the training was a little different compared with that
for the students: it was organized individually, basically to show how to apply different information in different functions of TeleTOP, like the Course
Information, News, in the Roster, and in the other areas.

Because of the Internet speed and instructors of the masters' courses are
ongoing, it was decided to divide the tasks between instructors and support
staff. These instructors asked support staff to set up their courses in TeleTOP,
and the task of the instructors was to use it when teaching their courses.

Course Design

To implement TeleTOP as was planned at EMU, it was necessary that the
instructors redesigned their courses so that the courses had few face-to-face
lectures and more individual or group activities. It was also necessary that
the students had activities in which they had to contribute something to
the course environments. The desired situation in the Faculty of Education
is to change the persistent traditional pedagogy recently used and start to
use the new pedagogical model and add a course-management system, for

instance, to support what had been planned in the educational model defined in the curriculum of the faculty.

In the following list, the general course design is introduced with the respective course organization, learning contents, learning activities, and general communication.

Course Organization

The courses will be organized using some functions available in Tele-TOP: News; Course Information; the Roster; Discussion; and Question & Answer. But other functions are available to allow and motivate instructors and students to use these functions. The Course Information and especially the Roster are very important. The Course Information will be used to post the general course information; for instance, the information about the course instructor, course objectives, and course materials. The Roster will be used to post the time schedule of the lessons and assignments. In the Roster, the activities are organized in accordance with the three cycles of learning (before, during, and after activities).

Learning Contents

The learning contents of the courses will be posted under Course Documents. The learning contents will be broken into a few lessons, and then each lesson will be broken again into small sections to fit frequent interruptions. Also, students have to find other contents related to the courses on their own, and the instructor provides goals and literature to be used in the courses; also, an electronic collection of knowledge, which the students must explore in order to achieve these goals.

Learning Activities

In both courses of the master's program, the learning activities of the course mainly consist of three parts.

Before the sessions, students should prepare lectures, reading materials (chapters of the books, articles from different resources, etc.) of what they have been learning.

During the session, instructors should explain or create a discussion upon what students have been preparing before the sections. The instructors should present the content of the section, clarifying the most important points of the content and what students should learn. The instructors should create discussions or create practice activities during the sessions. The instructors should bring the students back together and make culminating comments on what has occurred, as the students were busy.

After the session, the instructors should give assignments upon and extend what happened in the focal session. Students should do the assignments and submit through TeleTOP, in a certain period of time that they have been allocated. And instructors should give feedback.

Figure 14.3 showed what the roster of the one of the courses looks like.

General Communication

The instructor and students will communicate with each other using the tools available under Communication On the page of Communication; the three communication tools; Send E-mail, Discussion and Questions & Answers are listed. All the listed tools are the asynchronous communication tools.

External Links

On different pages, both the instructor and students can add external links during the course. Some links are already listed and added by instructors.

Assignments

On the Roster, the students can see assignments after sessions.

DESIGN DECISIONS

During discussions of implementation of a WWW-based course-management system, in the design, it was necessary to take into account some points related to the research questions. The investigator suggested options and the instructors of the courses decisions.

One of the decisions was that the course is organized in two parts. In the first part, the student has to do an assignment individually, and in the second part, where he/she has to work in a group, the student has to adjust the tempo of study for other participants.

One of the important decisions made by the instructors was the reduction of the number of contact lectures and the increase of other forms of contact, like individual meetings between instructors and students. During the previous year, it was planned for students to be in the faculty four days a week, from 14:30 to 19:00 hours. Now this was reduced to three days, and in some weeks it was reduced to two days. The other days, students were free to choose how to manage the time for their studies. In two courses, we can see the distribution of the lectures during the weeks (see the Roster in Figure 14.3).

Table 14.2 shows how the courses were designed to include a balance of acquisition and contribution activities in both TeleTOP and face-to-face interactions.

TABLE 14.2   Application of Acquisition and Contribution Aspects in Relation to Flexibility

Component	To increase flexibility and support an acquisition model	To increase flexibility and support a contribution model
General course organization	• All announcements about the course procedures are posted in the TeleTOP News section. • A calendar is provided in the TeleTOP Roster with all relevant dates and times highlighted.	
Lectures/contact sessions	• The traditional lectures and the contacts and unscheduled meetings. • Summary lecture notes are available in TeleTOP. • Students who were not at the session can review the instructor's notes, listen to the instructor explaining particular points (via contact asked by the students or e-mail), and can review the materials created and posted by the students who were present at the sessions.	• Interaction of the students with each other in a way that engages them in discussing the lecture material and articulating their ideas in a summary by using group work. • Extend the lecture after the contact and change to online learning by having all students reflect on some aspect and communicate via some form of structured comment from the instructor via TeleTOP. • The instructor uses the students' input as the basis for the next session or activity. • Capture student debates and discussions and use as basis for asynchronous reflection and further discussion.

Self-study and exercises; practical sessions	• Exercises and guided self-study are now integrated with the contact sessions; all can be engaged in from wherever the instructor and student have network connections.	• Students can use each other's submissions as learning resources once these are available withinTeleTOP.

• Communication and interaction via the TeleTOP site provides students with guidance as to how to respond productively to each other's work and questions.

• Personal questions will be addressed via e-mail and other methods of capturing communication.

Feedback/ testing/ assessment of the assignments	• Feedback in a quick and targeted manner, without the student needing to wait to see the instructor face-to-face. • Feedback is posted in TeleTOP.	• Peer feedback.
General communication	• TeleTOP has a group/ participant page listing all students and instructors profiles including their e-mail addresses.	• Discussions and question and answer activities about course topics within TeleTOP.

Source: Adapted from Collis & Moonen 2001, p. 21

RESULTS

This section of the chapter shows results concerning student and instructor access to computers and the Internet, student evaluations of the two courses, and the use of different TeleTOP features.

1. Student Access to Computers:

TABLE 14.3 Places Where Students Have Access to Computers

	Master's	Graduate	Frequency	Percentage
Faculty	1	22	23	44.2
Faculty and outside EMU	13	16	29	55.8
Total	14	38	52	100.0

We note that:

> More than half of the students have access to computers in faculty and in other places (for example, at home, at work, and in Internet cafés, 55.8 %). In a total of 14 masters' students, 13 have access in the faculty and outside EMU. Most of the graduate students only have access to computers in the faculty.

2. Student Access to the Internet:

TABLE 14.4   Where Students Have Access to the Internet

	Master's	Graduate	Frequency	Percentage
Faculty	1	30	31	59.6
Faculty and outside EMU	13	8	21	40.4
Total	14	38	52	100.0

We note that:

> More than half of students have access to the Internet only in the faculty (59.6 %). Of the total of 14 masters' students, 13 have access in the faculty and other places.

3. Instructor Access to the Internet:

TABLE 14.5   Places Where Instructors Have Access to the Internet

	Frequency	Percentage
Faculty	15	68.2
Faculty and outside EMU	7	31.8
Total	22	100.0

Most of the instructors depend on faculty computers (68.2%), and less than a third of instructors have access to the Internet outside EMU.

4. Feedback from Masters' Students Concerning the use of TeleTOP:

Most of masters' students agreed that working with TeleTOP improved their courses. Twelve of the 14 masters' students who completed the final evaluation questionnaire stated that the use of TeleTOP resulted in improved communication with instructors; more opportunities for feedback from the instructors; improved access to course information; more learning activities during class hours; and improved course quality. The same 12 masters' students also demonstrated an interest in TeleTOP support in

TABLE 14.6   Feedback by Masters' Students About the Effects of Using TeleTOP

	Disagree	Neutral	Agree
Improves the quality of the courses	$p = 7.1$ $n = 1$	$p = 28.6$ $n = 4$	$p = 64.3$ $n = 9$
More communication between students	$p = 14.3$ $n = 2$	$p = 50$ $n = 7$	$p = 35.7$ $n = 5$
More communication with instructors	$p = 7.1$ $n = 1$	$p = 7.1$ $n = 1$	$p = 85.7$ $n = 12$
Helps to be prepared for lessons	$p = 14.3$ $n = 2$	$p = 14.3$ $n = 2$	$p = 71.4$ $n = 10$
Gives more opportunities for feedback	$p = 7.1$ $n = 1$	$p = 7.1$ $n = 1$	$p = 85.7$ $n = 12$
Gives access to course information	$p = 7.1$ $n = 1$	$p = 7.1$ $n = 1$	$p = 85.7$ $n = 12$
More assignments before and after the classes	$p = 7.1$ $n = 1$	$p = 35.7$ $n = 5$	$p = 57.1$ $n = 8$
Leads to more activities during class hours	$p = 7.1$ $n = 1$	$p = 7.1$ $n = 1$	$p = 85.7$ $n = 12$
Students like to have TeleTOP support in more courses	$p = 7.1$ $n = 1$	$p = 7.1$ $n = 1$	$p = 85.7$ $n = 12$

more courses and more regular use of TeleTOP for assignments before and after classes.

5.   Impact on Teaching and Learning Models:

With the basic infrastructure to support flexibility in time and place, students had the opportunity to work on assignments or tasks at times of their own choice. Interactions within the period of the courses were completely flexible, except for the scheduled face-to-face contact with the instructor or other course participants and assignment deadlines. Thus, the tempo or place of study was partly fixed.

The social organization of the courses was quite flexible. There were face-to-face meetings of the whole class at the beginning and the end of the course, as well as group work for some assignments and individual work for others. The learning resources were open, so that the students had to find their own resources to do the tasks and assignments. This supported self-controlled learning. There was also an opportunity for using students' contributions, but there were some difficulties in students uploading attachments.

One instructor made extensive use of classroom discussions and individual meetings at the expense of interaction in TeleTOP. The instructor of the second course made much more use of TeleTOP, including more online discussion and feedback, and made online resources available to students. From the student perspective, there were improvements in communication, feedback to students, and perceived course quality in both courses. The instructors were, however, cautious about changing their courses and preferred slow incremental changes to radical shifts in pedagogy and learning activities.

The acquisition and contribution models are well-known in the Faculty of Education and fit well in a context in which one wants to build competencies based curriculum (Kouwenhoven, 2003). The teaching and learning model chosen for the two course interventions involved students in the acquisition of skills, concepts, and also in contributions to the growth of a learning community. This project has shown that many ideas for more flexibility and student contributions were achieved, despite the limited use of flexible communication within TeleTOP.

The findings of the investigation show that the two courses in the Faculty of Education moved to a position from the first to the third and partially to the fourth quadrant of the flexibility figure as shown in Figure 14.4. The shift to quadrant four relates to an increase in both flexibility and in the use of the contribution model. We agree that flexibility and contribution are important aspects in generating an effective implementation, but also suggest that acquisition elements are still needed.

COST AND BENEFITS

Table 14.7 applies the Simplified Return on Investment (ROI) model (Moonen, 2000) from an efficiency perspective. In this table, some relevant items regarding quality perspective are mentioned in the first column. The last three columns indicate ROI scores from the institutional, instructor, and student perspective. A weighting factor is mentioned in order to represent the importance of each item per actor as reliably as possible. The data in the cells (on a scale from –10 to +10, indicating 100% loss to 100% gain) represents the relative amount of loss or gain that was perceived by the respective actors in the new situation when using the course-management system in comparison with the original traditional situation. Some of the remarks made are used in the table to clarify the score given by the researcher. The results as shown in Table 14.7 suggest that the introduction

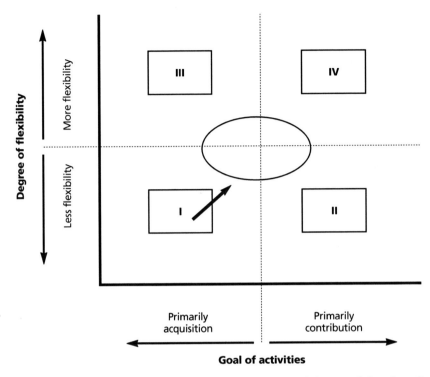

Figure 14.4 Flexibility–activity framework with position of the actual situation of two courses applied in TeleTOP.

of the learning-management system has improved efficiency from institutional, student, and instructor perspectives.

From an economic perspective, there are some investments and yearly costs. In the case of this pilot intervention, the costs were quite high in relation with the efficiency gains. For future projects, including a faculty or universitywide roll-out, far higher gains of quality and efficiency are expected. EMU has an Informatics Center (CIUEM), which offers ICT services. One of the main recommendations of this study is that EMU should buy or license a WWW-based course-management system and host it in this center. The infrastructure for introducing new e-learning is already there; hence, a big amount of investment for it could be saved. Another point to be taken into account is that EMU's part-time students urgently need flexibility because of their full-time work commitments.

TABLE 14.7 Simplified ROI with Respect to Efficiency

Actors:	Institution		Instructor		Students	
Items:	Weight	Score	Weight	Score	Weight	Score
Flexibility	1.0	+5 Can serve students at a distance[a]	1.0	+5 Can work on the course outside of the faculty or when traveling, don't have to be in the faculty all time[a,b]	0.8	+3 Time can be used more efficiently, don't have to come to lectures all afternoon, but it is necessary to work at a computer[c]
Studying course content via TeleTOP.					0.6	+2 Since the course itself is teaching users to use e-learning system, so the TeleTOP system will be more efficient[a,b,c]
Efficiency in terms of student results	1.0	+5 Students will stay on tempo, finish the course on time[a]	1.0	−4 Will costs much more time to look at and give feedback on all the extra assignments, handle e-mail, etc.[a,c]		
Finding information and literature online	0.8	+2	0.8	+2 Information, also via TeleTOP, will always be available[d]	0.6	+2
Doing and submitting assignments					1.0	+3 Saves time and is handy, and according to the content of course, it would be better to do assignments in web environment[c]

Assessing assignments and giving feedback			0.8	−3 Easier and faster to give feedback with a red pen directly on paper[a]	0.8	+1 Good that you can read feedback, even outside of the faculty, as soon as the instructor puts it there[c]
Feedback on assignments via Web-based system			1.0	+1 Despite above, it is handy to give feedback directly into the TeleTOP[a]	0.8	+1
Communication	0.6	+2 Can get information about what users need faster[a]	0.8	+2 More communication with students[b]	0.8	+2 More communication with instructors[b]
Support of group work			0.8	−2 Much better if students do it face to face[a]	0.6	−2 Easier to get together face to face[a]
General information about the course available on TeleTOP	0.6	+1 Will be handy[b]	0.8	+1	0.8	+2 Will be up to date and handy[b]
Technology skills and competencies	0.8	+2 Everyone will benefit from having more technology experience[a]	0.8	+2 Will get much more handy with the computer since using Web-based approach[a]	0.8	+2 Will improves your skills at using the Internet[a]
ROI: Efficiency	15.4		3.6		12.2	

Source: Adapted from Moonen, 2000
[a] Information from the investigator observations
[b] Information from questionnaires
[c] Information from discussion with instructors
[d] Information from TeleTOP data.

CONCLUSIONS

On the basis of this study, a number of conclusions were reached.

First, with regard to flexibility and face-to-face teaching time, the interventions in these two master's-level courses resulted in improvements of flexibility in place and time, flexibility related to content, flexibility related to instructional approach, and flexibility related to delivery and logistics. In both courses, the time spent in face-to-face lectures was reduced. The students used their access to computers in the faculty and outside EMU to engage flexibly in learning and assessment activities beyond scheduled face-to-face meetings.

Second, it was noted that the course changes resulting from the use of a course-management system were varied. The instructors were cautious about changing their courses. Only one of the two instructors made extensive use of TeleTOP. However, from a student perspective, the increased flexibility and access to online resources and communication resulted in changes in communication patterns, feedback to students, and a perception of improved course quality in both courses.

Third, it was noted that the combination of the contribution model and acquisition model fits best in this context. The combination of increased flexibility and a shift toward contribution activities is likely to be of greatest benefit to part-time students.

Fourth, with regard to costs and benefits, it was possible to demonstrate efficiency gains from institutional, instructor, and student perspectives. It was also observed that a far higher return on investment could be achieved through the use of a learning environment on the EMU network.

Fifth, in order to gain maximum benefit from the roll-out of a course-management system across EMU, several changes are needed. At a technical level, these include improvements in local network capacity, Internet connectivity, and IT support systems. Access speed and cost of bandwidth both offer strong arguments for the use of a course-management system on a local EMU server. Finally, there is a clear need for staff development activities to ensure the instructors' confidence in the use of the technology and in designing and leading activities, based on a contribution model.

REFERENCES

Collis, B., & Moonen, J. (2001). *Flexible learning in a digital world*. London: Kogan Page.

de Boer, W. F. (2004). *Flexibility support for a changing university*. Thesis, University of Twente, Enschede, Mozambique.

EMU (1998). *Strategic plan 1999–2005*. UEM, Maputo, Mozambique.

Jones, D., & McCormack, C. (1997). *Building a web-based education system.* New York: John Wiley and Sons.

Kouwenhoven, W. (2003). *Designing for competence in Mozambique: Towards a competence-based curriculum for the faculty of education of the Eduardo Mondlane University.* PhD thesis, University of Twente, Enschede, Mozambique.

Moonen, J. (2000). Cost effectiveness and the new economy in education. In H. Taylor and P. Hogenbirk (Eds.), *The bookmark of the school of the future* (pp. 193–210). London: Chapman Hall.

Reeves, T. C. (2000). *Enhancing the worth of instructional technology research through "design experiments" and other development research strategies.* Paper presented at the annual meeting of the American Educational Research Association, New York. Retrieved October 2003 from http://it.coe.uga.edu/~treeves/AER-A2000Reeves.pdf

Republic of Mozambic (2002). *Information & communication technology policy, implementation strategy.* Comissão para a Política de Informática, Maputo, Mozambique.

Rich, D., Gosper, M., Love, P., & Wivell, C. (1999). *Flexible learning plan 1999–2002.* Macquarie University, Australia. Retrieved August 2003, from http://www.dest.gov.au/archive/highered/quality/quality_plans_01/files/macquarie.rtf

CHAPTER 15

EVALUATING THE IMPACT OF CABLE

A Cognitive Apprenticeship-Based Learning Environment

Ioana Chan Mow, Wing Au, and Greg Yates

INTRODUCTION

Teaching computer programming skills within the university context has proven to be a difficult and challenging task. After two years of learning programming, most novice programmers are still struggling to be proficient (AECT, 2001; Moursound, 2002). The cognitive load placed upon students (Garner, 2000) is heavy, and it is unclear if traditional instructional practices are optimal within this area. Traditionally, at the National University of Samoa, student attrition levels have been high, and ways to address such problems needed to be considered. From an examination of current research in this field, one reason why computer programming instruction is challenging lies in a lack of understanding about good instructional approaches in this direction (Tholander, Karlgren, & Ramberg, 1998).

Bridging the Knowledge Divide, pages 267–287
Copyright © 2009 by Information Age Publishing
All rights of reproduction in any form reserved.

The research on which this chapter is based is concerned with ways to improve university course materials and instructional provisions, specifically within the context of teaching advanced programming skills to undergraduate students at the National University of Samoa. Over a three-year period, an instructional program was developed and referred to as CABLE (Cognitive Apprenticeship-Based Learning Environment). Recent research on learning theory has indicated that a learning environment should be managed so that students are encouraged to set personal goals, actively gather meaningful information, monitor and evaluate their own learning, and reflect personal learning experiences in different authentic environments and social contexts (Brown & Campione, 1996; Wilson, 1996). Pedagogical approaches have been developed where the aim has been to modify the learning environment so as to facilitate the development of students' higher-order thinking skills and to support the shared construction of knowledge (e.g., Brown, 1992; Cognition and Technology Group at Vanderbilt, 1993; Collins et al.,1989; Palincsar & Brown, 1984; Scardamalia et al., 1994).

THE CABLE MODEL

CABLE, the pedagogical model researched in this study, is an attempt to devise a viable instructional model based around the construct of apprenticeship. Cognitive apprenticeship is a model of instruction that involves the effective communication of domain knowledge in such a way that the students become aware of the thought processes involved in knowledge construction within that domain (Brill, Kim, and Galloway, 2001). Cognitive apprenticeship is directed at teaching processes that experts use to handle complex tasks, and is characterized by a number of teaching methods (Moursound, 2002). These include modeling, scaffolding, coaching, articulation, reflection, and exploration (Jarvela, 1995). Another instructional strategy that is gaining prominence as an effective teaching method and is integrated into the learning environment being trialed is collaborative learning.

Our starting assumption is that the computer can be used as a tool assisting in both cognitive apprenticeship and collaborative learning. In this sense, computers are used as cognitive tools. Cognitive tools are defined as any technology that enhances the cognitive powers of humans during thinking, problem solving, and learning (Jonassen & Reeves, 1996). They facilitate critical thinking and higher-order learning if used in ways that promote reflection, discussion, and collaborative problem solving. Another factor that is thought to stimulate the learning process is metacognition. Computers are thought to provide a highly interactive medium for problem

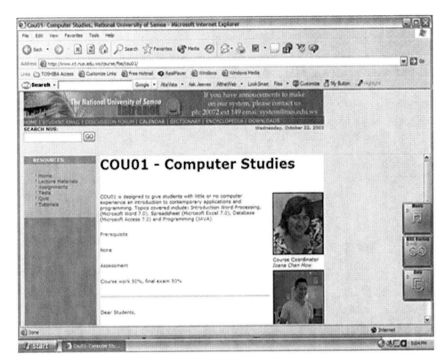

Figure 15.1   Main screen of class Web site.

solving and metacognitive training to take place. As the literature identifies metacognition as an important factor in stimulating the learning process, elements such as scaffolding, coaching, and reflection, which help students with their metacognitive processes, are also included as part of CABLE.

An important element of the CABLE learning environment is its use of computer-mediated communication techniques for implementing aspects of cognitive apprenticeship such as scaffolding, coaching, feedback, and modeling (Levin & Waugh, 1998). This is tele-apprenticeship. Computer-mediated communication techniques used in implementing tele-apprenticeship in the current study include e-mail, online notes, interactive tests, and a bulletin board.

This chapter presents the findings of a study, which is one of a series of trials that evaluated the impact of CABLE in the teaching of Java programming at the National University of Samoa. Specifically, this chapter focuses on the evaluation of the impact of the online implementation of CABLE. Since the CABLE procedures were developmental in nature, some improvements to the procedures took place between the phases.

METHODOLOGY

The research design used in this study can be described as quasi-experimental, since an independent variable (instructional approach) was manipulated, and subsequent changes in dependent variables (student attitudes to learning environment and student performance) were investigated within naturally occurring university courses.

PARTICIPANTS

The average age of the participants in both phases was 19 years. Participants were allocated to either the CABLE treatment or were taught in accord with the traditional university model of teaching (i.e., non-CABLE methods). This division was achieved through students being enrolled within different class times. To the awareness of university staff, the two available class times were regarded as equivalent timetable options, and no biasing factors such as gender, ability, or age were known. Students were not aware that differential instructional treatments were to be applied. There were 53 participants (32 CABLE, 21 traditional) for Phase 1 from the University Preparatory Computer Studies class, but by the time the study was completed, the numbers had dropped to 30 students (22 females, 8 males) in the CABLE treatment and 16 students (7 females, 9 males) in the traditional treatment.

It can be noted that the traditional treatment for both phases was administered by an experienced lecturer who has a strong reputation in his area and had taught computer programming skills for over 5 years. The CABLE approach was implemented by experienced lecturers. The teaching staff for CABLE across Phase 1 and Phase 2 were different, a factor that potentially acted against the smooth running of the treatment during Phase 2. However it needs to be established that this study had undertaken sufficient measures to minimize teachers' effect, for example, the training of teachers in the CABLE procedures so that individual differences were minimized.

The participants for Phase 2 were students enrolled within their first year of studies at the National University of Samoa from the Foundation (64%) and non-Foundation (36%) programs. Initially, 78 students (38 CABLE, 40 non-CABLE) consented to participation in the study. At the end of the study, complete sets of data were available from 67 students who completed the questionnaire (30 CABLE, 37 non-CABLE).

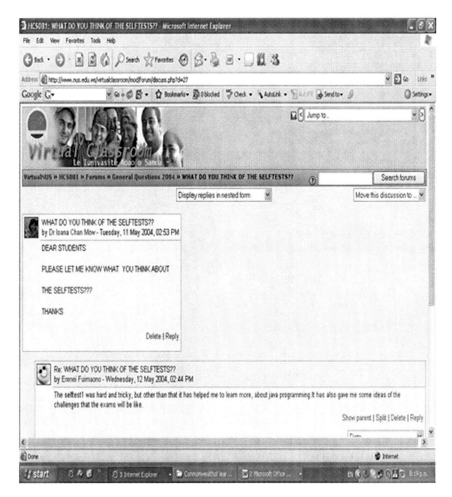

Figure 15.2 Discussion forum for CABLE students.

INSTRUMENTATION

Instruments used to collect data for this study consisted of separate questionnaires for collecting attitudinal data for CABLE and the traditional groups; post-test scores; and student interviews. The questionnaires for both CABLE and traditional groups had in common the first 11 questions and the two unstructured questions, but the questionnaire for the CABLE group had additional questions (Question 12 to 17), which evaluated the

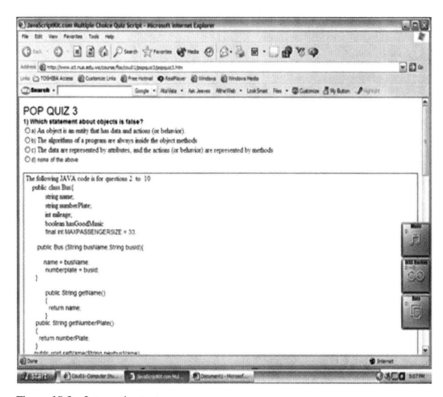

Figure 15.3 Interactive tests.

impact of online learning and collaborative learning. The Likert items for all these questions were constructed with a 4-point scale with responses of 1) strongly disagree, 2) disagree, 3) agree, and 4) strongly agree. Questions 1 to 11 evaluated student attitudes toward computers, the effectiveness of feedback, effect on self-confidence, students' love of learning, and motivation for learning.

PROCEDURES

The first phase was conducted in Semester 2, 2003, while the second phase took place in Semester 1, 2004. In both phases, the Java courses were taught over a 6-week period. This was dictated by the coverage time for Java programming within these classes, which was 6 weeks. After six weeks of exposure to the treatments, all students completed the final test paper and a questionnaire intended to tap into their evaluations of their course experience. The post-test consisted of six questions that evaluated their knowledge of Java commands and practical questions that tested the application of Java for solving a problem. Student attitudes toward the two approaches were gauged using the poststudy questionnaire, student interviews, and feedback from the online help desk.

THE CABLE ENVIRONMENT

An important task of the study was the construction of the actual CABLE environment. The course reader had been specifically designed for these Java courses by an experienced Java lecturer. The notes were structured so that Java programming was situated as part of the systems-development life cycle for the development of systems ("programming in the large"). This was to avoid the common problem, prevalent in traditional programming texts, of where programming is taught in isolation, denying the student the opportunity to see how programming can be applied within the context of information-systems development.

Secondly, the notes and exercises had been structured to encourage the articulation of steps in the Java activities such as those of creating an object. This was to encourage students to use some problem-solving heuristic to arrive at a solution. This was also aimed at facilitating the students' learning of the syntax and semantics of Java. Java notes for these courses were available in both hard copy and electronic form.

The online component of CABLE consisted of a class Web site hosted initially as part of our universitywide intranet. However, by Phase 2, the university had adopted the Moodle Learner management system, and the class Web site, e-mail, and bulletin board were then all migrated to and hosted within the Moodle environment. (Note: Moodle is a learner-management system like WebCT and Blackboard). The programming environment used for teaching Java is JBuilder, which is an integrated developer's environment (IDE), with text editor, debugger, and compiler. The Web site had a link within it from where students could initiate JBuilder. At the start of each phase, the students had to be trained in the use of the environment. The online component of CABLE underwent revisions as the trials progressed, in an attempt to improve on the model. From the recommendations of Phase 1, the e-mail facility was modified so as to facilitate internal (intranet) and home access, as well as links to tutorials and sample solutions. From recommendations generated in Phase 2, a UML scaffolding software was designed and initially trialed in a later study (Project 3).

There was some overlap in the instructional approaches in the two treatments. Students in both the CABLE and traditional groups were given the same set of notes and exercises on JAVA programming and also used the same Java environment, JBuilder. Both groups were exposed to elements of the cognitive apprenticeship-based approach such as feedback and coaching. In both groups, the teacher modeled computer programming theory and JAVA programming concepts using worked examples and real-life examples.

However, the differences in approaches between the CABLE and traditional groups were considerable. One main difference between CABLE and traditional approaches was in the provision of feedback to students. In the traditional approach, feedback was student initiated. Feedback was provided by lecturers when requested by students. Within the CABLE approach, feedback was more structured and was provided by an online system where the lecturer provided individualized feedback via e-mails. On a weekly basis, the students were expected to send to the lecturer an e-mail that answered several questions. The first question required them to describe activities or topics covered during the week. The second and third questions required them to identify problematic areas and post specific queries. The last question required the students to reflect upon the usefulness of what they had learned. From student feedback, the lecturer was able to compile some frequently asked questions (FAQs) and their solutions on the class Web site. Students were also encouraged to e-mail as often as possible whenever they encountered problems in class.

A second main differentiating factor between the CABLE and the traditional approaches is the cultivation of metacognition. Students were encouraged to reflect on their progress and also articulate their thinking processes in the form of "think-alouds."

The third main differentiating factor between the CABLE and traditional approaches is the incorporation of elements of collaborative learning. For example, students collaborated in such programming tasks as UML modeling and also in completing class programming assignments or projects.

One of the main distinguishing features of cognitive apprenticeship is modeling. Within CABLE, the teacher provided modeling in various ways: by demonstrating object-oriented programming concepts and skills, and by using certain problem-solving heuristics to demonstrate how to model JAVA applications.

Another component of the CABLE approach is coaching. This was implemented in several ways: a) by the lecturer giving expert coaching in class, b) by means of expert help via e-mail, c) by peer coaching from other students as they collaborate in certain programming activities, and d) by means of interactive online tests. Students could test their level of knowledge and skills by taking these tests, and by clicking on a button, the test would be graded and instant feedback of their test score would be returned. Coaching and modeling was also facilitated by the use of the debugger facility of JBuilder, the integrated developer environment for creating Java programs. The debugger allowed students to "step through" any JAVA program and visualize the sequence of execution of the JAVA program.

A salient feature of the CABLE approach is contextualization of abstract tasks. JAVA programming was taught within the context of the systems life cycle, so that students could see the steps of the process as integrated within a larger context and at the same time focus on the individual details. Situated learning was also facilitated by means of collaboration in pairs for programming activities; as in real life, programming is usually carried out by a team of developers.

Another important feature of cognitive apprenticeship is visualization. In CABLE, this was achieved by the lecturer articulating his thought processes and by posting notes and sample solutions on the class Web site. Within the CABLE approach, the lecturer provided scaffolding by providing the most appropriate teaching strategy to facilitate support for the student. This help or guidance was gradually withdrawn (fading) when students demonstrated that they could now step through the process with confidence. The learners would then be given more complex tasks.

Table 15.1 summarizes the operationalization of the different elements in the two groups. In the course of the study, the independent variable (instructional approach) was manipulated, and subsequent changes in the dependent variables (student attitudes to learning environment and student performance) were gauged using questionnaires, surveys, and post-tests.

TABLE 15.1 Operationalization of Instructional Variables for Phase 1 and Phase 2

Traditional mode	CABLE mode
Lecturer modeling present	Lecturer modeling present
Feedback process via conventional teaching methods	Student feedback through enhanced means such as scheduled e-mails, individualized monitoring, and elaborated instructions
Collaboration not factored in	Collaboration factored in (pair programming)
Visualization by use of debugger	Visualization by means of debugger
No online implementation	Online notes, online sample solutions, and interactive self-tests
Reflection not factored in	Learners encouraged to reflect on the state of their learning

RESULTS: PHASE 1

Student Achievement

Overall, the results indicated that the CABLE group performed better in the post-test than the traditional group. One-way ANOVA procedures confirmed that the difference between the CABLE group (mean = 68.7, SD = 23.0) and the non-CABLE group (mean = 49.4, SD = 15.9) was significant, $F(1, 44) = 8.9$, $p = .005$. For further investigation, the two treatment groups were then split into two groups on the basis of the prior test scores. The prior test scores were taken as a measure of ability level. The median value of 70 was used to generate a classification of high-ability and low-ability students. Initial analysis based on the post-test indicated that CABLE had advantaged high-ability more than low-ability students. However, a more sensitive measurement using hierarchical regression analyses indicated that CABLE had a positive effect on achievement irrespective of ability level. The treatment effect was significant and independent of initial ability level and gender.

Student Attitudes to Learning Environment

For the analysis of student attitudes for Phase 1 and 2, three aggregate variables were computed as measures of positive affect, to enable comparisons of attitudinal data between the two treatment groups. The following procedures were carried out for the aggregation of these variables:

Positive affect score (*PAS*) measured positive affect toward the learning environment. This was calculated for each student by summing all the responses for each question from Question 1 to Question 11, to permit a range from 11 to 44.

Online learning score (*OLS*) measured positive affect or liking for online learning. This was computed by summing the responses for Questions 12 to 15, to permit a range from 4 to 16.

Collaborative score (*CS*) measured positive affect toward collaborative learning and was calculated by summing student responses for Questions 16 and 17 (*CS* could take values between 2 and 8).

Positive Affect toward Learning Environment
From the analyses of these aggregate variables and the responses to individual items on the attitudinal questionnaire, the following results became apparent:

Overall, there were no significant differences in student attitudes to the learning environment (as indexed on *PAS*) between the CABLE and traditional groups, as students in both treatment groups showed high levels of affect for their learning environment, irrespective of gender and initial ability level (mean of 36.8 and 36.4 for CABLE and traditional respectively, $F(1, 44) = .1$, *ns*).

Effectiveness of Collaborative learning

Students in the CABLE group indicated positive attitudes toward collaborative learning, as indicated by the high values of *CS* (mean of 6.6, SD of 1.48). The possible range was from 2 to 8, with 5 as the natural midpoint, representing neutrality. The *CS* scores ranged from 2 to 8, with 84.4% of the respondents exhibiting scores above the natural midpoint of 5. Both high- and low-ability groups evidenced similar high levels of CS, with respective means of 6.67 and 6.43, $F(1,30) = .199$, *ns.*

Responses to the Question 18 probe asking what problems were encountered (if any) during the treatment revealed the following:

For the non-CABLE treatment, 5 out of 18 students reported having no problems in using this learning mode. The main problem students identified was the difficulty of understanding the terminology of the lecturer. Other problems reported included 1) difficulty of catching up with the work, 2) difficulty in communicating with the lecturer, 3) slow typing, 4) difficulty in finding errors, and 5) difficulty in understanding the purpose of the program.

In the CABLE treatment, 11 out of 32 reported having no problems with the learning environment. Those who did reported the following problems: 1) technical problems with computers breaking down, 2) found Java difficult, 3) problem accessing Web site, and 4) difficulty applying knowledge to writing a Java program.

Responses to the Question 19 probe asking to indicate reasons why the mode of treatment was perceived as effective revealed the following:

Ten out of 18 students in the non-CABLE treatment agreed it was an effective learning environment. The following reasons were given: 1) it provided a high level of understanding, 2) it prepared students for programming, 3) the use of good analogies in class, 4) the use by the lecturer of a step-by-step mode, 5) helped build self-confidence and self-esteem, 6) helped in learning new technologies, and 7) provided more computing knowledge and skills. Only one student found the learning environment ineffective, claiming it difficult to understand because of the terminology used by the lecturer.

For the CABLE treatment, the majority (27 of 32 students or 85%) reported the learning mode as effective. The main reason given for this was the ease of accessibility of lecture notes. Other reasons given by students for effectiveness included 1) the use of e-mail helped in understanding Java, 2) could send e-mail anytime, 3) the availability of extra reading materials online, 4) online notes saved writing, 5) online notes were easy to use, 6) lecture notes were well-organized and easy to use, 7) easy to visualize notes and read on screen, 8) accessibility of lecturer, 9) use of online FAQs helpful, 10) lots of sharing and closeness between students and lecturer, 11) improved understanding of subject, 12) provided encouragement to come to class, and 13) good teacher.

The majority of the students interviewed agreed on the usefulness and effectiveness of e-mail as a means of feedback. The main source of frustration was technical problems preventing effective access to e-mail. These included hardware failure and inability to access the Internet and the intranet. Most of the students regarded e-mail as very helpful, as it gave useful and immediate feedback. All of the students interviewed liked online notes, giving the main reason for liking as the ease of access, and also that they could access it at any time. Again, the main complaints were technical, such as computers breaking down and inability to access the Internet. All of the students interviewed liked the idea of sample solutions online, as they said they could 1) access it any time, 2) useful for revision, and 3) were useful for doing test corrections.

Figure 15.4   Computer Studies students in the Computer Lab at the National University of Samoa.

Effectiveness of Online Learning

Three data sources were used to gauge the effectiveness of online learning for Phase 1 and Phase 2: 1) the responses to the Questions 12–17 administered only to the CABLE group, and responses to Questions 18 and 19; 2) the responses from personal student interviews, conducted in weeks 6 and weeks 12 of the study; and 3) content of e-mail messages from the help desk and the weekly e-mail feedback from students.

Questionnaire questions and interviews with students focused on four main issues: 1) the effectiveness of e-mail for feedback; 2) the effectiveness of online notes on class Web site; 3) the usefulness of posting sample test solutions online; and 4) whether students like working in pairs.

Data from these sources were then analyzed based on the Triple Framework approach for evaluating online environments (Ryba, Selby, & Mentis, 2001).

The Triple P Framework

The Triple P Framework evaluates online communities by 1) documenting the views and experiences of students (Perceptions), 2) analyzing the content of interaction patterns of electronic contributions (Processes), and 3) verifying the products that result from the online learning process (Products).

The products of online learning for this study are the e-mail messages and FAQs. Based on the Triple P Framework, contents of these products were categorized using Poole's (2000) method of coding students' participation and then analyzed using Salomon's 5-stage model to evaluate the stage of growth of the online community. According to Salomon (2000), there are 5 stages in the development of an online learning community. Stage 1 is when community members develop the motivation to access and use the Web environment proficiently. Stage 2 is the establishment of online identities and the initiative to socialize with others online. Stage 3 is characterized by participants initiating the process of assisting and providing mutual support in information exchange. Stage 4 is characterized by course-related group discussions; increased collaboration among members of the online community as they collaborate in online work. Finally, stage 5, is characterized by the achievement of personal goals and an ability to reflect on the learning process.

Analysis of the processes of online learning is linked to Poole's (2000) work of coding students' participation in an online course in which messages are categorized as one or more of the following: 1) Technical messages relating to the Web site and managing online learning (Stage 1 of Salomon's model—access and motivation); 2) Social—messages that are nonacademic in nature (Stage 2 of Salomon's model—socialization); and 3) Coursework—information related to the course content and academic work (Stages 3 to 5 of Salomon's model—information exchange, knowledge construction, and development).

Evaluation Using the Triple P Framework

Perceptions

In terms of perceptions, CABLE group participants evidenced high levels of liking for the online environment, as indicated by the values of the *OLS* aggregate (mean of 12.75, SD of 1.98). The *OLS* scores ranged from 7 to 16, with 84.4 % of the respondents exhibiting scores above the natural midpoint of 10. Comparison of high-ability (mean of 12.93, SD of 2.5) and low-ability (mean of 12.61, SD of 1.6) groups indicated no significant differences on the levels of *OLS*: $F(1.30) = .196$, *ns*.

Processes

In terms of processes, the students were not only proficient in using the online environment, but were also proficient in using the online environment for receiving coaching, feedback, and scaffolding (88%). In fact, one could also claim that students were also using the e-mail facility for online discussion forums (7%) and, for a few of them, the ability to use it for reflection on their work (5%).

Products

In terms of products, student participation in e-mail included technical messages relating to the Web site or managing of the help desk and questions related to coursework (88% of the content was course related in nature, none of the messages were social in nature; and 12% of the content was technical and related mainly to problems of access and computer failure. The volume of messages had increased by 50% by the end of the project).

Evaluation using the Triple P Framework showed that the online community in Phase 1 had progressed to stage 3 of the 5-stage model, where students were involved in information exchange using e-mail and the discussion forum.

RESULTS: PHASE 2

Student Achievement

Results showed that there was an effect for CABLE treatment on post-test scores. That is, people who participated in CABLE scored higher on the Java post-test than those who were in the traditional treatment. Statistical ANOVA procedures were used and showed a significant overall effect for treatment, $F(1,53) = 8.48$, p = .005. Inspection of the CABLE group indicated a significant difference between high- (mean = 17.5, SD = 3.0) and low-ability (mean = 14.04, SD = 4.0) groups, $F(1,27) = 7.29$, $p = .01$. Hence, it was apparent that, although the CABLE treatment had benefited both ability groups, the effect was more prominent in the less-able group.

Student Attitudes to Learning Environment

Positive Affect toward Learning Environment
Overall, no significant differences could be discerned between CABLE and non-CABLE groups in student attitudes to the learning environment (as indexed on *PAS*), as both groups exhibited high levels of liking for their course instruction: $F(1, 65) = 2.34$, *ns.* For the CABLE (mean = 34.9, SD = 3.9) and the non-CABLE group (mean = 33.5, SD = 3.9), the actual values of *PAS* ranged from 26 to 43, with 97% of the scores lying above the natural midpoint of 27.5.

Effectiveness of Collaborative learning
In terms of collaborative learning, students in the CABLE group showed high levels of positive affect for collaborative learning, as indicated by the high values of *CS* (mean = 7.3, SD = .93). The possible range was from 4 to 8, with 6 as the natural midpoint, representing neutrality. The *CS* scores ranged from 6 to 8, with 70% of respondents exhibiting scores above the natural midpoint of 6. Further analysis reported a significant difference between high- (mean = 7.5, SD = .79) and low-ability groups (mean = 6.8, SD = .97): $F(1, 25) = 4.33$, $p = .048$, with high-ability showing more positive attitudes toward collaborative learning.

Responses to the Question 18 probe asking what problems were
encountered (if any) during the treatment revealed the following:
For the traditional treatment, 6 out of 24 students reported having no problems in using this learning mode. The main problem the students identified was the difficulty in understanding Java programming (12 out of 24 students). Other problems reported included 1) not enough time to do

work; 2) difficulty in accessing the lecturer; and 3) difficulty in specific Java concepts, such as declaring types and running the program.

In the CABLE treatment, 4 out of 24 students reported having no problems with the learning environment. As in the traditional group, the main problems students reported were the difficulty in understanding Java and too much Java terminology to learn.

Responses to the Question 19 probe asking to indicate reasons why the mode of treatment was perceived as effective revealed the following:

Fifteen out of 24 students in the traditional treatment agreed it was an effective learning mode. The following reasons were given: 1) it kept students alert, occupied, and provided experience of working under pressure; 2) it prepared students for programming independent of the lecturer; 3) improved student understanding of Java; 4) the provision of a balance of both practice and theory improved understanding of Java; 5) provided encouragement to learn; and 6) provided more computing knowledge and skills. Five students found the learning environment ineffective. One claimed it was because it was the first time they had studied computers, while another resented disruptions from other students.

For the CABLE treatment, 15 of 24 students reported the learning mode as effective. The main reasons given were 1) the use of both practicals and lectures facilitated a better understanding of Java, 2) increased motivation and improved confidence in learning Java, 3) improved understanding of Java, and 4) the use of e-mail. Two students found the learning environment ineffective, one of them giving the reason as insufficient coverage time for topics.

All of the students interviewed liked the use of e-mail as a means for feedback, quoting reasons such as 1) ease of access, 2) advantageous for shy students, and 3) being able to ask questions freely. The main problems were the reliability of the technology, such as inability to access the Web site and also the lack of knowledge and skills to use the Web site and e-mail facility. All of the students interviewed agreed on the effectiveness of online notes, giving as the main reason the ease of access. Again, the main problem was the reliability of the technology. Except for one student who had not attempted this feature, all of the students indicated the usefulness of the sample tests, giving as the main reason its usefulness in revision for tests.

Effectiveness of Online Learning

Evaluation Using the Triple P Framework

Perceptions

In terms of perceptions, participants in the CABLE group evidenced high levels of liking for the online environment, as indicated by the values of the OLS aggregate (mean = 12.5, SD = 1.9). The actual scores ranged from 8 to 16, with 72% of the scores lying above the natural midpoint of 10. Comparison using ability status as criteria reported no significant differences between high-ability (mean = 12.4, SD = 1.8) and low-ability groups (mean = 11.6, SD = 1.9) on the levels of OLS: $F(1, 25) = 1.37$, *ns.*

Processes

In terms of processes, the students were not only proficient in using the online environment, but were also proficient in using the online environment for receiving coaching, feedback, and scaffolding. Students were also using the e-mail facility for online discussion forums and for a few of them, the ability to use it for reflection on their work.

Products

In terms of products, student participation in e-mail included technical messages relating to the Web site or managing of the help desk and questions related to coursework. Lecturer participation was in the form of providing encouragement to the students, providing feedback on student queries, and bringing to the notice of students valuable features of the online environment (80% of the content was course-related in nature, 4% of the messages were social in nature, and 16% of the content was technical and related mainly to problems of access and computer failure. The volume of the messages had increased by 56 % by the end of Phase 2).

Hence, the results of the evaluation of the impact of the online learning environment using the Triple P Framework were very similar to those in Phase 1. Results showed that the online community in Phase 2 had progressed to stage 3 of the 5-stage model, where students were involved in information exchange using e-mail and the discussion forum.

LIMITATIONS OF THE STUDY

It is pertinent at this stage that the limitations of this research be acknowledged. Like most educational research, it is very difficult to draw direct cause-and-effect relationships between the CABLE treatment and variables evaluated in this research, mostly owing to the fact that a whole host of factors may also impact on student attitudes and performance. Classic examples of these factors include a student's prior knowledge, their experience, and also student expectations.

Secondly, it must be emphasized that CABLE is a package approach, and the emphasis was on the integration of the various instructional elements into a package and not the isolation of its individual components. Hence, we could not attribute the effects of the treatments to specific components of the CABLE model.

The third limitation is the small sample size and small scale of the study. It would be interesting to replicate the study with a larger research sample. With a larger sample size, the results could be more strongly validated. Furthermore, with larger samples, we can specify an extra level in the multilevel analyses, namely, the level of experimental condition. Under experimental conditions, and with larger samples, we may be able to isolate specific instructional elements that are linked with beneficial outcomes.

Fourthly, as with any study in which the individuals are aware of their participation, it is possible that student behavior may change because they are part of the study. Students, for example, may assume that the researcher or faculty member wants them to use e-mail, resulting in skewed and artificial results.

The reliability of technology also raised some concern. The breakdown of computers during class time, resulting in temporary inability of students to access the online learning environment, could also have had an effect on the evaluation of the effectiveness of the online learning environment. Possible consequences of this breakdown are a reduction in volume of e-mail traffic, and this is not to mention the demoralizing and discouraging effect on students.

Lastly, the truthfulness and veracity of student responses is a potential weakness and critical issue, as the validity of the findings of the data collection is based on the assumption that the student responses in the questionnaire are truthful and accurately reflect their attitudes on the subject.

SUMMARY AND CONCLUSION

From the results of this study it was found that

CABLE, as a viable model of conceiving and delivering a high-quality instructional-aid system, receives a measure of strong positive support from the present results. The results showed that on the overall, students were advantaged through their participation within this program.

In terms of positive attitudes toward the learning environment, results of the study indicate that all the participants showed strong positive feelings toward their allocated treatment.

There is positive evidence on the impact of online learning in all of the student interviews and questionnaire responses and also from the analysis of e-mail content and the processes students were engaged in.

The results of both studies confirm the effectiveness of CABLE as a viable instructional model for teaching computer programming. In the first phase, initial analyses seemed to suggest that CABLE advantaged high-ability students. However, more sensitive analyses using hierarchical regression showed that the effects of CABLE were irrespective of ability or gender. In the second phase, the low-ability students appeared to benefit slightly more than the high-ability students, although both ability groups showed clear advantages in the CABLE. Why might two similar studies yield slightly different findings? The solution we favor is that our CABLE model continues undergoing development firstly in terms of improvement and familiarity with procedures. Also in the second study, the lecturing team placed relatively greater emphasis upon individualized feedback.

It can be noted that the two studies differed slightly in the composition of the participant groups. In the first study, all the participants were from the Foundation program. These were generally the more able students, entering with high GPAs. In the second study, 64% of the participants were from the Foundation program. However there were also 36% from the non-Foundation program, generally entering with low GPAs. Despite the difference in ability levels of these two groups, there was no interaction between program and treatment, as CABLE had a positive effect on achievement levels of participants from both programs.

Hence, the results of the present study have boosted the confidence of our team in the viability of CABLE. It seems to indicate that the provision of excellent instructional procedures in a richly motivating and responsive educational context can have appeal and positive effects on students who may not otherwise perform to a high level. In this respect CABLE can enable us to achieve the ultimate goal of reducing variance within student achievement levels. This is encouraging, especially within the context of teaching computer programming, as the subject area is very challenging and cognitively demanding. Hence, an effective instructional model would certainly improve the quality of instruction of such an inherently demanding subject and ultimately result in improved achievement levels of computer-programming students within the university.

Furthermore, the results from both phases of the study provide positive evaluations of the impact of the online implementation of CABLE and points to the benefits of the use of technology such as e-mail, Web sites, discussion forums, and bulletin boards in implementing pedagogical approaches such as cognitive apprenticeship. However, it needs to be acknowledged that these are early stages in the development of CABLE, and further research and larger sample sizes are needed for further validation of its effectiveness.

REFERENCES

AECT (2001). *The handbook of research for educational communications and technology.* Retrieved June 12, 2003 from http://www.aect.org/intranet/publications/edtech/24/24-05.html

Brill, J., Kim, B., & Galloway, C. (2001). Cognitive apprenticeships as an instructional model. In M. Orey (Ed.), *Emerging perspectives on learning, teaching, and technology.* Retrieved April 5, 2004 from http://itstudio.coe.uga.edu/ebook/CognitiveApprenticeship.htm

Brown, A. L. (1992). Design experiments: Theoretical and methodical challenges in creating complex interventions in classroom settings. *The Journal of Learning Sciences, 2*(2), 141–178.

Brown, A. L., & Campione, J. C. (1996). Psychological theory and the design of learning environments: On procedures, principles and systems. In L. Schauble and R. Glaser (Eds.), *Innovations in learning: New environments for education.* Mahwah, NJ: Lawrence Erlbaum Associates.

Cognition and Technology Group at Vanderbilt (1993). Anchored instruction and situated cognition revisited. *Educational Technology, 33*(3), 52–70.

Collins, A., Brown, J. S., & Newman, S. (1989). Cognitive apprenticeship: Teaching the craft of reading, writing, and mathematics. In L. Resnick (Ed.), *Knowing, learning and instruction: Essays in honor of Robert Glaser.* Hillsdale, NJ: Erlbaum.

Garner, S (2000). *Cognitive load reduction in problem solving domains.* Edith Cowan University.

Jarvela, S. (1995). The cognitive apprenticeship model in a technologically rich learning environment: Interpreting the learning interaction. *Learning and Instruction, 5*(3), 237–259.

Jonassen, D. H., & Reeves, T. C. (1996). Learning with technology: Using computers as cognitive tools. In D. H. Jonassen (Ed.), *Handbook of research for educational communications and technology.* New York: Macmillan.

Levin, J., & Waugh, M. (1998). Teaching teleapprenticeships: Electronic network-based educational frameworks for improving teacher education. *Journal of Interactive Learning Environments, 6*(1–2), 39–58.

Moursound, D.G. (1996, 2002) *Increasing your expertise as a problem solver: Some roles of computers.* Eugene, OR: ISTE.

Palincsar, A., & Brown, A. (1984). Reciprocal teaching of comprehension-fostering and comprehension-monitoring activities. *Cognition and Instruction, 1,* 117–175.

Poole, D. (2000). Student participation in a discussion-oriented online course: A case study. *Journal of Research on Computing in Education, 22*(2), 162–177.

Ryba. K., Selby, L., & Mentis, M. (2001). *Analysing the effectiveness of on-line learning found in communities.* Retrieved September 25, 2003 from http://www.ecu.edu.au/conferences/herdsa/main/papers/nonref/pdf/KenRyba.pdf

Salomon, G. (2000). *E-moderating: The key to teaching and learning online.* London: Kogan Page.

Scardamalia, M., Bereiter, K., & Lamon, M. (1994) The CSILE project: Trying to bring the classroom into world 3. In K. McGilly (Ed.), *Classroom lessons: Integrating cognitive theory and classroom practice)* Cambridge, MA: Bradford Books/MIT Press.

Tholander J., Karlgren K., & Ramberg R. (1998) *Cognitive apprenticeship in training for conceptual modeling.* Retrieved July 15, 2003 from http://www.dsv.su.se/~klas/Publications/webnet98.pdf

Wilson, B. G. (Ed.) (1996). *Constructivist learning environments: Case studies in instructional design.* Englewood Cliffs, NJ: Educational Technology.

CHAPTER 16

FROM DISTANCE LEARNING TO E-LEARNING IN CENTRAL AND NORTHERN MOZAMBIQUE

Aurelio Gomes and Elizabeth Walker

BACKGROUND

Mozambique is considered one of the poorest countries in the world. It is a country where its mere physical length acts as a barrier to movements and agglomeration, and where floods and heavy rains constitute a worsening and regular factor. It is a country where lengthy civil war has destroyed the educational systems. The railway network, telephone system, and main and secondary road network still need heavy investment for improvement and maintenance. The destruction of the rural health system in central Mozambique during 30 years of war has caused the region to be terribly underserved in the provision of basic health care. Infrastructure must be rebuilt for education; health care personnel trained; public-health information gathered and acted upon; and education about nutrition, maternal child health, and HIV/AIDS made available to the rural population.

Bridging the Knowledge Divide, pages 289–298
Copyright © 2009 by Information Age Publishing
All rights of reproduction in any form reserved.

Mozambique ranks 168th out of 177 countries on the Human Development Report 2005 (http://hdr.undp.org/reports/global/2005). Per capita income averages $210 per annum; life expectancy of 41.9 years is among the lowest in Africa, owing largely to the impact of HIV/AIDS; and the adult literacy rate is 46.5%, although primary education has improved considerably. Mozambique ranks 133rd out of 140 countries in the gender-development index. From 1997 to 2003, under-5 mortality fell from 219 to 178 per 1,000 live births and maternal mortality from 1,000 to 408 per 100,000 live births. The Mozambique 2002–03 nationwide household survey indicated that poverty has declined from 69.4% in 1996–97 to 54.1% in 2002–03.

THE CATHOLIC UNIVERSITY OF MOZAMBIQUE (UCM)

The Catholic University of Mozambique (UCM), located in central and northern Mozambique (Figure 16.1), is the first private not-for-profit university in the country. The Catholic University of Mozambique (UCM) began in August 1996 with two Faculties: Faculty of Law in Nampula and the Faculty of Economics and Management in Beira. In 1998 UCM opened the Faculty of Education in Nampula and in January 1999, the Faculty of Agriculture (Niassa). In August 2000 UCM initiated the Faculty of Medicine in Beira. The Faculty of Tourism and Informatics was established in Pemba in 2001. The campus sites are designated by yellow squares in Figure 16.1. The mission sites, designated by red crosses in Figure 16.1, also serve as educational facilities for distance (print-based) learning and potential sites for e-learning.

The emergence of UCM as a significant player in the country's recovery efforts is due to the decentralization of the institutions of higher learning in central and northern Mozambique. Each campus provides a center for distance learning in the surrounding areas.

THE UCM CENTER FOR DISTANCE EDUCATION (CED)

The Catholic University of Mozambique officially created in 2003 the Centro de Ensino a Distancia (CED) or in English, Distance Education Center. At the present time, the majority of its students are teachers with no specific training in education. Such teachers work in rural areas of central and northern Mozambique.

The center has 676 students studying for a Bachelor or Bachelor's with Honors degree in the field of Education. The different areas (or specialties) of training are history, geography, mathematics, physics, chemistry, biology, Portuguese language, and design.

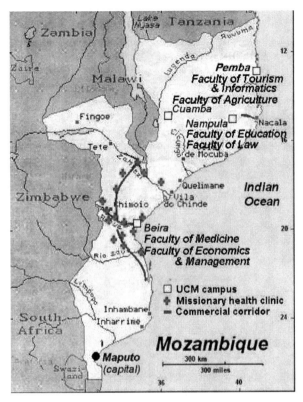

Figure 16.1 The Catholic University of Mozambique has campuses in the central and northern regions. The campus sites are designated by yellow squares; the mission sites designated by red crosses.

Objectives

The general objective of CED is to contribute to the training of teachers in order to improve the quality of teaching in the country.

The specific objectives are

- Guarantee to all citizens interested in teaching, and in particular those already teaching without a college degree in education, a higher-education degree to enable them to exercise the teaching activity at an adequate and efficient level;
- Allow teachers in rural areas where there are no colleges or universities to obtain a college degree without the need to stop teaching;
- Give adequate scientific, technical, and methodological knowledge to the students to allow them to reach the delineated objectives in their specialty.

TABLE 16.1   CED Programs in Four Cities Presently Serving 676 Students

City	Degree	# of students	Year	Provinces covered
Beira	BSc	110	3rd	Sofala, Inhambane, and Tete
Beira	BSc with honors	69	2nd	Sofala, Inhambane, and Tete
Cuamba	BSc	181	2nd	Niassa
Chimoio	BSc with honors	67	2nd	Manica, Tete
Chimoio	BSc with honors	95	1st	Manica, Tete, Inhambane
Beira	BSc with honors	122	1st	Sofala, Tete, I'bane, Maputo
Nampula	BSc with honors	32	1st	Cabo Delgado, Nampula e Zambezia
TOTAL		676		

Programs

CED currently has 7 different programs in 4 different cities (Beira, Chimoio, Cuamba, and Nampula). The first 76 BSc in education were graduated on Aug 25, 2007.

Modalities to Implement the Courses

CED's course teachers have two approaches for delivering the course material: face-to-face mentoring sessions between teacher and students at the rural site and distance (print-based) education.

The mentoring sessions occur four times a year; the first is in January and takes 5 days; the second, third, and fourth meetings have a duration of 3 days to avoid excessive disruption to the labor activities of the students.

Main Challenges

CED is facing several difficulties that limit and even compromise the actual success of the program. The main problems are

- Rapid increase in the number of candidates. In 2007 the number increased from 450 to the actual 676, and the trend continues;
- Requests to introduce new specializations, such as English Language, Informatics, Economy and Management, Psychology, etc.;
- The need to improve the quality of the courses already in progress. This involves
  - improvement of the self-instructional materials,
  - efficient management of the didactic and psych-pedagogic areas,

- – creation of strategies and mechanisms to guarantee a better "as-siduidade" and better support to the students;{/BSL}
- Lack of adequate infrastructure: the CED program has borrowed installations of the Archdiocese of Beira, which will have to be given back in 2 years
- Lack of transportation for the mentors. Due to the lack of vehicles, it is difficult to do a proper didactic supervision. The distances are far, and the team has to use public transportation, called "chapas," which are unreliable and not suitable for transporting faculty and instructional materials.

Removing Remoteness through Internet Capabilities

The actual experience of running a high-school distance (print-based) education program in the province of Niassa and Nampula showed that there are barriers to be overcome. This program runs summer courses for teachers. However, the lack of interaction with UCM faculty and the feeling of remoteness by the students hampers the success rate. To eliminate the above-mentioned constraints, the plan is to move from distance education to e-learning.

HEALTH SCIENCES E-LEARNING AT UCM

The Plan

Although e-learning will be promoted in all faculties of the university, there is some urgency to establish capability for health sciences e-learning. The first class of 13 UCM physicians has graduated (August 25, 2007) and are now dispersed throughout central and northern Mozambique. The focus of the UCM medical program is to produce physicians who will work in rural areas, not just in one-to-one care but in upgrading the training of the health workers and promoting education in rural areas concerning such health issues as the HIV/AIDS epidemic. The backbone of this project will be a new distance medical-education center at the Faculty of Medicine, including studio/electronic classroom, medical education laboratory, and full-time connection to the Internet. The center will coordinate preparation and delivery of distance courses, short-courses, workshops, tutorials, and other Web-based materials using WebCT or similar course-management software to health care workers, i.e., physicians, nurses, and other health workers in the rural areas.

Using initial funds available through a USAID grant called Partnership for Rural Health Education in Mozambique, the UCM Faculty of Medicine successfully collaborated with the WVU School of Medicine in laying out the framework for a rural education program among the medical students and other health care workers in central Mozambique. This seed grant provided $100,000 USD and led to a larger NIH grant and collaborations with the University of Pittsburgh and other universities. Due to the difficulty of funding, the main strategy was to apply for research grants, including funds to build needed infrastructure for training, care, and research.

The cornerstone of the e-learning will be a network of community outreach centers, based at the Catholic missions affiliated with Catholic University of Mozambique (UCM)/Faculty of Medicine. These centers must have the technological communications capabilities to run long-distance courses, and also will serve as the place to exchange technical information, update the health workers skills, and also interact with members of the community in general. The community outreach centers will have full-time, direct connect, two-way satellite Internet capability that will mainly consist of a satellite upload-download dish, transmit and receive modems, and router, as seen in Figure 16.2. The system is an "intermediate speed" Internet system and will have approximately 400 kbps upload and download capacity.

The community outreach centers will have a small computer center with up to 12 computers, each with a video camera. Every computer hooked to the network will have direct, full-time access to the Internet. Furthermore, with the help of the 12 Web cameras, staff and students will be able to simultaneously see and talk to someone over the Internet at other locations anywhere in the world via Internet Video Conferencing. These capabilities will allow not only running the distance education program, but also uploading and downloading images necessary for telemedicine.

This community "peripheral" basic infrastructure needs to be complemented with Internet, technological and educational capabilities based at the main campus of the faculties involved in the program, medicine, education, and economics and management to deliver the courses mentioned above.

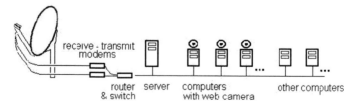

Figure 16.2 Equipment at outreach centers.

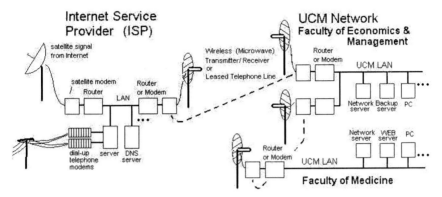

Figure 16.3 The Faculties of Management and Medicine network and Internet connections.

At this moment, only Beira has a fiber-optic network in the city, offering a very reliable phone system. Therefore, we are proposing to link by satellite. We propose to set a fast connection from the campus of the UCM medical school to all the community outreach centers involved in distance education. The community outreach centers would have full-time, direct connect, two-way satellite Internet capability, which will mainly consist of a satellite upload-download dish. However, the Internet service will also include a fixed, public IP address in order that a Web server may be established. Figure 16.3 illustrates this concept.

MANGUNDE MISSION SITE

Presently, there is already a V-SAT system in one of the missions, in Mangunde, that has been used to connect the local mission clinic to the main campus in Beira. E-learning is available to those based close to the mission (Figure 16.4).

Since this system only covers those based at Mangunde, soon we will install a distance wireless network linking all the health posts, providing constant education to the health care workers.

From September 1, 2003 until August 31, 2005, the project designated AWARE (HIV/AIDS Control Within A Research Endeavor) in a rural area (Mangunde Mission, District of Chibabava) was implemented by the Catholic University of Mozambique in collaboration with the University of Pittsburgh, UCLA, West Virginia Universit and Fundação Instituto Oswaldo Cruz (FIOCRUZ) from Brazil. The intention was to go beyond community awareness to strengthen the resolve of the community to face the problem of AIDS. The cornerstone of all the activities are rural health clinics and,

Figure 16.4 V-SAT in Mangunde.

at the community level, a vast network of volunteers to deliver prevention activities and provide home care to the patients. A pilot rural HIV clinic has been completed in Mangunde, a remote area of Sofala Province, where there is no electricity or infrastructure. This is a huge undertaking, as distances are enormous, the roads are poor, and travel to these rural areas is difficult. At the time, this was the first and only rural HIV clinic in Mozambique. It was featured in an article in SLATE magazine (http://www.slate.com/id/2119853/).

Mangunde is 303 km away from the city of Beira, in a rural area around 4½ hours driving time over roads that are marginal in many sections. It may take up to 5 hours to reach Mangunde Mission during the rainy season. There is no running water or power supply from the grid. The foundation has been established for communication with the School of Medicine in Beira via the satellite dish that provides good interconnectivity (V-SAT).

Solar energy is able to run two servers and five computers. A borehole for water has been established. The requirements for a rural education/training program are in place. In other words, this project has created a rural health clinic and a community outreach center (COC) for health rural education/e-education. As funding is available, more adds-in will be done, such as accommodation for permanent staff and permanent offices.

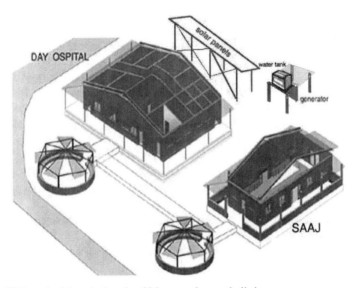

Figure 16.5a Architect's sketch of Mangunde rural clinic.

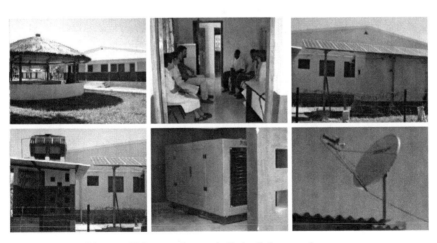

Figure 16.5b Photos of Mangunde rural clinic. Solar panels, a generator, water tanks, satellite dish have made it possible to establish the rural clinic in this remote area of Sofala Province.

SUMMARY

The emergence of the Catholic University of Mozambique (UCM) as a significant player in the country's recovery efforts is in part due to the decentralization of the UCM campuses in central and northern Mozambique. Each campus provides a center for distance learning in the surrounding areas. UCM is addressing three (education, health, and basic infrastructure) of the six priorities outlined by the government as "fundamental areas of action": 1) education, 2) health, 3) agriculture and rural development, 4) basic infrastructure, 5) good governance, and 6) macro-economic and financial management.

In 2003 UCM officially created the Centro de Ensino a Distancia (CED), i.e., Distance Learning Center. The majority of its students are teachers with no specific training in education. They teach in rural areas of central and northern Mozambique. Currently the Center has approximately 700 students studying for a Bachelor or Bachelor's with Honors degree in the field of Education. Distance (printed material) education in this environment has been difficult. Experience has shown that lack of interaction with faculty and the feeling of remoteness by the students is hampering the distance learning success rate.

As the first classes of physicians are graduated, UCM has the obligation to offer a distance continuing medical-education program. For remote areas, the plan (already in motion) is to move from distance (print material) education to e-learning, based on the CED experience. The cornerstone of the e-learning will be a network of community outreach centers, based at the Catholic missions affiliated with UCM. These centers will have the technological communications capabilities to run distance courses and also serve as the place to exchange technical information for health workers and members of the community.

CHAPTER 17

A FRAMEWORK
FOR THE DELIVERY
OF CROSS-REGIONAL
DISTANCE EDUCATION
TO PROFESSIONALS
IN DEVELOPING COUNTRIES

Kim I. Mallalieu and Pamela Collins

INTRODUCTION

The MRP (Telecommunications) is the University of the West Indies Master's degree in Regulation and Policy, with a specialization in telecommunications. It is offered through the Department of Electrical and Computer Engineering as a multidisciplinary Master's Degree with an emphasis on practical application to national and regional development, and has been developed to strengthen the capacity of the public and private telecommunication sectors in areas relating to regulation and policy.

Through this program, telecommunications professionals are exposed to practical and current knowledge in a broad spectrum of disciplines, which they may use to critically assess appropriate approaches to telecommuni-

Bridging the Knowledge Divide, pages 299–319
Copyright © 2009 by Information Age Publishing
All rights of reproduction in any form reserved.

cations regulation and to guide the development of telecommunications policy. It is also expected that participants of the program would develop a deep awareness of local, regional, and global developments in the field and would bring to their professional posts an appreciation of the perspectives of all the main stakeholders in the sector: the regulator, the private sector, and the state.

Launched in December 2003 by the Faculty of Engineering, the MRP (Telecommunications) program will have serviced three cohorts of students before transitioning into a universitywide program. Students have enrolled from over 30 developing countries, and eleven time zones, bringing diverse cultural as well as disciplinary backgrounds to the program.

The MRP (Telecommunications) program has already made a significant contribution to the telecommunications sector, with students and graduates holding key positions in public and private sector around the globe. The program has created a strong and dynamic international network of like-minded professionals and, through this online community, has become both a regional and international academic focal point for the sharing of ideas and experiences in the area of telecommunications regulation and policy.

PROGRAM PLANNING

Program planning required addressing a variety of issues, which include how to meet regional capacity building needs, of central importance to the University of the West Indies; the key target audience; the academic content and delivery mode of the program; and its administrative framework.

Identifying Regional Needs

Caribbean stakeholder demand for capacity building in telecommunications regulation and policy had been resonantly expressed at a number of regional forums as jurisdictions faced the prospects of sector liberalization. Among the articulated regional needs was the demand for advanced-level tuition for sector executives and other professionals. The MRP (Telecommunications) program was initiated to meet these capacity-building requirements.

During the MRP's planning stages, a three-day regional stakeholders meeting was conducted to contemplate the various dimensions of regional capacity-building needs in telecommunications regulation and policy. The outcomes of this meeting formed the basis for the design of a program that would address identified regional needs.

The program was, from the conceptual stage, perceived to be in support of a rapidly changing industry whose needs were expected to shift, even over the lifespan of the project.

Identifying the Target

The MRP (Telecommunications) program was designed for a student body comprising mature professionals, many of them executives, in the telecommunications sector. The program was planned to be open to professionals of various backgrounds who are involved in the development of the telecommunications sector. At least two years relevant experience in the sector was stipulated as a requirement.

Although primarily conceived as serving the Caribbean, participation from around the world was sought to ensure cross-regional perspectives on the telecommunications liberalization experience.

Identifying Curriculum Needs

Coming out of the initial stakeholders meeting, the curriculum was planned to incorporate legal, economic, technical, planning and public-policy elements, and to relate these sectors to the telecommunications industry.

Identifying Delivery Modalities

The outcomes of the initial stakeholders meeting included the proposal that the delivery modality of the program be predominantly online, with periodic face-to-face delivery. An element of the face-to-face delivery was expected to be mandatory.

Various aspects of program delivery were developed by the Program Coordinator, with inputs from representatives of well-established international distance education programs as well as the University of the West Indies' Distance Education Centre and Instructional Development Unit. The online components of delivery followed from initial local initiatives developed in the Department of Electrical and Computer Engineering at the university (Mallalieu, 1999, 2000a, 2000b). Other research and relevant resources (including Claxton & Murrell, 1987; Laurillard, 1993; Palloff & Pratt, 1999; Woodley et al., 1987) also guided the initiative.

Identifying Administrative Needs

Since the MRP (Telecommunications) program was planned to be delivered almost entirely online, it motivated the rethinking and redesign of many policies and processes at the University of the West Indies. These included the need for

- Online application
- Online registration
- Online receipt of University ID information
- Recognition of electronic signatures, e.g., for staff contracts
- Recognition of scanned and e-mailed correspondence, such as extension requests, examiners' reports, requests for leave of absence
- Electronic submission of grades
- Electronic distribution of graduation information packages.

The contemplation of new electronic policies and processes was timely for the University of the West Indies, which was, at the time of MRP (Telecommunications) program implementation, very keenly focused on expansion of its reach through distance education. The framework comprising these policies and practices was implemented as a pilot for the Electrical and Computer Engineering Department in the first instance. It was envisioned as a resource for the delivery of both regional and cross-regional distance education to professionals in developing countries, particularly for such programs operating with few resources.

PROGRAM OVERVIEW

The MRP (Telecommunications) program is delivered in English over two calendar years on a part-time basis. The program comprises eight 3-credit online courses, seminars worth a total of 3 credits, and a 9-credit project. All 3-credit courses are delivered completely online, seminars are delivered in either face-to-face or online mode, and the project is implemented by individual research, with one-on-one supervision.

A postgraduate Diploma in Telecommunications Regulation and Policy, the DRP (Telecommunications), features six of the MRP's eight 3-credit online courses, with no seminar or project requirement.

The MRP (Telecommunications) program aims:

- To strengthen the capacity of national regulators and policy makers in the telecommunications industry through advanced level academic tuition with an emphasis on practical application to regional development.

- To serve as a regional and international academic focal point for the sharing of ideas and experiences in the area of telecommunications regulation and policy.

PROGRAM OPERATIONAL FRAMEWORK

The framework within which the MRP (Telecommunications) program was developed, and is delivered, comprises three main thematic centers: Administrative, Academic, and Technical, under a single coordination point (Figure 17.1).

Administrative Center

Central to the MRP Administrative Center is a small but dedicated staff team assembled to support the program's aims and objectives. The team roles are tied together as depicted in the core organizational chart illustrated in Figure 17.2. Apart from the core MRP team, a campus librarian provides ongoing support on matters relating to electronic resources and preparation of project reports. From time to time, specialist skills are contracted for appropriate support in areas such as instructional design, course design, and quality-assurance monitoring.

The MRP team is grounded in shared program values that relate to academic excellence, academic integrity, and to complete and comprehensive support for teaching staff and learners. Each member of the MRP team is committed to clarity, responsiveness, tracking, and follow-up actions related to his or her portfolio.

The Administrative Assistant, on the frontline, provides personal guidance to new applicants as well as ongoing support for registration and other

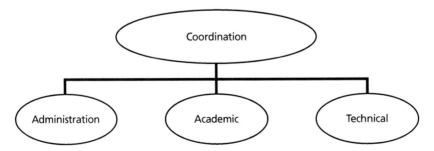

Figure 17.1   Operational framework for MRP.

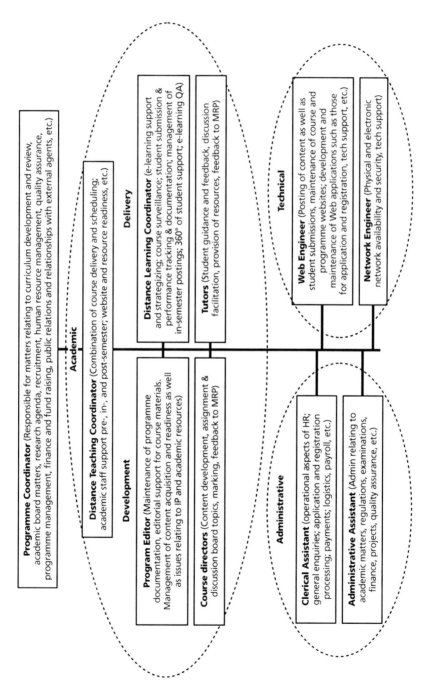

Figure 17.2 MRP core organization chart.

administrative matters, including fees. She interfaces with university services and staff to ensure that the MRP maintains a tight schedule. A number of practices have been introduced to ensure that the program's administration runs smoothly with rapid response. The Administrative Assistant's persistent and comprehensive follow-up are key to the success of these practices.

Academic Center

The academic center manages matters concerning academic policy, learner support, teaching support, content development, content delivery, and resource management, as shown in Figure 17.3.

Academic Policy

Academic excellence and academic integrity are core values of the MRP program. The program, however, recognizes that online delivery offers many avenues for dishonesty. The program has, therefore, produced a variety of resources that are intended to deter incidences of plagiarism and to provide information on avoiding unintentional plagiarism.

The MRP Academic Integrity Policy and other related resources are prominently featured on all course Web sites and are shared with staff and students through handbooks, as well as through orientation and readiness programs. All students are required to sign an Academic Integrity Pledge when they first register. The electronic plagiarism checker, Turnitin, is available to students to check their own work, and is used by the program to review all submitted assignments. Teaching staff are alerted immediately to any suspected violations of professional ethics.

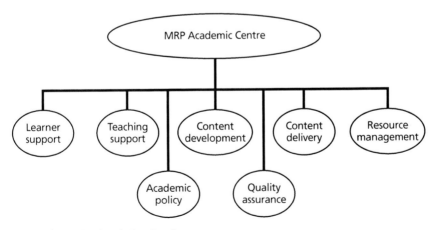

Figure 17.3 Academic focal points.

Learner Support

The cornerstone of the MRP is its learner support. The program recognizes the challenges of distance learning and the particular demands made upon the busy professionals who participate in the MRP. It therefore puts great emphasis on the support systems required to ensure that students can access whatever they may require of the program efficiently and effectively.

Fundamental to MRP learner support is the establishment of personal relationships between students and the program's various points of contact. The program places a great deal of emphasis on communication. Interaction between students and staff, as well as among the student body, is key to MRP learner support. The regular form of program communications is via e-mail and postings to course Web sites, with a nominal commitment from academic staff to respond within two days and from other program staff within one day. Staff and students communicate by phone as the need arises. The program's annual 3-day face-to-face seminars are very useful in establishing personal relationships and building the MRP community.

General academic and pastoral support for learners is provided by the Distance Learning Coordinator, whose academic and professional backgrounds are in education and counseling. Before courses start, she introduces herself to students and provides guidance on the program's Student Manual and Online Orientation Course. During the semester, she monitors student performance weekly, providing individual follow-up, and issues regular reminders on course- and program-related matters. She also provides personal counseling. Together with the program coordinator, editor, and librarian, she provides comprehensive scheduled programs of support for students leading up to and during the execution of their projects. The progress of all project students is closely tracked, and regular individual, as well as group, support and guidance provided.

Course directors and tutors are sensitive to the challenges of distance learners and therefore make a special effort to personalize their communications, such as opening their courses with welcome messages. Tutors provide feedback and guidance on content issues through the semester, while the program editor provides ongoing support with respect to academic integrity, citations and references. The librarian provides support on issues relating to research, electronic resources (e-resources), and document style. The MRP Web engineer/systems administrator provides direct support to learners on all technical matters and passes their assignment submissions through the program's electronic plagiarism checker, Turnitin, on a regular basis.

Teaching Support

Guidance is provided to teaching staff to ensure that they have a shared view of program values, aims, objectives, and academic standards, as well as the importance of responsiveness and fostering interaction. Tutor and Course Director handbooks, as well as electronic support programs and individual communication with teaching staff provide comprehensive guidance on these issues.

The Distance Teaching Coordinator, who has experience in academic matters and in distance teaching methodologies, provides guidance individually and collectively to course directors and tutors. She delivers an online orientation program for each new member of staff and an online readiness program before and during each semester for each course. She communicates regularly with individual tutors, who in turn are expected to interact closely with students during the semester.

A key focal point for academic staff support is the 9-credit MRP project, which follows all coursework. Project supervisors are guided through a comprehensive orientation program, followed by an ongoing support program throughout the project execution phase.

Content Development

The multidisciplinary teams that develop MRP course materials and resources bring together diverse strengths in curriculum development, academic content, online pedagogy, and online course management. Content specialists are recruited from a mix of academia and industry in various jurisdictions around the world. These content specialists and other team members work successfully at a distance to develop materials cooperatively in a process that parallels the challenges that course participants face in the online environment, which assists in ensuring that materials are presented in a user-oriented manner. The team approach also ensures that course material is routinely checked through several iterations from many perspectives.

The preparation of online MRP course materials follows a structured, iterative process led by the program's multidisciplinary/gender/cultural/national course-development teams. The steps, key staff, and staff competencies are illustrated in Table 17.1.

Content Delivery

To date, all online courses have been delivered through the commercial course-management system, WebCT. At the time of writing, the program was migrating its content to the open-source course-management system, Moodle, in concert with the rest of the campus.

Course Web sites provide a variety of facilities and resources for content, interaction, and academic guidance. Materials have been designed to encourage students to build and access these resources through independent research as well as through networking within and external to the program community. Course expectations are comprehensively articulated in the in-

TABLE 17.1   Course Development Process and Team Competencies

	Step	Team Member	Competencies
1	Curriculum development	Program coordinator in consultation with stakeholders	Rich academic and public/private sector experience.
2(a)	Course outline, content preparation and course design	Course directors in consultation with Distance Teaching Coordinator/Program Coordinator	Subject matter; instructional design
2(b)	Editorial review	Editor	Technical writing/editing, distance learning materials preparation.
2(c)	Selection of appropriate technologies	Course designer Web engineer	Online pedagogy Web development
3	Web site development	Web engineer	
4	Web site review (inputs: student and staff feedback from mid and exit surveys each semester in each course/ QA assessment)	Academic staff QA assistant Distance Learning Coordinator Distance Teaching Coordinator	Content Mechanical/visual critique Student experience critique Scheduling/assignments/ academic critique
5	Course and course site evaluation	Students, teaching staff, MRP QA team	Mixed
5	Web site revision	Web engineer	Web development
6	Quality Assurance (QA) Site development	All	Mixed

troduction to courses, and rubrics for each type of assignment as well as samples of assessed student work reinforce expectations.

Although the program does not distribute printed material, printable documents in PDF format are used in all courses to accommodate students who may prefer offline, asynchronous access to course materials. This has been appreciated since most MRP students are mature professionals with busy work and travel schedules.

As the MRP is delivered primarily over the Internet, online tools feature prominently in the program. Some are used to support all MRP courses, while others are used for selected courses, depending on their thematic content and particular learning objectives.

The program recognizes that, despite being involved in the telecommunications sector, many MRP students share the challenge of others in developing countries with regard to accessing online learning. Some have access to only very basic telecommunications infrastructure and services, while others have access to more sophisticated facilities. There are, therefore, no requirements for high-speed Internet access or synchronous online communications.

Various online engagement methods have been used to cater to the diversity in course content and objectives as well as of skills, experience levels, learning styles, and technology access of MRP students. For example, the course materials for RPTL 6801, Contemporary Telecommunications Networks and Technologies, include a rich portfolio of animations and interactive Web resources, which facilitate individual visualization and hands-on exploration of technical concepts. RPTL 6812, Online Seminar, on the other hand, emphasizes the building of an online community and therefore incorporates communication tools and strategies that encourage interactivity and personal expression. These tools have included discussion boards, wikis, blogs, and audio-recorded lectures, as well as assessed discussion contributions, e-folios, and e-presentations.

Table 17.2 summarizes the technologies and tools common to all courses as well as those used for two example courses, RPTL6801 and RPTL6812. The table identifies the purpose for which each technology is used and provides the considerations for each choice. It also provides a sense of how effective each particular technology or tool has proven for its purpose.

Resource Management

The MRP (Telecommunications) program provides all required readings online. The e-resources, which are managed by the campus' Main Library, represent an important productivity tool for staff and students.

All course Web sites feature access to the program's electronic reserves (e-reserves). The MRP e-reserves comprise a collection of electronic books, journals, databases, and a rich selection of other documents, which provide primary as well as secondary support for MRP courses and the final project.

Links to all course-specific required reading are provided on the course sites. MRP students also have access to the University of the West Indies' databases, e-books, and other documents online, which, along with Internet searches and access to local libraries and relevant agencies, provide a foundation for individual research.

Quality Assurance and Evaluation

The program affects quality assurance and continued evaluation through a variety of means. At program inception, an External Program Review Board was constituted with representation from

- The Caribbean Telecommunications Union (CTU),
- The Caribbean Association of National Telecommunications Organizations (CANTO)
- The International Telecommunications Union (ITU)
- The private sector.

TABLE 17.2   MRP Course Delivery: Technologies and Tools

Course	Media/Tech	Purpose	Considerations	How effective
All courses	WebCT	Course management	Uniform, full featured, intuitive user interface	Very effective. Well liked
	PDF documents asynchronous online	Course notes Content delivery and communications	Adults from developing countries. Busy work/travel schedules, unable to devote long, regular periods online	Very effective. Flexible access highly rated
	e-reserves; e-books/journals, databases, etc.	Reading resources	Access by students from diverse developing countries	Very effective in principle. Somewhat cumbersome to navigate
RPTL 6801	interactive animations	Visualization of, and interaction with, complex principles	Interdisciplinary background of students	Very effective. Well liked by students
	automated self-tests	Immediate feedback on basic content		
RPTL 6812	wikis	To develop a repository of course resources by student community	Enabling rich interaction across different learning styles	Varied success. Substantial learning curve for some students, in part due to technical issues as well as to discomfort with unfamiliar types of communication
	blogs	For reflection and to facilitate learning in affective domain		
	e-folios	To demonstrate individual learning journeys		
	multimedia	Student and demonstration presentations	Opportunities for delivering and assessing presentations	Some students unable to submit oral presentations
	voice overlays on Powerpoint presentations	Content delivery	Creation of a seminar atmosphere	Well liked, but in some cases, quality limited by low bandwidth

In addition to external stakeholders, the program draws heavily on the MRP community itself for ongoing feedback. Close ongoing contact between staff and students provides an open avenue for feedback, which has yielded important insights into areas for improvement as well as areas of strength.

Surveys are issued to students, course directors, and tutors for each offering of each course and seminar. Course surveys are issued midway in each semester as well as at the end of each semester. A program exit survey is issued to all program graduates. Regular quality-assurance meetings are held to review survey results, and response actions, as appropriate, are implemented.

The program's academic, human resource, and administrative frameworks, policies, and processes are comprehensively documented on the MRP quality-assurance (QA) site. The results of regular student and staff surveys are also documented for each semester of the program's delivery. The QA site, which captures all the essential features of the program, serves multiple purposes, the major ones being

- To provide a 360° view of the program for the external quality assessments
- To provide a 360° view of the MRP for internal review and revision and to act as the palette for continuous program development
- To function as a repository of program information for archive purposes and for continuity in the event of staff discontinuities of any kind

The MRP has been evaluated by assessors external to the region, external to the institution and internal to the institution. Across the three evaluations, sector-specific as well as generic pedagogical and process assessments were made. In the first year of program delivery, an independent program assessor from the UK was contracted to conduct a program evaluation. Subsequent program evaluations were conducted by the Campus' Quality Assurance Unit and by the External Program Review Board.

Technical Center

The technical center manages matters concerning academic policy, teaching support, learner support, content development, content delivery, and resource management, as shown in Figure 17.4.

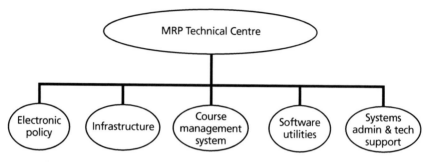

Figure 17.4 Technical focal points.

Electronic Policy

Electronic policies cover

- Privacy
- Physical, network, and social security for the course-management system
- Physical, network, and social security for the MRP program Web server
- Electronic backup for all course materials

As a policy position, the MRP (Telecommunications) program respects the privacy of its visitors and community members. To effect this policy, private information such as user passwords is stored, encrypted via one-way encryption, on the program database. Although the site uses session variables and cookies to track users to ensure a seamless user experience, cookies do not contain any personally identifiable information of any visitor or community member and are destroyed at the conclusion of each session.

The physical-network security policy for the server running the MRP course-management system assures that it is located at a physically secure data center. By policy, physical access to the machine is restricted to authorized personnel. The network-security policy for the course-management system server assures that it is protected behind a firewall in its secure data center. The only allowed access to the server is via an authenticated Web interface. Social-security policy is built on a strong MRP honor code. It is the responsibility of every user in the MRP community to ensure that they have chosen a secure password. As a matter of policy, users are expected to avoid sharing their passwords with anyone. If the course-management system administrator ever dispatches a password via e-mail, the recipient is responsible for changing the password immediately and deleting the e-mail message.

In addition to security policies relating to the course-management system server, the MRP has also developed policies relating to the general program Web site and server. The physical-security requirements of the MRP Web server are identical to those of the course-management system server. The program Web site is required, by policy, to recognize various categories of users: administrators, super users, general staff, staff tutors, students, and visitors, each with predefined access privileges. All users are authenticated and extra security is implemented at the database level through one-way encryption. Students, for example, are allowed access to the student area of the Web site, where they can receive personalized grades and information pertaining to them alone. Security is assured through a mix of electronic and manual procedures consistent with policy guidelines. Sensitive information, such as grades, is first entered on a local testing server to verify and validate the data before publishing to the live server. A list of all grades from the Web site is then obtained and manually compared against the original list of grades to ensure no human or computer errors. Student access to the Web site does not allow editing of grades.

By policy, the program Web site and course content are required to be backed up on a server outside of Trinidad and Tobago. Also by policy, access to the backup site is restricted to the MRP Web developer and systems administrator.

Infrastructure

In planning the MRP network infrastructure, the program's electronic policy guidelines were followed, a risk assessment of electronic processes was undertaken, minimum requirements for network bandwidth and connectivity were developed, and requirements for power backup were articulated. The final network configuration is shown logically in Figure 17.5.

The course-management system and Web server are run on machines physically located in a secure data center monitored and controlled by the Campus Information Technology Services (CITS) of the University of the West Indies' St. Augustine campus. The campus' electronic student-information system (SAS Banner) server, which manages student records, is collocated in this center. Internet access is provided through a firewalled leased line connection to a local provider.

The MRP backup site is hosted in San Diego, California, as an alternative download site for course notes and also as a host for program delivery in the event of primary site unavailability. The Web server stores all its data in databases, which are routinely backed up to safeguard against data loss. Access to the database is limited to the Web developer working on the program Web site.

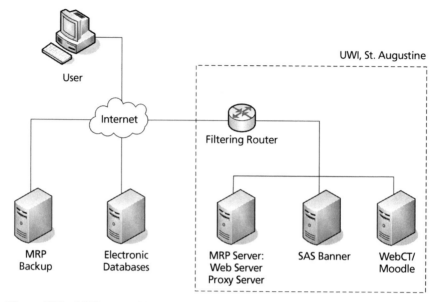

Figure 17.5 MRP network infrastructure.

Course-Management System

MRP course content was delivered through the campus' course-management system, WebCT, from December 2003 until May 2007, when the campus switched its platform to the open-source course-management system, Moodle.

Although the organization and appearance of Moodle differs from that of WebCT, it was found to be generally very user-friendly. Moodle presented several advantages, such as

- E-mail alerts of forum contributions
- Easy content creation
- A variety of rich-text options
- Diverse easy-to-use tools
- The option of developing new functionality.

Software Utilities

The MRP has designed and implemented a number of software utilities that have proven very useful in the delivery of its teaching by distance. These include online application and registration utilities, electronic claim forms, electronic grade slips, data security, and backup systems, as well as emergency crossover systems. It has also developed a Web-based system for tracking the progress of project students and an e-resources database application, which has facilitated the management of the program's electronic resources.

Systems Administration and Technical Support

Systems administration and technical-support services are provided by a program Web engineer and a program network engineer.

CHALLENGES AND SUCCESSES

In its short life, the MRP has had some significant successes:

- Eighty-three students (58 men and 25 women) were enrolled over three cohorts.
- The program has enjoyed an 87% retention rate over three cohorts, which the student body attributes to the program's comprehensive learner support.
- Over two cohorts, 11 students have graduated with distinction.
- MRP final projects relate directly to practical sector needs and therefore feed into the development process in the represented jurisdictions.
- The program has received consistently positive multistakeholder feedback, including a midprogram quality-assurance review board report.
- The program is recognized by leading sector agencies (International Telecommunication Union, Caribbean Telecommunications Union, CARICOM Secretariat and Caribbean Association of National Telecommunications Organizations), which feature it on their Web sites.

Online program delivery raises several challenges, and addressing these challenges is a continuing process, which has achieved mixed levels of success. Examples of recurring issues that the Quality Assurance team addressed through a variety of means, some programwide, and others individually include

- Sustaining student engagement in online activities, including discussions
- Developing student skills in academic English
- Developing student skills in critical analysis
- Maintaining motivation of isolated project students working individually

- Variations in the richness of student feedback from tutors and course directors
- Vigilance with regard to academic integrity
- Constancy and quality of Internet access. Maintaining constant student and staff Internet access, due to technical reasons or work-related travel, and accommodating the limitations of program delivery when some students lack broadband access.

Solutions found to be effective were incorporated as standard practice through iterative program development.

IMPACT

Overall, one of the greatest impacts that the MRP program has made is the establishment of a formidable international community of practice in which informal learning reinforces formal learning. This has been possible because of the many dimensions of diversity of the MRP program. Its student body represents over 30 developing countries around the world; its staff represent Africa, the UK, North America, and the Caribbean; its disciplines including law, economics, engineering, and policy; its content covers theoretical, practical, academic, and professional materials, and the delivery media comprise a mix of modern and traditional technologies.

The MRP program has impacted development directly through its curriculum and the particular student body it has been able to reach. Its thematic content, telecommunications regulation and policy, is pitched mainly at policymakers and regulators whose responsibility it is to establish the environment for social and economic development. The program places a great deal of emphasis on the values of the Millennium Development Goals, the progress of the World Summit on the Information Society (WSIS), and the societal realities of the developing world. There is a strong pro-poor theme that runs through the program's courses.

MRP graduates and students are from 32 countries in the developing world. The majority are from the Caribbean, but many are from Africa and the Asia/Pacific region (Figure 17.6). Almost half (44%) of the program participants are in senior management roles within the telecommunications sector. Many are employed with government (37.3%), most frequently in ministries with responsibility for telecommunication, or with government-established regulatory agencies (30.1%). Others are working with service providers (19.3%), and consultancies, law firms, financial institutions, and international telecommunications agencies are also represented (Figure 17.7).

While building human capacity in the public and private telecommunications sectors in represented developing countries, the MRP program

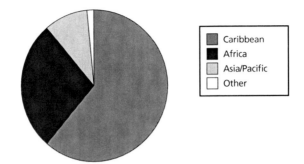

Figure 17.6 MRP program student nationalities (% students).

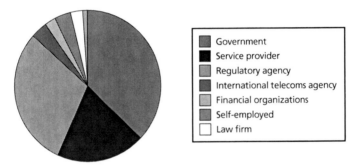

Figure 17.7 MRP program student affiliation (% students).

has facilitated the development of an enduring international community of practice. Among the key lessons that graduates and students bring to their respective professional portfolios are the many ways in which regulatory and policy intervention can impact societal development.

Although originally developed with Caribbean professionals in mind, the MRP has successfully attracted a global audience. It has been able to reach its student body, which comprises professionals of influence in national and global developmental agendas, because of its asynchronous, online mode of delivery. Online delivery has enabled the participation of these working professionals in a way that would otherwise be impossible.

CONCLUSION

The MRP (Telecommunications) program was the University of the West Indies' response to the needs of the evolving Caribbean telecommunications sector as well as a number of UWI institutional priorities. In particular, it responds to 1) the regional call for human-resource development programs in telecommunications regulation and policy, 2) the UWI's emphasis on programs of direct regional relevance, and 3) the UWI's focus on expansion of its reach through distance education.

The program uses a mix of traditional and contemporary media to accommodate the realities of developing-country professionals who are committed to lifelong learning. It targets these societal change agents and offers a model for the design and delivery of suitable distance education programs that can be delivered even within institutions that lack the requisite institutional framework. The program demonstrates how modest technologies can be used to provide a flexible, supportive, and effective online learning environment.

This chapter describes the planning and operational framework for the MRP (Telecommunications) Master's degree program. It discusses the human-resource allocations and core values on which the program is centered. The overarching framework within which the MRP (Telecommunications) operates and key elements of the program's Academic, Technical, and Administrative Centers are also described. The chapter provides a step-by-step account of the process of preparing online course materials, indicating relevant staff needs, and key required competencies. It raises considerations for the choice of media and technology in various program courses and describes how effective the MRP's choices have proven. The program's network infrastructure, electronic utilities, and technical resources are reviewed.

The framework described in this chapter offers a model for the design and administration of an online program that is well-suited to the delivery of distance education on a modest budget to professionals from geographically dispersed, developing-country environments.

REFERENCES

Claxton, C. P., & Murrell, P. H. (1987) *Learning styles: Implications for improving educational practices.* ASHE-ERIC Higher Education Report No. 4, Washington, DC: Association for the Study of Higher Education. (ERIC Document Reproduction Service No. ED293478)

Laurillard, D. (1993). *Rethinking university teaching,* New York: Routledge.

Mallalieu, K. (1999). *Migration towards the on-line delivery of engineering courses.* Proceedings of the Twelfth Annual Technical Conference: Second Latin-American and the Caribbean Forum on Engineering and Technology Education, Association of Professional Engineers of Trinidad and Tobago. Trinidad and Tobago.

Mallalieu, K. (2000a, June 26–28). *Optimal partitioning of content and evaluation, by media, in the electronic delivery of engineering courseware.* Proceedings of the Sixteenth International Conference on CAD/CAM, Robotics and Factories of the Future (CARS & FOF, 2000). Port of Spain, Trinidad and Tobago.

Mallalieu, K. (2000b, July 27–28). *Viable technologies and strategies for developing and administering distance education courses through electronic means in small states.* Proceedings of a conference on Distance Education in Small States, Commonwealth of Learning/The University of West Indies Distance Education Centre (COL/UWIDEC), Jamaica.

Palloff, R., & Pratt, K. (1999). *Building learning in cyberspace: Effective strategies for the online classroom.* San Francisco: Jossey-Bass, Inc.

Woodley, A., Wagner, L., Slowey, M., Hamilton, M., & Fulton, O. (1987). *Choosing to learn: Adults in education.* Society for Research into Higher Education and Open University Press, Milton Keynes.

CHAPTER 18

DISTANCE LEARNING— CHALLENGES AND OPPORTUNITIES FOR POSTGRADUATE MEDICAL EDUCATION

A Case Study of Postgraduate Training in Family Medicine Using Distance Learning at the University of the West Indies (2001–2006)

Pauline Williams-Green

INTRODUCTION

The most critical components of a well functioning primary health care system are the people or the teams who provide the health care. Family physicians are of particular importance to well-functioning primary health care teams. They are called upon to

Bridging the Knowledge Divide, pages 321–335
Copyright © 2009 by Information Age Publishing

> *treat a wide range of patients at the community level. They lead the teams that are*
> *critical for a well functioning, coordinated, cost-effective health system that responds*
> *to the trends and challenges affecting health services delivery while balancing*
> *quality, equity and relevance.*
>
> —Boelen, Haq, Hunt, Rivo & Shahady, 2002, pp. 35–36

General Practitioners are best prepared through training programs that modify their educational goals to fit the needs and resources of local environments. This training should be specifically designed to provide expertise in addressing the problems encountered in the community. In the Caribbean, general practitioners have limited access to this level of training because of the cost of these courses and the isolation of the practitioners.

Several attempts have been made to establish postgraduate training in general medical practice/family medicine in the Caribbean. These have failed because of the archipelagic geography of the region, the disparate nature of this medical specialty, and the remote location of its practitioners. This work describes the first attempt to utilize distance learning as the vehicle for this level of medical training at the University of the West Indies (UWI). The UWI is located in the English-speaking Caribbean at three campuses. One each in Jamaica, Trinidad and Tobago, and Barbados. Each campus has a medical faculty that offers undergraduate and postgraduate education.

HISTORY OF FAMILY MEDICINE TRAINING

The Ministers of Health in the Caribbean recognized the need for specially trained General Physicians who had administrative, research, and clinical skills. These physicians would be competent to manage and participate in polyclinics, general hospitals, and a district or community health center (Segree et al., 2007).

However, postgraduate training for general medical practitioners has been in the main poorly structured, fragmented, and irregular in frequency. This training has been characterized by an absence of core curriculum objectives, limited motivation among general practitioners, limited understanding of the general practice specialty, and a lack of career opportunities or incentives (Boelen et al., 2002).

In the English-speaking Caribbean, the postgraduate training of general practitioners began in 1971 at the University of the West Indies (UWI), Mona, Jamaica. The Department of Social and Preventive Medicine conducted seminars on the last Friday of each month for several years (Dept. of Social and Preventive Medicine, 1982).

In Barbados and the Eastern Caribbean, the UWI appointed a coordinator of Continuing Medical Education (CME) in 1979. The main type of CME was the medical conference or seminar (Hoyos, 1998). In Trinidad, the General Practitioner's Association of Trinidad and Tobago (GPATT) held a formal course on diabetes care followed by examination and certification. This was a rare Caribbean example of postgraduate certification of general practitioners (Hoyos, 1998).

A formal postgraduate training program was established with the support of a Kellogg Foundation grant at the Mona campus of the UWI. Initially there were two tracks: a) a full-time program for postregistration doctors with no experience in family medicine, b) a part-time program for doctors with more than 3 years experience in general practice (Family Medicine Program Manual, 2005).

The full-time program was a 3-year Master of Sciences program that involved three monthly hospital rotations as well as didactic lectures. A doctorate was offered for those physicians who completed a thesis or a casebook of clinical cases. This academic activity led to the formation of General Practitioner Associations, the Caribbean College of Family Physicians (CCFP), and publications such as the Caribbean Family Physician (Segree, 2007).

The training of general medical practitioners was hampered by several factors. The proclaimed endorsement by Caribbean governments for the training of general-practice specialists did not translate into a specific policy. There was no clear career path for these practitioners. In Jamaica, a few specialists were appointed to consultant or senior posts in ambulatory-care settings, but the majority were drawn into private solo medical practices.

Neither the university nor local governments would provide financial support for the training of these specialists. The physicians could not earn while engaged in a full-time conventional course, so the potential trainees dwindled until the program was discontinued in the early 1990s. The exception to this situation occurred in Barbados, where the program has endured since 1981, producing 17 graduates in 25 years.

The Role of General-Practitioner Groups

The medical community has acknowledged that recent medical graduates are not sufficiently prepared for unsupervised general practice. It is commonly recognized that further training is required for independent medical practice that ensures high-quality individualized care. It is also accepted that recent medical graduates require greater preparation to assume the roles of managers and leaders in the health sector (Segree, 2007)

In 1992 plans for the upgrading, training, and education of family physicians through Continuing Medical Education (CME) on a part-time basis and the expansion of the existing family medicine program at UWI were put forward by the Caribbean College of Family Physicians(CCFP) and the General Practitioner Association of Trinidad and Tobago (GPATT). The lobbying of these general-practitioner groups was supported by the Pan American Health Organization. In 1997 a workshop held in Jamaica brought together academics of the Faculty of Medical Sciences, UWI, technocrats from the Ministries of Health of the Caribbean, and general practitioners (GPs) of the CCFP and other GP associations.

The meeting examined a proposal for joint family medicine and public-health programs, which would share a core curriculum, followed by later differentiation into separate specialties. Although it was proposed that a steering committee be established to implement the program, this proposal has not become a reality. Of note, this meeting was significant for identifying the distance education modality for delivery of the program. The UWI distance-teaching satellite network, which uses audio-conferencing was identified as a means of overcoming the problems of access to the program.

In January 2000 the Trinidad and Tobago government sponsored 18 physicians to pursue a 2-year part-time postgraduate diploma program. They were led by a lecturer in family medicine in weekly 3-hour face-to-face sessions on general-practice topics that would later form the core of the modules in the Master's in Family Medicine. He developed printed outlines, which formed the basis for the seminars and small-group teachings (Maharaj & Sieunarine, 2002).

Why Distance Modality for Family-Medicine Training?

The distance modality was selected because it permitted access to physicians regardless of their location. The archipelagic geography of the Caribbean region has been a challenge for the delivery of training. The UWI has addressed this need by developing a satellite network that links campus and noncampus territories. Physicians enrolled in the program attend audio or teleconferences related to each course.

More importantly, the distance format permits teaching and learning outside of conventional training institutions. Distance education allows for context-specific training, since it facilitates the physician remaining in the office setting, while working and studying. Through distance learning, the physician is given the opportunity to remain in the office setting where he/she is presented daily with clinical incidents that are related to his/her teaching-learning experiences (Paul & Williams-Green, 2000). Thus, one's own experience becomes an important training resource independent of an onsite teacher.

THE PROGRAM

Aims

The Mission Statement of the program is to train doctors in general practice in the knowledge, skills, and attitudes necessary for the provision of comprehensive and continuous personal medical care in the primary-care setting through the promotion of health, and the prevention and treatment of illness and disease (Bain & Williams-Green, 2000). Trainees would be licensed, registered medical practitioners within the country in which training occurs. They were required to be employed in primary care for the duration of the course, and to be computer literate and have access to an Internet-linked computer.

The general aims of the program included

1. To provide education and training in primary care and family health appropriate and relevant to the health needs of the Caribbean community;
2. To stimulate the professional development of general practitioners based on their existing experience and to enhance their competence and ability to function effectively and efficiently as primary-care physicians in the reformed health sector;
3. To make possible access by general practitioners from noncampus island countries to a postgraduate program in primary care by adopting a distance education mode of course delivery;
4. To provide a continuing-education base for the development of a career structure for the primary care physician.

Course Development

The initial developers of the curriculum were guided by physicians/ content experts who met in focus groups over several months to develop educational goals for each course. These discussions served as a basis for the selection of learning objectives, which guided the design of the modules. The personnel selected for developing the instructional design of this program were drawn from many disciplines and fields of scholarship. The course writers were noted experts in their fields. They were guided by curriculum specialists/instructional designers and editors located in the Distance Education Centre at UWI, which ensured that materials adhered to sound distance education principles, emphasizing preplanning of content for effective delivery and the use of access devices to help learners navigate the materials. The manuals were produced with the assistance of graphic artists and other members of the distance education team. Course writers would later serve as course tutors.

Administration

The daily management of the program, its learners, tutors, and other participants was coordinated by a lecturer in the Department of Community Health and Psychiatry and a secretary. The lecturer was a full-time member of the faculty of Medicine, with a regular teaching load. The logistics of running this program, which initially consisted of 13 students across the island of Jamaica and later included 4 students in the British Virgin Island of Tortola, was challenging. This scenario demonstrates some of the challenges of a conventional academic institution that launches a program in the distance mode.

Distance Courses

Launched in September 2001, initially the program was composed of 19 distance courses. These were independent modules devoted to areas of general practice not previously addressed in the undergraduate training, such as the Consultation and Communication Skills, Medico-legal Issues, Doctor/patient relationship, Ethics for Primary Care Physicians, and Counseling for Primary Care Physicians. Other areas covered reinforced the knowledge and skills most frequently required in a general-practice setting. This included Child and Adolescent Care, Chronic Non-Communicable Diseases, Elderly Care, and the Management of Sexually Transmitted Diseases. Modules such as Health Determinants, Practice Management, and Epidemiology were included to encompass the proposal of some initial stakeholders to make this program a joint one for medical practitioners in public health as well as general practice.

In 2004 the Barbadian and Trinidadian campuses of the University of the West Indies became participants in this program, resulting in modifications in the course content. The public health components were omitted or made electives in year three, resulting in 16 independent courses. Thus, 12 courses are completed in the first two years (Phase 1) and 4 courses in the third year (Phase 2). These were initially provided to trainees as printed manuals containing core content and selected readings, but more recently have been sent to them electronically as program-documented files (PDF) or on compact discs. The manuals consist of a study guide, readings, exercises, and assignments. The trainees complete assignments for grading of the course. These are usually e-mailed as attached files to the course tutors, but are sometimes faxed or hand delivered. Each trainee is expected to spend 10 to 12 hours per week on the distance education material.

A course tutor is assigned to each course. The tutor is usually a family physician, but may also be a nonmedical-content expert, as occurred with the tutor for Gender Issues. The tutor maintains contact by electronic means (e-mail) in order to guide the learner's access to the material. Where necessary, the tutor may request a face-to-face session or a teleconference via the UWIDEC network. Recently, in the eastern Caribbean, more significant use of the Internet has been used as a means of course delivery via on-line discussions for delivery of content, discussions, and tutorials. Courses run sequentially, each lasting 6 weeks.

DISTANCE MODALITIES

Audio Conference

Audio conferences are conducted via the satellite network of the University of the West Indies. Individuals can access these audio conferences by telephoning the distance education center or attending the centers. Learners make oral presentations on their assignments and receive immediate feedback from tutors. The conferences exemplify the virtual classroom, since learners and teachers are situated in various locations. These sessions facilitate verbal interactions with course tutors and allow learners to clarify queries or share experiences. Verbal and written feedback from learners indicate that these sessions are highly valued for their interactivity, resulting in greater learner and teacher satisfaction. However, learners admit that they find it challenging to make these synchronous sessions.

In July 2005, when a hurricane wreaked havoc with examination schedules, the oral defense of the master's thesis was executed by audio conference, inclusive of slide presentations. This was repeated 2 years later, when a master's student was too ill to travel to the examination site, but was able to defend his thesis via audio conference and PowerPoint presentations.

Electronic Mail

In the early years, the courses were available as printed manuals using Microsoft Publisher, but were later made available electronically as program-documented files (PDF). Electronic mail (e-mail) was used to transfer course content as puff files. E-mail was used frequently for communication between tutors and learners, such as to communicate modifications in the courses, reminders about assignments, teleconferences, and workshops, and general teacher-learner communications. Thirdly, e-mail was vital for the delivery of completed assignments from learners to teachers. This methodology was extremely satisfying at times because of the asynchronous access, low cost, and ease of use. However, learners and teachers had to learn how to communicate effectively by this means. Mail was sometimes missed by the intended recipients. Learners and teachers soon realized the importance of acknowledging mails as well as well-timed responses.

Online Discussions

Recently, the campus in Barbados has initiated the use of online synchronous lectures and discussions using the Elluminate learning environment. This permits lectures with slide presentations. It allows for question-and-answer sessions with a capability of many learners participating. This has received positive feedback from learners and tutors.

Print

This modality was initially the major means of course delivery in the first 3 years of the program. Conversion to computer discs and later e-mailed files was achieved in the later years of the program. Printed manuals continued to be used as guides for orientation to the program and information on the clinical examination.

Audio/Videotapes

Learners were required to complete audiotapes or videotapes as a component of their assignments for several courses. For example the course Counseling for Primary Care Physicians required trainees to implement the principles taught and produce a taped (audiotapes or videotapes) recording of a counseling session with a patient. The course Consultations and Communication required the trainees to tape a medical interview for analysis. The tutors were able to observe the performance of the family-physician trainees in their practice setting. These activities were required for successful completion of the courses.

Compact Discs

The third cohort of learners was given compact discs (CDs) with the course material. These CDs contained schedules of courses, workshops, and teleconferences, as well as any other important events in the school year. The learners would also use them as the medium for assignments. One learner used this medium for his portfolio. The CDs were sent by post or inter-island couriers.

WORKSHOPS

In the early years of the program, face-to-face sessions were conducted to meet specific objectives of the program. These workshops also served to reduce the alienation experienced by the distance learner. They included family-medicine topics as well as hands-on sessions, which covered physical examination skills, basic cardiac life-support skills, common emergency-medicine skills, and presentations on several noncommunicable chronic diseases. Workshops were also used to introduce new skills such as conduct of an audit and data analysis.

Clinic Sessions

In many ways the family-medicine program by distance was an attempt to convert the former hospital-based rotations to a distance-learning program. Before the program was launched at the Mona Campus, Jamaica, several family physicians met to determine the number of hours to be devoted to the clinical sessions. These family physicians had been trained in the previous "hospital system," which was composed of three monthly rotations in various medical disciplines. They sought to retain the hospital component as once weekly half-day sessions throughout the 3 years of training. Clinical teachers were drawn from interested consultants in regional hospitals. This allowed trainees to attend hospitals in their locale. Clinical training involved the rotation of family-physician trainees through selected disciplines. They participated in ward rounds, care of patients in the specialist outpatient clinics, and on the wards. Each trainee devoted a half-day per week throughout the 3 years for clinical training. Their training was guided by specific learning objectives implemented by senior physicians in these specialties. The trainees in the program were expected to complete 120 clinic sessions during 3 years.

A special feature of the program was the involvement of experienced family physicians as family-practice preceptors (trainers) to the trainees. The family-medicine preceptors were selected to match trainees in the same location. The preceptors implemented the specified learning objectives of the family-practice sessions over the 3-year period. They guided the trainees in developing interviewing skills, managing diverse consultations, and conducting practice audits.

RESEARCH COMPONENT

One of the exciting inclusions in this family-medicine training curriculum was the research-training module. This was an early component in the curriculum design. The module on research methods was developed with the aim of introducing research skills to the family-physician trainees. Thus, the primary practice setting would not only serve as a classroom for experiential learning but also as a laboratory to conduct clinical observations and interventions. This research thrust was being emphasized at the university postgraduate level (Young, 1999). When the program was presented to the local Ministry of Health in the year 2000, the officers commented positively on this component.

The trainees found this course new and demanding. One of the weaknesses of the instructional design was the absence of a learner guide for the development of skills in medical-data analysis. Hence, the coordinator found it necessary to introduce face-to-face workshops for tutorial support.

ASSESSMENTS

Early in the course design, the consensus among the course developers was to avoid traditional written- and oral-examination methods. They felt that there should be a heavy reliance on continuous course assessments. A shift was made to less-conventional methods, such as portfolios, objective-structured clinical examinations, and the research projects. It was felt that portfolios would document the learners' journey over the 3 years, while the clinical examinations would allow the learners to demonstrate their practice of family medicine before an evaluator. Finally, the research protocols would be used to evaluate the learners' skills of critical appraisal and scientific reasoning.

Portfolio

The physicians who designed the program in the late 1990s proposed that written examinations did not capture the essence of the teaching/learning experience to be gained from the general-practice training. Instead, they presented the portfolio as an assessment instrument most able to capture the growth of physicians from general doctor to general/family practitioner. This showpiece portfolio was a three-ring binder that contained written evidence of the participants' attendance at clinic sessions, all corrected assignments with grades displayed, a personal learning diary, and a reflective essay describing personal observations on readings and courses. This portfolio accounted for 50% of the final assessment.

In 2004 the assessment methodology was modified to reflect the views of more conservative educators, and a written examination was added to the clinical examinations at the end of Phase1. The successful physician would be conferred with a diploma. Physicians who completed the third year would be assessed by means of written examinations and portfolios as well as the research protocols. The weighting of the ongoing course assessment was decreased but remained significant.

Program Evaluation

Between 2001 and 2006, 17 physicians graduated from the Mona Campus. The program has been evaluated regularly. The first evaluation took place two years after the initial cohort of learners began. It took the form of a SWOT (Strengths, Weaknesses, Opportunities, and Threats) analysis of the program. This consisted of four focus-group discussions followed by a plenary session. These included two groups consisting of students only, and two groups consisting predominantly of teachers and other stakeholders. The latter included representatives of the Distance Education Centre, government and private health professionals, as well as members of the medical faculty in Barbados and Trinidad. Each group was asked to identify and discuss the strengths, weaknesses, opportunities, and threats to the program, which was then reported in the plenary session (Williams-Green, Matthews, Paul, & McKenzie, 2007).

Other methods of program evaluation implemented were student surveys at the completion of individual distance modules. These questionnaires addressed issues such as course content, presentation, relevance, the adequacy of time for completion of the course, and the efficiency of the distance learning format for the specific course content. Students and examiners were regularly surveyed after the clinical examinations to determine their satisfaction with the program. At the end of a final examination for each cohort, an external examiner from a prominent family medicine/general practice educational center was invited to oversee the examination as well as assess the learners. This allowed for international comparison between various forms of postgraduate training of family physicians. In 2007 the Department of Community Health and Psychiatry, Mona, UWI (Segree, 2007) also carried out a review of the program.

LESSONS LEARNED

Reduced Opportunity Cost

The format of the distance program achieved the goals of physicians learning and earning simultaneously. Learners were able to continue in their jobs while pursuing training in family medicine, their chosen career. Learners repeatedly stated verbally and in writing that they would not have been able to access this level of training in the conventional face-to-face format. Physicians confirmed that this form of postgraduate medical education was only accessible to them because of the distance format.

Flexibility

The distance format of the program promoted flexibility in the course delivery. Hence, learners were able to complete the required objectives of each module within their own time and space. Learners had greater control over their involvement in the program than would have occurred in traditional postgraduate courses in conventional tertiary institutions.

Instructional Design

Although the modules were designed for the learners to work through the material and execute exercises over a specified period of time, this was not realized. Often, learners would ignore the recommendation to complete the activities on a weekly basis and would instead compress 40 hours of work into a few days to meet assessment deadlines. Tutors complained that during the period of course delivery, learners were unresponsive to their attempts at communication. It was clear that the assignments would have been of better quality if learners were motivated to interact with the instructional material throughout the time allotted for each course.

Modular Format

The modular format facilitated ease of administration of the courses. Each course had its learning objectives: specific content with activities and assignments for grading of the learner. Tutors were able to provide feedback by e-mail or phone to learners throughout and at the end of the course. Recently, the Medical Councils of the Caribbean have embarked on a more rigorous regulation of physicians to achieve proper standards of medical practice. This has resulted in a process of relicensing of physicians through continuing medical-education credits. The modular format of the program is ideal for the retraining of physicians in practice.

Administration

The woefully inadequate administrative team of one lecturer and one secretary highlighted the lack of appreciation of the needs of a dual-mode institution for a program delivered chiefly by distance. In many ways, the curriculum was a conversion of a face-to-face program to a program delivered by e-mail. There were many hurdles to overcome. These included preparation of course writers for the philosophical concepts of distance learning as well as convincing them that this modality was just as good as conventional methods of training family physicians.

The training of academic and clinical tutors was particularly challenging since many were part-time staff or only employees of the local hospital and so had little obligation to the program or indeed the university. This led to many difficulties in translating instructional objectives into learning experiences for the trainees. Learners complained of the disinterest or, indeed, scant regard they received from tutors in some of the clinical rotations. An important lesson was that part-time tutors constituted a cadre that had special training needs.

Teleteaching

Learners enjoyed the teleconferences as a means of connecting to other learners and tutors. They enjoyed the rapport developed at these sessions, but admitted that restrictions on their time did not allow for full attendance at the teleconference centers.

Information and Communication Technologies

This program underscored the benefits of teleteaching and the use of information and communication technologies (ICT) in distance learning. Some authors stress the benefits of ICT as well as the economic benefits, but the medical-education research literature has not produced many evaluations to prove this point (Valcke & Wever, 2006).

Achieving competence with the use of Internet features such as e-mail and searches on medical databases was a challenge for some trainees. Both tutors and learners suffered the frustrations of assignments lost in cyberspace or computer crashes. A few learners remained largely paperless, using their laptops to read their manuals and submitting assignments in an electronic form only.

There was a need to assess the information-technology skills of learners at the commencement of the program. Establishing an early information-skills profile of all incoming students is essential for improved adaptation to the distance modality of training. Two possible methods are self-assessment questionnaires and online skills assessment (Oberprieler, Masters, & Gibbs, 2005). A self-assessment questionnaire was administered to the first cohort of learners in 2001 and indicated that all had access to computers, but half of the class was unfamiliar with the use of the Internet. Oberprieler et al. described an online assessment that included questions with multiple choices, use of the mouse to drag and drop, identifying the minimize button, selecting data for a chart in Excel, and inserting appropriate search phrases in a search engine. In this program, learners were obligated to acquire these skills along the way. It would have been preferable to introduce these skills in an appropriately designed distance module.

SUMMARY

"The aim of specialty training in family medicine is to prepare family doctors to provide comprehensive, high quality care for individuals, families and communities. Most specialty programs involve at least three years of full-time study after completion of medical school" (Boelen, Haq, Hunt, Rivo, & Shahady, 2002, p. 96). Attempts at this model of postgraduate training were made in the Caribbean in 1980, but became unsustainable after approximately 10 years.

Graduate training in family medicine in the Caribbean region has for years been stymied by limited resources and the difficulties of having practicing physicians in remote regions "come in" to university centers for training. The introduction of a postgraduate training program using distance learning addressed many of these challenges (Williams-Green & McCaw-Binns, 2006). The family-medicine-by-distance education program was launched in September 2001 at the University of the West Indies, Mona. In September 2004 the campuses in Barbados and Trinidad and Tobago came on board, and this chapter describes its development up to 2006.

The graduate training program makes use of the information and communication technologies easily available to physicians in the English-speaking Caribbean. These include audio conferencing via satellite, e-mail and online discussions via the Internet. The nature of medical education requires some face-to-face contact. Hence, workshops and patient-contact sessions are an integral part of the courses. The family-medicine program at the UWI provides an innovative and convenient means of postgraduate training for general medical practitioners in this region.

REFERENCES

Bain, B., & Williams-Green, P. (2000). Overview of the program the master of science degree in family medicine through distance education. *Program Manual.* Faculty of Medical Sciences, UWI Mona Campus, Jamaica.

Boelen, C., Haq, C., Hunt, V., Rivo, M., & Shahady, E. (2002). *Improving health systems: The contribution of family medicine.* World Organization of Family Doctors.

Department of Social and Preventive Medicine. (1982). *25th Anniversary Booklet, April 1957–April 1982*. Faculty of Medicine, The University of the West Indies.

Family Medicine Program Manual. (2005). Faculty of Medicine, The University of the West Indies.

Hoyos, M. (1998). *Continuing medical education.* UWI Barbados and the Barbados Association of Medical Practitioners.

Maharaj, R., & Sieunarine, T. (2002). The postgraduate diploma in primary care and family medicine at the University of the West Indies, St. Augustine, Trinidad and Tobago: Program Description. *West Ind Medical Journal, 51,*108–111.

Oberprieler, G., Masters, K., & Gibbs, T. (2005). Information technology and information literacy for first year health sciences students in South Africa: Matching early and professional needs. *Medical Teacher, 27*(7), 596.

Paul, T., & Williams-Green, P. (2000, July 27–28). *Barriers to training of family physicians in the Caribbean: Distance education as a promising prescription.* Conference Proceedings Distance Education In Small States.

Segree, W. (2007). *Review of the family medicine program 2001-2006.* Department of Community health and Psychiatry, UWI.

Valcke, M., & Wever, B. D. (2006). Information and communication technologies in higher education: Evidenced-based practices in medical education. *Medical Teacher, 28*(1), 44.

Williams-Green, P., Paul, T., & McCaw-Binns, A. (2006). *Challenges of the distance modality for postgraduate training in family medicine.* The Fourth Pan Commonwealth Forum on Open Learning, (p. 5). Retrieved August 28, 2007 from http://pcf4.dec.uwi.edu/viewpaper.php?id=435.

Williams-Green, P., Matthews, A., Paul, T., & McKenzie, C. (2007). Family Medicine training by Distance Education. *West Indian Med Journal, 56*(1),12.

Young, R. (September 1998/February1999). *Mona campus coordinator's report graduate studies & research.* UWI Mona Campus, Jamaica.

SECTION 4

PREPARING TEACHERS USING FLEXIBLE APPROACHES

CHAPTER 19

PRESERVICE TEACHER PREPARATION AND EFFECTIVE eLEARNING[1]

Susan Crichton and Gail Shervey

E-Learning, which involves the use of Internet-based technologies to both deliver and support learning and professional development, has experienced enormous growth in K–12 education in the past 10 years. Not surprisingly, significant research in this field has accompanied its growth. While many educational researchers (Coppola, Hiltz, & Rotter, 2001; Gold, 2001; Harasim, 1987; Miller & King, 2003; Oblinger & Maruyama, 1996; Palloff & Pratt, 2000) have written of the potential of this new learning environment to bring about significant transformation in teaching and learning, others (Brennan, 2003; Good, 2001; Kemshal-Bell, 2001) are investigating the emergence of a distinct e-pedagogy, attempting to clarify what the e-learning environment asks of both learners and teachers. This literature chapter offers a brief summary of current research regarding the evolution of e-learning, its promise and potential, as well as current models for preparing teachers to work in both blended/distributed and wholly online learning environments.

Bridging the Knowledge Divide, pages 339–356

339

Four key concepts guide this chapter. Firstly, several critical constructs, such as distance education, distributed learning, online learning, and e-learning, are defined and clarified. Secondly, the transformational potential that distributed and online learning offer is examined and discussed. Thirdly, the emergence of a distinct e-pedagogy is discussed and analyzed with regard to the significance it plays in designing online teacher-preparation programs. Fourthly, current professional development models for training online teachers are examined and discussed.

DISTANCE EDUCATION

Distance education, originally characterized by a geographical separation of the teacher and student and the use of some form of technology to facilitate student learning, was the forerunner to e-learning (The Council on Alberta Teaching Standards, 2002).

During the 1920s distance education in Canada grew in response to the need for schooling for rural students who were unable to attend school and became a nationwide correspondence-school system by the 1930s (Smith & Crichton, 2003). Because the rural population of Canada declined during the mid-20th century, the need for distance education also declined. However, it has enjoyed a renaissance since the mid-1980s due to the advent of computer-mediated communication. This kind of communication can be *asynchronous,*[2] which allows students and teachers to communicate at different times, or *synchronous,*[3] which requires students and teachers to communicate with each other at the same time. Although still geographically separated from the teacher, today's distance education students benefit from a wide variety of technologies that enhance and enable their distance learning, including e-mail, phone, fax, and asynchronous and synchronous computer-mediated learning technologies.

DISTRIBUTED LEARNING

Distributed learning represents a more recent form of distance education and is further characterized as (Oblinger & Maruyama, 1996)

- The delivery of content and the facilitation of learning through the use of a number of interactive technologies, including computer-mediated communication
- A learner-centered philosophy
- A dispersed student population

- A tendency to integrate face-to-face components, such as classrooms, libraries or labs, with online components
- A "pull" model of learning where the student has more control over his or her learning than the teacher does

Distributed learning embraces a learner-centered philosophy, which allows students to take control of their own learning in an environment that has broken the barriers and constraints of time and space (Maeroff, 2003). This form of learning can be delivered wholly online, using the Internet and a number of information and communication technologies, including synchronous and asynchronous communication tools as well as phone and fax, and is also referred to as online learning, e-learning, or virtual learning. In addition, distributed learning may take the form of blended-learning experiences that combine both online and face-to-face components. Whether offered entirely online or in a blended format, this option is based on a learner-centered philosophy wherein the teacher, as a member of a collaborative teaching team, is a facilitator and mentor, and the student is an independent learner with direct access to resources and increased interaction with other students (Harasim, Hiltz, Teles, & Turoff, 1995).

ONLINE LEARNING

In North America, e-learning in the K–12 sector is often referred to as online learning. Definitions of online learning abound in the literature (Goodyear, Salmon, Spector, Steeples, & Tickner, 2001; Miller & King, 2003; Palloff & Pratt, 2001), but it is comprehensively defined by the course-authoring software company, Blackboard,[4] as "an approach to teaching and learning that utilizes Internet technologies to communicate and collaborate in an educational context. This includes technology that supplements traditional classroom training with web-based components and learning environments where the educational process is experienced online" (Blackboard, n.d.).

Salmon (2004) uses the term to refer to a full spectrum of distributed learning opportunities, from blended to fully online, wherein "the teacher, instructor, tutor, facilitator—or e-Moderator—is operating in the electronic environment along with his or her students, the participants" (p. viii). Because the research study referred to in this chapter concerns K–12 teachers, the term "online learning" will be used to refer to the full spectrum of learning opportunities that embrace the learner-centered philosophy of distributed learning and employ digital networks to deliver and support learning (Advisory Committee for Online Learning, 2001).

Online learning has the potential to support a rich and effective learning environment. For the student, there are numerous advantages to learning online, including access to a readily available, democratic environment that provides the learner with choice over when to participate, allows time for reflection, and shifts authority and control from the teacher to the student (Salmon, 2004). For the teacher, there is the need to understand the notion of an emerging e-pedagogy. This is discussed in the next section of this chapter.

The tools available to the online teacher and learner provide a number of advantages. Asynchronous tools, such as online bulletin boards, facilitate collaboration and interaction. Students can take the time to reflect on important concepts and issues and subsequently participate in text-based discussions by making postings to the online bulletin board. Once complete, online discussions are archived within the course, giving learners the added ability to record, search, and organize messages for future reference. Miller and King (2003) state that the use of online bulletin boards in this way provides greater potential for students' thoughtful analysis, thus enhancing knowledge building and collaboration.

Another advantage for the online learner is the ability to access a wide variety of learning resources as needed. This facilitates a "pull" model of learning (Oblinger & Maruyama, 1996), which allows the student a much greater degree of control as opposed to a "push" model, where the teacher determines which resources and content students need and pushes or delivers them at the same time for all learners. The Web is a two-way medium and is the first that truly accommodates multiple intelligences, thus allowing students to match their own particular learning style to the media used for learning (Seely Brown, 2000).

From the student's perspective, the flexibility of the environment and, thus, the opportunity it provides for controlling and pacing learning, is its most appealing characteristic (Cashion & Palmieri, 2002). In fact, online students may value the flexibility of online learning so much that, in course evaluations, they often rate an online course more highly than it deserves based on its convenience rather than on the quality of the learning experience (Brooks, 2003).

The growth of K–12 online learning and its potential for the transformation of teaching and learning are enormous. The literature reveals that it has the potential to provide flexible, collaborative, student-centered, multimedia-rich, and authentic, quality learning experiences (Miller & King, 2003, Palloff & Pratt, 2001). With the evolution of Web 2.0 software, typically termed "social software," it is anticipated that additional options for interaction will emerge. However, the research also clearly indicates that this potential cannot be realized without a fundamental shift in not only the institution and the learner, but also the pedagogy and the teacher (Miller & King, 2003). Such a shift requires, in turn, new models for training online teachers who embrace innovation and change (Childs, 2004; Crichton & LaBonte, 2003; Kemshal-Bell, 2001).

ONLINE TEACHING

E-Pedagogy

Pedagogy, defined by Australian researchers Brennan et al. (2001) as "a core of effective and traditional practices of teaching and training that have worked over time" (p. 24), underpins and strongly influences the way that learning experiences are both designed and delivered.

Numerous studies and surveys reveal that, up to now, technology has often driven pedagogy in online teaching (Brennan et al., 2001; Miller & King, 2003). However, it is now becoming clear that the technology itself will not magically bring about a change in teaching or an improvement in student learning outcomes (Gold, 2001), nor will the adoption of traditional teaching practices, such as transmission-style teaching, be successful in the online environment. This was illustrated when, in the rush to put courses and programs online during the 1990s, existing face-to-face practices and content were often transferred to the Web and, as a result, met with limited success (Kemshal-Bell, 2001). The general consensus among researchers in the field is that, given the potential that online learning represents for the transformation of teaching and learning and the need for online teaching and learning to be collaborative and student-centered, a new e-pedagogy must be conceptualized and implemented (Brennan, 2003; Coppola, Hiltz, & Rotter, 2001; Crichton & Childs, 2003; Good, 2001). As Australian researcher Roslin Brennan states in her 2003 study involving more than 300 online teachers and students, "It is no longer acceptable to assume that the skills developed in face-to-face teaching can be instantly transferred to the online environment with either ease or good results. The practice of teaching has to be re-conceptualized" (p. 24).

This fundamental shift in pedagogical methodology and the reconceptualization of teaching that Brennan calls for requires "teachers and trainers who are both confident and comfortable with this new way of working" (Brennan et al., 2001, p. 51). Currently, online teacher training is focused on in-service teachers, who often have many years of experience in the traditional classroom (Salmon, 2000). However, preparing for online teaching represents a massive shift in theory and practice for many of these teachers. It appears that the time has come for a new model that introduces preservice teachers, at a formative point in their teaching careers, to the emerging body of knowledge of effective online pedagogical practices.

The work of determining the profile of the effective online teacher and specifying the knowledge, skills, and attitudes required has begun, but is far from complete; in fact, it will more likely be ongoing as the environment evolves and as a clearer picture of e-pedagogy emerges. What is apparent, however, is that teaching online is fundamentally different than teaching in the traditional classroom (Brennan et al., 2001; Childs, 2004; Good, 2001; Miller & King, 2003); therefore, the unique competencies of the online teacher require specific and unique training as well as ongoing professional development. However, even with such training, this represents a shift that many experienced in-service teachers may find difficult to make.

Professional Development

The most significant concern when training experienced face-to-face teachers, who have completed many years in the traditional classroom, is the pedagogical shift they must undergo in order to be effective in the online classroom and to truly understand the transformational potential of online teaching and learning. In fact, experienced classroom teachers' skills may not be useful or adaptable to the online environment at all (Brennan, 2003). These experienced practitioners are often concerned about their change in roles, from teacher as transmitter of knowledge to teacher as facilitator and co-learner and may be nervous about giving up some of the control they have traditionally had in the classroom (Schofield et al., 2001). In addition, despite extensive professional development, it often becomes clear that not every teacher is suited for online teaching. Indeed, those who are particularly extroverted and engaging in the face-to-face classroom may not be effective in the online environment (Palloff & Pratt, 2001; Salmon, 2000). Further, unless efforts are made to increase teacher competence and comfort with ICT integration, the focus will remain how to actually use the technology rather than how IT can enable changed teaching and learning.

Another challenge for in-service teachers who begin teaching online is that they may not have experienced, either as teachers or as learners, e-learning environments in which the teacher guides student learning as a facilitator and resource provider. Studies of teacher learning, cited by Stein, Schwan-Smith, and Silver (1999), suggest that teachers filter information about new ways of teaching through their own experiences as students. Unless experienced in-service teachers are trained in e-pedagogy and the specific competencies of the online teacher, they may revert to traditional teaching practices that spring from their own past experiences (Vrasidas & Glass, 2004), thus undermining the transformational potential of the e-learning environment.

Training Needs for Online Educators

Without well-trained, effective, competent, and pedagogically strong online teachers, the potential for transformational teaching and learning represented by the online learning environment may never be realized. Numerous studies point to the need for online teachers to "learn the steps to a new dance" (Maeroff, 2003, p. 94) and for professional development, which allows them to develop the skills and attributes necessary to be effective in the e-learning environment (Cashion & Palmieri, 2002; Good, 2001; Kemshal-Bell, 2001; Miller & King, 2003).

Currently, online practitioners are almost exclusively drawn from the ranks of experienced, face-to-face teachers (Salmon, 2000). The literature describes a variety of professional development courses and programs, including structured professional development, Web-based community-building activities, and volunteer teaching, as well as conferences and mentoring designed to train inservice teachers to become effective online teachers (Schofield et al., 2001).

In a qualitative case study of online educators from two rural school districts in Alberta, Canada, researchers gleaned information on the issues faced by online teachers, the skills and knowledge required to be effective, and the ongoing professional development required to support online teachers. Crichton and Childs (2003) suggest that professional development for online educators should include three major components:

- Technology and Support
- Application knowledge of software and delivery systems
  - Technical knowledge of software and delivery systems
  - Support for and in the online learning environment
- Online Pedagogy
  - Understanding online classroom management techniques
  - Organizational skills
  - Strategies for engaging and motivating learners
- Opportunities to Practice
  - Experience as an online learner before teaching online

In addition, the need for prospective online teachers to immerse themselves, as online learners, in the environment and to learn by doing is critical to an online teaching-training program (Childs, 2004; Crichton & LaBonte, 2003; Gold, 2001; Hansen & Salter, 1999; Salmon, 2000). Becoming an online learner allows a teacher to experience the environment firsthand and determine its complexity, benefits, and compatibility with his or her own goals and philosophies (Surry, 2002). In terms of innovation adoption, teachers who have an opportunity to try out an innovation, such as online teaching and learning, are more likely to adopt it than those who do not have such an opportunity (Rogers, 1995). Those who begin teaching online, without having experienced the environment as online learners, may attempt to re-create the face-to-face classroom and retreat to ways of teaching that are more comfortable and ingrained and, as a result, seriously limit the enormous potential of this innovative learning approach (Zuber-Skerrit, 1992, as cited in Hansen & Salter, 1999).

As more research emerges on the topic of online professional development, the current model of training experienced in-service teachers to teach online will continue to evolve to overcome its challenges. Is this, however, the only way to train online teachers? One innovative model suggested in a number of research studies (Brennan et al., 2001; Childs, 2004; Kemshal-Bell, 2001) promotes the introduction of online teaching experiences into preservice teacher education programs. This is the model on which the second phase of this research is focused—a course-based distributed learning experience offered to preservice teachers at the University of Calgary in Calgary, Alberta, Canada. This course was first offered in 2004 and, having gained in popularity, was subsequently offered in 2005 and 2006. A brief synopsis of the course and a summary of a research study into the impact of the distributed learning experience on the first cadre of students are described in the next sections of this chapter.

Distributed Learning Preservice Course

The Special Topics: Distributed Learning course was designed based on the research of Crichton and Childs (2004), as described above, and in response to literature from the field suggesting the need for a new model of preparing online teachers. The 13-week course, offered during the final semester of a 2-year Bachelor of Education program at the University of Calgary, involves both an online component and a practicum component, in which the preservice teachers are partnered with experienced online teachers at the Calgary Board of Education's online high school, CBe-learn.[5] The design of the course is consistent with the philosophy of the University of Calgary's Bachelor of Education Program or Master of Teaching (MT) program, in that it is "learner-focused, inquiry-based and field-oriented" (University of Calgary, 2003, p. 2), providing preservice teachers with technological support, online pedagogy, as well as opportunities to practice.

The goals of the course are to

- Immerse preservice teachers in the e-learning environment, both as students and teachers
- Provide a practicum experience in which preservice teachers can observe and work alongside experienced online teachers

- Expose preservice teachers to a new model of learning and teaching in which learning and teaching are not constrained by the traditional barriers of time and place
- Encourage preservice teachers to examine underlying assumptions about designing and delivering effective learning experiences.

One component of the course involves using Blackboard as the learning-management system, in which the students are expected to participate as learners and facilitators of various online discussions. The course provides a hybrid or blended online learning experience as face-to-face sessions are held at the University of Calgary so that the students, as well as their partner teachers, could participate in hands-on technology workshops to supplement their technical knowledge and assist them in the development of learning objects.[6] Synchronous learning opportunities are also provided using Elluminate Live software, so novice teachers can experience what learning at home, alone, is like.

The majority of the preservice teachers considered themselves to be either "confident explorers" or "beginners" in terms of their technological expertise. Only three had taken an online course before, and none had experience in online teaching or teaching in a distributed learning environment.

Early in the semester, the students met with the CBe-learn online teachers who had volunteered to be partner teachers, and partnerships were set up according to the students' subject-area interests and areas of expertise. Over the course of the subsequent weeks, the preservice teachers and their partner teachers collaborated to design and develop online learning objects for high school courses in a number of curriculum areas, including Science, Math, English Language Arts, Social Studies, Career and Technology Studies, Art, and Physical Education. As resources for this project, the students had access to in-house technical expertise at both the University of Calgary and CBe-learn. These online learning objects provided a rich source of data for the Phase 2 study.

In addition, the students were required to write an Inquiry Project paper, reflecting their understandings of online teaching and learning. In summary, the components of the Special Topics: Distributed Learning course consisted of

- Inquiry Project Paper
- Online Participation
- Content Development
    - Development of a subject-specific learning object
    - Development of a lesson or activity using the learning object
    - Development of an assessment item to determine learner understanding of the lesson/activity

Impact On Preservice Teachers

In order to determine the impact of the course-based distributed-learning experience on the first cadre of students to go through the Special Topics course (Phase 2), research (Shervey, 2005) was conducted in the form of a qualitative case study. The research focused on a central question:

> What was the impact of the online teaching and learning experience in the course Special Topics: Distributed Learning on preservice teachers' understandings of the practice of teaching online?
>
> In particular, what was the impact on their understandings of
> - the unique skills and competencies required of an online teacher?
> - the unique challenges faced by online teachers?

For the purposes of this study, "impact" refers to the participants' professional growth in terms of what they knew, understood, and were able to do as online teachers at the conclusion, as compared with the outset, of their experience in the Special Topics course.

Data, in the form of entrance and exit surveys, a focus group interview, artefacts from the online portion of the course, and the student-designed online learning objects, was gathered and analyzed using a codes-and-frames approach (Goffman, 1959). The researcher was involved in the course as a participant-observer, interacting with the preservice teachers in the Blackboard course and in technology workshops throughout the course term.

In terms of knowledge, the data revealed that, at the end of their experience in the Special Topics course, the preservice teachers appeared to understand a great deal about the practice of online teaching, including the changed role of the teacher and various strategies for motivating and establishing rapport with students without the benefit of visual cues. They appeared to recognize the unique nature of electronic communication and the need for an online teacher to provide not only clear and frequent but also positive feedback to online students. They seemed to understand the highly complex role of Web-based instructional design, demonstrated by their thoughtful work in designing and developing engaging, student-centered learning objects. Finally, they demonstrated some understanding of the emerging field of e-pedagogy.

In terms of skills, the preservice teachers, who came to the course with some expertise in electronic communication but limited or no experience with online learning, were greatly affected by their experience as both online teachers and learners. Their learning objects were evidence of their emerging abilities to create authentic, student-centered tasks with clear instructions and navigational paths as well as their willingness to make mistakes and take risks along the way. Within the 13-week time frame of the

Special Topics course, the preservice teacher participants began to learn and had the opportunity to practice the skill of moderating online discussions, although the art of online dialogue and online questioning can take years to master. In the process of creating their learning objects, the preservice teachers demonstrated their newfound abilities to use the Web-based tools within the online Blackboard course as well as a variety of multimedia software programs, with which most had previously been unfamiliar.

The preservice teachers' attitudes were also impacted by their experience in this course. Many expressed a changed attitude toward the use of graphics and flashy technology in online design. Even those who, at the end of this experience, favored the hybrid or blended approach over the wholly online approach appeared to be open minded and positive about the potential of this new learning environment. In designing and developing their learning objects, they demonstrated technological fearlessness and risk-taking as they chose to experiment with new instructional strategies and unfamiliar Web-based tools. By virtue of the fact that these novice teachers chose to take the Special Topics: Distributed Learning course from among many other choices, it is likely that most of them brought open-minded, risk-taking attitudes with them. However, at least 3 of the participants who came to the course with great reservations about online learning finished with positive attitudes toward the new learning environment to which they had been introduced.

In terms of online teaching challenges, the preservice teachers involved in this case study recognized and wrestled with many of the significant challenges faced by online teachers in the field. These include establishing rapport and communicating with students without seeing them face-to-face, monitoring and assessing student progress, keeping technical skills sharp and up-to-date, using technology to effectively enhance student learning, addressing learner diversity online, and coping with the amount of time required for the complex and time-consuming task of online design. The Special Topics course provided the preservice teachers an opportunity to experience some of these challenges and to discuss solutions among themselves as well as with their partner teachers.

This is not to say that the participants learned all that there is to know about the practice of online teaching. Within the timeframe of a 13-week course, that would be impossible. However, their professional growth in terms of knowledge, skills, and attitudes indicates that they were greatly impacted by their experience as online teachers and learners and in their collaboration with their partner teachers at CBe-learn.

Although it is impossible to predict exactly how this experience will affect the future practices of these novice teachers, they were asked, on the exit survey and in the focus group discussion, about the impact of this experience on their classroom teaching practice and the use of technology in learning in the future. Their comments reveal the significance of this experience in shaping their future teaching practices as well as a sense of confidence and excitement as they anticipated moving from preservice preparation to the real world of teaching. For most, the Special Topics course experience opened their eyes to learning options and alternatives that they had not known existed. As a result, many of the preservice teachers said that they planned to incorporate more multimedia and technology into their teaching practices by investigating and using Web resources, creating class Web pages for communication with parents, creating online modules, using learning-object repositories, and setting up hybrid online classrooms to supplement face-to-face teaching.

The results of this study confirm that preparing preservice teachers to teach online can significantly impact their understandings of these unique online teaching competencies and also raise their awareness of new ways of incorporating technology in their teaching practices. Experiences such as this course have the potential to help teachers understand how technology can be integrated seamlessly into both online and traditional teaching and learning. Most importantly, the results support the need for online teacher training to become embedded in existing preservice teacher-education programs.

Following "Them" into the Field

In Phase 3 of this research, students from the first two offerings of the course were contacted. Thirteen were located and sent consent letters and surveys via e-mail. Nine of those former students agreed to participate.

Seven had full-time teaching positions (one in England, in Manitoba, and the rest in Calgary). Two were employed part-time as substitute teachers. Only 5 reported that their schools had the infrastructure to support technology use in their teaching. The majority of students reported that taking the course had helped them obtain their present jobs, commenting

- "I think that my comfort level with technology made it possible for me to get this job with CBe-learn."
- "I was hired in the hopes to bring some technology into these classrooms as the students work purely on … modules which are all paper and textbook based lessons."
- "The knowledge I gained during the course in terms of working with technology gave me an advantage over other applicants. I was told so by the vice-principal."

Of greater significance was the reoccurring comment that the course had

> ...introduced me to a new way of thinking about teaching with technology. Prior to my registration in this course I assumed that e-mail was the extent of integrating technology into the classroom. I have gained a greater appreciation and comfort level with using technology in the classroom. The Special Topics Course taught me something very valuable: using technology has to be **a deliberate and conscious act.** I should not use technology in the classroom for the sake of introducing something new. It has to be integrated in a way that is meaningful for students.

A statement, repeated by the majority of the students, was the degree to which technology was not being used in their schools. They reported limited access to technology, limited time to develop content, and limited encouragement within the schools to try innovative distributed learning options. It is important to note that all but one of these students were placed in traditional schools, those not offering distributed learning or online learning as a curricular option. However, the one who is employed by CBeLearn, stated she is drawing on all the knowledge and skills learned in the course.

As a concluding question in the survey, students were asked for their suggestions about improving the course. The majority stated they had enjoyed it, found the experience invaluable to their subsequent teaching, and were happy with the way it was structured. They added they wished they had had more time to test their learning objects with "real" students and then to modify it based on that feedback. Of major significance was the comment that they felt all University of Calgary Master of Teaching (MT) students needed exposure to the option of e-learning and that

> ...MT students should be introduced to the resources available for them to use in their courses. I think that there should be a section or day focused on teaching the MT students to use the resources available online.

In many ways, the findings from Phase 3 were not remarkable. The students had self-selected the course as their fourth semester option within the MT program, so they were already either interested in Distributed Learning or confident that the course would offer them something of value to their future work. The sad finding was the degree to which novice teachers in 2006 were facing similar barriers to meaningful technology integration as their predecessors.

LINK TO DEVELOPMENT WORK

Ironically, we discovered similar concerns/barriers in our recent development work. Crichton and Shervey both were involved in a 4-year Canadian International Development Agency (CIDA) and Crichton was involved in a 3-year Asian Development Bank (ADB) project in western China. The focus of both projects was the development of a distance education system to deliver teacher education to rural educators. ICT for teaching was a core component. Content and materials from CIDA can be located from the project site http://202.205.160.161/cidaweb/en/index.html.

Increasingly, development projects are turning to e-learning and school-based ICT to gain efficiencies in terms of improved teacher education and learning experiences. E-learning offers a way to reach large numbers of educators who are often in rural, remote locations. The lure to maximize the potential of e-learning is great, but the temptation to invest in foreign expertise and hardware infrastructure rather than local training and domestic capacity-building tends to be greater. The three professional development (PD) components identified by Crichton and Childs (2003) are often overlooked in project funding, with PD being seen as a luxury—if there is money left over from "necessary" infrastructure purchases, some could be allocated to PD.

Further, partnerships in development work tend to be with government agencies rather than teacher colleges or other preservice training institutions. Consequently, as a project uses e-learning to retrain existing teachers, new teachers enter the workforce trained to work in old ways; in essence, putting increased demand on retraining efforts. Therefore, we propose a recasting of partnerships to include preservice providers.

Our research with novice teachers at the University of Calgary suggests that preservice teachers are able to learn and embrace e-learning. Further, these campus experiences help them to integrate technology meaningfully in their teaching, whether online or in the classroom. Without intentional PD for technology use, we know, from both our own practice and the literature (Cuban, 2001), that hardware and software will be underutilized in classrooms, and the potential and promise of e-learning will be limited.

Analysis of the findings of two international development projects supports this. In the case of the CIDA project, emphasis was on professional development rather than hardware. Initially, this was a source of conflict with project partners, who increasingly wanted amounts of money allocated to infrastructure. However, the report from the independent monitor confirmed the merit of investing in PD, but cautioned that sustainability would be an ongoing concern. Fortunately, one of the last activities in the CIDA project invited a professor from a leading teachers college in Beijing to work with a Canadian professor for the development of the last training module. Through this collaboration, the two professors have continued to work together, integrating the CIDA project materials into the course content of the Beijing professor, thereby ensuring a degree of sustainability beyond the actual project itself. In the case of the ADB project, a train-the-trainer model (cascade model) of PD was used. Canadian expertise was used to train instructors at a regional teachers college. Those instructors then trained the local teachers and provided the follow-up training and evaluation. It is hoped that the methods and content from the training will inform the instructors' preservice teaching. The value of the cascade model rests in the notion of distributed expertise. This approach is often used when attempting to effect large-scale change at the classroom level, as the expertise rests with those who receive the training and lasts well after the initial expert leaves the project and moves on to other work. However, the risk with this approach is that it tends to be slow and often the content is "diluted" or reduced each time someone else receives the training from a person increasingly further removed from the initial training.

While neither the CIDA nor ADB work has any long-term findings (both projects concluded spring 2007), we trust the involvement of teacher-preparation providers included in both projects, while still limited, will help to sustain the goals of the individual projects.

CONCLUSION

Without intentional courses and training, the literature suggests that professionals working in e-learning environments will continue to create experiences based on their traditional learning experiences. While the University of Calgary continues to offer its course in Distributed Learning, ironically, it continues to be one of the few universities to do so (Shervey, 2005; Crichton & Childs, 2003).

The Calgary Board of Education (CBE), through CBeLearn, continues to support the university's efforts, encouraging the partnership among its teachers and the MT students. CBE teachers attend on-campus portions of the course as part of their professional development activities, and there are plans to continue and expand this partnership. The professor from the teachers college in Beijing remains in contact with the authors, and she continues to integrate the CIDA project's training materials into her teaching.

The importance of our findings and our development work points to the need to encourage schools and agencies to embrace the promises and potential for both distributed and online learning through intentional professional development from all ages and stages of teachers. This intentionality is critical if the teaching and learning needs of the 21st century are to be realized.

If we feel preservice experiences such as those described in this chapter are important for university students in North American contexts, then we must conclude that they would be valuable in supporting and sustaining critical development work worldwide.

The last words in this chapter belong to the students of the in the MT course.

> I found this course a most worthwhile learning experience, a veritable treasure trove of supremely practical and useful knowledge for a beginning teacher. . . . I had previously thought of online learning as a completely separate alternative to traditional classroom-based instruction. Never had I thought of blending the two in such a way to benefit from both environments, adding further differentiation strategies to my pedagogical knowledge base. . . . Flexibility is what blended learning offers, and I look forward to making it a part of my repertoire in September.

REFERENCES

Advisory Committee for Online Learning (2001). *The e-learning e-volution in colleges and universities: A pan Canadian challenge.* Retrieved September 15, 2004, from http://www.digitalschool.net/edu/summary_E_learn.html.

Blackboard (n.d). Retrieved September 6, 2004 from http://www.blackboard.com/

Brennan, R. (2003). *One size doesn't fit all.* ISBN 1 4096 157 9. Retrieved August 12, 2004 from http://www.ncver.edu.au

Brennan, R., McFadden, M., & Law, E. (2001). *All that glitters is not gold.* Leabrook, South Australia: National Centre for Vocational Education Research.

Brooks, L. (200). *How the attitudes of instructors, students, course administrators and course designers affects the quality of an online learning environment.* Retrieved November 14, 2004 from http://www.westga.edu/~distance/ojdla/winter64/brooks64.htm

Cashion, J., & Palmieri, P. (2002 December). *The secret is the teacher.* Retrieved October 9, 2004 from http://www.ncver.edu.au

Childs, E. (2004). *The impact of professional development on teaching practice: A case study.* Unpublished doctoral dissertation, University of Calgary.

Coppola, N., Hiltz, S. R., & Rotter, N. (2001). *Becoming a virtual professor: Pedagogical roles and ALN.* Proceedings of the 34th Hawaii International Conference on System Sciences.

Crichton, S., & Childs, E. A. (2004). Teachers as online educators: Requirements for distributed learning and teacher preparation. *Educational Technology, 44*(4), 25–30.

Crichton, S., & LaBonte, R. (2003). Innovative practice for innovators: Walking the talk. *Education Technology and Society, 61.* Retrieved December 2, 2008, from http://www.ifets.info/journals/6_1/crichton.html.

Cuban, L. (2001). *Oversold and Underused.* Cambridge, MA: Harvard University Press.

Goffman, E. (1959). *The presentation of self in everyday life.* Bantam Doubleday Dell Publishing Group Inc.

Gold, S. (2001). *A* constructivist approach to online training for online teachers. *Journal of Asynchronous Learning Networks, 5*(1).

Good, M. (2001). On the way to online pedagogy. In J. Stephenson (Ed.), *Teaching & learning online* (pp. 166–174). London: Kogan Page.

Goodyear, P., Salmon, G., Spector, J. M., Steeples, C., & Tickner, S. (2001). Competencies for online teaching: A special report. *Educational Technology Research and Development, 49*(1), 65–72.

Hansen, S., & Salter, G. (1999). *Modelling new skills for online teaching.* Paper presented at the meeting of ASCILITE99, Brisbane, Australia.

Harasim, L. (1987). Teaching and learning on-line: Issues in computer-mediated graduate courses. *Canadian Journal of Educational Communication, 16,* 117–135.

Harasim, L., Hiltz, S. R., Teles, L., & Turoff, M. (1995). *Learning networks: A field guide to teaching and learning online.* Cambridge, MA: MIT Press.

Kemshal-Bell, G. (2001, April). *The online teacher.* New South Wales Department of Education and Training.

Maeroff, G. (2003). *A classroom of one.* New York: Palgrave MacMillian.

Miller, T., & King, F. (2003). Distance education: Pedagogy and best practices in the new millenium. *International Leadership in Education, 6*(3), 283–297.

Oblinger, D., & Maruyama, M. (1996). *Distributed learning.* Cause Professional Paper Series, #14. Boulder, CO: Cause. Retrieved September 16, 2004 from http://www.educause.edu/ir/library/pdf/PUB3014.pdf

Palloff , R. M., & Pratt, K. (2000, October). *Making the transition: Helping teachers to teach online.* Paper presented at the meeting of the EDUCAUSE 2000: Thinking IT Through. Proceedings and post-conference materials. Retrieved December 3, 2008, from http://net.educause.edu/ir/library/pdf/EDU0006.pdf

Palloff, R., & Pratt, K. (2001). *Lessons from the cyberspace classroom.* San Francisco: Jossey-Bass.

Rogers, E. M. (1983). *Diffusion of innovations* (3rd ed.). New York: The Free Press.

Salmon, G. (2000). *Learning submarines: Raising the periscopes.* Retrieved October 10, 2004 from NETWorking 2000 Conference Web Site: http://flexiblelearning.net.au/nw2000/main/key03.htm

Salmon, G. (2004). *E-moderating: The key to teaching and learning online.* (2nd ed.). London: Routledge Falmer.

Schofield, K., Melville, B., Bennet, D., & Walsh, A. (2001, March). *Professional practices online: renovating past practices or building new ones?* Paper presented at the meeting of the Research to Reality: Putting VET Research to Work. Retrieved October 14,2004 from http://www.avetra.org.au/abstracts_and_papers_2001/Walsh-Melville-Schofield_full.pdf

Seely Brown, J. (2000). Growing up digital. *Change,* March/April, 10-20.

Shervey, G. (2005). *Preservice teachers and online teaching.* Unpublished thesis, University of Calgary.

Smith, R., & Crichton, S. (2003). *Online learning in Alberta: Sustainability factors*. Report for Alberta Learning

Stein, M. K., Schwan-Smith, M., & Silver, E. (1999). The development of professional developers: Learning to assist teachers in new settings in new ways. *Harvard Educational Review, 693*.

Surry, D. W. (2002, April). *A model for integrating instructional technology into higher education*. Paper presented at the meeting of the Annual Meeting of the American Educational Research Association. New Orleans, LA.

The Council on Alberta Teaching Standards (COATS) (2002, March 28). *Teacher education by distance learning: A discussion paper*.

University of Calgary (2003). *Mentoring student teachers*. (brochure). Calgary, Alberta: Author. Retrieved January 10, 2004 from http://www.educ.ucalgary.ca

University of Melbourne. (n.d.). Archival Catalogue of Digital Learning Objects. Retrieved December 3, 2008, from http://dlocat.unimelb.edu.au/

Vrasidas, C., & Glass, G. V. (Eds.) (2004). *Current perspectives in applied information technologies: Online professional development for teachers*. Greenwich, CT: Information Age Publishing.

NOTES

1. Examples of asynchronous computer-mediated communication include learning-management systems (e.g., Moodle, etc.), bulletin boards, and e-mail, where messages are posted or sent and then later responded to by classmates or the teacher.

2. Synchronous computer-mediated communication is facilitated by tools, such as "chat," which allow online participants to meet in a chat room at a specific time. The chat may be totally text-based or may be enhanced by audio capabilities that allow the participants to hear and speak to each other, but is considered to be synchronous communication because it takes place in "real" time.

3. Course-authoring software, such as Blackboard, WebCT, and Desire2Learn, is used to create online learning courses, which may include Web pages, online discussion tools, private e-mail, and other tools to facilitate the delivery of course content and communication between the students and the teacher in a secure and bounded online environment.

4. CBe-learn is the Calgary Board of Education's online school. Originally part of the CBE's upgrading high school, Chinook Learning Services, it became a full-fledged online high school in 2002 and added an online junior high school in September 2004.

5. An online learning object can be defined as "any digital object or media asset that is an independent and self-standing unit of learning content predisposed to reuse in multiple instructional contexts" (University of Melbourne, n.d.).

CHAPTER 20

DISTANCE TEACHER TRAINING IN RWANDA

Comparing the Costs[1]

Alison Mead Richardson

BACKGROUND

The simple question, "Is distance teacher training cheaper than conventional teacher education?" has only a complicated answer (Perraton & Potashnik, 1997).

Like many governments in sub-Saharan Africa, the Government of Rwanda (GoR) set itself a goal of Universal Primary Education (UPE) by 2015. One legacy of Rwanda's unique recent history is that the country has a high proportion of unqualified teachers. A research study carried out by UNESCO in 2000 showed that more than 65% of secondary teachers in government and government-aided schools in Rwanda were unqualified (Drique & Wassenove, 2000). The GoR has made many advances in the education sector postgenocide, and enrollment in secondary education trebled from 50,000 in 1995 to 150,000 in 2003.

Bridging the Knowledge Divide, pages 357–374
Copyright © 2009 by Information Age Publishing
All rights of reproduction in any form reserved.

The Revised Education Sector Policy Document, published by the Ministry of Education (MINEDUC) in 2002, makes the following policy statements:

- Teachers at all levels shall be trained in sufficient number and quality.
- Both preservice and in-service teacher training methods with the use of distance learning shall be strengthened.

It is against this policy background that MINEDUC took the decision to use distance education to upgrade the qualifications of inservice secondary teachers.

There is a long history of distance teacher training projects in Africa. In the 1970s and 80s Botswana, Malawi, Swaziland, Uganda, and Zimbabwe all developed one-off projects based in teacher training colleges (Perraton, 1993). We know that distance education has continued to be an important option for educational policymakers (Dodds & Youngman, 1994). Distance teacher training was suggested as a possible solution to the problem of lack of qualified teachers in Rwanda. In 1998 GoR created Kigali Institute of Education (KIE) to take responsibility for teacher training in the country. In 1999 KIE admitted 300 students to a campus-based preservice program. It was quickly realized that the conventional preservice training at KIE could not train the large number of unqualified serving teachers needed to cope with increasing secondary enrollment.

In 1999 KIE started planning for an in-service distance training program in order to meet the need for more secondary-school teachers and to contribute toward the GoR target of UPE by 2015. KIE started delivering the first national distance training program for teachers in 2001. The Department for International Development of the British Government (DFID) agreed to fund program set-up costs, development, and delivery for the first cohort of 500 students. The Rwandan Ministry of Education (MINEDUC) covered the costs of staffing, office accommodation, and running costs.

This study was undertaken to compare the costs of the campus-based preservice teacher training program with the costs of the distance education inservice program.

Aims of the Study

There were four aims to the study:

1. To demonstrate how costs can be calculated in both the conventional preservice program and the distance training inservice program at KIE,

2. To establish what researchers say about the costs of other distance teacher training programs in Africa,

3. To calculate the comparative costs of the distance teacher training program at KIE and the conventional preservice program,

4. To provide information on the comparative costs of the KIE programs and make recommendations for future planning for teacher education in Rwanda.

Justification for the Study

There are many case studies on the use of distance teacher training programs in African countries, which indicates it is a popular choice for governments faced with expanding student populations and large numbers of untrained teachers. Distance education is chosen because of its power to stretch educational resources (Young et al., 1991).

The prominence of distance teacher-education programs in Africa indicates that governments consider it is a cost-effective alternative to conventional training programs. Distance education for teacher training is often the only alternative if large numbers of un- or underqualified teachers need to be trained inservice. This study set out to test this assumption in the Rwandan context.

The Government of Rwanda (GoR) has a strategy of ICT-led development, which impacts on all subsectors including education. This was the first national distance training program, and the plans included the later development of e-learning materials. It was important to be able to make accurate statements about the cost of the distance teacher training program in Rwanda in order to inform the future design of this, and other, distance teaching programs. GoR saw this as a test case for distance education in Rwanda in general, and specifically for teacher training.

One of the founding concepts of the program was that the distance training program should be equivalent to the campus-based preservice program. The distance training program offers the same courses and credit units as the first 3 years of the preservice BEd program, and leads to a diploma. If the two programs are equivalent and distance education could be shown to produce qualified teachers for less cost, then there would be a case for investigating the expansion of either distance training or a more mixed-mode approach at KIE.

In addition to the local needs for the study, there are wider implications of a comparative cost study of national teacher training programs. Commentators on distance teacher education, such as Creed (2001), Perraton (1993), and Robinson and Latchem (2003), identify the need for more studies on costing to be included in the research agenda for distance teacher education.

Scope of the Study

One of the purposes of costing is to allow us to make cost-efficiency comparisons between different ways of achieving an output (Rumble, 1997). This study focused on the cost of the in-service distance teacher training program compared with the cost of the preservice campus-based program. It was, therefore, a study of cost-efficiency. A system is cost-efficient if, relative to another system, the outputs cost less per unit of input (Rumble, 1997).

This was not a study of cost-effectiveness because at the time, the first cohort of students had not graduated from either the preservice or inservice programs. Further research is needed to establish the cost-effectiveness of the distance training program in terms of the quality and effectiveness of the teachers who graduate from both programs. Cost-effectiveness usually takes into account both costs and quality.

The study took into account all funds provided for the KIE distance teacher training program through the DFID Rwanda Education Sector Support Program (RESSP) and all operating funds provided to KIE through MINEDUC and other donors.

Hidden costs and opportunity costs were identified and quantified where possible, for example, the school buildings that were used as distance training centers for weekend tutorials and residents. These are hidden costs, as they are provided at no cost to the program, but they do have a value. There is an opportunity cost to students on the distance training program. The time they spend studying could be profitably used in other income-generating ways. The study also considered the cost to the Ministry of increasing the salaries of newly qualified teachers in line with their improved qualifications.

It was necessary to establish information other than financial data, such as drop-out rates from each program and the number of preservice graduates who will eventually become teachers. It was believed that many of the preservice students come to KIE only because they have failed to gain entry to the National University of Rwanda or other higher-education institutions. It is possible that a high proportion of the KIE preservice graduates will not go on to teach in secondary schools, and a survey was carried out to investigate this.

Apart from the generic literature concerning the methodology of costing distance teacher training, the literature review was confined to case studies in sub-Saharan Africa.

WHAT DOES THE LITERATURE TELL US?

There have been many studies of African distance teacher training programs (Akyeampong et al., 2000; Hawkridge et al., 1982; Murphy & Curran, 1992; Robinson et al., 1995; Gatawa, 1990; Perraton, 1993, 2000; Chivore, 1992; Bako & Rumble, 1993; MUSTER, 1999–2002). Projects were launched in the 1960s in countries like Botswana, Kenya, Malawi, Swaziland, and Uganda to produce primary teachers to meet increasing demand. In the 1970s and 1980s, countries like Nigeria, Tanzania, and Zimbabwe used distance education for training unqualified teachers, often in an effort to achieve UPE. Some of these studies contain useful cost information, others focus more on the effectiveness of the program. From these studies, it is possible to draw up a picture of commonly-held beliefs about distance teacher training.

Does Distance Teacher Training Produce Qualified Teachers at a Lower Cost than Conventionally Taught Programs?

We have little information on the costs of the early distance teacher training programs, although Young et al. (1991) tell us that the earliest recorded were in Palestinian refugee camps in 1963 and Perraton (1993) reports that the cost per student in these programs was less than half the comparable in-college course. In the same meta-analysis, Perraton concludes that distance training programs can be designed for teachers at a cost between one-third and two-thirds of college-based programs. Costs need to be seen in the context of teacher education generally. In countries where teacher training is funded in the same way as other higher-education programs, the costs tend to be high. So one of the reasons distance education appears to be cheaper, or more cost-effective, is because the conventional programs are actually expensive (Perraton, 2000).

Rumble (1997) reports on the findings of Hawkridge et al. (1982) on the Kenya Correspondence Course Unit's inservice teacher training program from the 1970s. In this case, the researchers concluded that the distance program was more expensive than the comparable traditional program, but this was likely to be because of low student numbers. Perraton (2000) reports on a cost analysis by Makau in 1993, which showed that the external BEd at the University of Nairobi in the late 1980s produced graduates at "significantly lower annual costs per student than the residential equivalent."

Neilsen (1996) reports on a study by Mählck and Temu (1989) of Tanzania's distance teacher education program in the mid-1970s. They concluded that the distance program was 25% cheaper than the conventional program, and that it was a worthwhile investment, as the distance program produced teachers of comparable quality. Chale (1993) also found that the distance inservice teacher training program in Tanzania in the 1970s was cheaper than the college-based alternative.

Moon and Robinson (2003), in a study of the use of distance education for initial teacher training (both in-service and preservice), found that distance education can produce trained teachers at lower cost. They note that distance education also enables scarce educational resources to be used more effectively, for example, by enabling greater access to programs based in teacher training colleges.

It is clear that it is not possible to make a definitive statement that distance teacher training either costs more or less than college-based programs. Costs depend on the design of the distance training program, and there are many variables. Robinson and Murphy (1996) cite media choice, use of contact time, and element of cost sharing as being influencing factors.

So, from the literature, it would appear than there is a general consensus that distance teacher training costs *tend* to be lower than comparable college-based programs. Influencing factors are the structure of teacher education costing in that country and the design of the distance program.

THE NEED FOR COST ANALYSES
OF DISTANCE TEACHER TRAINING

Cost analysis is often an important part of evaluating donor-funded projects, especially when linked with setting up new distance education programs. There were many studies carried out during the '70s and '80s, but since the 90s, the research focus has moved away from this important area (Oliveira & Orivel, 2003).

The development of new technologies for teaching and learning has shifted the focus onto new delivery methods, and it was possible to find many more examples of cost analyses of the use of ICT in distance education than cost analyses of print-based programs using more low-tech media.

There are five main reasons for carrying out cost analyses within teacher education (Oliveira & Orivel, 2003):

- to understand how much different courses cost
- to improve the efficiency of courses
- to establish cost-recovery strategies to finance courses
- to analyze the cost benefit of different technologies
- to compare different forms of teacher education

This study aimed to compare different forms of teacher education in one institution.

ISSUES IN COST ANALYSIS OF DISTANCE TEACHER TRAINING PROGRAMS

While there is a substantial literature *describing* African distance teacher training programs, it is difficult to find detailed cost-analysis information for programs in Africa. Many commentators refer to the need for both *more* research in costing distance teacher training and for more robust methodology to be used (Perraton & Potashnik, 1997; Robinson & Latchem, 2003). Perraton (2000) points out that "we have a modest number of cost studies that use a standard approach and a larger number of partial accounts which are often methodologically less rigorous."

Studies of cost-efficiency are sought after by education managers who are trying to make decisions about choices between different modes of delivery or between different teaching media. Such studies are complex and costly in terms of time and expertise if they are to be done with a high degree of reliability and validity.

Key sources were MUSTER (1999–2002), which analyzed five countries, including Ghana, Lesotho, Malawi, and South Africa (with Trinidad and Tobago); MITEP in Uganda; NTI in Nigeria; and ZINTEC in Zimbabwe. Meta-analyses have been carried out by Perraton (1993, 2000), Moon and Robinson (2003), Creed (2001), and Nielsen (1996).

There are nine main issues that emerged from the literature:

1. Economies of Scale

One of the defining characteristics of distance education is the opportunity for economies of scale. This feature is related to the relationship between fixed and variable costs and the concept of marginal cost (Rumble, 1997). Distance education tends to have higher fixed costs and lower variable costs than conventional education (Creed, 2001; Perraton, 1993). This means that the start-up costs may be high (for developing distance learning materials), but as more students follow the program, the unit costs decrease. In conventional education, with higher variable costs, any appreciable increase in students necessitates more teachers, classrooms, and other infrastructure.

Perraton (1993) specifies the importance of economies of scale. This is borne out by the studies in Uganda such as MITEP, which had small student numbers, estimated at 900 (Robinson & Murphy, 1996). The later NITEP with 2,750 students, showed much lower unit costs (Perraton, 2000). In Nigeria, where there were 20,000 teachers in the program, researchers concluded that the operating costs of the program were "relatively low."

The pilot distance training program at KIE was very small—just 500 students—and this indeed affected the findings in terms of unit costs. To understand the implication of this, we need to consider the marginal costs.

A marginal cost is the cost of providing one more unit of the product or service, i.e., in this case, of adding one more student to the program. For example:

If the distance education student cohort was increased by one, the marginal cost would be only the cost of printing one more set of materials and the marking of one more examination script. The fixed costs of the program would not be affected. This could also be true of conventional programs. Increasing the number of students by a small amount would probably not have any effect on the costs.

However, if the distance training program cohort was doubled (studying the same subjects), the marginal costs are still relatively small—500 sets of materials, 500 more exam scripts, plus student travel and accommodation. Existing student-support staff and facilities could accommodate the increase in student numbers. These marginal increases are even less if there is a smaller component of face-to-face tuition than currently provided in the distance training program.

If the cohort on the preservice program was doubled, KIE would need to expand the infrastructure of the college to provide more classrooms and laboratories, more student accommodation, double the government bursaries, increase capacity in the library, computer labs, etc. A considerable increase in teaching staff and some support staff would be needed if teacher-student ratios were not to increase to an unacceptable level.

The difference in the balance of the variable/marginal costs between the two modes of delivery means that if the number of students on the distance training program were significantly *increased*, then the cost per student would *decrease* substantially. This is not true for the campus-based preservice program.

2. Cost Sharing

Cost sharing does not essentially change the total costs of the program, as all costs should be included in the calculation, regardless of who bears those costs (Perraton, 1993). However, if these costs are donor or Ministry funded, it is easier to account for them than if they are paid by students.

Most distance teacher training programs are fully funded, either by government or donors. At KIE, it was a condition of the donors, DFID, that there should be no costs to the students participating in the distance training program. KIE managers felt some cost sharing would be more appropriate and assist in making the program sustainable after the end of the funding. The distance education program was fully funded at MITEP, which was also donor funded by DFID. In other programs, student contributions may include travel and accommodation costs to attend contact sessions, textbooks, and stationery.

We calculated that the cost of travel and accommodation for weekend tutorials and residential sessions was approximately 10% of the whole program. Therefore, the government could expect up to a 10% decrease in its costs if each student was required to make a contribution to cover these items. There is also an argument that people who pay something—however small—for their DE program, feel they are investing in their education and have a greater incentive to continue.

3. Equality of Entry Requirements

Ideally, comparative cost analyses should compare two different forms of delivery with two student groups who have the same profile, but this does not usually happen. Distance education students tend to be older, live in more rural areas, be working, and have a very different profile from students on conventional programs (Perraton, 2000). The MITEP researchers found that entry requirements were lowered for the distance training program, which they believe adversely affected the exam results (Robinson et al., 1995).

At KIE, there is a very different student profile on the distance training program, compared with the preservice program. One key issue at KIE was that many of the preservice students did not wish to be teachers, but KIE was their only option for higher education. There were important differences in the student profiles of the in-service and preservice programs. The distance training program learner profile indicated that the KIE distance students tend to

- be older
- have family commitments
- be working full time
- have lower educational qualifications
- have not studied for many years
- be fully committed to the teaching profession

These differences are important in terms of costing in the extent to which they impact on student drop out and final destination of the preservice graduates. Anecdotal evidence from KIE lecturers suggested that a high proportion of preservice graduates were unlikely to enter the teaching profession. A quantitative survey of the second-year preservice cohort was carried out to establish the validity of this assertion. The survey indicated that more than 40% of the cohort was likely *not* to enter teaching when they graduate from KIE. If the number of preservice graduates taking up employment as teachers is decreased by 40%, the unit cost *per graduate* increases by 40%.

4. The Cost of Staff Training

When distance teacher training programs are donor funded, there is usually a high element of technical advice, training, and capacity building costed into project funds. Creed (2001) makes the assumption that this raises the quality of the work. Researchers have dealt with this differently, but it is not always stated explicitly if training costs have been included or excluded. The MUSTER team, when analysing the costs in Malawi and Ghana, excluded all these costs. In the MITEP research, Robinson and Murphy (1996) included the costs of the long-term technical adviser to the program.

In the KIE Distance Training Office, staff received formal training inputs for 25% of their time in the first 2 years. In addition to this, there was a long-term Distance Teacher Education Adviser. All staff-development activities were covered by DFID funds. In this survey, the long-term adviser and all staff-development funds were excluded.

The costs of training in the comparative costing between the two programs were not included because it was felt that the considerable costs of initial training would not be required again and would therefore skew the cost analysis.

5. The Difficulties of Obtaining Accurate Cost Information from Ministries of Education

One recurring theme in the literature is the difficulty in obtaining financial information from ministries and institutions. Financial systems are sometimes not rigorous enough to produce valid data on program costs.

Aderinoye (2002) reports problems of identifying appropriate financial data due to the lack of comprehensive audited financial records for the National Teachers' Institute in Nigeria.

Rwanda is in the early stages of rebuilding the nation after the genocide. A total breakdown of civil society was suffered, with massive loss of human resource. Considerable advances have been made in building capacity and the development of new systems and procedures for delivering the educational goals of the government. With the assistance of donors such as DFID,

World Bank (2001), and others, development targets are being set and reached. However, in many areas there is still some distance to go, and Administration and Finance is one such area. Improvements are being made in record keeping, budgeting, and financial modeling in order to provide the information needed for assessment of levels of development.

It proved difficult, for instance, to identify the current range of salaries for qualified and unqualified teachers. Figures were available from MINEDUC, but due to recent decentralization, it was difficult to obtain a complete set of salary information for all teaching categories.

6. The Effects of Student Drop Out

If high numbers of students drop out of teacher training programs or do not join the teaching profession after graduation, there is a cost implication. Perraton (1993) notes that drop out for fully-funded distance teacher training programs tend to be low in most countries, and we found this to be the case at KIE. There was a 6% drop out on the KIE preservice program and 5% drop out on the distance training program.

Student drop out is related to the issue of economies of scale. Distance teacher training programs usually have high completion rates. High student motivation, because of expected promotion and job security, means high completion rates and favorable comparative costs per graduate (Perraton, 2000). However, Bako and Rumble (1993) found very high drop-out rates at NTI in Nigeria. This was interesting because there was a penalty for not upgrading their professional qualification, which was loss of job, because the Nigeria Certificate of Education became the minimum qualification for primary-school teachers.

One can assume that most in-service teachers will remain in the profession, but it is important to establish how many preservice graduates will eventually become teachers. The number of students who do not graduate will impact upon the unit costs.

Another issue is, should the funds spent so far on dropouts be included in the unit costs? If the numbers are small, this is probably not necessary. At the NTI in Nigeria, where there was a high drop-out rate, data was analyzed to see which year students dropped out and then costs so far on these students added to remaining unit costs (Bako & Rumble, 1993) .

7. Cost Implications for Government

When costing in-service teacher education programs, an important part of the equation is the increase in the government teachers' salary bill when large numbers of unqualified teachers graduate and become eligible for pay increases (Creed, 2001). A related question is: What would be the cost of taking the in-service teachers out of schools in order to teach them full time? What would be the cost of replacing them?

There were two important implications for the Rwandan government in terms of costs:

1. The increase in the government teachers' salary bill once 500 teachers gain diplomas through the distance training program. Qualified teachers earn more than unqualified teachers.
2. If all teacher training in Rwanda was full-time, campus-based, what would be the cost of taking in-service teachers out of schools in order to teach them full time? What would be the cost of replacing them in the classroom during their studies? This figure would need to be factored into the cost of producing a graduate on the campus-based program.

It was possible to calculate the actual costs of these two scenarios, but it was beyond the scope of this survey to analyze the impact upon the teachers' salary budget.

8. The Effects of Working in Different Currencies

This is a broad issue in costing activity. Several researchers note the difficulty of making cost comparisons between programs in different countries (Perraton, 1993; Lewin, 1999). Studies vary in their methodology for working in local currency or US dollars. A difficulty encountered in this cost study was the effect of the falling rate of exchange between the Rwandan franc (FRW) and the British pound.

It is difficult to budget effectively when funds are allocated in one currency (pounds sterling) and spent in another (Rwandan francs). In addition to this, a good deal of major procurement (vehicles, computer and science equipment) is in a third currency (US dollars). From the point of view of the operational budget of the program, currency fluctuations were beneficial, as the overall DFID budget allocation to KIE did not change, but the continuously weakening Rwandan franc over the 4-year period meant that the program could buy more with the funds provided.

The cost analysis was carried out in the local currency—Rwandan franc—which makes it difficult to compare findings with similar cost analyses carried out in different currencies. Some researchers convert local currencies to the US dollar for comparison purposes, although Rumble (1997) points out that this is a potential source of distortion, because the value of the dollar moves against other currencies. For comparative costing, Rumble suggests using a proxy such as the efficiency ratio, where the ratio of the DE costs divided by the face-to-face costs in one country is compared with a similar ratio in another country.

9. Materials Development as Capital Cost

The final issue relates to whether the inclusion of, often high, materials-development costs should be removed from the calculation of program costs and only materials reproduction be included. The MUSTER survey of MIITEP in Malawi removed these costs (Kunje & Lewin, 2000). Robinson & Murphy (1996) included them in their analysis of costs in MITEP, Uganda.

We must also ask if the distance training materials are used in the preservice program in any way. In most institutions, distance materials are available either in the library or for purchase by full-time students.

This survey included the cost of materials development, because the materials are the main form of teaching in distance education, and it was felt that they should therefore be included in the overall evaluation of cost. It would not be acceptable to exclude lecturers' salaries from a cost analysis of conventional education. The cost of the materials was annualized over their expected life.

This issue is related to economies of scale because if materials-development costs are included, and there are few students, then the unit costs will be high. But if the same materials are used for some years for subsequent cohorts, then the unit costs start to decrease. This is one of the main economic benefits of distance education.

In addition to this, the distance training materials were in high demand within the preservice program. Lecturers reported using the modules for teaching, and a complete set was kept in the library for preservice-student reference. It was not possible to analyze the cost of this sharing of resources.

These are nine important issues for any researcher embarking upon a cost analysis—especially a comparative analysis—of distance teaching programs.

COSTING METHODOLOGY

It is important for any analyst to have a clear idea about the purpose of the costing exercise (Rumble, 1997). Researchers have used different models for calculating the costs of distance education programs. Many African case studies quoted their use of Orivel's methodology (1987) for calculating the costs of distance teacher training programs such as Robinson et al. (1995) in Uganda and Bako and Rumble (1993) in Nigeria.

Orivel identified 4 stages of cost analysis:

1. Identification and measurement of costs
2. Separation of capital costs from recurrent costs
3. Separation of variable costs from fixed costs
4. Analysis of cost function—the relationship between costs and the number of students— which allows estimation of total, average, and marginal cost

Robinson & Murphy (1996) took this model further and expanded it to 7 stages:

1. Identify all direct costs and annualize capital costs
2. Identify all hidden costs
3. Distinguish fixed from variable costs
4. Analyze costs and determine costs for particular outcomes
5. Repeat these steps for conventional teachers college
6. Compare costs between the two programs
7. Observe

Having found Orivel's model useful, and agreeing with the refinement suggested by Robinson and Murphy (1996), we set out to use the refined model as the principal methodology. However, it proved not to be possible to follow the model exactly, as difficulties in obtaining information caused further adaptations to be made to this methodology.

Calculating the Costs of the Programs

When it came to calculating the costs of the preservice program, it became clear that it was not possible to follow the chosen methodology, because the required level of financial detail was simply not available for the relevant period. Therefore, the methodology was adapted to fit in with the financial information available.

1. Identify all income to KIE from government and donors per annum from 1999–2003
2. Identify the costs relating directly to teacher training.
3. Subtract the costs of all salaries and accommodation related to the distance training program.

4. Identify the number of students for each year of the preservice program.
5. Divide the total income each year by the number of preservice students registered that year to calculate the unit cost per year. Add all the yearly unit costs together to give a total unit cost per preservice student over the 5 years of the program.
6. Take the costs of only 3 years (2001–2003) of the preservice program, which would be equivalent to the distance education Diploma.
7. Compare this with the known costs of the inservice students for the 4-year period of their distance diploma. The costs of the distance teacher training program were known because they were all covered by DFID, and all budget and expenditure information was available. For the distance program, we were able to follow Orivel's model.

This methodology is somewhat unconventional, but it was the most reliable method that could be devised in order to reach a sensible unit cost for KIE preservice students, based on the information available to the researcher. The detail of the cost analysis will not be given here, only the findings.

WHAT DID WE FIND?

A summary of the unit costs calculated for each program are given in Tables 20.1 and 20.2.

In gross terms, the cost of an in-service diploma student studying for 4 years at a distance was 81% of the cost of a preservice diploma student studying for 3 years on campus. On the face of the findings, it would appear

TABLE 20.1 Unit Costs for the KIE Campus-Based Teacher Training Program

Year	KIE budget	+ Buildings cost/year	/Student numbers	Unit cost (FRW)
2001	854,192,000	107,160,000	889	1,081,386
2002	1,677,098,531	107,160,000	1229	1,451,797
2003	1,895,457,711	107,160,000	1671	1,198,454
Total				3,731,637

TABLE 20.2 Unit Costs for the KIE Distance Teacher Training Program

Year	Total cost	/Student Numbers	Unit cost (FRW)
2001–2004	1,435,012,024	474	3,027,451

that the distance training program is cheaper than the preservice program by nearly 20%. This figure was broadly confirmed by a subsequent study of the comparative costs of the two programs carried out by Rumble in 2005.

Because we believe that a high proportion of preservice students will not enter the teaching profession, the cost of producing a qualified teacher is actually much higher on the campus-based program. Taking this variable into account means the unit cost of producing a qualified teacher through distance education drops to nearer 50% of the cost of a campus-based graduate. However, this says more about the selection procedures for the preservice program than the costs of campus-based program delivery.

When the effects of economies of scale were taken into account, it was seen that a 100% increase in the size of the distance cohort would result in a *decrease* in distance training program-unit costs to about 16% of the cost of the conventional program.

CONCLUSIONS

The gross comparative figures showed that the unit costs were lower for distance training than for the conventional program by nearly 20%. If the projections for drop out of the preservice program were taken into account and the potential benefits of economies of scale were realized, then the distance training program would be even more efficient.

This study has borne out most of the claims made for distance teacher training identified in the literature review.

- The distance program can train teachers at a lower cost that is between one-third and two-thirds of conventional teacher training programs, as claimed by Perraton (1993).
- The cost of the conventional teacher training program in Rwanda is relatively high, in line with costs generally for higher education.
- The student profile for the distance training program is different from that of the preservice program.
- Drop out is not high in the distance training program. The lower number of preservice graduates who join the teaching profession will have an adverse effect on the unit costs of the preservice program.
- Distance and conventional education programs have different mixes of capital and recurrent expenditure.
- The distance education program has lower fixed and higher variable costs than the conventional program.
- The distance education program has lower marginal costs than the conventional program.

- Cost sharing would reduce the costs to government for distance student travel and accommodation. This is in line with recent GoR legislation.
- The distance training program will benefit from economies of scale.

The study concluded that, all other elements of the program being equivalent, the distance training program produces qualified teachers at a lower cost than the campus-based preservice program.

NOTE

1. The work on which this chapter is based was undertaken as part of the Rwandan Education Sector Support Program, funded by DFID and managed by CfBT Education Trust. However, any opinions expressed are those of the author and not necessarily of the Rwandan Ministry of Education, CfBT or DFID.

REFERENCES

Aderinoye, R. (2002) *An alternative route to primary teacher qualifications, Nigeria.* Unpublished case study, IRFOL.

Akyeampong, K,. Furlong, D., & Lewin, K. (2000) *The costs and financing of teacher education in Ghana.* (MUSTER Research Rep. No. 18) University of Sussex, England.

Akyeampong, K., Ampiah, J., Fletcher, J., Kutor, N., & Sokpe, B., (2000). Learning to Teach in Ghana: an evaluation of curriculum delivery. MUSTER Discussion Paper No 17, Centre for International Education, University of Sussex.

Bako, C., & Rumble, G. (1993). *The National Teachers' Institute, Nigeria.* In H. Perraton *Distance education for teacher training* (chap. 7). New York: Routledge.

Chale, E. M. (1993) *Tanzania's distance teaching program.* In H. Perraton (Ed.), (1993) *Distance education for teacher training* (chap. 2). London: Routledge.

Chivore, B. R. S. (1992). *Pre-service teacher education at a distance: The case of Zimbabwe.* In P. Murphy and A. Zhiri, *Distance education in anglophone Africa* (chap. 8). The World Bank.

Creed, C. (2001). *The use of distance education for teachers.* International Research Foundation for Open Learning, Cambridge, UK.

Dodds, T., & Youngman, F.(1994). Distance education in Botswana: Progress and prospects. *Journal of Distance Education/Revue de l'enseignement a distance, 9*(1). Retrieved December 3, 2008, from http://cade.athabascau. ca/vol9. 1/ dodds-youngman. html

Drique, G., & Wassenhove, G. (2000) *Setting up a system for distance training for secondary school teachers in Rwanda.* UNESCO, Kigali.

Gatawa, B. (1990). The Zimbabwe integrated teacher education course. In B. Koul, and J. Jenkins (1990) *Distance education: A spectrum of case studies.* London: Kogan Page.

Hawkridge, D., Kinyanjui, P., Nkinyangi, J., & Orivel, F. (1982). In-service teacher education in Kenya. In H. Perraton (Ed.), *Alternative routes to formal education* (pp. 173–213). Baltimore, MD: Johns Hopkins University Press.

Kunje, D., & Lewin, K. (2000). *The costs and financing of teacher education in Malawi.* (MUSTER Research Rep. No. 2). University of Sussex, UK.

Lewin, K. (1999). *Counting the cost of teacher education: Cost and quality issues.* (MUSTER Research Rep. No. 1) University of Sussex, UK.

Mahlck, L., & Temu E. (1989). *Distance versus college trained primary school teachers: A case study from Tanzania.* Research report No. 75. Paris: International Institute for Educational Planning.

Moon, R., & Robinson, B. (2003). Open and distance learning for initial teacher training. In B. Robinson and C. Latchem (Eds.), *Teacher education through ODL: World review of distance education and open learning* (chap. 4, vol. 3). London: RoutledgeFalmer.

Murphy, P., & Curran, C. (1992). Distance education at the second level & for teacher education in six African countries. In P. Murphy and A. Zhiri, *Distance education in anglophone Africa* (chap. 3). World Bank.

MUSTER. (1999–2000). Multi-Site Teacher Education Research Project (MUSTER). Retrieved December 3, 2008, from http://www.sussex.ac.uk/education/1-4-30-8.html

Neilsen, H. D. (1996, October 21–25) *Evaluative research on the quality of primary teacher training through distance education.* Paper for Asian Development Bank regional seminar on Capacity Building in Distance Education for Training of Primary School Teachers, Bangkok.

Orivel, F. (1987). *Analysing costs in distance education systems: A methodological approach* (mimeo) Dijon, France: IREDU, Université di Bourgogne.

Oliveira, J. B., & Orivel, F. (2003). *The costs of distance education for training teachers.* In B. Robinson and C. Latchem (Eds.), *Teacher education through ODL: World review of distance education and open learning.* London: RoutledgeFalmer.

Perraton, H. (2000). *Open and distance learning in the developing world.* London: Routledge.

Perraton, H. (1993). *Distance education for teacher training.* New York: Routledge.

Perraton, H., & Potashnik, M. (1997). *Teacher education at a distance.* Education and Technology series, 2(2) 1997. World Bank.

Perraton, H., Creed, C., & Robinson, B. (2002) *Teacher education guidelines: Using open and distance learning.* Paris: UNESCO.

Robinson B., & Murphy P., (October 1996), *Upgrading the qualifications of serving primary teachers using distance education in Uganda: A comparative study of costs and effectiveness.* Penultimate Draft (Unpublished)

Robinson, B., Tuwangye, E., Serugga, S., & Pennells, J. (1995). *Report of an evaluation of Mubende integrated teacher education project (MITEP).* Uganda IEC & Action Aid-Uganda.

Robinson, B., & Latchem, C. (Eds.) (2003). Teacher education through ODL. *World Review of Distance Education and Open Learning, 3.* London: RoutledgeFalmer.

Rumble, G. (1997). *The costs and economics of open and distance learning.* London: Kogan Page.

Rumble, G. (2005). *Consultancy to assist Kigali Institute of Education to plan for the sustainability of the inservice distance training program.* RESSP Report.

World Bank (2001). *Teacher qualifications and pay in 2001.* From draft Country Report.

Young, M., Perraton, H., Jenkins, J., & Dodds, T. (1991) *Distance teaching for the third world* (2nd ed.). International Extension College.

CHAPTER 21

BECKONING E-LEARNERS THROUGH EXPLORATION OF COMPUTER TECHNOLOGY

Pier Angeli Junor Clarke

A sense of daring is badly needed in any plan of strategy for the way forward and bolder futures-oriented strategic thinking and planning might provide that sense of daring

—Hickling-Hudson, 2000, p. 230; Nettleford, 1997, p. 93

INTRODUCTION

In this chapter, the journey of a group of preservice secondary-school mathematics (PSSM) teachers in an English-speaking Caribbean setting is provided to demonstrate how computer-technology integration served as a vehicle to e-learning. Despite the many challenges they face, the PSSM teachers were willing to pursue in their quest for the knowledge and benefits e-learning had to offer to them and their students.

E-learning is increasingly shaping the current borderless world. Some of its main concerns are to foster collaborative learning and improve teaching methods. In terms of access, e-learning is universally recognized as a

Bridging the Knowledge Divide, pages 375–389
Copyright © 2009 by Information Age Publishing

useful proposition for overcoming many barriers imposed by distance and time in educational institutions. Among other features, e-learning is characteristic of gaining access to education and training anywhere or anytime (synchronous and asynchronous). This form of educational technology can facilitate learning to many underserved communities; enables flexibility in integrating learner's schedules; permits the integration of geographically dispersed learners into a single virtual learning community; and the use of geographically dispersed human resources (Mallalieu, 2004).

The reality of the effects of this mode of learning nationally in the Caribbean is a bit far-fetched and sometimes thought of as something to happen in the far-future years. But as Nettleford (1997) stated, "a sense of daring is badly needed in any plan of strategy for the way forward" and bolder futures-oriented strategic thinking and planning might provide that sense of daring (Hickling-Hudson, 2000, p. 230). In the context of the Caribbean, we have to think and think fast about the holistic approach needed for such a transformation to take place before it is placed upon many of us. Currently, there is that "daringness" to continue where various projects such as the Caribbean Association for Distance and Open Learning (CARADOL); E-Link Americas in the Caribbean, which is linked with Caribbean Knowledge and Learning Network (CKLN); and Caribbean Universities Project for Integrated Distance Education in association with UNESCO (CUPIDE) (Marshall, 2003), just to name a few, are focusing. Collectively, these projects have intentions to develop a learning society in the Caribbean through 1) providing low-cost connectivity and bandwidth, 2) contributing to the developmental goals of the region through equity and access to quality education, and 3) advocating for and facilitating the use of Open Distance Learning as a means of transforming education to the concept of "Lifelong Learning." With this approach, there should be some caution of the challenges of such transformation (Carr-Chellman, 2005). In this chapter, I will provide the perspectives of a group of five preservice mathematics teachers from a Caribbean setting, followed by a discussion of a "way forward" for the local context and the region.

In the research study (Junor, 2003), a group of preservice secondary-school mathematics (PSSM) teachers were engaged in developing activities and implementing the use of computer technology (CT) in their mathematics instructional practices in a Caribbean setting. The intent was for them to be aware and have some experience of the challenges and benefits of technology integration in developing and/or enhancing mathematical concepts and thinking. The outcome was for them to provide their perception of the integration of computer technology in their instructional practices. Their focus was mainly on affordable classroom technology and using the Internet. Through the Web Knowledge Forum [WebKF], a Web site that serves as a communication facility, the PSSM teachers were able to share their experiences with one another in synchronous and asynchronous discussions. The Web site offered that enabled students. As part of a technology-application course, the PSSM teachers were provided with hands-on experience of the hand-held graphing calculator TI-83+; a computer software program, Math Trek 789 (7, 8 and 9 are the grades of middle and high schools; in the Caribbean' these grades are in secondary school), and WebKF. The PSSM teachers conducted discussions in WebKF. They modeled the synchronous environment while in class after some of their activities. This was to give them the feel for such an environment if they were to access the WebKF from another place but at the same time of day. These teachers also continued or began new discussions after class in an asynchronous environment on WebKF, where they voiced their experiences of challenges and successes and responded to each other in their own time and space. Outlined below, in the *context,* is a description of the Caribbean region within where the study was conducted. Next, *prior experiences of CT integration in the Caribbean,* and the *cultural adaptation* that was extended in the study for a meaningful experience are discussed. Finally, highlights of the *e-learning experience* of the study are presented prior to *advantages and challenges for the e-learning environment* in the Caribbean region.

CONTEXT

> Bounded on the south by the coasts of Columbia and Venezuela, on the west by the Central American Republics and on the north and east by the Gulf of Mexico and the Atlantic Ocean, the Caribbean countries form an island chain ... The Caribbean countries fall naturally into related groups according to their former dependence upon Britain, the Netherlands, France, or upon the United States. (Morris & Thomas, 1980, p. 7)

The English-speaking Caribbean, referred to as the "Commonwealth" Caribbean, and formerly British-owned, comprises Antigua, the Bahamas, Barbados, Belize, the British Virgin Islands, the Cayman Islands, Dominica, Grenada, Jamaica, Monserrat, St. Kitts-Nevis-Anguilla, St. Lucia, St. Vincent, Trinidad and Tobago, and the Turks and Caicos Islands. These Caribbean countries are now self–governing and independent, but collectively with support from the University of the West Indies (UWI), they are also autonomous with respect to the provision of formal education for the common region (Morris & Thomas, 1980).

Development of education in the Caribbean has been an ongoing challenge given the fact that the annual per capita income is below the equivalent of $2,000 USD for most of the independent countries, except for Trinidad and Tobago and the Bahamas (Stromquist & Monkman, 2000). Additionally, most Caribbean governments do not have the resources to fund significant new developments in the education system. However, higher education at the end of the 20th century has taken the first steps to respond to the challenges of globalization (Stromquist & Monkman, 2000). In search of making sense of what is conducive and can be adapted in the Caribbean, researchers have been investigating and implementing different strategies to include the Caribbean in the global change. Though in retrospect, it is not intentional to prepare Caribbean educators for the global market, but rather to prepare them to develop their students for the global community in which they live and to be able to benefit from ICT in their own countries as part of their development and connection with global economies (Carr-Chellman, 2005, p. 201).

PRIOR EXPERIENCES OF CT INTEGRATION IN THE CARIBBEAN

The prior experiences of CT integration in the Caribbean have highlighted many interesting lessons for future implementations of any type of technology. These experiences should not be discarded, but serve as references to improve on future implementations for the development of the Caribbean. In Africa, Latin America, the Caribbean, and most of Asia, where people are capable of greater substantial improvements in their income level, there is need to consider the new educational technologies that are available in order to meet the enormous educational challenges they face (Heyneman, 1990). Among the new educational technologies, politicians and decision makers identified computers as becoming the most favored piece of technology. Computers could be used to deal creatively with major deficiencies of educational systems in developing countries, or even aimed at the needs of individual students that cannot be adequately met by conventional means (Oliveira, 1989). Computers have unleashed a whole new way of thinking about teaching and learning. It can no longer be a question of whether school systems will make increased use of technology, but rather it is knowing *when, how,* and to *what extent* its use could be adopted in education within developing countries (Fine, 1991). In an attempt to understand the current situation of the Caribbean, a discussion of their past experiences in efforts to implement or integrate computer technology is important.

Most governments justify their need for computers with the greatest emphasis on the *vocational rationale.* The vocational rationale is addressed when students are given courses allowing them to gain substantial knowledge of computer usage, skills in programming, and program applications. This would enable them to function adequately as professional workers in the society and thereby support economic development (Hawkridge, Jaworski, & McMahon, 1990; Rock, Glick, & Sprout, 1991). Other governments (such as Jamaica as well as Trinidad and Tobago) who desired to follow the pedagogical rationale became frustrated because the British origins of their curricula clashed with U.S. origins of the software and hardware they used (Hawkridge et al., 1990).

In Barbados, the Ministry of Education did not provide funds to train the teachers in several secondary schools where networks were placed, nor in the schools that had obtained computers through a corporate donation. There were schools where funds were raised to buy additional equipment; however, they suffered from a severe shortage of suitable software (Hawkridge et al., 1990). This government had pursued a British-type curriculum, but had mainly purchased U.S. machines. In mathematics, where the origin of the software would not have mattered, Barbados could have utilized the software better than they did. By focusing on subject areas at that time, the teachers resorted to teaching programming as a subject rather than trying to use the computers across the curriculum (Hawkridge et al., 1990). Many developing countries, including those in the Caribbean, paid a horrendous price for unsuccessful CT integration, mainly due to 1) senior officials' insufficient knowledge to make policy decisions, 2) teachers receiving little or no training and support, and 3) the advisory committees lacking suitable expertise.

The integration or adoption of computers into the educational curriculum should not merely be used as a teaching aid but as a defining technological tool that would bring about major changes in the delivery of instruction and in the role of teachers (Oliveira, 1989). More recently, Reid (2002) has also cautioned that all technology must be assessed and should not to be used simply because it is fashionable, but rather for its suitability to the skills, resources, culture, and economy of a country, and the region as a whole. Carrington (1993) and Oliveira (1989) supported the use of all four major rationales because of their significant effects in areas requiring scientific reasoning or abstract skills. Accordingly, the integration of computers into such subjects as mathematics, sciences, and other areas requiring higher-order intellectual skills would make a major contribution to developing countries (Carrington, 1993; Oliveira, 1989). This approach does not only pertain to developing countries, but also to the global community.

A number of problems, such as the high cost and unreliability of equipment; low quality of software; deficient or inadequate telecommunications; a lack of funding, staffing, and planning; and poor definition of goals, have plagued developing countries. In particular, the governments of Barbados, Jamaica, and Trinidad and Tobago have indicated that their earlier attempts were deficient and that incompatibility of software and hardware, lack of training, and frustration due to the constraints were the major reasons for their lack of success (Hawkridge et al., 1990). Nevertheless, acquiring high technology remains a favorite goal in order for a new reality to take shape. Decision makers became more knowledgeable about the potentials of various technologies in education; educators and decision makers were better able to determine the kinds of educational and other pressing problems that could be best solved with the use of CT (Oliveira, 1989).

It is rewarding and inspiring to hear of the developments in the developing countries, and since these countries lag significantly behind the developed world in terms of technological progress, they could benefit from appropriately applying the solutions of problems solved in other countries of similar constraints. However, prior to the delivery of training, it is recommended that a needs assessment be conducted to assist decision makers in determining who gets what type of training and how it should be provided. Hazari (1992) argued that when technology in education was properly introduced, and the rationale for its use was clearly stated, it was appreciated and used with enthusiasm. According to Hawkridge and McMahon (1992), training all staff, including the policymakers, when introducing computers into Third World schools is a very important component of a successful CT implementation.

When U.S.-developed *computer-assisted instruction* (CAI) in Grenada, it was observed to be beneficial to students from English-speaking countries, even when those students had vastly different cultural and linguistic experiences relative to a typical student in the US(Royer, Greene, & Anzalone, 1994). A few significant outcomes and suggestions were noted: 1) systematic training of school personnel prior to student interaction with the system did involve a more positive and thorough approach in the integration; 2) support was needed to address the behavior of students who "adopted the strategy of randomly selecting response choices until they found one that allowed them to move on" (p. 59); and 3) a group of teachers from a target country would need to take note of any problems with the lessons and provide materials modified by a native speaker of the country, particularly with regard to the language and specific icons.

Out of a partnership among the government, the private sector, and the secondary-school communities aimed to improve the quality of secondary education through the use of CAI, particularly in English and mathematics, Miller (1996) identified a few strengths and weaknesses. He recommended some lessons that ought to be learned, such as 1) imaginative, bold, and committed leadership at all levels is the most critical ingredient of fundamental change in the education system; 2) in the paradigm of partnership, all partners have different priorities and agendas from those set out in the policy prescriptions and priorities of governments and international donors; 3) the organizational, logistical, and technical problems faced by Third World countries in using information technology in their school systems to expand access and improve quality are probably best worked out on an individual basis than by long-term central planning; 4) in the absence of state authority and government policy direction, the vested interests of the partners to reform are brought to the fore in a more transparent and forthright manner than otherwise may have been the case; 5) where professional bodies, the private sector, and communities take the lead in reform, the state is not only made almost invisible, but its role and substantial contribution is grossly underestimated; and 6) high value placed on education by communities is more advantageous to schooling than the possession of greater resources (Miller, 1996).

The documentations of these efforts do provide a platform for future developments knowing the strengths and weaknesses of the rationales and implementation process. However, most developing countries that have made attempts to integrate CT into their education systems realized those attempts were poorly planned and initiated by their desire to be included in the global professional community, and designed to bridge the technological gap in fear of being left behind (Oliveira, 1990; Sadowsky, 1993). These experiences, though they were costly and unsuccessful, have provided information to educators as well as policy and decision makers, which hopefully have been useful in the current and future innovations of CT and ICT or e-learning.

THE CULTURAL ADAPTATION

Learning was greatly shaped by the environment, and in e-learning, the cultural influence should be taken into consideration when designing any activities/programs in schools. The theory of constructivist learning (von Glasersfeld, 1995) underscores the fact that culture plays a fundamental role in the learning process. Students construct knowledge based on their own mental categories, such that, new knowledge is added into a network of already existing relationships with which the learner associates. The social context becomes a facilitator and scaffold for the e-learning environment (Henning & Westhuizen, 2003). The design of the teaching model adapts to what the learners want; and those goals of the learners will largely determine what is being learned (Savery & Duffy, 1995).

The PSSM teachers in the study were mathematics majors who had computer options in their program. For the purpose of the research and to assist in designing their hands-on activities, it was important to conduct a needs assessment for the targeted community of PSSM teachers (Hazari, 1992) in the application of CT. The results of the needs assessment survey indicated that the PSSM teachers 1) were on average in the 20–30 years age group; 2) had not used mathematical software before, though they were all computer literate; 3) did not work cooperatively often; 4) never used a Web database for learning; and 5) were motivated to learn to use and implement the mathematical software. The culture of this small group lent itself to the innovation with which they were challenged. This enabled me to adapt and design the professional-development sessions to meet the cultural needs of the PSSM teachers (learners) so they could maximize the benefits. For example, early in the sessions with sharing the CT tools like the computers and calculators, it was important to gradually have the PSSM teachers learn how to share the tools facing the reality of their local situation of limited resources and at the same time have the potential to maximize the benefits of using the tool. Within this environment, the PSSM teachers, placed in cooperative learning groups, used WebKF in an asynchronous environment. By localizing the use of computer technology and e-learning within their community and social context, I observed what was important to guide their communication. Sharing was a critical issue, though they knew theoretically of cooperative learning groups and how it should work, but not using this teaching and learning strategy frequently caused some challenges in forming groups and working with a limited number of CT tools. Those challenges were used as teachable moments because teachers will be faced with similar issues in their own classrooms. Designing the sessions to begin communication in class, then to continue in WebKF, was employed to encourage the comfort of sharing their thoughts with each other and in groups. The total effect of this adaptation could not be measured meaningfully since there were other barriers for continued access to the computer lab at the institution.

E-LEARNING EXPERIENCE OF THE PSSM TEACHERS

In particular, the PSSM teachers' experiences in the e-learning context are the focus. Experiences using the Web Knowledge Forum (WebKF) database (housed in Toronto, Canada) varied among the PSSM teachers. They found WebKF to be user-friendly and required less technical manipulations because it was easily accessible through the Web. They were making comparisons with the use of the graphing calculators and the mathematics software. One PSSM teacher found WebKF to be a forum where he could share his classroom experiences and acquire knowledge from his peers, which confirms to the findings of Pugalee and Robinson (1998). They stated that teachers, who have interest, utility beliefs, attitudes, skills, training, and access or a combination of some of these factors, are usually more inclined to initially try CT as well as explore its capabilities over time. The study was not designed for the teachers to use WebKF with their students in their practicum, but utilizing this medium provided them with hands-on experience and awareness of such existing tools and its benefit for discussion in a synchronous environment.

In addition, they had the privilege to continue using the database asynchronously, but there was a minimal number of contributions, which was mainly a result of 1) the limited schedule to access computers, 2) limited number of computers with access to the Internet at the teacher education institution, and 3) limited personal computers and accessibility to the Internet in their out-of-class experience. From the study, the transition of improvement over time was the comment of one participant:

> Logging on to WebKF was at first a tedious task. Sometimes an error was made in the address and much time had to be spent trying to locate the error. This became very frustrating and time-consuming. As time went by, however, the task of going into WebKF became much easier. Now I am much more comfortable logging on to WebKF. Although I have to constantly be reminded of the address, I am better able to manipulate the system. (WebKF contribution)

The benefits proved to have outweighed other tasks within the process, according to another participant:

> Computing though possessing numerous plusses has never failed to fizz me. Not that I do not take its best intent at heart. It can, however, become a drag on the illiterate. Logging on to WebKF, for instance, has proven itself to be a very tedious task. The URL is by far too long for comfort. This would call for an excellent memory or too much on-and-off eye movement. I suppose, though, that all this can be ignored for the sake of the benefits that are available [with its use]. (WebKF contribution)

NCTM–Principles and Standards (2000) gives a base in the usage of technology to increase the standard of instructional programs dealing with mathematical concepts. A response among a PSSM teacher was

> Yvette, I have read your comments on the NCTM–Principles and Standards, and I am curious to know whether or not you were really able to form links between what you learned in kindergarten and what you learned in later years. To be frank, I do not think my teachers did a very good job in allowing me to form links between simple principles, which I would need to move on to more complex topics. I think too much time was spent trying to complete a syllabus rather than ensuring that concepts were properly grasped. (WebKF contribution)

The NCTM–Principles and Standards could be used in a number of ways in the view of another PSSM teacher:

> NCTM–Principles and Standards are very beneficial to Mathematics teachers, as they are being provided with information that they can relate to and even improve on their prior knowledge in a particular content area. Not only does

it serve as a tool for Mathematics teachers, but it can also be very useful to teacher educators and staff developers to use in examining and improving the quality of mathematics instructional programs.

As a Mathematics teacher in training, I find that the implementation of NTCM was a wonderful idea, as I can now refer to its principles and standards when I am planning my lessons, among other things. (WebKF contribution)

These comments from the PSSM teachers indicate that their experiences on WebKF and what was required of them through the Principles and Standards of the National Council of Teachers of Mathematics (NCTM) did arouse their interest and made them aware of how the NCTM is aligned with the teaching and learning of secondary mathematics. They appreciated the technology principle, and it was actually a "buy in" for them to get acquainted with and actively engaged in learning and teaching using technology tools. They found the database WebKF to be useful in providing them the opportunity to share their classroom experiences and also acquire much knowledge from their peers. They also realized that there is much more for them to learn in order to be successful in the global market, and it seemed to motivate them to get involved in the change process of using CT and e-learning. The use of e-learning, in not only mathematics but also all subject areas, is becoming more of an integral part of teacher-education programs in developed countries. The benefits are evident, especially in teacher preparation and higher-education programs in disseminating information and conducting various synchronous and asynchronous discourses.

The opportunity to use WebKF in allowing the PSSM teachers to have knowledge of the richness of each others' teaching and learning experiences as well as the challenges encountered that need attention for future uses was noteworthy. One of the purposes of providing this experience for the PSSM teachers could not be said simpler than what Blume (1991) suggested in his study: that teachers would translate their own encounters that were facilitated by their instructor in a technology [-rich] environment into similar encounters for their students. In time, these teachers can become advocates of technology activities in their classrooms.

Currently, there are more ICT tools to bring about these changes. Courses are designed for learners to collaborate on content knowledge and pedagogical content knowledge. Online synchronous and asynchronous environments are now competitive and more affordable. Changes in telecommunication infrastructure, such as the upgrading of phone lines from copper to fiber-optic cables, and satellite technology, are now accessible (Schreiber & Berge, 1999), which allows developing countries, including those in the Caribbean, to implement ICT innovations more effectively. However, the challenge for the Caribbean remains one of financial support for innovations in both secondary and tertiary levels of the educational systems. In spite of the challenges, current projects are persistently trying to develop their desired goal of a learning society in the Caribbean through their collective expertise.

Lessons Learned

As was stated in the study, there was cultural accommodation in designing the activities in which the PSSM teachers participated. Meeting the PSSM teachers at their comfort level was important for us in moving forward together in their development or enhancement of technology literacy. The professional development designed for these teachers was adapted to use the limited resources of TI-83+ and Software Math Trek 789 placed on a limited number of computers (for the lack of sufficient computers for each PSSM teacher), and lack of Internet access on every computer at the institution. Other challenges were in gaining access after class to participate on WebKF. There were limitations on scheduled computer time at the computer lab of the institution. In addition, some of the PSSM teachers did not have their own computers and/or Internet access. However, what they did possess was the willingness to learn with and about the technology afforded at the time. They suggested that the key factors in the reform efforts of technology integration were 1) more technology resources available for the teachers and learners, 2) human support for the efforts, and 3) training for the human support in the local context.

Reflections of the PSSM Teachers' Challenges and Concerns

This study, being one of few that explored a Caribbean perspective, has provided evidence that a Caribbean setting has faced many similar challenges of developed and developing countries when new qualified teachers attempted to apply new technologies. The above recommendations from the PSSM teachers are directly aligned with the experiences of earlier researchers in developed and developing countries. They were motivated to explore the use of CT in their student teaching instructional practices. These new teachers were willing to take risks in exploring with new ideas, teaching and learning strategies, and new technologies. However, the lack of resources, support from principals and other faculty, technical support, and environments that are conducive for teaching and learning during teacher preparation are seen to be prohibitive to the appropriate integration of CT. To encourage new teachers to continue the path to an effective teaching career in the reform of mathematics education in the Caribbean, policymakers need to review the availability, accessibility, and pedagogy of computer technology in the mathematics curriculum.

These teachers' interests were piqued after the integration of CT in mathematics classroom instruction. It was encouraging to observe the motivation they continued to hold with the intent to remain in this learning mode and to be committed to their personal growth. Subsequently, ongoing professional development became a collaborative theme among the teacher educators from the USA (developed country) and the Caribbean setting (developing country), whose PSSM teachers participated in the study. Moving forward with the motivation to use e-learning to facilitate our continued collaboration, uLearn (similar to WebKF), a Web conferencing environment, will be used to create an environment for professional development. The teacher educators from both developed and the Caribbean context of the study are collaborating to bring about desired changes in their programs. Through the use of uLearn, cohorts of new PSSM teachers will be provided with the opportunity to reflect critically on their instructional practices in the urban (inner city) and suburban environments. The scenario of getting the PSSM teachers to be engaged in the e-learning environment was timely because of their interest in learning about computer technology for their classrooms. However, there are many factors to be mindful of as we reflect on possible advantages and disadvantages that e-learning can create for both contexts.

ADVANTAGES AND CHALLENGES FOR THE E-LEARNING ENVIRONMENT

Teacher educators of the Caribbean have to continue seeking beyond the borders of their own local communities and continue to nurture a vibrant relationship so they can help each other. With strength, the Caribbean can collaborate with other developed countries in innovations that benefit both contexts. E-learning/online education could be financed for our low income/poor students and, in particular, incentives toward local educators to build culturally relevant online education to empower their local students (Carr-Chellman, 2005, p. 11).

The plan for utilizing an e-learning environment as a vehicle to continue building and sustaining a professional learning community in both contexts of the developed country and Caribbean might be considered daring and challenging. However, what we do have existing as a community is the willingness and commitment to each other. What we do need is the financial, human, and technical support for this environment. In our learning community, we have allies from both contexts that help tremendously with the cultural adaptations when there is need to address it. Built into this collaborative is the understanding that we are building for sustainability of each context. Each context has the online capabilities, but as a group of mathematics educators, we will be building our teacher-education programs through the collaborative support of each other. Funding has been sought to support the initial face-to-face professional development. Here again, we are depending on funding to kick this project off the ground. These are real challenges and, as Carr-Chellman stated in her work, it is one of the realities of many of the poorer communities, and I would not exclude those in the developing countries, including those in the Caribbean.

Another challenge is the lack of opportunity for the poor/have-nots to participate in e-learning environments/online education/CT integration in the lower grades to improve their knowledge of the content and technology. Further, with the power to control the technological products and services away from the poorer communities, the digital divide and social gap will continue to widen and be distinct respectively. That is, no means to an end and the vision about "No Child Left Behind" will become "[y]our child left behind."

CONCLUSION

The study showed that the use of CT with meaningful application within PSSM teachers' discipline had some influence on the use of the e-Learning tool, despite their early challenges with its use. However, from the biographic data depicting their high academic records, it can be concluded that the teachers' academic acquisition in technologies is not only initiated by their aptitude but rather is indicative of the knowledge imparted and gained during their exploration. The mixed mode of delivery was operational in this study, and so we cannot dismiss the influence of interactions between face-to-face and e-learning environments. This provided a space for this small group of learners to begin to recognize the social qualities of effective group work. The lessons learned demonstrated that teachers are willing to explore the uses of affordable technologies to enjoy the benefits and learn about the challenges. However, they are requesting similar conditions that their counterparts in developed settings do want; such as support, training, and an adequate amount of training for their local context. Drawing from this small group of PSSM teachers, further inquiry is initiated through collaboration with teacher educators in this Caribbean context. In this initiative, professional development will be provided to a cohort of teacher educators who have constantly reviewed the use of educational technologies and the e-learning environment to adapt them to their local context.

It is intended to build the human resources for the implementation and to sustain the initiative beyond the life of the project.

REFERENCES

Blume, G. W. (1991). Preparing mathematics teachers to use computers: Shifting the focus from teaching to learning. *Education, 8*(4), 538–541.

Carrington, E. W. (1993). *The future of education in the Caribbean.* Report of the CARI-COM Advisory Task Force on Education. Evaluative Report. ERIC Document Reproduction Service.

Carr-Chellman, A. A. (2005). *Global perspectives on e-learning: Rhetoric and reality* (p. 201).Thousand Oaks, CA: Sage Publication.

Fine, C. (1991). *The potential of technology for urban schools.* In North Central Regional Educational Laboratory, Urban Education Network Post-conference Yearbook. North Central Regional Educational Laboratory's Tech Expo and conference, 1990. Oak Brook, IL: Author (ED 337 557).

Hawkridge, D., Jaworski, J., & McMahon, H. (1990). *Computers in third world schools.* London: Macmillan.

Hawkridge, D., & McMahon, H. (1992). Training teachers to use computers in third world schools. *Journal of Information Technology for Teacher Education, 1*(11).

Hazari, S. I. (1992). Faculty computer needs assessment in third world countries. *Journal of Educational Technology Systems, 20*(4), 321–326.

Henning, E., & Van der Westhuizen, D. (2004). Crossing the digital divide safely and trustingly: How ecologies of learning scaffold the journey. *Computers & Education, 42*(4), 333–352.

Heyneman, S. P. (1990). Economic crisis and the quality of education. *International Journal of Educational Development, 10*(2/3),115–129.

Hickling-Hudson, A. (2000). Globalization and universities in the Commonwealth Caribbean. In N. P. Stromquist and K. Monkman (Eds.), *Globalization and education: Integration and contestation across cultures* (pp. 219–236). New York: Rowman & Littlefield Publishers, Inc.

Junor, P. A. (2003). Preservice secondary school mathematics teachers exploring the integration of computer technology in their instructional practices: A Caribbean perspective. Doctoral dissertation, OISE, University of Toronto.

Mallalieu, K. I. (2004). *An e-learning strategy – Foundation block for a knowledge-based society.* Speech delivered at the Plenary Discussion Panel of the CTU's 8th Telecommunications Policy Seminar, University of the West Indies, Barbados.

Marshall, S. (2003). The Caribbean universities project for integrated distance education. *International Journal of Education and Development Using Information and Communication Technology, 1*(1),128–129.

Miller, E. (1996). *Partnership for change: Using computers to improve instruction in Jamaica's schools.* Advancing Basic Education and Literacy Project. Academy for Education Development, Washington, DC.

Morris, R. W., & Thomas, L. F. (1980). *Caribbean co-operation for curriculum development and reform in teacher training.* Paris: UNESCO.

National Council of Teachers of Mathematics (2000). *Principles & standards for school mathematics*. Reston, VA: NCTM.

Nettleford, R. (1997). The continuing battle for space—The Caribbean challenge. *Caribbean Quarterly, 43,*(1–2), 90–95.

Oliveira, J. B. A. E. (1989). Computer education in developing countries: Facing hard choices. *Education & Computing, 9*(2), 301–311.

Oliveira, J. B. A. E. (1990). Can technology advance education? *International Journal of Educational Development, 10*(4), 231–244.

Pugalee D. K., & Robinson, R. (1998). A Study of the impact of teacher training in using Internet resources for mathematics and science instruction. *Journal of Research on Computing in Education, 31*(1), 78–88.

Reid, R. B. (2002). *Challenges to Caribbean development – 2000 and beyond.* Paper presented at Comparative International Education Society (CIES, 2002).

Rock, M. T., Glick, P. J., & Sprout, R. V. (1991). A cost analysis of computer instruction in Belize. *Journal of Educational Development, 11*(1), 67–82.

Royer, J. M., Greene, B. A., & Anzalone, S. J. (1994). Can U.S. developed CAI work effectively in a developing country? *Journal of Educational Computing Research, 10*(1), 41–61.

Sadowsky, G. (1993). Network connectivity for developing countries. *Communications of the ACM, 36*(8), 42–47.

Savery, J. R., & Duffy, T. M. (1995). Problem based learning: An instructional model and its constructivist framework. *Educational Technology, 35*(5), 31–38.

Schreiber, D. A., & Berge, Z. L. (1999). Distance training: How innovative organizations are using technology to maximize learning and meet business objectives. San Francisco: Jossey-Bass.

Stromquist, N.P., & Monkman, K. (2000). *Globalization and education: Integration and contestation across cultures.* New York: Rowman & Littlefield Publishers, Inc.

von Glasersfeld, E. (1995). A constructivist approach to teaching. In L.P. Steffe and J. Gale (Eds.), *Constructivism in Education* (pp. 3–15). Hillsdale, NJ: Lawrence Erlbaum Associates.

CHAPTER 22

EDUCATIONAL TECHNOLOGY AND FLEXIBLE EDUCATION IN NIGERIA

Meeting the Need for Effective Teacher Education

**Nwachukwu Prince Ololube
and Daniel Elemchukwu Egbezor**

INTRODUCTION

Improving the quality of education through the diversification of contents and methods and promoting experimentation, innovation, the diffusion and sharing of information and best practices as well as policy dialogue are UNESCO's strategic objectives in Education.
—UNESCO, 2002

The effective use of ICTs for teacher education addresses both the problem and solution to technology-based learning, seeking synergistic results that benefit preservice teachers as they graduate and carry out their duties as

Bridging the Knowledge Divide, pages 391–413
Copyright © 2009 by Information Age Publishing
All rights of reproduction in any form reserved.

teachers. Accordingly, in order to demonstrate the above assertion, the author will be embarking on a discussion of ICT and teacher education and some factors that hinder (institutional, infrastructural, and economic problems) the uptake of educational technology and flexible education in Nigeria (see Figure 22.3). And consequently there is the need to better design teacher education curricula, infrastructure, and organization of programs so that preservice teachers can better plan for the unanticipated and unintended results that confront them in the classroom. Because ICTs play a key role as enabler to help us better manage the complex information flow and to integrate such information toward effective policy formulation and planning toward the utmost maximization of human capital and potential in society, we must develop effective and integrated tools as well as training modules to enable their application through effective teacher education agenda (Mac-Ikemenjima, 2005).

Government leaders have relied on universities to get the job done—with guidance in the form of certification tests, accreditation, and program approval (Fry et al., 2006). It is practical that despite efforts by both the federal and state government to establish valuable teacher education programs through distance learning in Nigeria to help in the preparation of effective teachers, it has a fundamental problem that has incapacitated its development. This problem has hindered the successful implementation of effective teacher education programs. For example, Yusuf's (2005a) study, which investigated teachers' self-efficacy in implementing of computer education in Nigerian secondary school found that

- Most teachers in federal-government colleges in Nigeria do not have the needed experience and competence in the use of computers either for educational or industrial purposes.
- A majority of male and female teachers in federal-government colleges do not have needed competence in basic computer operations.
- Most of the teachers in federal-government colleges do not have needed skills and knowledge in the use of common computer software.
- There was no significant difference between male and female teachers in their experience in using computers, their levels of proficiency in computer operations, and in their use of common software. This is reflected in the establishment of no statistically significant difference for 15 out of a total of 16 questionnaire items.

With the advent of the new information and communication technology (ICT) revolution, the world is witnessing an expansion in learning. This new information revolution has enabled academic institutions to provide a flexible and more open learning environment for students. The convergence of new information technologies, such as telecommunications, computers, satellites, and fiber-optic technologies, is making it easier for institutions to implement distance education (Akhahowa & Osubor, 2006). Information and communication technologies (ICTs) have become key tools and have had a revolutionary impact on how we see and live in the world. This phenomenon has given origin to our contemporary ways of life. However, this revolution is not widespread and needs to be strengthened to reach a large percentage of the population (Mac-Ikemenjima, 2005).

The pervasiveness of ICT has brought about rapid changes in technology and has caused a social, political, and global economic transformation. The field of education has also been affected by the penetrating influence of information and communication technology. Thus, ICT is having a revolutionary impact on educational methodology globally. Unquestionably, ICTs have impacted the quality and quantity of teaching, learning, and research in teacher education, which provides opportunities for student teachers, academic and nonacademic staff to communicate with one another more effectively during formal and informal teaching and learning (Yusuf, 2005b). Because of these innovations, teachers need training not only in computer literacy but also in the application of various kinds of educational software in teaching and learning; they need to learn how to integrate ICTs into their classroom activities and school structure (Ololube, 2006b, c).

The quality of teachers is known in virtually all countries to be a key predictor of student learning. Therefore, teacher training is crucial in using ICTs, because ICTs are tools that on the one hand can facilitate teacher training and on the other hand help them to take full advantage of the potential of technology to enhance student learning (UNESCO, 2003). Correspondingly, ICTs have introduced a new era in traditional methods of teaching and offering new teaching and learning experiences to both teachers and students. Hence, the Nigerian education environment should take advantage of this capability to provide easy access to information, since technologies enable the visualization of educational materials in an innovative and realistic manner. However, in a complex society like Nigeria, many factors affect ICT usage and integration (Mac-Ikemenjima, 2005). The relationship between the development of ICT usage and penetration in teacher education programs and its diffusion into the programs in Faculties of Education and Schools of Education, however, is dependent upon governmental policies (Beebe, 2004).

Contextual Environment in Nigeria

The academic landscape in Nigeria includes the teaching and learning process alongside the educational programs and courses, and the pedagogy or methodology of teaching; the research process, including dissemination and publication; libraries and information services, including higher-education administration and management (Beebe, 2004). Many higher-education institutions are not getting the job done and are in no particular hurry to redesign their programs to ensure that preservice teachers are thoroughly prepared for their role in improving curriculum, instruction, and student achievement (Fry et al., 2006).

Nigeria, like most African countries, has fared poorly on the various indices used in assessing a country's e-readiness to participate in the information age despite the abundant resources (Ifinedo & Ololube, 2007; Ifinedo, 2005b; Ifinedo & Uwadia, 2005). The reason for this is mostly attributed to corrupt practices. Nigeria has enormous economic potential. It has a vibrant private sector, highly motivated entrepreneurs, and a large domestic market. It is the seventh-largest oil exporter in the world (about 2 million barrels per day) and is richly endowed with other natural resources as well. Her natural resources are petroleum, natural gas, tin, coal, limestone, zinc, columbite, and lead. Yet in spite of these resources, her development toward meeting the millennium goal has been very slow.

According to the World Bank Report (2006), countries in Africa remain the world's biggest development challenge. More than 314 million Africans—nearly twice as many as in 1981—live on less than $1 a day. Thirty-four of the world's 48 poorest countries, and 24 of the 32 countries ranked lowest on the United Nations Development Program's Human Development Index, are in Africa, and most African countries are heavily indebted. However, 14 African countries are already relieved of 100% of their debt as agreed at the G-8 Summit in Gleneagles in 2005. This number will grow to 25 as countries reach their completion points under the Heavily Indebted Poor Country (HIPC) Debt Relief Initiative. For example, the Paris Club wrote off around $17 billion USD of Nigeria's debt (G-8 Summit in Gleneagles, 2005). Nigeria's mortality rate has been impressive since independence with an infant mortality rate 112 per 1,000 live births, and an annual number of deaths of children under age 5 of 187 per (thousands). Over 70% of the population depends on agriculture to survive. Table 22.1 illustrates a few comparative socioeconomic indicators for some African and western European countries showing their e-readiness, Nigeria inclusive.

Nigeria is bounded in the north by the Niger republic, in the east by Cameroon, in the northeast by the Chad republic, in the west by the Benin republic, and in the south by Equatorial Guinea and the Gulf of Guinea. Nigeria has an area of 923,768 sq. km., about the size of California, Nevada, and Arizona. Annual rainfall ranges from 381 cm. along the coastal region to 64cm. in the north. Nigeria has an estimated population of 128.8 million and a growth rate of 2.7%. About 60% of the population lives in the rural areas. Nigeria is made up of over 250 ethnic groups, with Hausa-Fulani,

TABLE 22.1 Socioeconomic Indicators for Selected Countries from Africa and Europe

Country	Region	Population	Literacy rate (%)	Life expectancy (years)	GDP per capita	Internet users	Electricity production (kW)
Nigeria	Africa	131,859,731[a]	68.0[b]	47.08[d]	US$ 1,400[c]	1,769,700[c]	15.59 billion[b]
Ghana	Africa	22,409,572[a]	74.8[b]	58.87[d]	US$ 2,500[c]	368,000[c]	5.356 billion[b]
Cameroon	Africa	17,340,702[a]	79.0[b]	51.16[d]	US$ 2,400[c]	167,000[c]	2.988 billion[b]
U.K.	Europe	60,609,153[a]	99.0[b]	78.54[d]	US$ 30,300[c]	37,800,000[c]	369.9 billion[b]
Finland	Europe	5,231,372[a]	100.0[c]	78.5[d]	US$ 30,900[c]	3,286,000[c]	79.94 billion[b]
Germany	Europe	82,422,299[a]	99.0[b]	78.8[d]	US$ 30,400[c]	48,722,055[c]	558.1 billion[b]

Source: CIA: The World Factbook (last updated June 13, 2006)
[a] July, 2006
[b] 2003
[c] 2000
[d] 2006
[e] 2005

Figure 22.1 Map of Nigeria. *Source:* Adapted from GraphicMaps.com, with permission.

Ibo, and Yoruba as the majorities. Nigeria consists of 36 states including the federal capital territory Abuja as the capital. Her major cities are Lagos, Port Harcourt, Kano, Enugu, Ibadan, Sokoto, Kaduna, etc. (Background notes on countries of the world, 2000). Figure 22.1 shows a map of Nigeria and her borders.

FLEXIBLE EDUCATION IN NIGERIA

The term "flexible education," known to most people in Africa as distance education, has until very recently been considered as inferior to the traditional conventional method of face-to-face education or training. However, this attitude is gradually changing as telecommunications and new educational challenges emerge. Several studies have been carried out in North America that compared traditional teaching methods with those delivered via telecommunications. Using final grades as indicators to determine outcomes, the studies revealed almost no difference in outcome; in fact, the studies often showed slightly better results from students learning via an ICT medium. Telecommunications have closed the gap between and within instructional methods; much teaching and learning now use telecommunications media to augment, extend, and enhance face-to-face meetings. Students in one institution can take courses from another institution, making the concept of distance no longer the issue (Mason, 1994).

Flexible education in this context is an approach aimed at fostering active learning through using educational technologies to improve course and program design to support learning aims to provide choices for students in terms of how, where, when, and what they study. Flexible courses or programs usually offer some combination of options, such as flexibility in the timing, pace, place, content, requirements, and methods of study.

However, diverse courses and programs may allow different forms of flexibility, depending on the context and needs of students, teachers, and the institution. In Nigeria, a distance education system is being considered as the most viable solution to the menace of satellite campuses, which were banned by the federal government. The government of Nigeria is resuscitating the National Open University of Nigeria (NOUN), which will be innovative and involving state-of-the-art teaching and learning multimedia packages. The ultimate trend to the reactivation of the National Open University of Nigeria (NOUN) is toward delivery of courses through electronic networks (Akhahowa & Osubor, 2006).

NOUN is Nigeria's leading and only specialist provider of open and distance learning at the tertiary level. It is also the country's largest tertiary institution in terms of student numbers. The National Open University of Nigeria operates from its Administrative Headquarters, located in Lagos, Nigeria, with study centers throughout the country. The pioneer student enrollment stands at 32,400. The university currently offers over 50 programs and 750 courses, from certificate to diploma and degree level, and maintains a strong commitment to internationalization. NOUN academic units are composed of four schools (Arts and Social Sciences, Science and Technology, Business and HR Management, and Education) and a center for continuing education. NOUN's expertise in program design; course development; learner-support systems; and a great spread of study centers nationwide, focusing on lifelong education and online education, make it well-suited to making excellent contributions to Nigeria's universal basic education effort and education for all program (National Open University of Nigeria, 2007). The course delivery of the Open University is through a combination of Web-based modules, textual materials, audio and video tapes as well as CD ROMs (Commonwealth of Learning International, 2001).

The School of Education came into being with the resuscitation of the National Open University of Nigeria as one of the five major academic schools/centers in 2002. The School of Education is committed to providing qualitative, functional, and cost-effective teacher education for the educational system in Nigeria, vis-à-vis

- Providing wider access to teacher education, generally in an open distant learning environment
- Providing flexible but qualitative teacher education
- Enhancing professional ethics by laying emphasis on both national and international teaching codes of conduct
- Integrating information-technology media in the provision of teacher education program

- Embarking on training and retraining of those in the teaching profession with a view to enhancing their productivity
- Providing opportunities for academic and professional growth of those in the teaching profession
- Providing programs that will produce highly motivated, conscientious, and efficient classroom teachers for all levels of educational systems
- Providing opportunities for acquisition of teacher education to the less privileged and those with special needs
- Encouraging teachers to develop the spirit of enquiry and creativity

The School of Education is mandated through the Federal Republic of Nigeria, National Policy on Education 1998, section 6b to

- Produce highly motivated, conscientious, and efficient classroom teachers for all levels of our educational system
- Encourage further the spirit of enquiry and creativity in teachers
- Help teachers to fit into the social life of the community and the society at large and enhance their commitment to national goals
- Provide teachers with the intellectual and professional background adequate for their assignment and make them adaptable to changing situations
- Enhance teachers' commitment to the teaching profession (National Open University of Nigeria 2007).

Another medium used in Nigeria to provide distance education is via the National Teachers Institute (NTI). With over 600 study centers spread across the country, along with media, particularly print and other media, and to allow individual students to learn at their pace, the institute was established to provide refresher and upgrading courses for teaching personnel; to organize workshops, seminars, and conferences; and to formulate policies and initiate programs that would lead to improvement in the quality and content of education in the country (Yusuf & Falade, 2005). In pursuit of these responsibilities, the institute initiated training and training programs for helping unqualified primary-school teachers and refresher courses in teacher training colleges. Recently, the institute also embarked on the Nigeria Certificate in Education (NCE) program through a Distance Learning System (DLS). The institute also provides training for the Pivotal Teachers Training Program (PTTP) by means of a distance learning system. The PTTP was introduced in 2002 as a means of producing teachers to fill the gap in teacher supply for the federal government's newly introduced Universal Basic Education (UNBE) program (Osunde & Omoruyi, 2004).

ICTS AND TEACHER EDUCATION

Nigeria as a nation came late and slowly into the use of ICT in all sectors of the nation's existence, especially in teacher education. This is a result of chronic limitations brought about by economic disadvantages and government policies. These factors have direct consequences on the nation's educational development. The consequences are immediate; for example, many Nigerian teachers are unable to find effective ways to use technology in their classrooms or any other aspect of their teaching and learning life. The possible explanation for this lack of success is that the use of technology in the classroom has not been encouraging and teachers are not well-trained in using ICT in teaching as a means for educational sustainability (Ololube, 2006b), notwithstanding the specifications in the National Policy on Education (Federal Government of Nigeria, 1998, 2004).

A recent study conducted by the Global Information Technology (2005) used the Networked Readiness Index (NRI), covering a total of 115 economies in 2005–2006, to measure the degree of preparation of a nation or community to participate in and benefit from ICT development. Nigeria was ranked 90th out of the 115 countries surveyed. The United States of America topped the list, followed by Singapore, Denmark, Iceland, Finland, Canada, Taiwan, Sweden, Switzerland, and the United Kingdom, and so on. Nigeria was ranked 86th out of 104 countries surveyed in 2004 (Global Information Technology, 2004). This shows a decline in Nigeria's preparedness to participate in and benefit from ICT development globally. Fundamentally, the slow access to basic ICT equipments; low Internet connectivity and computers; and inadequacies in the use of audiovisual materials and equipment, including films, slides, transparencies, projectors, globes, charts, maps, bulletin boards; plus programmed materials; information retrieval systems; and instructional television in teacher education programs are barriers to the effective and professional development of teachers in Nigeria (Ololube, 2006a, c). Therefore, administrators and trainers need to make educational technology an integral part of teaching and learning to provide a clear demonstration of how the use of instructional technology tools can address the personal and general concerns of teaching and learning in Nigeria.

Nonetheless, in recent times the integration of information and communication technologies (ICTs) in university teaching and particularly in teacher training programs has been the topic of much debate, because educational systems around the world are under increased pressure to use the new information and communication technologies (ICTs) to teach students knowledge and skills they need in the 21st century (Larose et al., 1999). Teacher education institutions are faced with the challenges of preparing a new generation of teachers to effectively use the new learning tools in their teaching practices (UNESCO, 2002). As a result, teacher education programs have not been unaffected by the penetrating influence of information and communication technology (ICT). Certainly, ICT has impacted the quality and quantity of teaching, learning, and research in traditional and distance education institutions around the world. In concrete terms, ICT literacy has enhanced teaching and learning through its dynamic, interactive, and engaging content and has provided real opportunities for individualized instruction (Newhouse, 2002a). Information and communication technology has the potential to accelerate, enrich, and deepen skills; motivate and engage students in learning; help to relate school experiences to work practices; help to create economic viability for tomorrow's workers; contribute to radical changes in school; strengthen teaching; and provide opportunities for connection between the institutions and the world. Information and communication technology can make education more efficient and productive, thereby engendering a variety of tools to enhance and facilitate teachers' professional activities (Yusuf, 2005b). To Newhouse (2002b), technology has been developed to solve problems, improve living standards, and to increase productivity. Therefore, it is reasonable that we should expect educational technology to be developed with similar objectives. Thus, educational technology should influence educational outcomes and costs. If a teacher selects the most appropriate educational technology, student learning can be optimized, which means an increase in the value of the outcomes. Within the educational context, these objectives are to increase productivity and solve problems in teaching/learning programs.

Newhouse explains educational productivity as a concept most happily found in economics textbooks, where the productivity of a worker or economic unit is defined by dividing the output (revenue) by the input (costs). This is more difficult to define for the education industry since the output is not easily measured, particularly not in monetary terms, so as to compare with the costs. Nevertheless, he defined it in the educational context by stating that output is largely the quality and quantity of learning demonstrated by students or learning outcomes (as shown in the equation below).

$$\text{Productivity} = \frac{\text{Output}}{\text{Input}} \qquad \text{Outcomes} \quad \begin{array}{l}\text{Quality and quantity of student learning.}\end{array}$$

$$= \frac{\text{Educational Outcomes}}{\text{Costs}} \qquad \text{Costs} \quad \begin{array}{l}\text{Teacher and student time, classroom materials, equipment, etc.}\end{array}$$

The concept of teachers' ICT literacy is theoretically unclear and changing in that the definition of the concept is more or less precise, depending on whether it occurs at the level of the definition of operational abilities or at other levels. Most contemporary authors tend to center the definition of ICT literacy on a few competencies or abilities, which might characterize that teacher's ability to use ICT's instructional material. However, the definition goes beyond basic competencies to include the ability to prepare and use the selection of appropriate and operation of ICT materials, and to identify and affect efficiently incorporate students' specific purposes in order to build knowledge and develop critical and creative thinking in students. Thus, teacher education and training is a means for professional updating, which deals with all developmental functions directed at the maintenance and enhancement of one's professional competence and literacy. Teachers' professional growth supports the idea that ICT in teacher education and training is an important factor in teachers' job effectiveness and development. This is so because teachers' education and training is generally considered to be essential for school effectiveness and improvement (Larose et al., 1999).

It was argued (Creemers, 1994) that teachers who are bent on improving their competence are likely to contribute directly or indirectly to the growth of student's achievement. Similarly, studies concerning staff training and education clearly demonstrated the need to offer teachers better opportunity to educate and develop themselves in order to create understanding between their job and their effectiveness (Javis, 1983; Keen, 1991; Kautto-Koivula, 1996). To make this work, teachers need effective techniques, tools, and assistance, which can help them develop ICT-based projects and activities specially designed to raise the level of teaching in required subjects and to be able to improve student learning and academic achievement (Aduwa-Ogiegbaen & Iyamu, 2005). Realistically, the inclusion of ICT materials in secondary schools is not valuable if teachers are not conversant with the traditional teachings necessary for adequate and effective teaching involvement. It then follows that teachers should initially be trained and developed professionally to be able to assist students in their ICT material-utilization competencies (Ololube, 2006a).

On the other hand, Larose et al. (1999) argue that regardless of the quality of ICT equipment available to teachers in the school environment and independently of the quantities of courses that they have taken during their undergraduate studies, the level of transfer of acquired competencies and learning to practice is very weak. However, the major impact of education on the educated remains at the level of the "private" use of these technologies and not in their integration into daily teaching practices. Larose and colleagues further pointed out that many of the educated, no matter the level of education, have minimal computer literacy but do not use it in their pedagogy because of the fear that the rapidity of obsolescence of the hardware and of the software will make their task more complex and interminable. They supplementarily asserted that other writers explain this trend by pointing to the low level of computer literacy of student teachers at the time of their insertion in preservice education. However, Newhouse (2002b) has identified the impacts of the use of ICT on students; learning environments; teachers and pedagogy; schools' provision of ICT capacity; and school and system organization, policy, and practice. Newhouse presented these in five dimensions:

- Students (ICT Capability, Engagement, Achievement of Learning Outcomes)
- Learning-Environment's Attributes (Learner-centered, Knowledge-centered, Assessment-centered, Community-centered)
- Teacher Professional ICT Attributes (Vision & Contribution, Integration & Use, Capabilities & Feelings)
- School ICT Capacity (Hardware, Connectivity, Software, Technical Support, Digital Resource Materials)
- School Environment (Leadership & Planning, Curriculum Organization, Curriculum Support, Community Connections, Accountability)

The relationships of these dimensions to each other are represented in Figure 22.2.

PROBLEMS OF ICTS AND DISTANCE EDUCATION IN NIGERIA

Despite the eagerness of institutions of higher learning to establish distance education programs, they are confronted with enormous problems that may impede proper implementation. The greatest of these problems is poor ICT penetration and usage among Nigerian distance education practitioners. Almost all African countries' basic ICT infrastructures are inadequate; this is a result of lack of electricity to power the ICT materials, poor telecommunication facilities, poor postal systems, and lack of access to the needed infrastructures because of insufficient funds due to Nigeria spending less than 12% of its annual budget on education in general.

Institutional Problems

Another basic problem that teacher education programs in Nigeria face is how to address the issue of technology. The goal of educational technology in teacher education programs is to provide as complete an education as possible to preservice teachers. ICT knowledge and skills are essential for today's student teachers. Educational technology allows students to stay current with computer and telecommunications technology. However, this

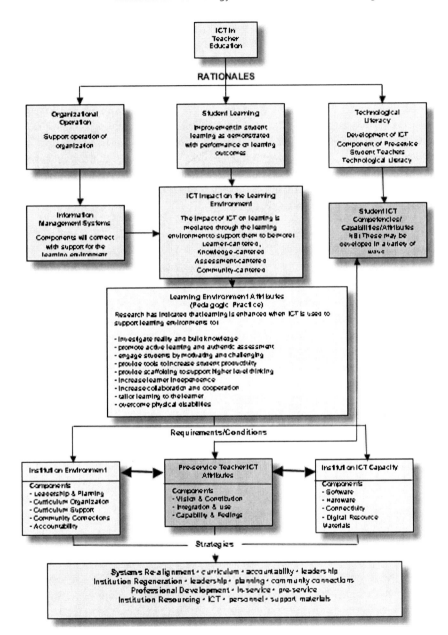

Figure 22.2 Schematic diagram representing the relationships between the dimensions of impact of ICT in teacher education. *Source:* Adapted from Newhouse (2002b, p. 4) with permission, but modified by the researcher to suit the purpose of this study.

is impossible as there are limited efforts that support the integration of ICTs in the unique teacher education programs in Nigeria. Fundamentally, there are limited or no programs that students can use to develop their perception as well as conception of ICTs. As a result, students lack words to address all the contemporary terminology that is used in describing educational technology (Ololube, 2006a, b). It is also evident that policymakers, administrators, and faculty members in developing countries lack the necessary expertise to manage new innovation, including the implementation and delivery of ICT-enabled education (Mac-Ikemenjima, 2005). In general, culture and social attitude/anxiety are also major constraints; Nigerians, like other Africans, do not have a mechanistic view of the world (Ifinedo, 2005a, b; Ifinedo & Ololube, 2007).

Infrastructural Problems

In terms of a range of ICT indicators, African countries score lower than the global average; in other words, the gaps between African and other developed countries and emerging economies persist; indeed, they have intensified over the last decade, indicative of a growing digital divide (Gillwald, 2005). The term "digital divide" is used to refer to such differing standards or imbalances between countries fully poised to reap the benefits of the information age and those that are unable to do so (Ifinedo, 2005a). The growing digital divide includes both ICT products and outputs (Internet access, e-mail, fax, television, radio, cell phones, etc.) and inputs (engineers, scientists, etc.), and this divide could make other developmental gaps impossible to bridge. For example, in a survey of 10 African countries, Botswana has the highest fixed-line household penetration at 22.4%, followed closely by South Africa at 22.1%. Zambia is next at 18.6%, with Namibia at 14%. Tanzania has a fixed-line penetration of 6.1%, Ethiopia just over 5% and Rwanda 4.4%. Uganda trails far behind the rest, with penetration under 1% (Gillwald & Esselaar, 2005). Basically, African countries tend not to have the same infrastructural facilities and support as the developed West, which are prerequisites for the new order (Ifinedo, 2005b). According to Yusuf (2006), successful distance education cannot be assured without the use of communication and technological tools (e-mail, fax, Internet, television, radio, etc.). Several cities and rural areas in Nigeria are yet to have electricity or have fluctuations in its supply. Additionally, most Nigerians (82%) do not have access to telephones and other telecommunication facilities. Even telephone lines in the urban centers are not adequate to serve the teeming population. Services for those who have access are in most cases epileptic. These may make the integration of telecommunications in the delivery of distance education difficult. In addition, the poor state of telephone communications has led to an increase in dial-up cost for most Nigerians. Even with the introduction of GSM in August 2001, access is still limited, services are yet to be perfect, and service charges make GSM unattractive for distant learners.

Economic Problems

The poor economic situations and their effects on middle-level manpower stand as the major obstacle in the implementation of ICTs in distance education. Over 85% of the population live below poverty level. An average middle-income earner cannot afford basic technological and communication gadgets. Thus, computer-related telecommunication facilities might not be useful for most Nigerians, as computers are still a luxury in institutions, offices, and homes. The cost of computer-related gadgets in Nigeria is three times the monthly wage of an average worker. The cost of subscribing to a telephone line or owning one is beyond the reach of an average Nigerian citizen. The same is true for the procurement of Internet access in Nigeria; ordinary citizens find it difficult to own such services. This has made the integration of necessary online resources (e-mail, newsgroups, World Wide Web, etc.) into distance education in Nigeria most difficult. Nigeria spends less than 12% of its annual budget on education in general and even far less on ICT in particular due to insufficient funds. This is for the most part compounded by illiteracy, which, incidentally, is widespread in the country; thus, about 33% of the population is unable to read and write according to *CIA: The World Factbook* (2006).

Figure 22.3   Some factors affecting successful implementation of distance education.

DISCUSSION

The quality and quantity of ICT materials in our universities are poor, since the teachers trained through these programs are not well enough equipped technologically to be able to face the challenges of carrying out their duties effectively, that is, meeting the global transformations in science and technologies. It demonstrates that the existing curriculum designed for the training of preservice teachers in Nigeria does not include the practical usage of ICT material such as computers and their software, slides, overhead projectors, etc. Even if it is included, it is only based on theoretical paradigms. Student teachers hardly come in contact with ICT instructional materials, including those who are in the department of educational technology proper. Besides, the institutions responsible for the provision of teacher education programs provide programs within the confines of the mandate given to them by the federal and state governments through various bodies that coordinate their activitie, like the National Commission for Colleges of Education (NCCE), National Universities Commission (NUC), and the National Board for Vocational Colleges and Technical Education (NABTECH). However, their ability to be effective is dependent for the most part on the availability of funds to be able to purchase the needed ICT equipment.

As previously noted, Nigeria is poor and indebted. The dire economic situation for both the country and its population exacerbate its inability to make use of ICT products, especially those related to educational initiatives (Ololube, 2006b). The cost of a PC in Nigeria is three times the monthly wage of an average worker. The cost of subscribing to or owning a telephone line is beyond the reach of an average citizen. The same is true for the procurement of Internet access; ordinary citizens find it difficult to own such services. In the same vein, the Nigerian educational sector is constrained by a lack of funding (Ololube, 2006a, b; Yusuf, 2006). Thus, it is not uncommon to read that limited financial resources have stalled some notable ICT-enabled initiatives in the Nigerian educational sector (Bolaniran & Ademola, 2004; Ifinedo & Uwadia, 2005; Ifinedo & Ololube, 2007). The issue of scarce resources in Nigeria harks back to the unfavorable contextual socioeconomic situation in the country. Notably, huge sums are spent serving foreign debts.

Further, Nigeria lacks qualified information technology (IT) professionals; this is so because Nigerian universities do not graduate enough skilled IT professionals to match their current ICT needs (Ifinedo, 2005a; Ifinedo & Ololube, 2007). Oyebisi and Agboola (2003) note that the highest enrollment in the University for Science and Technology in Nigeria between 1991 and 1998 was 0.31 per 1000 and only 0.05 per 1000 students earned a postgraduate degree in the field. Additionally, the human-capital problems in Nigeria are compounded by illiteracy, which is rife in the country; i.e., about 32% of the population is unable to read and write (CIA: World Factbook, 2006; Ifinedo 2005b; Ifinedo & Ololube 2007). Effective organizational skills are needed to maintain the vision of delivering effective teacher education using ICT (Commonwealth of Learning International, 2001; Ololube, 2006b). The reality is that institutional leadership in developing countries lacks the necessary expertise to manage new innovation, including the implementation and delivery of ICT-enabled education (Mac-Ikemenjima, 2005).

In the same way, Yusuf's (2005a) study found that most teachers in Nigeria do not have the necessary experience and competence in the use of computers either for educational or industrial purposes. Neither do they have the necessary competence in basic computer operations, skills, and knowledge in the use of common computer software. Yusuf concluded that there was no significant difference between male and female teachers in their experience in using computers, their levels of proficiency in computer operations, and their use of common software. Furthermore, computer education introduced in Nigerian secondary schools since 1988 has largely been unsuccessful as a result of teachers' incompetence, because empirical studies (e.g., Yusuf, 2005b) recognized that teachers' ability and willingness to use ICT and integrate it into their teaching is largely dependent on the quality of professional ICT development they receive. Thus, they have been unable to find effective ways to use technology in their classrooms or any other aspect of their teaching and learning life (Ololube, 2006a, b).

CONCLUSION AND RECOMMENDATIONS

Social, economic, and technological changes in the past decades are making education and training more crucial than ever. Yet, educational systems to different degrees worldwide are struggling to afford educational opportunities for all, to provide their graduates with the necessary knowledge and skills for evolving marketplaces and sophisticated living environments, and to prepare citizens for lifelong learning. To meet these challenges, countries have to focus concurrently on expanding access, improving internal efficiency, promoting the quality of teaching and learning, and improving system management (Haddad & Jurich, [n.d]). Accordingly, quality education is regarded as the main instrument for the social, political, and economic development of a nation. Thus, the strength, security, and well-being of Nigeria rest squarely on the quality of education provided for its citizens. Education has therefore continued to be a great asset to many, as well as a steady source of manpower for the national economy, especially in the West, where education is seen and accepted as an effective instrument for success. Therefore, it is essential that we recognize that teachers are indispensable for successful learning about ICTs and learning and teaching through ICTs to improve the standard of education in Nigeria. In the same vein, Newhouse (2002b) made clear that a good balance between discovery learning and personal exploration on one hand, and systematic instruction and guidance on the other characterizes a powerful ICT learning environment.

African universities and high schools have been confronted with numerous changes in their external and internal environments. They are forced to respond to emerging challenges such as continual developments in ICT in recent years to meet their educational needs. The rapid decline in educational standards is evident due to crumbling infrastructure, an unpredictable academic calendar, flight of researchers and professionals abroad, and the declining respect for its graduates across the globe. Providing access to quality education for every student in the universities is a significant task that must be accomplished so that they can reach their potential. Therefore, African universities must follow the prevailing trend in most parts of the world by applying new technologies to overhaul and enhance their educational materials and resources. Though these universities and high schools are confronted with critical challenges to meet the new demands of ever-increasing student growth, they lack expansion in terms of educational resources to accommodate the increasing number of students. For that reason, they need educational environments that make them more responsive to the challenges. One way to provide access to educational necessities is electronic learning, which helps to provide students with the opportunity to have access to available experts, best resources, and up-to-date information. E-learning is fast becoming an accepted and indispensable part of the mainstream of educational systems, especially in the developed world (Akhahowa & Osubor, 2006).

However, there is hope for Nigeria ICT and flexible-education improvement following China's launch of a communications satellite for Nigeria, a first for an African country and the first time China has provided both the satellite and the launch service. The Nigerian Communication Satellite (NIGCOMSAT-1) is a superhybrid geostationary satellite that will provide communications services for Africa, parts of the Middle East, and southern Europe. Experts estimate that the satellite will revolutionize telecommunications, broadcasting, and broadband multimedia services in Africa. They say it will help create thousand of new jobs and IT professionals for Nigerians and provide Internet access to remote villages. It is also expected to improve e-commerce and government efficiency by promoting the development of the digital economy in Nigeria and the rest of the African continent.

Finally, though, educational technology and flexible education are beginning to play a major role in the future of teacher education agendas in Nigeria. The evidence points to the fact that the emerging new technologies show that the teaching profession is evolving from emphasis on teacher-centered and lecture-centered instruction to student-centered interactive learning environments (Newhouse, 2002a, b; UNESCO, 2002). Therefore, designing and implementing successful ICT-enabled teacher education programs is the key to fundamental, wide-ranging educational reforms. Consequently, teacher education institutions in Nigeria should either assume a leadership role in the transformation of education or be left behind in the swirl of rapid technological changes. Accordingly, for Nigerian education to reap the full benefits of ICTs in learning, it is essential that preservice and in-service teachers are able to effectively use these tools for learning. Teacher education institutions and programs must provide the leadership for preservice and in-service teachers and model the new pedagogies and tools for learning through effective strategic plan. That is, leadership in higher education should be visionary about conceiving a desired future state, which includes the picturing of where and what the teacher education program should be in the future, without being constrained by such factors as funding and resources, and then working backward to develop action plans to get to the desired point.

However, a successful and effective strategic plan depends on the extent to which proper implementation and monitoring are carried out. This is heavily vested on the government, which must ensure that all parts of the country receive telecommunication services: the rural parts ought not to be neglected. In short, universal access should be encouraged, and certain sections and parts of the society should not be sidelined. The Nigerian telecommunications sector needs more investments. Ongoing activities and efforts in this area have helped to improve the teledensity rates for Nigeria. There is an urgent need to increase the number of computers available to the population; access to the Internet needs to be improved for distance education to spread in the country. The Nigerian government may have to waive certain import duties and tariffs for goods and equipment imported for delivering distance education. Shortages in other infrastructural facilities, e.g., electric power generation, need to be addressed. The national policy for distance education and e-learning initiatives in the Nigerian national IT policy need to be reinvigorated. Government's commitment in this area should be unequivocal. The government should set up enabling regulatory and legal policies for distance education using ICT. Those with limited skills and knowledge may require training to enable them to reap the benefits of using ICT for and in education. More relevant technical and computing education in the country are needed. External sources of technical expertise and skills should be sought in areas where such are lagging (Ifinedo & Ololube, 2007). Thus, the schematic diagram (Figure 22.2) representing the relationships between the dimensions of impact of ICT in teacher education is a handy tool for analysis toward ICT planning and implementation in teacher education.

IMPLICATIONS

This chapter focused on the topic of educational technology and distance education and the impact on teacher education in developing countries using Nigeria as a case study. The practical implications of flexible learning in relation to teacher education are that teachers and students may need to use different methods and approaches to teaching and studying. Teachers take on new roles and may be increasingly dependant on institutions' infrastructure and support. This chapter might have made a considerable stride in the understanding of the impact of ICTs on teacher preparation toward producing a new caliber of teachers, whose professional abilities are essential in a developing economy.

REFERENCES

Aduwa-Ogiegbaen, S. E., & Iyamu, E. O. S. (2005). Using information and communication technology in secondary schools in Nigeria: Problems and prospects. *Educational Technology & Society, 8*(1), 104–112.

Akhahowa, A. E., & Osubor, V. I. (2006). E-learning: A technology-based teaching method for providing access to sustainable quality education. *The African Symposium, 6*(3&4), 17–25.

Background Notes on Countries of the World (2000). US Department of State. Retrieved April 27, 2007 from http://lcweb2.loc.gov/frd/cs/ngtoc.html

Beebe, M. A. (2004, September 1–2, 2004). *Impact of ICT revolution on the African academic landscape.* CODESRIA. Conference on Electronic Publishing and Dissemination, Dakar, Senegal. Retrieved December 3, 2008, from http://www.codesria.org/Links/conferences/el_publ/beebe.pdf

Bolaniran, A., & Ademola, O. (2004). E-Learning in Africa: Related issues and matter arising. Proceedings of the 9th World Conference on Continuing Engineering Education, Tokyo.

CIA: The World Factbook (2006). Country Report. Retrieved April 30, 2007 from https://www.cia.gov/library/publications/the-world-factbook/geos/ni.html

Commonwealth of Learning International (2001). *Building capacity to deliver distance education in Nigeria's federal university system.* Report prepared for the World Bank. Retrieved April 22, 2007 from http://siteresources.worldbank.org/NIGERIAEXTN/Resources/capacity_de.pdf

Creemers, B. P. M. (1994). Effective instruction: An empirical basis for a theory of educational effectiveness. In Reynolds et al., (Eds.), *Advances in school effectiveness research and practice*. (pp. 198–205) Willington: Elsevier Science.

Federal Republic of Nigeria (1998). National policy on education"(3rd ed.). Lagos: NERDC Press.

Federal Republic of Nigeria (2004). National policy on education (4th ed.). Lagos: NERDC Press.

Fry, B., O'Neill, K., & Bottoms, G. (2006). *Schools can't wait: Accelerating the redesign of university principal preparation programs*. Atlanta, GA: Southern Regional Education Board.

G8 Summit in Gleneagles (2005, July 8). *Chair's summary, Gleneagles summit*. Retrieved April 23, 2007 from http://www.g8.gov.uk/servlet/Front?pagename=OpenMarket/Xcelerate/ShowPage&c=Page&cid=1119518698846

Gillwald, A. (2005). *Toward an african e-index: Introduction*. Retrieved June 26, 2007 from http://www.researchictafrica.net/images/upload/Toward2.pdf

Gillwald, A. & Esselaar, S. (2005). *A comparative analysis of ICT access and usage in 10 African countries*. Retrieved June 26, 2007 from http://www.researchictafrica.net/images/upload/Chapter02new(latest).pdf

Global Information Technology Report (2004). *The networked readiness index rankings, 2004*. Retrieved July 7, 2007 from http://www.weforum.org/pdf/Global_Competitiveness_Reports/Reports/GITR_2004_2005/Networked_Readiness_Index_Rankings.pdf

Global Information Technology Report (2005). The networked readiness index rankings, 2005. Retrieved October 7, 2007 from http://www.weforum.org/pdf/Global_Competitiveness_Reports/Reports/gitr_2006/rankings.pdf

Graphic Maps (2007). *World atlas travel*. Retrieved April 21, 2007 from http://worldatlas.com/webimage/countrys/africa/ng.htm

Haddad, W. D., & Jurich, S. (n.d.). ICT for education: Potential and potency. Retrieved November 11, 2007 from http://cbdd.wsu.edu/edev/Nigeria_ToT/tr510/documents/ICTforeducation_potential.pdf

Ifinedo, P. (2005a). *E-government initiative in a developing country: Strategies and implementation in Nigeria*. Proceedings of the 26th McMaster World Congress on Electronic Business, Hamilton, Ontario, Canada.

Ifinedo, P. (2005b). Measuring Africa's e-readiness in the global networked economy: A nine-country data analysis. *International Journal of Education and Development using ICT, 1*(1), 53–71.

Ifinedo, P. & Ololube, N. P. (2007). A discourse on the problems, prospects, and progress of distance education in a developing country. In E. P. Bailey (Ed.), *Focus on distance education developments* (pp. 183–194). New York: Nova Science Publishers.

Ifinedo, P., & Uwadia, C. (2005). *Towards e-government in Nigeria: Shortcomings, successes, swish or sink*. Proceedings of the International Federation of Information Processing (IFIP) WG 9.4 Conference, Abuja, Nigeria.

Javis, P. (1983). *Professional education*. London: Croom Helm.

Kautto-Koivula, K. (1993). *Degree-oriented professional adult education in the work environment:* A case study of the mian determinants in the management of a long-term technology education process. Unpublished PhD dissertation, University of Tampere, Finland.

Kautto-Koivula, K. (1996). Degree-oriented adult education in the work environment. In P. Ruohotie and P. P. Grimmett (Eds.), *Professional growth and development: direction, delivery and dilemmas* (pp.149–188). Canada and Finland: Career Education Books.

Keen, K. (1991). Competence–What is it and how can it be developed. In Conference Proceedings of Ette Conference, 1991, (pp. 61–77).

Larose, F., David, R., Dirand , J., Karsenti, T., Vincent Grenon, V., Lafrance, S., & Judith Cantin, J. (1999). Information and communication technologies in university teaching and in teacher education: Journey in a major Québec university's reality. *Electronic Journal of Sociology.* Retrieved December 3, 2008, from http://www.sociology.org/content/vol004.003/francois.html

Mac-Ikemenjima, D. (2005, April 13–15). *E-education in Nigeria: Challenges and prospects.* Paper presented at the 8th UN ICT Task Force Meeting, Dublin, Ireland.

Mason, R. (1994). Using communication media in open and flexible learning. Oxon: RoutledgeFalmer.

National Open University of Nigeria (2007). *About NOUN.* Retrieved April 21, 2007 from http://www.nou.edu.ng/noun/

Newhouse, C. P. (2002a). *The impact of ICT on learning and teaching.* Perth, Australia: Special Educational Service.

Newhouse, C. P. (2002b). *A framework to articulate the impact of ICT on learning in schools.* Perth, Australia: Special Educational Service.

Ololube, N. P. (2005a). Benchmarking the motivational competencies of academically qualified teachers and professionally qualified teachers in Nigerian secondary schools. *The African Symposium, 5*(3), 17–37.

Ololube, N. P. (2005b). School effectiveness and quality improvement: Quality teaching in Nigerian secondary schools. *The African Symposium, 5*(4), 17–31.

Ololube N. P. (2006a). The impact of professional and non-professional teachers' ICT competencies in secondary schools in Nigeria. *Journal of Information Technology Impac*t, *6*(2), 101–118.

Ololube, N. P. (2006b). Appraising the relationship between ICT usage and integration and the standard of teacher education programs in a developing economy. *International Journal of Education and Development using ICT. 2*(33), 70–85.

Ololube, N. P. (2006c, April 19–21). *Teachers instructional material utilization competencies in secondary schools in Sub-Saharan Africa: Professional and non-professional teachers' perspective.* In conference proceedings of the 6th International Educational Technology Conference EMU, North Cyprus (pp. 1303–1314).

Osunde, A. U., & Omoruyi, F. E. O. (2004). An evaluation of the National Teachers Institute's manpower training program for teaching personnel in mid-western Nigeria. *International Education Journal, 5*(3), 405–409.

Oyebisi, T. O., & Agboola, A. A. (2003). The impact of the environment on the growth of the Nigerian IT industry. *International Journal of Information Management, 23,* 313–321.

UNESCO (2002). *Information and communication technologies in teacher education: A planning guide.* Paris: UNESCO.

UNESCO (2005). *United Nations decade of education for sustainable development 2005–2014.* Retrieved November 4, 2006 from http://portal.unesco.org/education/en/ev.php-URL_ID=27234&URL_DO=DO_TOPIC&URL_SEC-TION=201.html

World Bank Report (2006). *African development indicators report–2006.* Retrieved December 3, 2008, from http://siteresources.worldbank.org/INTSTATINAFR/Resources/ADI_2006_text.pdf

Yusuf, M. O. (2005a). An investigation into teachers' self-efficacy in implementing computer education in Nigerian secondary schools. *Meridian: A Middle School Computer Technologies Journal, 8*(2). Retrieved January 06, 2007 from http://www.ncsu.edu/meridian/sum2005/computer_ed_nigerian_schools/index.html

Yusuf, M. O. (2005b). Information and communication technologies and education: Analyzing the Nigerian national policy for information technology. *International Education Journal, 6*(3), 316–321.

Yusuf, M. O. (2006). Problems and prospects of open and distance education in Nigeria. *Turkish Online Journal of Distance Education, 7*(1), 22–29.

Yusuf, M. O., & Falade, A. A. (2005). Media in distance learning: The Nigerian National Teachers Institute distance education program. *Turkish Online Journal of Distance Education (TOJDE), 6*(4) Article 3.

CHAPTER 23

FOSTERING DIGITAL LITERACY OF PRIMARY TEACHERS IN COMMUNITY SCHOOLS

The BET K–12 Experience in Salvador de Bahia

Lorenzo Cantoni, Francesca Fanni, Isabella Rega, and Stefano Tardini

INTRODUCTION

In Brazil, the federal government's law n. 4019/2004 requested teachers to obtain a university degree in order to keep on teaching. Even if the first foreseen deadline—year 2012—has been postponed, this law has promoted an important and positive mobilization among teachers, which resulted in a significant growth in the demand for updating courses, especially for in-service teachers who do not own the required university degree and need preparatory courses for the *Vestibular* (*Pre-Vestibular* courses), i.e., the exam for accessing university. These courses usually last no longer than 12

Bridging the Knowledge Divide, pages 415–433
Copyright © 2009 by Information Age Publishing
All rights of reproduction in any form reserved.

months and are promoted either by public and private universities or by private institutions other than universities; institutions are starting to test the use of ICTs to deliver their teacher-training curricula (Marinho et al., 2004; Magalhães & Schiel, 2004; Prata Linhares et al., 2004; Modro, 2002; Bof, 2004). However, attending these courses and passing the *Vestibular* is still a big problem for teachers of disadvantaged schools because of their inadequate background; in addition, these teachers are excluded from the teacher-training programs sponsored by the federal government, because these kind of courses are only for public-school teachers.

Even if the goal of the government's decision is the improvement of teachers' preparation and, as a consequence, of the quality of the Brazilian school system, it could cause other problems, such as the closure of disadvantaged schools for the lack of graduate teachers. For this reason, the training of teachers, particularly of those who live in disadvantaged areas, is still a crucial issue for the Brazilian school system. Hence, the government decision to embark on online training programs.

The BET K–12—Brazilian eLearning Teacher Training in K–12 project aims to help primary teachers in community schools in a disadvantaged area of Salvador (State of Bahia, Brazil) to obtain the university degree by training them in the use of ICTs and in the introduction of ICTs in their teaching activities; in this way, they are also supposed to become more equipped to live and work in the knowledge society.

As a matter of fact, being able to access information and hence, knowledge, is one of the most important issues and challenges of development, both at the personal level, where it means education and employability and at the social one, where it could mean growth and welfare. To access, produce, and share information and knowledge, one has to master the technologies through which information and knowledge are "exchanged," the so-called "technologies of the word" (Ong, 2002). Nowadays, who cannot master ICTs—the most recent technologies of the word—risks to be excluded from the social life of his/her community or society by the so-called digital divide; this term is used to refer to "the inequalities that exist in Internet access based on income, age, education, race/ethnicity, and [...] between rural and metropolitan areas, through such factors as pricing and infrastructure" (Hill, 2004, p. 27).

Before describing the details of the project, a brief presentation of the Brazilian school system is needed. The Brazilian school system is divided into two main branches: *Educação Bàsica* (basic education), which encompasses *Educação Infantil* (preschool), *Ensino Fundamental* (primary education) and *Ensino Médio/Profissionalizante* (high/technical school); and *Educaçao Superior* (higher education). Higher education extends from 4 to a maximum of 6 years of studies at university level and can be followed by 18 months of postgraduate course or by a *Mestrado* of a minimum of 2 years.

The highest superior education degree is the doctorate, which lasts at least 4 years. The Brazilian school system is summarized in Figure 23.1.

In this system, an important distinction has to be made between public and private institutions. Public institutions can be managed at a federal, state, or municipal level, and are free of charge. Private schools are mostly linked to religious institutions, notably to Catholic ones, and are not free of charge, but offer quite often scholarships for disadvantaged students.

In general, at the level of *Educação Basica,* the preparation offered by public schools is lower than that offered by private schools. At the level of higher education, on the contrary, public universities are free of charge and usually better than private ones. This means that students aim to attend public universities, but the number of available places is not enough. Therefore, passing the entrance exam (*Vestibular*) is a goal that only few people can achieve; usually those who have attended a quality basic school, which very often means a private school, have more chances. On the contrary, those who have attended public basic schools may end up having an

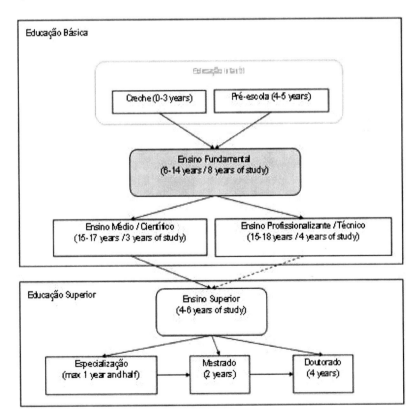

Figure 23.1   The Brazilian school system.

inadequate preparation to pass the *Vestibular*. So, underprivileged people may not be able to attend public universities because they have not the knowledge and the competencies to pass the *Vestibular* and do not have enough money to afford private university fees.

In some areas, in particular in suburbs or in rural areas, there are other kinds of schools, the so-called community schools, which have been created to compensate for the lack of public schools; community schools are managed and funded by associations of citizens. Often located in very small and not comfortable buildings, these schools have been created in order to give underprivileged children a chance at education, even if the quality of teaching is often very low, mainly because of the inadequate training of teachers.

The chapter is structured as follows: the first paragraph introduces the BET K–12 project: its roots in previous experiences of collaboration among Swiss and Brazilian researchers (1.1), its goals and design (1.2), and the group of teachers involved in the training experience (1.3). The second paragraph describes the three courses offered to them: Computer Literacy (2.1), ICTs in Educational Context (2.2), and Communication Theory (2.3). The last paragraph defines the Self-Efficacy concept (3.1), describes the constructs of Computer and Teacher Self-Efficacy (3.2), and shows the results of the project (3.3).

BET K–12 PROJECT

BET K–12 is a project managed by the NewMinE (New Media in Education) Lab of the Faculty of Communication Sciences at the University of Lugano (Switzerland), in collaboration with the CEAP – Centro de Estudos e Assessoria Pedagogica, in Salvador (Bahia, Brazil); the Swiss National Science Foundation and the Swiss Agency fund the project for Development and Cooperation. The aim of the project is to investigate the role and the impact of ICTs in the field of teacher training in Brazil.

BET K–12 BACKGROUND

The project BET K–12 is grounded in a previous collaboration between the NewMinE Lab and CEAP, which brought to the development of some e-learning courses for community school teachers to be integrated in the CEAP curriculum. The collaboration started in 2004 and was funded by a private foundation.

CEAP is a training center that addresses teachers working in community schools; it offers in-service training for primary-school teachers and supports them in the challenging goal of passing the *Vestibular* exam; for this purpose, it organizes a 3-year training curriculum. Moreover, CEAP advises and coaches community-school teachers also, once they have entered university, and continues its training activities also for teachers who have completed their university study.

NewMinE Lab was asked to design and develop some e-learning/blended learning[1] courses to be integrated into the CEAP curriculum. The benefit of introducing ICTs into the CEAP curriculum is twofold:

1. The introduction of blended learning courses answers the need of time and space flexibility. Community-school teachers attending CEAP courses usually go to the CEAP center after an 8-hour day of work in their schools; and to reach the center they undertake a journey with public transportation lasting up to 2 hours; moreover, the large majority of teachers are women who must take care of their families and children. Therefore, introducing a model of learning that helps them to spare transportation time or at least to allow them to autonomously decide when to go to the lab was a key issue for CEAP.

2. The introduction of blended courses allows teachers to be exposed, for the first time, to new technologies. The possibility of becoming skilled in using ICTs is for them an important chance to enter the so-called Knowledge Society: "Computer literacy and familiarity with the net have a major impact on people's employability in many sectors and areas; and access to the internet means an increased access to information, education and economic opportunities as well as more opportunities for communication and political participation. Not getting access to it could entail fewer chances in the same areas; in fact, as long as countries enter the so-called information society [...] access to information and the use of it become the most important competitive factors at a national and regional level, as well as at a company and individual level" (Cantoni & Tardini, 2006, p. 35).

Consequently, the NewMinE Lab designed and developed two blended-learning courses to be introduced into the CEAP curriculum:

- *ICTs in educational contexts*: Approaching three main topics: Web-site qualitative assessment, strategies to learn online, and strategies to teach online;
- *Communication Theory*: Addressing three main issues: principles of logics, principles of linguistics, and text production.

Moreover, a basic face-to-face course on *computer literacy* has been added to the CEAP curriculum to provide teachers with the necessary technical skills and knowledge to become e-learners. The setting up of this first project soon raised the urgent need of studying the impact of e-learning in primary-school teacher training in Brazil and assessing its possible applications and advantages, as well as success conditions and shortcomings; hence, the idea of BET K–12 started to grow.

Research Goals

BET–K12 wants to investigate three main issues:

- *Access to ICTs*: It deals with the technical, economic, sociological, and psychological factors influencing persons' opportunities to use the technologies;
- *Quality*: It explores the conditions under which it is possible to implement an effective and efficient e-learning program for primary teachers in disadvantaged Brazilian areas (BET K–12 includes also a phase aiming at understanding the quality of the e-learning environment and models in teacher training in Brazil);
- *Impact*: It studies the readiness of Brazilian primary teachers of community schools to use e-learning in their training and their acceptance and adoption patterns.

While this chapter focuses on the impact of ICTs on teachers' teaching and learning practices—studying the changes in computer and teacher self-efficacy and the relationships between them—BET K–12 extends its study also to the impact on other fields of their life (snowball effect), as well as the impact on the transmission of the potentialities of ICTs to their community.

Teachers Involved in the Research

The group of people who attended the above-mentioned courses was composed by 44 primary-school teachers, 43 of which were women. This reflects the Brazilian culture, where the teaching profession is historically associated with the role of women as mothers and of schools as extensions of home. The average age of the group was about 37 years; 12 teachers were over 45; the large majority of the group started teaching before 30; only 8 of them after 35. Twenty-eight teachers were working in only one community school, 10 in two schools, 2 in 3 schools, 4 in more than 3; 10 teachers who were teaching in more than one school were teaching also in a primary noncommunity school. Eight teachers (18%) declared that they earned less than the minimum wage (about RS 350, corresponding to $160

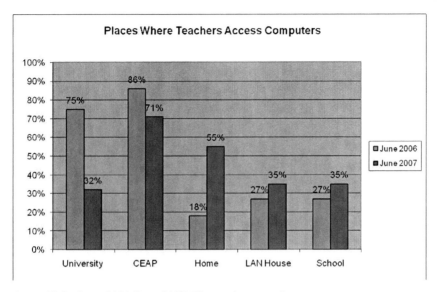

Figure 23.2   June 2006–June 2007: Places where teachers access computers.

USD); 15 earned the minimum wage, 21 more than the minimum (24%) (Rega, et al., 2006).

In the group, there were teachers who did not pass the *Vestibular* exam yet, teachers who were enrolled in a university, and teachers who had already completed their university curriculum. As concerns the teachers' possibilities of accessing ICTs, two sets of data are compared: access data in June 2006 and in June 2007 (more than one answer was allowed). Figure 23.2 presents the places where teachers could use a computer.

Two were the more striking changes that occurred in one year: the percentage of teachers using computers at the university fell from 75% in June 2006 to 32% in June 2007; this can be explained by the fact that most of the teachers were able to complete their university curriculum and obtain the diploma.

The other very encouraging datum is that the percentage of teachers owning a computer passed from 18% to 55%. Furthermore, during this period, the percentage of teachers using the computer more than once a week increased from 77% to 100%.

Figure 23.3 shows a similar trend in the possibilities of Internet access.

The percentage of teachers accessing the Internet at the university decreased from 79% to 26%, while the percentage of teachers owning a connection at home increased from 19% to 45%. Another relevant datum is that the number of teachers exploiting LAN Houses (Brazilian Internet

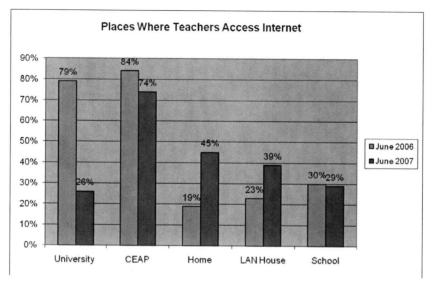

Figure 23.3 June 2006–June 2007: Places where teachers access Internet.

cafés) increased from 23% to 39%. Finally, the percentage of teachers surfing the Internet more than once a week increased from 72% to 91%.

CEAP ELEARNING COURSES

Computer Literacy
(September 2005 to September 2006)

Taking into consideration the teachers' lack of exposure to ICTs, it was decided to deliver the first course completely in person (20 hours). The contents of the course were designed adapting the ECDL (European Computer Driving License) program to the context. Course modules are presented in Table 23.1.

TABLE 23.1   Computer Literacy Course Modules

Module 1: Basic Concepts of Information Technologies
Module 2: Using the Computer and Managing Files
Module 3: Word Processing
Module 4: Spreadsheet
Module 5: Presentation
Module 6: Internet and E-mail
Module 7: Introduction to Moodle LMS

The last module, Introduction to Moodle LMS, was added because the two following courses used this learning-management system.

ICTs in Educational Context
(November 2006 to July 2007)

The course lasted 20 hours and was organized in three main sections: Qualitative Analysis of Websites, How to Learn Online, and How to Teach Online. This course was offered on Moodle in a blended modality. The contents were developed by the NewMinE Lab team in collaboration with CEAP and were localized by a student of the University of Lugano, who did a 3-month internship at CEAP. The schema in Figure 23.4 summarizes the topics of the course and its educational scenario.[2]

Participants worked in groups during the first 2 sections of the course, afterwards they developed an individual project consisting of a lesson using technologies in their school. Every week each participant had to do a short activity, such as writing comments in the course journal or participating in a forum or answering a test. These activities were developed to help participants to keep pace with the course. Furthermore, at the end of each section, a self-assessment quiz was provided. Four lessons were planned face-to-face; however, since this was their first e-learning experience, teachers could use the CEAP informatics lab in case they did not have any other place to access the Internet (online activities were, however, very limited, due to well-known access problems), and/or they wanted to be tutored by CEAP staff. The course lasted more than expected due to three main factors: holidays calendar, connectivity breakdown, added tutoring sessions.

Communication Theory
(August 2007 to December 2007)

The course—also delivered through Moodle in a blended modality—lasted 60 hours and was divided into three sections of 20 hours each: Logic and Argumentation, Language, and Text Production. This course was provided in order to offer a wider and better interpretation of the role ICTs play in the knowledge society, moving from knowing how to knowing why, hence, offering a more scientific understanding of the nature and role of the technologies of the world.

The structure of this course parallels the medieval *Trivium*, i.e., the three "roads" forming the foundation of ancient liberal arts (grammar, logic, rhetoric) (Cantoni et al., 2008). Each section of the course presented its topics in a rich multimedia way: for instance, in the first section, the main topics (Knowledge and Truth; The Elements of Thought: Concepts and

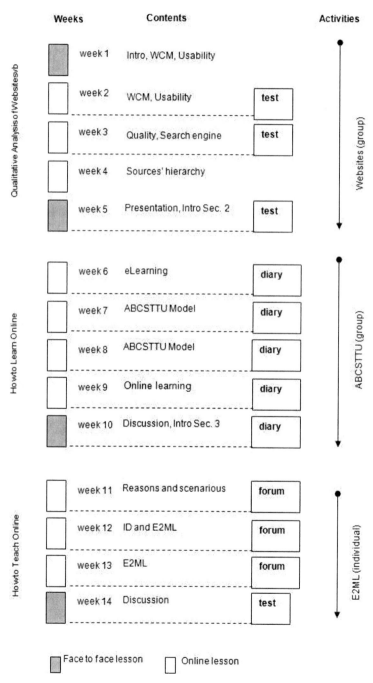

Figure 23.4 Topics and educational scenario.

Propositions; Reasoning; Argumentation) were presented by means of audio files containing simple fairy tales; teachers were required first to listen to the whole fairy tale, then to a commented version of it, where the main theoretical concepts were presented and explained. In the second section, the framework of a story contained different animations and interactive presentations where the main topics (Speech; Sign; Language; Text) were presented. In addition to these multimedia contents, each section provided online activities to be accomplished either in groups or individually, self-evaluation tests, and text files, where all the contents of the section were presented in a more detailed and structured way.

The choice of presenting rich multimedia content was made in order to satisfy the demands of teachers, who, in spite of possible technical difficulties due to low bandwidth, requested to have as little written/printable materials as possible in order to be allowed to know and exploit the multimedia features of ICTs.

COMPUTER AND TEACHER SELF-EFFICACY

A set of questionnaires was designed by the Swiss-Brazilian team in order to test the group on the following matters: the use of and exposure to ICTs, learning behaviors, teaching behaviors, and teachers' role as change agents (Rogers, 1983).

During informal interviews in July 2006, teachers stressed the fact that the greatest added value for them in attending those courses was an amount of self-esteem as persons and as teachers: the fact of having new technological competences helped them to regard themselves with more esteem, both as persons belonging to a community and as teachers. Therefore, in order to assess the impact of technologies on teachers' working activity, Bandura's Self-Efficacy model was adopted.

Defining Self-Efficacy

The concept of self-efficacy was elaborated in the frame of the Social Cognitive Theory by Albert Bandura. According to this theory, human behavior is subjected to three main influences: the personal, the behavioral, and the environmental. With the term "self-efficacy," Bandura means "people's judgment of their capabilities to organize and execute courses of action required to attain designated types of performances" (Bandura, 1995, p. 2). Self-efficacy beliefs are considered crucial to human behavior study as they influence one's feelings and thoughts, motivation processes, and the engagement in life activities.

People with a low level of self-efficacy tend to shy away from difficult tasks they consider as a threat. They usually have low aspirations and show little effort in achieving their aims. In difficult situations, they dwell on their shortcomings and obstacles. It takes time before they overcome failures, and they lose faith in their capabilities. Conversely, people with a high level of self-efficacy approach difficult tasks as a challenge, with great motivation. They set ambitious targets and fight to achieve them; they attribute failure to insufficient effort or lack of knowledge and skills and are confident that they can acquire them (Pajares, 2002).

Computer Self-Efficacy and Teacher Self-Efficacy

In BET K–12, the concept of self-efficacy has been applied to measure the impact of ICTs on the education of the primary-school teachers who attended the Computer Literacy and the ICTs in Educational Contexts courses. In particular, the concepts of Computer Self-Efficacy and Teacher Self-Efficacy were adopted to measure the self-efficacy with respect to the skills of using a computer and to teaching skills.

According to Compeau and Higgins (1995, p. 191), computer self-efficacy represents "an individual perception of his or her ability to use computers in the accomplishment of a task." In order to measure the computer self-efficacy of the teachers of the involved courses, a questionnaire was built on the basis of the one proposed by Compeau and Higgins (1995). The questionnaire contained 10 items that referred to the use of a piece of software in an educational context; for each item a Likert-scale from 1 to 10 was provided, where 1 was "not at all confident" and 10 was "totally confident." The 10 items were repeated for each one of the seven software/technologies (MS Word, MS PowerPoint, blogs, wikis, Internet search engines, e-mail, chat) teachers had learned in the Computer Literacy course.

"A Teacher's Self-efficacy belief is a judgment of his or her capabilities to bring about desired outcomes of student engagement and learning, even among those students who may be difficult or unmotivated" (Bandura, 1977). In order to measure the teacher self-efficacy, the Teacher's Sense of Efficacy Scale proposed by Tschannen-Moran and Wolfolk Hoy (2001) was used. In this scale, 12 items referred to different aspects of the teaching activity; for each question, a Likert-scale from 1 to 9 was provided, where 1 corresponded to "nothing" and 10 to "a great deal." Teachers had to answer these questions by indicating how much they felt able to accomplish given teaching activities. Questions were divided into three categories: student engagement, instructional strategies, and classroom management; for each category, four questions were provided (see Annex).

in order to measure if and how computer self-efficacy and teacher self-efficacy did change over time, the questionnaires were delivered twice during the ICTs In Educational Contexts course, namely, in the middle (March 2007) and at the end of the course (July 2007), having respectively 30 and 31 respondents. During the second delivery, teachers were asked about their perception of computer and teacher self-efficacy in regard to the beginning of the course and to the end of it (see Annex; unfortunately, it was not possible to submit the questionnaire at the very beginning of the course). Due to the fact that it had not been possible to have a control group, the designed research is a quasi-experimental one, testing the following three hypotheses:

H1: *Computer self-efficacy and teacher self-efficacy grow over time*

H2: *Their growth is significantly correlated*

H3: *Computer self-efficacy (independent variable) positively influences teacher self-efficacy (dependent variable)*

Once H1 and H2 are proved, H3 is verified, on the assumption that no other main events happened in the considered period, having a significant impact onto teacher self-efficacy of the involved group.

Results

The results of the questionnaires are presented in Figures 23.5, 23.6, and 23.7.

Figure 23.5 shows how the perception of the self-efficacy in the use of the seven studied technologies has increased during the ICTs in Educational Contexts course. As it can be seen, the self-efficacy has grown for all the technologies. However, it is worth noticing that the self-efficacy for the wiki has grown less than for the other technologies: a possible interpretation is that at the beginning of the course, teachers felt confident in using a wiki, probably because they had just learned it in the Computer Literacy course, which had just ended; but when it came to learning how to use a wiki in their teaching activity, they perceived this tool as more difficult than the others.

Figure 23.6 shows the amount of computer self-efficacy for each technology over time.

The figure shows that search engines, e-mail, and chat are the three technologies with a major amount of self-efficacy perception between the beginning and the end of the course. This is a very interesting datum, since

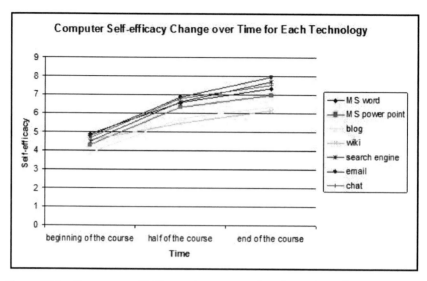

Figure 23.5 Computer self-efficacy change over time for each studied technology.

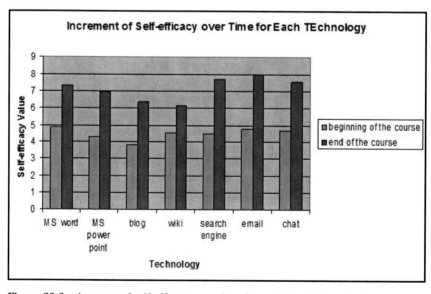

Figure 23.6 Amount of self-efficacy over time for each studied technology.

teachers already knew and often used these technologies before the course, however during the ICTs in Educational Context course they learned how to deeply master them.

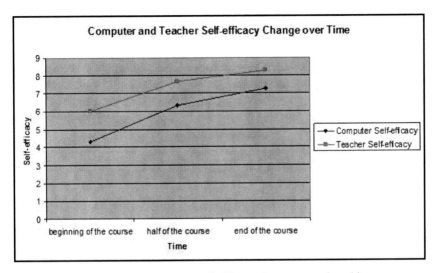

Figure 23.7 Computer and teacher self-efficacy change over time (data are normalized to a 9-grade scale).

Figure 23.7 shows that both computer and teacher self-efficacy have grown over time during the course. Not surprisingly, at the beginning of the course teacher self-efficacy was considerably higher than computer self-efficacy; at the end of the course, the difference decreased from 1.6 to 1.0. These data show that the ICT learning experience has been very useful, not only to help teachers become more confident with computers, which was the main goal of the courses, but also to help them become more confident as teachers, which is a very important effect of computer self-efficacy. As a matter of fact, performing a statistic regression, it can be demonstrated that computer self-efficacy is positively correlated with teacher self-efficacy; furthermore, this correlation increases over time, as shown in Table 23.2.

TABLE 23.2   Regression Coefficient

Teacher self-efficacy

	Beginning of the course		Half of the course		End of the course	
	β	R^2	β	R^2	β	R^2
Computer self-efficacy	0.19[b]	0.16	0.23[a]	0.11	0.28[b]	0.26

[a] $\alpha < 0.10$
[b] $\alpha < 0.05$
[c] $\alpha < 0.001$

Thus, H1 and H2 are confirmed; H3 also seems to be very reasonable, due to the fact—underlined in formal and informal interviews with the involved teachers and their trainers—that the above-presented learning experience has been the most important experience for their professional growth in the period of the research.

CONCLUSION

In this chapter, the presentation of the BET K–12 project has given the chance to show how learning ICTs and using ICTs in a meaningful learning experience has impacted on the computer and teacher self-efficacy of primary-community-schools teachers of a disadvantaged Brazilian area.

As mentioned above, in the knowledge society, getting expertise in ICTs and, through them, access to information and knowledge, is of the utmost importance to start a virtual development circle. Of course, knowledge and education have to be combined with freedom, commitment to work, and the right cultural framework, able to integrate new findings (Stark, 2005), but they remain one of the most powerful engines for development. BET K–12 has helped to go just a little step forward, but in the right direction.

REFERENCES

Bandura, A . (1977). Self-efficacy: Towards a unifying theory of behavioral change. *Psychological Review 84*(2), 191–215.

Bandura, A. (1995). *Self-efficacy in changing societies.* New York: Cambridge University Press.

Bof, A. M. (2004). Distance learning for teacher training in Brazil. *International Review of Research in Open and Distance Learning, 5*(1). Retrieved December 3, 2008, from http://www.irrodl.org/content/v5.1/bof.html

Botturi, L. (2006). E2ML. A visual language for the design of instruction. *Educational Technologies Research & Development, 543,* 265–293.

Cantoni, L., Botturi, L., Succi, C., & NewMinE Lab (2007) *E-learning. Capire, progettare, comunicare.* Prefazione di Tony Bates, Milano: FrancoAngeli.

Cantoni, L., Di Blas, N., Rubinelli, S., & Tardini, S. (2008). *Pensare e comunicare.* Milano: Apogeo.

Cantoni, L., & Tardini, S. (2006). *Internet.* Routledge introductions to media and communications. London–New York: Routledge.

CEC—Commission of the European Communities, (2001) Communication from the Commission to the council and the European Parliament, The eLearning Action Plan: Designing tomorrow's education, COM(2001)172, Brussels, 28.3.2001. Retrieved December 3, 2008, from http://ec.europa.eu/education/archive/elearning/annex_en.pdf

Compeau, D. R., & Higgins, C. A. (1995). Computer self-efficacy: Development of a measure and initial test. *MIS Quarterly, 192,* 189–211.

Hill, E. (2004). Some thoughts on e-democracy as an evolving concept. *Journal of E-Government, 1*(1), 23–39.

Magalhães, M., & Schiel, D. (2004). *Technology integration and production of educational multimedia material by the pre-service teacher.* Proceedings of the World Conference on Educational Multimedia, Hypermedia and Telecommunications 2004 (pp. 3129–3133). Norfolk, VA: AACE.

Marinho, S., Lobato, W., & Amaral, C. (2004). *The 'techno-absence' in pre-service teacher education–some findings.* Proceedings of the Society for Information Technology and Teacher Education International Conference 2004 (pp. 3492–3497). Norfolk, VA: AACE.

Modro, N. (2002). *Virtualizing: A Brazilian initiative for upgrading media knowledge of K–12 public school teachers.* Proceedings of the World Conference on E-Learning in Corporate, Government, Healthcare, and Higher Education 2002 (pp. 1929-1932). Norfolk, VA: AACE.

Ong, W. J. (2002). *Orality and literacy: The technologizing of the word* (3rd ed.). London–New York: Routledge.

Pajares, F. (2002). *Overview of social cognitive theory and of self-efficacy.* Retrieved July 25, 2007 from http://www.emory.edu/EDUCATION/mfp/eff.html.

Prata Linhares, M., Moraes Paroneto, G., Moraes Silva, S., & Ribeiro, O. (2004) *Spinning the web of continuing education: Perspectives and challenges of using education at a distance technology in university level teacher education courses.* Proceedings of the Society for Information Technology and Teacher Education International Conference 2004 (pp. 2551–2554). Norfolk, VA: AACE.

Rega, I., Cantoni, L., Tardini S., Olivatto, B., Nery, F., Marques, O., & Fanni, F. (2006, October 30– November 3). *What do Brazilian teachers in disadvantaged schools think of ICT?* Proceedings of the Fourth Pan-Commonwealth Forum on Open Learning PCF4. Ocho Rios, Jamaica.

Rogers, E. (1983). *The diffusion of innovation* (3rd ed.). New York: Free Press.

Stark, R. (2005). *The victory of reason.* New York: Random House.

Tschannen-Moran, M., & Wolfolk Hoy, A. (2001). Teacher efficacy. Capturing an elusive construct. *Teaching and Teacher Education, 17,* 783–805.

ANNEX

The questionnaire submitted to CEAP teachers in March 2007 and in June 2007 is presented here. Questions about computer self-efficacy have been repeated for each technology: MS Word, MS PowerPoint, blog, wiki, e-mail, chat, and search engines. In June 2007 the perceived self-efficacy for each question and for each technology was investigated at the beginning and at the end of the course.

Introduction

1. How often do you use the *computer*?
   - ☐ once or more a day   ☐ twice or more a week
   - ☐ once a week   ☐ once every two weeks
   - ☐ once a month   ☐ less than once a month
2. From where do you have access to the *computer*? Mark more than one answer if necessary.
   - ☐ home   ☐ school where you teach   ☐ university
   - ☐ CEAP   ☐ LAN house   ☐ other …

3. How often do you use *Internet*?
   - ☐ once or more a day   ☐ twice or more a week
   - ☐ once a week   ☐ once every two weeks
   - ☐ once a month   ☐ less than once a month

4. From where do you have access to the *Internet*? Mark more than one answer if necessary.
   - ☐ home   ☐ school where you teach   ☐ university
   - ☐ CEAP   ☐ LAN house   ☐ other …

Teacher Self-efficacy

1. How much can you do to control disruptive behavior in the classroom?

Nothing		Very little		Some influence		Quite a bit		A great deal
1	2	3	4	5	6	7	8	9

2. How much can you do to motivate students who show low interest in school work?
3. How much can you do to get students to believe they can do well in school work?
4. How much can you do to help your students value learning?

5. To what extent can you craft good questions for your students?
6. How much can you do to get children to follow classroom rules?
7. How much can you do to calm a student who is disruptive or noisy?
8. How well can you establish a classroom management system with each group of students?
9. How much can you use a variety of assessment strategies?
10. To what extent can you provide an alternative explanation or example when students are confused?
11. How much can you assist families in helping their children do well in school?
12. How well can you implement alternative strategies in your classroom?

Computer Self-efficacy

In my teacher activity, I can use Word...
1. ...if there was no one around to tell me what to do as I go.

Not at all confident				Moderately confident				Totally confident	
1	2	3	4	5	6	7	8	9	10

2. ...if I had never used a package like it before.
3. ...if I had seen someone else using it before trying it myself.
4. ...if I could call someone for help if I got stuck.
5. ...if someone else had helped me get started.
6. ...if I had a lot of time to complete the job for which the software was provided.
7. ...if I had just the built-in help facility for assistance.
8. ...if someone showed me how to do it first.
9. ...if I had used similar packages before this one to do the same job.

NOTES

1. In this chapter, "e-learning" is understood according to the following definition: "the use of new multimedia technologies and the Internet to improve the quality of learning by facilitating access to resources and services, as well as remote exchanges and collaboration" (CEC, 2001, p. 2); for a discussion of it, see Cantoni & Tardini, 2006, pp. 176–182 and Cantoni et al., 2007, pp. 23–37.
2. WCM stands for Website Communication Model (Cantoni & Tardini, 2006); ABSTTU stands for Assistance, Blend, Communication, Space, Time, Technology and Use of media (Cantoni et al., 2007); I D stands for Instructional Design; and E2ML stands for Educational Environment Modeling Language (Botturi, 2006).

Printed in the United States
214773BV00003BA/3/P

9 781607 521099